Contents

Acknowledgements

I would like to thank some of the most influential people in my life, without whom this work would not have been possible. My wife Shabnam for enduring the absence of a husband over the many long hours of research, writing and editing that goes into compiling a book of this nature, and my Rebbe, Rabbi Robert O. Miller of *Agudat Bris Ministries* in Temple Texas, for his gentle guidance and instruction. His teachings have been instrumental in my Torah learning and spiritual growth. Also thanks must go out to Elder Maurie Hollman for his "staying power" and holding the office that he was appointed in the face of many trials. Special thanks to Maurie's late wife and Eema of our congregation, Glenda Hollman, of blessed memory, who now ministers in the Golden Altar.

Thank you to Ross Murray for his editorial assistance on the final chapter of my last book, which I failed to acknowledge in print. Thank you to Scott Wyatt for putting in many hours of proofreading on this latest volume and to Julius Timmerman for a cameo proofreading return on the two-part chapter on repentance.

Toda raba to sister Batya Emunah for doing a series of meticulous final proofreads and her husband Zerubbabel Emunah for his faithful assistance.

Most importantly I give thanks and praise to YHWH for allowing me to produce this work. Without His mercy and grace (unmerited power) this book would not have been possible. I pray that it may play some small part in transforming the two houses of Israel back into one.

Please Note: Not all the information and views expressed in this work are necessarily that of those who assisted and influenced it.

Warning

The topics discussed in this book are in no way meant as a final word. Though some ideas and opinions presented are based on careful research and independent literary investigation, this author discourages a reader to be completely convinced of any subject presented herein without subsequently seeking additional verification.

This work is merely the product of an ongoing wrestle for truth with Torah as a guiding rule. The word "Torah" means "teaching" and usually appears wherever the legalistic word "law" is mentioned in most modern Bible translations.

It is the sincere hope of the author that this book sparks independent investigation over having any face value merit from any reader. Having said this, please note: This book's level of controversy is only directly proportionate to the level of ignorance of the reader.

The author of this work is in no way affiliated with any church denomination. He is a Nazarene (Natsri) Israelite (offshoot branch watchman ruled by El) who serves YHWH (God) through the redeemed finished work of the resurrected Messiah, Yahshua (Jesus Christ).

[Some theological subjects broached in my first book have been re-clarified in this volume. To this end some material from *All Lights on in the Master's House* has been reproduced and revised in this work.]

Translation used in this work

Throughout this work I have chosen to predominantly use *The Restoration Scriptures True Name Edition Study Bible* [RSTNE] (Third Edition) compiled by Rabbi Moshe Yoseph Koniuchowsky and put out by *Your Arms to Israel Publishing*. I have done this because it retains the Hebraic perspective of its original authors and its high use of transliterated Hebrew words help familiarise a reader with the language and mindset of Messiah. Bracketed English explanations of Hebrew words have been added by the author and do not appear in the original flow of the text. The use of this translation is in no way meant to imply that this author subscribes to all accompanying commentaries or endorses all the teachings, practices and views presented in the ministry of its compiler.

Other versions I heartily recommend are:

The Hebrew Roots Version Scriptures **(HRV) (2004)** The Society for the advancement of Nazarene Judaism - Compiled by James S. Trimm **http://www.nazarene.net**

The Scriptures (1998) - Published by the Institute of Scripture Research (South Africa) **http://www.messianic.co.za**

John 4:22; "You worship you know not what: we know what we worship: for salvation is from the Yahudim (Jews)"
– Yahshua's (Jesus') own words (RSTNE)

Romans 3:1; "What advantage then has the Yahudi (Jew)? Or, what profit is there in brit-milah (flesh circumcision)? Much in every way: primarily, because they were the first to believe in His word."
– Sha'ul's (Paul's) own words (RSTNE)

Introduction

STUDYING THE ORIGIN and evolution of Christianity, the Church, and the major Bible translations this religion espouses, has been a staggering and profound journey. A journey that has been frightening and wonderful; frightening because of the vast number of religious people who appear to be so thoroughly deceived by its teachings, and wonderful because of having the privilege to be shown a truth and having an opportunity to proclaim it through the medium of the printed word. For when one reads the Scriptures and compares it to what the Church has taught for the past two millennia, a mountain of startling discrepancies emerge.

This work is a compilation of material that is the product of my ongoing investigation into the one true faith that was practiced by the first humans and later formally reintroduced to a Chaldean[1] man and then an entire nation of his descendants. Some information contained in my previous book, *All Lights on in the Master's House*, has been revised and included in this second volume to anchor a secure foundation for the new range of subjects discussed.

1 ***Genesis 11:28***

While my first book delved into the identity of Israel and examined its replacement by an anti-semitic Greco-Roman political religious order, it also rather ambitiously addressed a range of strange and unusual topics. The most controversial subjects included the Scriptural context of the UFO phenomenon, ancient technology, human-angelic relations, suppressed archeological evidence of giants and a possible scientific rationale behind demonic possession. Whilst there was a need for these topics to be addressed from a Scriptural perspective, the information regarding the significance of Israel's identity sat somewhat in the background. Though I have endeavored to include and expand on some of the same topics again, the thrust of this work is to re-establish the Hebraic context of the Scriptures. I also hope to make the reader acutely aware of the awakening, restoration and return of the lost sheep of the house of Israel and the temporary nature of the tribe of Judah's (the Jews') blindness to the identity of the risen Messiah. The impermanence of this blindness has never been more evident than in recent times. Consider the following event: The late Sephardic Orthodox Haredi[2] Rabbi Yitzchak Kaduri, of righteous memory, who passed away in 2006, left a legacy that may usher in a gradual acceptance of Yahshua as Messiah among many Jews. Sixteen years before his passing "Israel's leading known Kabbalistic Elder" was told by the late Lubavitcher Rebbe, Menachem Mendel Schneerson, of righteous memory, that he would one day meet and learn the name of Messiah. According to the revered teacher's closest students such an encounter with Messiah did eventuate in the month of November 2004. Rabbi Kaduri subsequently wrote a short note with instructions not to open until one year after his death. The note was penned in Hebrew and signed in the rabbi's name. It read, "Concerning the Reishei-Tivot[3] (letter abbreviation) of the Messiah's name, he will lift the people and prove that his word and Torah is valid. This I have signed in Elul (the Month of Mercy)." The first letter of each Hebrew word in the note spelt out the name Yahshua (Jesus). One Jewish commentator pleaded "no comment" in response to the note, but aptly quoted Mark Twain,

2 Haredi Judaism is the most theologically conservative form of Orthodox Judaism in the world.

3 Reishei-Tivot is the name for a common Kabbalistic letter code.

"A thing long expected takes the form of the unexpected when at last it comes."

Rabbi Yitzhak Kaduri meeting with Lubavitcher Rebbe Menachem Schneerson

The uppermost desire in the heart of the Father is the return to unity of both houses of Israel - Judah (the Jews) and Ephraim (the lost ten tribes of Israel). They are described in the Scriptures as two houses ***(Isaiah 8:14)***, two nations ***(Ezekiel 35:10)***, two families ***(Jeremiah 33:24)***, two branches ***(Zechariah 4:11-14)***, two sticks ***(Ezekiel 37:15-28)***, two witnesses ***(Revelations 11:3,4)*** and two lamp-stands ***(Revelations 11:3,4)***. Unfortunately this message is largely ignored, misapplied or denied by both Christianity and Judaism. This is because if light on this subject was ever cast into either camp for any significant amount of time it would almost certainly weaken the enormous barriers that separate both faiths. HaSatan (The Accuser) is quite happy for Christianity and Judaism to remain completely isolated from one another and remain partially blinded, one to Torah and the other to Messiah. Today the majority of Israel resides within these two imperfect, but sincere religious systems. Interestingly two leavened loaves (representing the inflated pride of both houses) are waved before the Almighty in ***Leviticus 23:17*** on the first-fruits of Shavuot and two silver trumpets are sounded in unison (symbolising their future reunion) in ***Numbers 10:2,3***.

The Scriptures promise a Torah-giver to be found among Judah throughout its days ***(Genesis 49:10)***. The house of Ephraim on the other hand, made up of the remaining ten tribes of Israel (first mentioned as a collective in ***1 Kings 11:31***), departed from the ways of Elohim (God) after a dispute with the tribe of Benjamin (who later became absorbed into Judah). But now in this very day there has commenced a stirring in the hearts of many Christians (possibly Ephraimites) to return to the Hebraic roots of the faith to join with brother Judah as one new man in Messiah as foretold in ***Zachariah 8:23; "This says YHWH tzevaoth (of hosts); In those days it shall come to pass, that ten men shall take hold out of all languages of nations (Gentiles), even shall take hold of tzitzit (fringes on the four-cornered garment of a Jew) of him that is a Yahudi (Jew), saying, <u>We will go with you: For we have heard that Elohim (God) is with you</u>."***

Messiah Yahshua came only to save the lost sheep of the House of Israel. ***Matthew 15:24; "They (Elohim) did not send me but to the lost sheep of the Beit Yisrael (House of Israel) who went astray"***. These "lost sheep" included physical descendants of Abraham through the lineage of Jacob ***(Romans 11:23)*** and any converts with them. These converts were foreigners who desired to be completely grafted or joined to the Commonwealth of Israel ***(Isaiah 56:1-7)***. So anyone has the potential be a recipient of the message of salvation. Whether Jew, Ephraimite or Gentile, all men have an opportunity to become joint heirs with no distinctions through Messiah. ***Galatians 3:26-29; "For as many of you as have been immersed into Moshiach (messiah) have put on Moshiach. There is neither Yahudi (Jew) nor Aramean nor Greek, there is neither eved (slave) nor free, and there is neither male nor female: for you are kol (whole) Yisrael [and] echad (one) in [Yahshua HaMoshiach]. And if you are Moshiach's, then are you Avraham's Zera (seed), and heirs according to the promise."***

Rabbi Sha'ul HaShaliach (The Apostle Paul) went to the Gentiles to provoke the Jews to jealousy so they might also accept Messiah. ***Romans 11:11; "salvation has come to the nations (Gentiles) to make Yisrael envious."*** This motive was plainly revealed to Israel in the time of Moshe (The Prophet Moses). ***Romans 10:19; "But I say,***

Did not Yisrael know? First Moshe says, I will provoke you to jealousy by them that are not a people at all, Lo-Ami (not my people) and by this foolish nation I will anger you."

Dear reader, you hold in your hands one of the most controversial, yet critical messages of this era. The identity of those who walk according to the instructions of the Creator of heaven and earth are revealed within the pages of this book. As billions of people in thousands of manmade religious institutions and thousands of denominational divisions within these very same institutions promote, debate and argue their various viewpoints, the one true remnant of Israel is awakening in these last days and shifting their gaze to Mount Zion. An unexplained hunger for the Hebraic Torah compliant roots of the original faith is beginning to seize the heart of the Christian while at the same time a burning curiosity for Yahshua (who the world calls Jesus) tugs on the heart of the Jew.

It is my sincere hope that this book will benefit people who are thinking of or in the process of making the transition from Christianity to the original unpolluted faith of YHWH. I pray that this work will bless all those who read it.

In Messiah Yahshua,
Jason C.N. Jordan.

Chapter One

Come Out of the Church

"In those days and in that time', says the YHWH, 'The children of Yisrael shall come, They (the lost ten tribes) and the children of Yahudah (the Jews) TOGETHER, going and weeping: they shall go, And seek YHWH their Elohim. They shall ask the derech (way) to Tzion (Zion), With their faces towards it, saying, 'Come, and let us join ourselves to YHWH in an everlasting brit (covenant) that shall not be forgotten'"
– Yirmeyahu/Jeremiah 50:4-5

CONTRARY TO POPULAR belief, the Christian church did not commence in the Book of Acts despite modern Bible translations telling us otherwise ***(Acts 14:27, 16:5)***. This might be a bold statement, but it's absolutely true. A casual study of the Scriptures reveals that the true body of Messiah was actually established in a covenant that was personally delivered by the Creator to an entire nation at Mount Sinai. Furthermore, it can be argued that it was established well before that with Adam and elaborated upon to certain righteous descendants down through the ages. The faith of the patriarchs was never dissolved and handed over in a new and improved form to a Gentile Church. In fact, the very definition and function of a "church" is actually contrary to the teachings of Messiah and the early apostles. The concealment of this truth doesn't lie at the feet of Scripture itself, but generations of translators who have handled its sacred passages dishonestly. ***Jeremiah 8:8; "How do you say, We are wise, and the Torah of YHWH is with us? See, certainly the lying pen of the scribes has made it falsehood."*** From the corrupt fruits of these men countless believers have espoused doctrine that over time has edged itself further and further away from a once undefiled message.

Studying Word Origins Reveals that the Faith was Hijacked

Over the centuries Greco-Roman scribes reproduced inadequate and misleading information from manuscripts originally written by a nation who possessed a diametrically opposed mindset. An etymological study of the word "church" provides clear evidence that the true faith was hijacked. Etymology is the study of word origins. Words have meaning and serve as a memorial to an object or a person's identity. To translate or transliterate a foreign word is perfectly legal and practical, but to translate or transliterate a word that carries a completely different meaning is literary fraud. This practice causes confusion and often sets a false premise when studying an author's original intent. To deliberately or ignorantly mistranslate words under normal circumstances is dangerous, but to do it with a set of writings that claim to teach the only path to salvation is eternally dangerous. It is perhaps one of the reasons why Sha'ul encouraged intense study of the Scriptures in ***2 Timothy 2:15; "Study to show yourself approved before YHWH, a workman that needs not to be ashamed, rightly dividing the word of emet (truth)."*** But this is not to say that study on its own brings about salvation ***(John 5:39)***. Study should merely be a byproduct of a deep desire to receive closer intimacy with the Creator and nothing more. Let us examine the definition of the word "church" and see what we can find.

Dictionaries give the origin of the word "church" as the Anglo-Saxon root, "circe," which comes from the name of the goddess *Circe*, daughter of *Helios*, the Sun-deity. The origin of the word "church" **is not** from the Greek word "ekklasia." The correct English translation from this word is appropriately rendered as "congregation," "assembly," or "collection." The English word "church" **does not** come from this Greek word "ekklasia." Webster's dictionary says that the word "church" comes from the Greek word "kuriakon," which *apparently* means "the Lord's" or "the Lord's house or belonging." However, a good Bible concordance will reveal that the word "kuriakon" does not appear in any Greek translation. Even the early English translator William Tyndale uniformly translated "ekklesia" as "congregation" and in fact used the word "church" to denote heathen temples in ***Acts 19:37***. The only religious body in Biblical times that bears any resemblance to today's modern church is the *Temple cult of Circe.*

What Would Yahshua Do?

Yahshua attended a synagogue ***(Luke 6:6)***, proclaimed the correct uncorrupted Name of his Father ***(Luke 4:17, John 17:6)*** and kept all the Appointed Times as observed in Judaism. Keep in mind that most Christians (if they wish to sound biblical) will profess to try and follow a similar lifestyle as practiced by the Messiah, even some to the point of wearing small wrist bands that contain the initials WWJD, meaning "What Would Jesus Do?" Now read the following list, which displays Yahshua's observance of Jewish holidays as recorded in Scripture alongside mainstream Christianity's reaction:

- Yahshua observed Shabbat [Sabbath] ***(Mark 1:21, 3:1-2 & 6:2, Luke 4:16 & 13:10)***. This Appointed Time is thrown out by most of Christianity and replaced by worship on the Venerable Day of the Sun [Sunday], a practice observed in Yahshua's day by sun worshipers of Circe.
- Yahshua observed Pesach [Passover] ***(Matthew 21:1, 9-12, 17-18,23)*** This Appointed Time is replaced within mainstream Christianity by the celebration of the fertility ritual of Easter, which was originally observed by the Assyrians, the Phoenicians, and the Philistines who displayed eggs to represent Mother Earth's impregnation by the sun. Pagan priests would ritually impregnate temple prostitutes whose offspring

would be sacrificed one year later in a "child mass" where the newborns would be offered into a furnace located in the belly of a huge red effigy[1]. After the child is incinerated a wish list is read out for various gifts to be bestowed upon all participants for the coming year. Today this practiced is also partially replicated in the Christmas ritual of bringing a child into Santa's lap to request presents. The child offering and sacrifice aspect of the ritual is still echoed in the deliberate escalating act of abortion, though abortion is not generally motivated to appease a god. The most popular reason, an unwillingness to change lifestyle is an even more callous motive than a parent who brings their child as a precious offering to a false god.

- Yahshua observed Sukkot [Feast of Tabernacles] ***(John 7:2)*** This Appointed Time is ignored as an organised practice within Christianity. Please note that there may be small church congregations that observe a week in the outdoors as a custom specific to that particular congregation but it is not an officially observed holiday by the church.

- Bikkurim [The Feast of First Fruits] ***(1 Corinthians 15:20-23)*** Yahshua observed this feast throughout his life, but ultimately fulfilled it by rising along with many other righteous ones from the dead ***(Matthew 27:52)***. Believers are to commemorate this feast by beginning to count seven weeks to the Feast of Weeks. See *Israel's Feasts and their Fullness* by Batya Ruth Wooten for further details.

The Scriptures clearly show that Yahshua held fast to all the covenants with zealous love and affection. He wore tzitzit ***(Luke 8:44)***, he blessed food ***(Luke 9:16)***, he encouraged the offering of animals for sacrifice ***(Matthew 8:1-4)***, obedience to rabbis – ***(Matthew***

1 The Canaanites sacrificed children to a large hollow idol called Moloch. According to the 12th century rabbi, Rashi, the image was made of brass; and heated in its lower parts. Its hands were fashioned to stretch out and hold the child as it was burnt alive. "...when it (the child) vehemently cried out...the priests beat a drum, that the father might not hear the voice of his son, and his heart might not be moved." – Commentary by Rashi on ***Jeremiah 7:31.***

23: 1-3) and was against stoning an accused without witnesses[2] ***(John 8:10,11)***.

Any sort of adherence to all of the above Appointed Times and other seemingly archaic Jewish customs is barely recognised let alone formally practiced within Christianity. Yahshua never attended a church, or celebrated Christmas, Easter, Lent, Good Friday, Sunday worship services or any other custom in a way that is even remotely similar to any major events practiced within all Christendom throughout the last eighteen hundred years of its divergent lifespan. Ritual meetings on the first day of the week occurred because believers would usually still be gathered together at nightfall on the close of the Sabbath. This is why Miriam of Magdala (Mary Magdalene) and Miriam (Mary) sought Yahshua in his tomb at this time ***(Matthew 28:1)***, though Christianity often cites this reference and others to support Sunday worship.

Sha'ul also attended and spoke in synagogues after his conversion ***(Acts 13:5, 13:14-15)*** and even observed Sabbaths in communities that did not have synagogues by meeting with believers outside the city walls ***(Acts 16:13)***. He also pronounced the Name of YHWH ***(Acts 2:21*** & ***Romans 10:13)*** and kept the Torah ***(Acts 21:21-24)***.

Sha'ul calls believers to be imitators[3] of Yahshua, yet all Christianity avoids nearly every aspect of his daily, weekly and monthly routine that has any association with Judaic practices. Yahshua is off celebrating The Feast of Chanukah in ***John 10:22*** and amazingly when it commenced on Christmas day 2005 most, if not all, of Christianity didn't even bat an eyelid. This is because their Messiah is a Greco-Romanised miracle working crusader who apparently put an end to the Torah (law) and established a new replacement "do as thy will" grace covered religion. Is it any wonder that the Orthodox Jew runs a mile when he hears Christian preachers try to sell a Torah destroying miracle man delivered with the same cheap rhetoric as a used car salesman?

---

2 The woman accused of adultery was not able to undergo the test of an adulterous woman or be stoned because all of her witnesses had fled after seeing their transgressions written in the dust by Messiah. See Chapter Seven, 'A Faith Worth Losing Your Head Over' and refer to the subheading, 'Was Yahshua Against the Death Penalty?' for more information.

3 In actuality Rabbi Sha'ul calls believers to be imitators of him ***(1 Corinthians 4:16)***. In essence he is instructing students of Torah to imitate their teachers, but only as they imitate Yahshua as living examples ***(2 Thessalonians 3:7)***.

Rome - The Convenient Phantom Menace

Dear reader, the church is what believers are called to come out of, not just the Roman Catholic Church, the CHURCH! All of the church! This means any church that does not proclaim the royal names of Yahshua and YHWH and does not keep the Sabbaths or uphold the covenants.

The Church IS NOT a new Israel or a continuation of the concept of Israel from the TaNaK (Old Testament). By this I mean **any** movement, organisation or institution that goes under the banner of a church. I must make it clear that I am not just singling out the favoured punching bag - Rome. The church, no matter what the denomination, is not a replacement of Israel in any capacity whatsoever. The church is not and can never be the recipient of the promises made to Israel. The prophecies in Scripture concerning the blessing and restoration of Israel to the Land of Promise are not "spiritualised" blessings for the church. The prophecies of condemnation and judgment, however, still remain for national Israel and the Jewish people. The church has no relationship to the curses and blessings for Israel; the covenants, promises and warnings are only valid for Israel.

To accept that the church replaces Israel in the program of YHWH is called "Replacement Theology." Major problems exist with this view. The most prominent being the continuing extraordinary existence of the Jewish people throughout the centuries despite the best efforts of many of the world's greatest empires to eradicate them from the face of the earth.

The Indestructible Nation

The Jews, though for many centuries being deprived of a homeland, a formal army, enduring a long existence as slaves passed from one pagan nation to another, and never numbering more than one third of one percent of the world's entire population have made contributions to religion, science, literature, music, finance and philosophy that are so out of proportion to their numbers, that it almost defies logic. Even more astounding is the revival of the modern state of Israel nestled like an eyesore in amongst over twenty hostile Muslim countries. If Israel has been condemned by YHWH and there is no future for the Jews, how do we account for their supernatural survival in the face of such great hardships and atrocities placed on them by the Egyptians, the Babylonians, the Assyrians, the Greeks, the Romans, the Muslims, the Christians and the Nazis?

You are about to read something that might make you very angry. But it is completely Scriptural and must be published. The truth is that to stay a Gentile (that is to stay knowingly outside the Commonwealth of Israel and practice the common Western interpretation of the one true faith) is to stay without hope. What do the Scriptures say? ***Ephesians 2:11-12; "Therefore remember, that you being in times past gentiles in the flesh, who are called The Uncircumcision by those called the Brit-Milah (circumcised) in the flesh made by hands; that at THAT TIME you were without Moshiach (Messiah), being EXCLUDED, aliens from the Commonwealth of Yisrael, as gerim (strangers) from the covenants of promise, having no tikvah (hope), and without Eloha (the Mighty One) in the olam hazeh (the world)."***

But how do we reconcile this truth in the light of Rabbi Sha'ul HaShaliach's words, ***"For whoever shall call upon the Name of the Master YHWH shall be saved."(Romans 10:13)***? The church does not deny that the Name of the Father is YHWH, but they do not proclaim it on the grounds that its pronunciation is uncertain. So they settle on the non-descript title, "Lord God," which is a transliteration of a pagan city named, "Baal Gad" after the god of the Canaanites ***(Joshua 11:17, 12:7, 13:5)***. This is despite Scripture calling for believers to refrain from uttering the name of pagan deities in the context of worship and praise. This statute first appears in ***Exodus 23:13*** and is then ironically, reconfirmed in the very book that this pagan god is mentioned ***(Joshua 23:7)***. The Jew on the other hand also avoids pronunciation of the Name, but they at least spell it out daily in their prayers as "*Yud*" "*Hey*" "*Vav*" "*Hey*." The only congregation today that makes any consistent effort to pronounce the Name of YHWH is the Nazarene Israelite and Messianic Jewish communities who by definition accept that they are members of the Commonwealth of Israel. Calling on the name of the Creator requires using His Name. In addition, it also requires a process of declarations, which can be found in the Book of Ruth.

The Sacred Name Pronunciation Debate

The reality at the heart of "the Sacred Name debate" is this: There are very few Christian scholars that dispute that the Name of the G-d of the Hebrews is "YHWH[4]" (or some variation thereof) and there is no serious academically accepted work which disputes that "Joshua" or "Yeshua" (or some variation thereof) is the Hebrew name for the Messiah. However, debate over the pronunciation of the Sacred Name persists. While some individuals in Messianic communities indulge in heated debates over this issue, Christian anti-name groups are only too happy to sit back and criticise this behaviour as a sign of this movement's disunity. Yet nearly all of Christendom continues to use a more widespread pagan transliterated nonspecific title over using the indisputable personal memorial Name of the Creator.

The reasons for writing and pronouncing the Creator's Name are:

- It is His Name ***(Isaiah 42:8)***.
- There are no Scriptures that support suppressing or substituting it with any other name or title.
- It correctly identifies and accordingly exalts the one true El of Israel.
- The Name of YHWH is to be made known, honoured and proclaimed to all nations ***(Malachi 1:11; Isaiah 12:4)***.
- Use of the Name upholds the Commandment in ***Exodus 20:7; "Do not make His Name worthless."*** (Rendered in Hebrew as, ***"Lo tisah et Shem YHVH Eloheicha l'shav."***) And in ***Deuteronomy 5:11; "You do not bring the Name of YHWH your Elohim to vain emptiness, for YHWH will not hold him guiltless that brings His Name to vain emptiness."***
- Using it follows the example of the Hebraic Patriarchs and Prophets in the Torah and TaNaK (Old Testament) who clearly

4 Every accepted in-depth Christian source concerning the name of the Creator supports the Tetragrammaton name of YHWH as originally appearing approximately 7000 times in the Old Testament and 1000 times in the New Testament.

pronounced the Name YHWH as a testimony to non-Jews and non-believers.

- The martyr Stephen was stoned for using it.
- Yahshua used it ***(Luke 4:17, Matthew 4:7; 4:10; 5:33; 21:42; 22:37 & 22:44)***, came in it ***(John 5:43)*** and testified to the Father that he used it [***(John 17:6, 26)*** which confirmed the prophecy in ***Psalms 22:22***].

The pronunciation of the Creator's Name can vary slightly, though initially there appear to be quite a few versions out there which include: ***YHVH, YHWH, Yahweh, Yahveh, Yaveh, Yaweh, Jehova, Jehovah, Jahova, Jahovah, Yahova, Yahovah, Yahowah, Jahowa, Jahowah, Yahavah, Jahavah, Yahowe, Yahoweh, Jahaveh, Jahaweh, Yahaveh, Yahaweh, Jahuweh, Yahuweh, Jahuwah, Yahuwah, Yahuah, Yah Jah Yahu, Yahoo, Yaohu, Jahu, Yahvah, Jahvah, Jahveh, Yahve, Yahwe, Yauhu, Yawhu, Iahu, Iahou, Iahoo, and Iahueh.*** Careful study can narrow this list down to a few chief variations. They include, "yahwê[5]," "yahweh[6]," or "yahuah[7]."

Yeh, Yeh, Yeh, Whatever Yah Reckon

Note that there are several different types of spellings for these three pronunciations. From these "Yahweh" (YHWH), the sound of a deep inhale and exhale, is the most accurate. Quite a few Nazarene

5 *Unger's Bible Dictionary*, p. 1177 states, "Yahweh (ya' we), the Hebrew tetragrammaton (YHWH) traditionally pronounced Jehovah is now known to be correctly vocalized yahwê. New inscriptional evidence from the second and first millennia B.C. point toward this fact...."

6 20th Century Schaff-Herzog Encyclopedia, pg. 1194, 1195 "The pronunciation Yahweh of the Hebrew Tetragrammaton need no longer be based on traditions preserved in late patristic sources. Both the vocalization yahwe and yahu (a shortened form used chiefly in personal names) are now confirmed by a variety of ancient Near Eastern inscriptional materials from the first and second millennia B.C." The Modern Judaica Encyclopedia, Vol. 7, p.69 "The true pronunciation of the name YHWH was never lost. Several early Greek writers of the Christian Church testify that the name was pronounced 'Yahweh'. This is confirmed, at least for the vowels of the first syllable of the name, by the shorter form Yah, which is sometimes used in poetry (e.g., Ex.15:2) and the -yahu or -yah that serves as the final syllable in very many Hebrew names." New Bible Dictionary (1962) "The pronounciation Yahweh is indicated by transliterations of the name into Greek in early Christian literature, in the form iaoue (Clement of Alexandria) or iabe (Theodoret; by this time Gk. b had the pronunciation of v)"

7 This variation is born from the similarity in the pronunciation of the name Yahudah (Judah), meaning "praise Yah," which contains the Tetragrammaton.

Israelites mispronounce and misspell the Name YHWH and Yahshua as "Yehweh" and "Yeshua." This view is espoused from the handling of the Father's name in translations of the TaNaK by the Massoretes[8]. These were groups of Jewish Scholars who produced vowel markings to accompany the Hebrew text. Early Hebrew did not require vowels for those fluent in the language. The Massoretes created this vowel system to retain the correct pronunciations of Hebrew words during the Diaspora. These vowel markings indicate the name Yahudi (Jew) to be pronounced as "Ye-hoo-Dee" and the name Yahudah (Judah) to be pronounced "Ye-hoo-Dah." The Messiah's name is made up of the first three letters of the Father's name (*Yud, Hey* & *Vuv*) hence the rendering "Yeshua." However, the Massoretes, in an effort to preserve the sanctity of the Name YHWH and prevent its use, changed the relevant vowel markings to give an "ee" sound instead of an "ah" sound. ***Psalms 68:4*** exhibits the short form of the Father's name as "Yah" (written as "Jah" in the King James Bible) giving the whole game away. I wonder how many "Yeh" advocates also maintain continuity and proclaim "HalleluYEH" instead of "HalleluYAH."

Believers should use and call upon the one true El (Mighty One) of Israel, as best as their own understanding permits. Addressing the Creator by the anglicised transliteration, "Lord God" from the pagan title, "Ba'al Gawd" on the philosophy that the correct pronunciation of the Name is irretrievable is not biblical because there is no biblical evidence of a future climate where the Name is COMPLETELY forgotten (whether pronounced or written) by any generation. But I digress.

The New Covenant in the So-called Old Testament

Jeremiah 31 and ***Hebrews 8*** declare that the Renewed Covenant was only made ***"with the beit (house) of Yisrael and with the house of Yahudah."*** Yahshua backs this teaching up when he said, "***They (Elohim) did not send me but to the lost sheep of the Beit Yisrael (House of Israel) who went astray." (Matthew 15:24)*** The Jews (Yahudim) are not included in this statement because they were

8 The word Massorete comes from the Hebrew word *massorah*, meaning "tradition." This movement existed from 500 to 1000CE.

one of twelve Israelite tribes who remained Torah observant and therefore were not lost (though partially blinded to Messiah for a time). The sayings of the Sha'ul HaShaliach are also aimed at sifting out these lost sheep. This is evident when we observe his heartfelt appeal to his fellow Jews by describing how he came to call Yisrael from ***"...among the nations (Gentiles)..." (Romans 1:5)***. Sha'ul didn't come to call Gentiles to remain Gentiles, but to be grafted into Israel ***(Romans 11:23)***. The Gentile's openness to Messiah was designed to provoke the Jews to jealousy. ***Romans 11:11; "salvation has come to the nations (Gentiles) to make Yisrael envious."*** The purpose of this jealousy is to steer their eyes toward Messiah. This was not a new teaching as Sha'ul points out earlier in ***Romans 10:19; "But I say, Did not Yisrael know? First Moshe says, 'I will provoke you to jealousy by them that are not a people at all, Lo-Ami (not my people) and by this foolish nation I will anger you.'"*** Moshe's account of YHWH's reaction to a disobedient Israel and His intention is plainly recorded in ***Deuteronomy 32:21; "They have moved Me to Jealousy with that which is not El; they have provoked Me to anger with their vanities: and I will move them to jealousy with those who are Lo-Ami; (not my people) I will provoke them to anger with a foolish people."*** As usual Sha'ul's words completely line up with Torah, as do Yahshua's.

Messiah Yahshua had always been the continual goal of the Torah. ***Romans 10:4; "For Moshiach is the actual goal of the Torah for an eternal tzadik (righteous) standing to everyone that believes."*** His role to save mankind was determined before the very foundation of the earth. ***Hosea 6:3; "His going forth is prepared as the morning..."*** The Torah was not given as a burdensome stumbling block to predestine Israel to misuse or depart from. It was something that was already in their mouths. ***Deuteronomy 30:14; "But the Word is very near to you, in your mouth, and in your lev (heart), and in your hand, that you may do it."*** Yahshua was not an afterthought sent down in reaction to a flawed system of living given by His Father. This is called "crisis theology." Sha'ul reiterates this truth in ***Romans 10:8; "But what does the Torah actually say? The word is near you, even in your mouth, and in your lev (heart): that is, the word of emunah (truth), which we proclaimed."***

Offering Animals on the Fruit of our Lips

Any argument supporting Torah inevitably brings up the issue of animal sacrifice, in particular the sin offering. Even in the days before Yahshua's death and resurrection an offering was not accepted as a sacrifice unless the one bringing it saw it as a representation of Messiah's future work. Without this view this ritual was reduced to a pointless year after year slaughter of animals ***(Hebrews 10:1)***. The sacrificial system was set up as a shadow of things to come and as a physical reminder of past sins ***(Hebrews 10:3)***. The blood of animals never took away sins ***(Hebrew10:4)*** or made one perfect before YHWH. To believe that animal sacrifices were an old way of salvation and Messiah is now a new way is to believe that there were two paths to eternal life, the former one through animal sacrifice and the present one in an intellectual belief in Messiah Yahshua.

The accepted view in Christianity, according to ***Hebrews 13:15***, is that these offerings are now a ***"sacrifice of praise...that is the fruit of our lips."*** But ***Hosea 14:2***, written in the TaNaK (Old Testament) also states, ***"Take with you words of Torah, and make teshuvah (a return) to YHWH: and say to Him, take away all our iniquity, and receive us graciously: so we will render the bulls, the fruit of our lips."*** Or more commonly translated as: ***"for we will offer the sacrifices of our lips."***' The sacrifice of verbal praise refers to the sinner's response in witnessing the flowing of an innocent animal's blood on their behalf. Praise of the lips was heard from the mouths of those who brought offerings long before Yahshua rose from the dead. Lip service alone was never meant to replace the physical act of presenting an offering. Why would ***Hebrews 10:3*** (written after the resurrection) say, ***"But in those sacrifices there is a yearly reminder of sins,"*** and continue in ***Hebrews 13:10*** by saying "WE HAVE AN ALTAR..." as opposed to saying "we had an altar..." to which the bodies of animals are to be brought ***(Hebrews 13:11)***?

Daily prayers in Judaism are structured around the daily offerings that were undertaken in the Temple. Therefore it can be truly said that only the Orthodox Jews offer up the fruit of their lips in place of the blood of animals according to ***Hebrews 13:15***. Messianic or Nazarene Israelite congregations are gradually picking up on this revelation and have begun implementing the same prayer cycles.

A casual read-through of Hebrews by a person unfamiliar with the Torah and ignorant of the correct application of the New Covenant will find several verses that appear to speak of something being done away with and replaced with something new. ***Hebrews 7:12, 22 & 10:9*** refers to the old priesthood being replaced by the new priesthood under Messiah Yahshua and has nothing to do with an annulment of the sacrificial system or any aspect of the Torah. This is because Yahshua is the perfect High Priest in that he will never die of old age and will never have to give an ongoing personal sin offering like the men that served in the Aaronic priesthood in former times. ***Hebrews 9:11; "For Moshiach (Messiah) has now become a Kohen HaGadol (High Priest) of tov (good) things to come."*** Much more detail on the sacrificial system is included in Chapter Eleven of this book and is recommended reading as the subject of animal sacrifice is a major stumbling block to many people.

Judaism & Christianity - Joining Two Halves of One Theological Plow

The Gentile Christian must accept Yahshua's assurance that NONE OF THE TORAH IS DONE AWAY WITH ***(Luke 16:17)***. In turn, the Orthodox Jew must accept that ALL THE TORAH POINTS TO YAHSHUA. When this happens, both Jew and Gentile will become one new man by uniting together under the banner of the Commonwealth of Israel. Neither the Church [*Circe*] nor Orthodox Judaism [one tribe of Israel], on its own, embodies Israel in its totality.

Question: "But if this is true, what must I do?"

Answer: If you are a church going Christian I would encourage you to find people who accept Messiah Yahshua, proclaim the Name of YHWH, keep the Sabbaths and hold to the covenants ***(Isaiah 56:6)***. Some brothers and sisters I know live in rural areas and cannot attend any sort of gatherings with other covenant members, let alone find a Messianic synagogue. They either keep in contact with other members via the phone or internet or attend Sabbath keeping churches. I believe this last option depending on a person's circumstances may be acceptable for a time.

If you are a Jew who has come to belief in Messiah Yahshua I would discourage you strongly from joining a church. On the contrary, continuing synagogue attendance may be acceptable in many circumstances, but acknowledgement of Yahshua and study and discussion of New Testament books will have to be kept private (at least amongst fellow Jews). As a synagogue upholds the Name - at least in its spelt out form, the Sabbaths and the covenants, there is little need to consider attending a church. If possible make contact with a Messianic Jewish or Nazarene Israelite community. If you live in the vicinity of such congregations then and only then might it be more appropriate to leave the Orthodox synagogue environment.

As I pointed out, the Jew must accept that all the Torah points to Messiah Yahshua and the Gentile must accept obedience to Torah if they wish to please him! Both religions have elements of truth, but the Jews have the advantage. That is why Sha'ul said, ***"What advantage then has the Yahudi (Jew)? Or, what profit is there in brit-milah (circumcision)? Much in every way!"*** Because ***"...primarily...they were the first to be entrusted with the oracles of YHWH and the first to believe in His word." (Romans 3:1-2)***

Question: "Does the Church have any advantage?"

Answer: Well, one could say that they have Messiah, but he's so stacked with Babylonian mystery cult sun-god regalia, that it's not really fair to say they have the real guy.

Question: "But I'm happy at my church!"

Answer: This is not about you; it's about YHWH who, like His son, does not change. ***Malachi 3:6; "I am YHWH I change not..." Hebrews 13:8; "Yahshua is the same yesterday, today, and forever."*** Just because someone else changed things to a point where they barely resemble the harmonious walk that once existed in the Garden of Eden doesn't give you or anyone else the luxury of carrying on in its falsehood once the Ruach (Spirit) has revealed more truth to you. Honour what little truth you come into by acting in accordance with what you believe and YHWH will lead you into more truth.

Question: "But I was saved in the name of Jesus and it was at a church!"

Answer: Halleluiah, you were saved indeed! Don't let anyone convince you otherwise! But if Jesus and church were all you knew at that time, YHWH honoured that and counted it to you as righteousness.

Question: "Should I really consider leaving my church?"

Answer: Yes, if you fully understand this message and have the ability to join with an established group of committed Nazarene Israelites, who exhibit the following core characteristics:

- Keep the Sabbaths,
- Hold fast to all the Covenants,
- And love the Name of the Creator enough to use it.

(***Isaiah 56*** systematically reveals all the three pillars of the faith.)

The Torah has to be central to the group's focus, but only as it points to and heralds Messiah Yahshua. Some Messianic groups can push Yahshua into the background, making him feel like an afterthought. No religious group is completely perfect or without internal disputes and strife. Yahshua's very own Talmidim (disciples) argued and wrestled over different issues regularly ***(Luke 22:24)***. They would have known who was going to betray Yahshua if they weren't busy having a dispute at the same time their Master dunked bread with Judas ***(Mark 14:20)***.

Question: "Should I learn about Judaism and attend a synagogue?"

Answer: Steady-on-there cowboy! If you understand this message, you will soon realise that the Jew is your brother. But tread carefully. Do not rush off to an Orthodox or Reformed synagogue.

Some Orthodox Jews can be just as far off the mark as a Catholic Priest. Take for example this excerpt from Rabbi Adin Steinsaltz's book *The Essential Talmud:*

> "...the Talmud is the central pillar, soaring up from the foundations and supporting the entire spiritual and intellectual edifice. In many ways the Talmud is the most important book in Jewish culture, the backbone of creativity and of national life. No other work has had a comparable influence on the theory and practice of Jewish life, shaping spiritual content and serving as a guide to conduct."

The Jews are an ancient Semitic people who have endured the most consistent and severest levels of persecution throughout the history of mankind. Yet they have achieved a level of contribution in such fields as music, literature, finance, medicine, education and science to a degree that far exceeds the contribution of any other nation in proportion to their numbers, on the face of the whole earth. This is all the more interesting when one realises that the Jews make up less than 1% of the world's overall population and ought not to have even been heard of. Their mighty volumes of Talmudic writings and traditions are the product of a continuous attempt by sincere men to protect the Torah. But in many ways this guardian has evolved into a juggernaut that has overshadowed its Master. In turn this has caused some people to form the view that the Talmud supports the Torah. Jewish traditions, which should serve to amplify the Torah, have, to some extent, taken centre stage. But there has always been a remnant of Israel who uphold the Torah above all else and know that it points to Messiah. The books of the Talmud contain excellent teaching and insight into the Torah, but they also have some crazy stuff in them as well and anyone who studies them without a good knowledge of Scripture may drift into error.

You may only find a handful of people that accept Torah and the testimony of Messiah Yahshua. It is highly uncommon (at this time) to find many Orthodox Jews sympathetic to this view. Most Nazarene Israelites in the Western world have come out of the church. I believe this is because the majority of the lost tribes of the house of Israel are in the church. This view is based on the fact that

Christianity is the only other dominant religion in the world that professes to serve the same Elohim (God) as Judaism, albeit not according to the correct oracles.

If possible meet with like-minded people regularly, especially on the weekly Shabbat. Praise YHWH on that day; read the designated Torah portion and supporting prophetic and Messianic writings (New Testament). Try also meeting at an additional time to research Scripture together. Discuss it, debate it, and chew over it. If you have internet access, consider getting in touch with other lost sheep via this platform. Use it to acquire books on YHWH's festivals and other material that relates to understanding the Scriptures from a Jewish perspective.

Most importantly, when one understands the full extent of what the church is about and thoroughly brings the issue before YHWH, it won't be a question of, 'if one should leave,' but 'when' and 'how.' Every person's situation is different. One person may be asked to flee immediately and literally run for the nearest door. Another may be required to hang around a little while before completely detaching. Take for example the testimony of my teacher, Rabbi Robert O. Miller, a Messianic Rabbi. He relates that when he was a Christian minister he was eventually confronted with this statement from the Father, "I will no longer accept strange fire from you." A short time later he left the church and walked away from a congregation, a regular evangelistic TV slot, a house, a car, and a well-paid and respectable job. Ultimately his decision cost him his family. When the time came he stood up before his entire congregation, told them that he was their Jonah, made a farewell announcement and left. Everyone's situation is different. Be cautious and don't burn any bridges unless you have to. My wife and I still keep in touch with many members of the last church we attended. We maintain an ongoing mutual respect for our Christian friends there, without whose initial support, would not have enabled us to be in the place we are at now. Amein.

Chapter Two

Is Being a Christian Biblical?

I REMEMBER LISTENING TO the sincere testimony of a relative newcomer to a church I used to attend. As he spoke I began to note, with mounting curiosity, the amount of times he referred to himself as a Christian. This got me thinking, 'what is a Christian?' The following chapter consists of my findings, observations and my eventual earth shattering conclusion that being a Christian is not biblical.

The religion that Christianity purports to be based on had many of its foundations revealed to men in the days of Moshe. These foundations were set by the hand, voice and movement of YHWH. Followers of this original faith were known as His chosen people and called, "Israel" (Yisrael). This means: "powerful prevailing princes (or soldiers of YHWH) who struggle with Him and prevail." It also means, "those who struggle with El (The Mighty One of Oaths)" or "El rules these men." The name "Israel" was originally given to our forefather Jacob whose family grew to around 70 people upon entering Egypt and whose descendants increased to 600,000 at their eventual exit. This multitude of 600,000 was broken up into twelve tribes plus the tribe of Levi. One of these tribes was called Judah (Yahudah), which means, "Praise Yah[1]." Gradually the term "Jews" (Yahudim[2]) came to be used as the general name for Israelites and by the time Yahshua emerged in the flesh the title of Jew held national significance. This was because they were the only tribe among the whole nation who retained the "oracles" or Torah of YHWH. ***Genesis 49:10; "The scepter shall not depart from Yahudah (Judah), nor a lawgiver from between His feet, until Shiloh comes; to Him shall the gathering of the nations be."*** The term Jew could refer to a native Judean or a direct descendant of the Israelite forefathers, Abraham, Isaac and Jacob. All the other tribes, having forsaken the Torah, lost their identity and became absorbed into pagan nations. In the final days the lost tribes will be re-gathered to form one Yisraelite nation. This awakening to the Hebrew roots of the faith is happening right now!

Christianity Served with a Tallit

The Hebraic awakening that is taking place in some church bodies typified by ministers using the name Yahshua, the wearing of prayer shawls and the occasional blowing of a shofar is to sate the appetite of some Christians who are developing an appeal for the "Messianic movement." The motive behind these moves is to retain membership numbers and appeal to those who just want their Christianity served to them by a minister wrapped in a tallit. Any so-called awakening will only ever be limited within official church

1 ***Genesis 29:35; "And she (Leah) conceived again, and bore a son: and she said, 'This time I will hallel (praise) YHWH: therefore she called his name Yahudah and ceased bearing."*** The word comes from the root, *yadah* which means, "an extension of the hand in adoration or acceptance" or "to throw or cast." Interestingly Yahuda is called upon to go up *first* into battle against the Canaanites ***(Judges 1:1-12)***. Therefore this can literally be understood as meaning, 'let praise go up to YHWH at the commencement of a trial.' We see this illustrated in Job's reaction to hearing the worst news he could possibly imagine in ***Job 1:21; "...naked I came out of my eema's (mother's) womb, and naked shall I return there: YHWH has given, and YHWH has taken away; Baruch-et-Shem (blessed be the name of) YHWH."***

2 With the observance of the one true way dwindling down to one tribe, the faith itself began being called after that's tribe's name – Yahudah > Yahudaism (Judaism). This tribal specific name for "the way" continued into the apostolic era. Rabbi Sha'ul was accused of being a ring leader of a heretical Nazarene branch or sect of Judaism ***(Acts 24:5)***, by men who in actuality followed a heretical version of it. Judaism or "the way" was always a Messianic faith. The prophet Moshe was instructed to build a tabernacle, and populate it with a priesthood to mimic the priesthood in the heavens, so even he knew there had to be a high priest also interceding in the heavenly realms.

congregations as a full awakening will undermine the very core of its replacement theology.

Nonetheless, people are coming out of the church with an urgency to learn the covenants, acknowledge the true royal names of YHWH and Yahshua and participate in the Sabbath festivals. This joining of two houses, Judah and the lost tribes, are described in ***Ezekiel 37:16-22***. However, there will always be a group of people, predominantly Jews who are "the remnant" ***(Isaiah 37:32, Ezekiel 14:22, Romans 11:5)***. The remnant primarily refers to Torah observant Jews who accept Messiah. In biblical times splinter groups that fit this category remained in effect, though two major groups gained the most attention by historians and scribes. These were the Nazarenes (Ha-Natsarim) and the Ebionites. Christianity, though the term "Christian" pops up in modern Bible translations, did not commence until many centuries after the events in Scripture took place. The term was popularised by translators and later adopted as the name for a people who wished to disassociate themselves from Jews. Though the word "Christian" appears several times in the New Testament, it is a mistranslation from the original Hebrew word "Natsri" or "Natsarim" (plural) which is transliterated as "Nazarene." The term Nazarene comes from the Hebrew word "Netser," meaning "branch," and forms a Hebrew word play with "Natsar" which means, "to watch." This marriage of words signifies a member of an offshoot faith that watches diligently. The Hebrew word "Natsarim" is preserved in both the Aramaic and Greek texts. Therefore the term Christianity has nothing whatsoever to do with Scripture and because its meaning is not related to this original word, it cannot be considered a legal transliteration by any means.

I decided to see if there was any truth into the widely accepted claim that the word "Christian" was originally a slur. This led to one of the most perplexing observations that I have noted in my studies. It concerns scholars' admittance that the term "Christian" was originally used as a derogatory term in its three appearances in the New Testament. ***Acts 11:26*** being the first instance, ***"And the disciples were first called <u>Christians</u> in Antioch"*** **(New King James Version)** and so on in ***Acts 26:28*** and ***1 Peter 4:16***. Generally the same scholars that make this claim also say that Christian is taken from Christ, which means "anointed," which is confusing because the act of anointing was a sacred consecration partaken by both pagan and Judaic faiths alike. It is therefore difficult to view this term from either perspective as an insult. The only association I have found that links the word Christian with a slur meaning is the word "cretin."

> *The Webster New World Medical Dictionary* states: "The word 'cretin' is said to have come from the old French 'Chretien' meaning 'Christian' because heretical Christians, to escape persecution, fled into iodine-deficient valleys in the Pyrenees in southwest France and had children with congenital iodine-deficient hypothyoidism. However, the original term "cretin" is conjectural and could come from 'creature' (creature) or 'creta' (chalk, pale) or some other root."
>
> And the *1911 encyclopedia* adds: "The word is usually explained as derived from chritien (Christian) in the sense of innocent. But Christianus...is probably a translation of the older cretin, and the latter is probably connected with creta (era ie) a sallow or yellow-earthy complexion being a common mark of cretinism."

The word "cretin" does not appear to have been in use before the 1700's yet it is the only reference I can find that has a slur connotation to the word "Christian." Furthermore its French origin could be linked to Antioch as the French did occupy settlements there, but my understanding is that this was some considerable time after the events recorded in the Book of Acts. If cretin was not its original slur meaning, then what was it? And why is this all maintained anyway if the original word, "Natsri" was replaced by the word "Christian," which means something completely different?

Amazingly the "Greco-Roman" term "Christianity" was not used in this complete English form until the fifteen hundreds. The religion this word represents had its principle foundations planted some time earlier by Roman Emperor Constantine who convened a counsel at Nicaea. This council set the foundations for a replacement theological view of the original Scriptures. Most churches still openly support this religion while others who outwardly oppose it, still knowingly or unknowingly follow a great majority of its doctrines. The Scriptures speak of only one people that will be saved ***(Romans 11:26)*** and it is these followers who still observe a particular walk with YHWH that I wish to single out as I make the following observation. Unlike many other religions, observers of this faith have had a long and bloody history of persecution through the ages, as many nations have been offended enough by its people to be driven to exile them, fight them, enslave them and exterminate them. At this point one might be forgiven for thinking that I am talking about Christians. But I am certainly not. Surprisingly, a great many of these attacks have been launched under the very banner of Christianity. The people I refer to are "Israelites," both before and after the resurrection of Messiah. The church wrongly maintains that it has replaced the old Israel, but Rabbi Sha'ul HaShliach makes it exceedingly clear that Israel will never be replaced. ***Romans 11:1a; "I say then, has YHWH cast away His people? By no means!"*** and verse ***2a; "YHWH has not cast away His people whom He knew and chose beforehand."*** These people, who the world calls "Jews," have been blinded ***(Romans 11:7-10)***. But according to ***Romans 11:25***, they will awaken when a preordained number of scattered Israelites (largely Ephraimites and their converts) are sifted from the nations. "***...that partial blindness has happened to Yisrael, until the fullness of the nations - the melo hagoyim - comes in.***"

Many Israelites in the era depicted in the New Testament accepted the risen Messiah and still maintained a zealous affection for the whole Torah ***(Acts 21:17-27)***. This sect multiplied and grew into thousands of Jews ***(Acts 2:41-47; 4:4, 6:7; 9:31)***. Later, many grafted-in former Gentiles were added to their numbers, which led to a dispute between Sha'ul and Shimon Kepha (Peter) as to how they should be instructed ***(Galatians 2)***. This demographic were persecuted by both fellow Israelites ***(Thessalonians 2:14-16)*** and wider Gentile oppositions. Mass persecutions of those who observed a Natsarim (off-shoot) walk is difficult to ascertain from the records of early church fathers, because they saw little distinction between the appearance and lifestyles of Natsarim and Jews. Sadly, over time history labeled these groups with a general reference that later evolved into the term, "Christian." Sha'ul, who was formerly opposed to the Natsarim or "Followers of the Way," spoke directly to those of them who had suffered persecution by their own people in ***Romans 11:28-29; "As concerning the besorah (good news), they are enemies for your sakes, but as far as being the chosen people, they are beloved for the sake of the ahvot (fathers). For the gifts and the calling of YHWH are without teshuvah (turning back)."***

All Israel [By definition: covenant keepers who know that the Torah points to Yahshua ***(Romans 10:4)***] will be saved ***(Romans 11:26)*** because, ***"Favoured are you, O Yisrael; who is like you, a people saved by YHWH, the Shield of your help, who is the Sword of your excellency. And your enemies shall be found to be liars to you; and you shall tread down their high places." (Deuteronomy 33:29)***. This means that ***"Yisrael shall be in YHWH with an everlasting Yahshua (salvation); you shall not be ashamed nor embarrassed le-Olam-Va-Ed (without end)." (Isaiah 45:17)***

The question arises, 'where do Christians fit into this equation?' The problem is that the majority of the Bible believing world is blinded to the fact that YHWH calls only one people His own and it isn't Christianity or the church by any means. As pointed out earlier, Yahshua was only sent to the lost sheep of the House of Israel ***(Matthew 15:24;" They did not send me but to the lost sheep of the Beit Yisrael [House of Israel] who went astray.")***. Sha'ul was also sent out to sift these same lost sheep from among the nations (Gentiles). It isn't a question of whether one is a Jew, a Gentile or a Christian. It is a question of whether one has been grafted into the Commonwealth of Israel. According to Scripture the Jew has an advantage in maintaining this covenant relationship ***(Romans 3:1)***. The Gentile on the other hand is without hope ***(Ephesians 2: 11,12)*** unless he enters into this same covenant relationship by the door of Yahshua. A Christian, who knows the Scriptures well and wishes to remain a Gentile and reject any association with Israel, is without hope in this state.

Some sources state that "Christ" is the Greek word for "anointed," meaning "the application of oil for consecration" and the addition of the "ian" comes from the Latin suffix "ianus," which means "associated with." Therefore the name "Christian" is born out of the Greek rendering of this sacred act (Christos). There is no refuge in claiming that the word "Christian" is associated with Yahshua because the word "Christ" has no specific correlation to him and was a general term used for anointing. *The Oxford Companion to the Bible 1993 edition* admits that, "The origin of the term Christian is *uncertain.*" Still other sources claim that the word Christ is related to the Hindu god, "Krishna." One thing is certain about the word "Christian." Its exact meaning is conjectural. Therefore, to stringently use this name to profess the faith of one who follows Yahshua is completely devoid of any biblical foundation. Christians invariably respond to this observation with the statement, "names don't matter." Yet to them the term "Christian" seems to matter enough to be used to immediately pigeonhole someone as a follower of the true faith. As a consequence unnecessary pressure is continually brought to bear on newly converted members of Christianity to use this term exclusively to profess who they are. This attitude convinces a new believer that they are going against biblical doctrine if they don't assume this title, when in actual fact it is merely a requirement of manmade tradition. Though many Christian evangelists and ministers would agree that the term was never used in Yahshua's day, they support nonetheless that the prevailing attitude to anyone not professing to be a "born again Christian," should be one of suspicion. Their biblical support of this view is found in ***Acts 11:26, 26:28*** and ***1 Peter 4:16***, which all exhibit the word "Christian." Yet as pointed out previously, the term "Christian" does not share the same meaning as the original word "Natsarim."

Being Born Again was Not a New Concept

Being "Born Again" was not a Christian concept either. The *mikveh* (water immersion) in rabbinic literature refers to the water as "the womb of the world," and as a convert or existing believer emerged from the water it was considered a "new birth" that set him apart. As one emerged from these waters his was considered "a little child just born" or "a child of one day." Rabbinic literature uses the term "born again" at least six different times. It is referred to in the conversion of a Gentile, when someone is crowned king, at a bar mitzvah, marriage, becoming a rabbi and when an individual becomes the head of a Yeshiva (rabbinical school).

The term being "born again" is also used in Yahshua's exchange with Nicodemus, the head Pharisee of the Jews ***(John 3:1-8)***. Here Yahshua was talking about the "absolute renewal," "regeneration" or "transformation" of a person after they receive Moshiach (Messiah), which was always the very foundation of the Torah. His terminology that signifies this spiritual rebirth has simply been favoured and later adopted as a mass generic prefix in the title of all modern-day Christian followers since the 1960s. Evangelist Billy Graham principally ignited this trend. *After all,* Sha'ul HaShliach *(Paul)* had his own term for the experience which was, ***"a New Creation."*** This meant ***"...old things have passed away;*** (and) ***behold, all things have become new."*** **(2 Corinthians 5:17).**

Yahshua's surprise at Nicodemus's enquiry into being spiritually reborn is testimony to the concept's prior rabbinical acceptance. As ***John 3:10*** states; "***...Are you the moreh (teacher) of Yisrael, and you do not know these things?"*** The Messiah is genuinely surprised at Nicodemus' unfamiliarity with the concept of a "new birth" because every believer received a birth from above. The concept of being "born again" was not a new teaching introduced by Yahshua. To say otherwise reduces Yahshua's question to an arrogant comment. Even father Abraham was "born again" as is evident in his expectation of the coming deliverer. ***John 8:54; "Abraham looked forward to seeing Moshiach's day, saw it, and was glad."***

When one accepts YHWH by faith they die to their carnal self and are "reborn" or "live again" with a new spirit of faith. The re-establishment of this truth is what Yahshua was sharing with his friend Nicodemus. Oh yes, I said "Friend!" For years Christians have been giving old Nicodemus a hard time, but if you read his whole exchange with Yahshua you will find that he and his colleagues believed that he was truly the Messiah. He even respectfully addresses him as Rabbi! ***"Rabbi, we know that You are a moreh (teacher) come from Elohim; for no one can do these nisim (signs) that You are doing, except Elohim be with him."(John 3:2)***

So don't be fooled into believing that Yahshua came up with any new concepts that prior to his ministry were not known or ever realised by faithful believers. He was simply re-establishing a core aspect of Torah that had gradually been forgotten by many Pharisees in his day.

The preference for the name Christian is also supported by the fact that it is the current universally understood name for people who follow the Messiah of Nazareth. To be hesitant in the use of the term Christian in most evangelistic circles is looked upon as a sure sign of a questionable acceptance of the Saviour. While hesitancy in calling oneself a Christian may usually stem from a shaking spiritual foundation, to assume that it is always the case is dangerous. History has indeed put forward an unlikely array of men who also professed an allegiance to this name that modern history lecturers have managed to avoid mentioning. We can see why when we read this section of a speech by Adolf Hitler:

> "...My feeling as a Christian leads me to be a fighter for my Lord and Saviour. It leads me to the man who, at one time lonely and with only a few followers, recognised the Jews for what they were, and called on men to fight against them...As a Christian, I owe something to my people."

In the book called, *I Became a Jew*, *Shira Sorko-Ram* writes:

> "The culmination of all persecutions was masterminded by Hitler. Since Hitler was neither a Jew nor a Moslem, he was, in the eyes of the Jews, a Christian. (He had a Catholic background.) If a questioning Christian Gentile strongly resisted the idea that Hitler was a Christian, the Jew will answer that Hitler did not destroy these millions of Jews by himself. Thousands of Germans, Poles and others who called themselves Christians herded Jews onto trains or met them at sites of destruction. If you should have the opportunity to look through old World War II pictures, notice the Crusader's Cross pinned to the Nazi uniform. The cross is the symbol of Christianity to the Jews."

Prior to this universal use of the term Christian, members of this faith were known by many names. "Followers of the Way" is the second most widely known reference as found in ***Acts 9:2; "...and asked letters from him to the synagogues of Damascus, so that if he found any who were of the Way, whether men or women, he might bring them bound to Jerusalem."*** A considerably lesser-known reference appears in ***Acts 24:5; "For we have found this man a plague, a creator of dissension among all the Jews throughout the world, and a ring-leader of the sect of Nazarenes."*** The Scriptures also portray followers referring to each other as "brothers," "saints" or "disciples."

At the end of the day if anyone prefers to go by any of the above names *exclusively* they are taking a name given by men over a name that has been exclusively given by YHWH. Within any church environment, the taking on of the title "Christian" is seen as an extremely important step for a new believer. The result of this type of conditioning presented itself when I invited a woman to attend a Messianic meeting. She insisted on knowing if the people at this meeting were Christian to gauge whether she would attend or not.

I am not advocating that a Bible believing person should immediately drop the use of the term Christian because of reading anything contained solely within this work. My desire is that people, particularly Christians, might be inspired to investigate the issue and make a calculated decision based on information gathering and research rather than the hearsay of a guy with a back-to-front white collar.

One of the main characteristics of this Eternal Creator is that He is "unchanging," and suitably so should our actions be toward Him. While an almost unnoticeable aspect of our walk, such as a change in a name or a slight deviation in a style of worship may appear to be unimportant or of no consequence, over time a thousand changes of equal value, could one day see YHWH's chosen people practicing a completely foreign faith. Contrary to popular belief the Israelites did not abandon their Elohim when Moshe went up into Mount Sinai. They simply chose to worship Him in a manner that they assumed would be acceptable ***(Exodus 32:4-5)***. This assumption proved catastrophic. There is a fundamental practicality and simplicity in remaining securely anchored to the teachings of Scripture.

Over the centuries men of influence have caused the masses to deviate away from many of YHWH's commandments, despite Scripture warning believers to retain them via repetitious action. ***Thessalonians 2:15; "Therefore brethren, stand fast and hold the traditions, which you were taught, whether by word or our epistle."***

Today, there is no shortage of sermons that focus on carrying out and sharing YHWH's word in a loving manner (though the church refers to Him as God). But there are few, if any churches, that emphasise "guarding" or "holding fast" to it ***(Deuteronomy 11:22, Isaiah 56:6)***. Because this raises the question, 'hold fast to what?' Popular Christian theology unravels in this area because it is forced to explain an adherence to subsequent manmade traditions over former rulings set down by YHWH. ***Leviticus 22:9*** and ***31*** emphasizes guarding His commandments, because people ***"seek*** (the) ***truth from the lips of*** (His) ***priests" (Malachi 2:7)*** and if they do not hold onto His former knowledge (or teachings) His commands will become corrupted. Then these men will be held "contemptible" ***(Malachi 2:9)*** and receive a stricter judgment. ***James 3:1; "Let not many of you become teachers, knowing that we shall receive a stricter judgment."***

Paradoxically Christians are taught to avoid manmade traditions. As they do this they unwittingly let go of many of YHWH's statutes as well. The result is a vague teaching (grace heavy), which subconsciously promotes tradition as "legalism." Such a climate has given birth to a people who have claimed a foreign name, which has subsequently given birth to a foreign identity. YHWH, both through His Son and His own actions always leads by example and does not change. ***Malachi 3:6-7a; "For I am YHWH, I change not; therefore you sons of Yaakov are not consumed. Even from the days of your ahvot (fathers) you have gone away from My Torot (plural for Torah) and have not guarded them. Make teshuvah (a return) to Me, and I will return to you, says YHWH tzevaoth (of Hosts)."*** And ***Hebrews 13:8; "Yahshua ha Moshiach is the same yesterday, today and le-olam-va-ed (forever and ever)."*** If we find ourselves at a point where we've inherited religious lies from our ancestors, we should make an effort to return to the truth.

While it may be enlightening to reveal a truth and in doing so hint at taking something away, in this case the use of the name "Christian," it is important to attempt to fill the potential vacuum that this revelation might create. Calling into question a comforting and familiar term, that represents a person's belief, and walking away, can be a bit like turning up to a house and telling its occupants it's poorly built before demolishing it and leaving. What name then should a people who profess to follow the same Elohim as the Hebrews go by? The answer is found in ***Genesis 32:28; "And the Man said, your name shall no longer be called Yaakov (Jacob), but Yisrael: for as a sar (lower level prince) you have power with Elohim and with men, and have prevailed."*** This verse reveals the name of YHWH's chosen people and its meaning, which is a nation of "overcoming believers" who struggle with Messiah and succeed. Jacob's wrestling match with the Creator, masquerading as a man, is a snapshot of Israel's whole existence.

The Scriptures are overwhelmingly clear on who these people were and what their name was. There are no other people that YHWH has ever mentioned as being sovereign over throughout the whole of the Old or New Testament. The frequent appearance within Scripture of "all nations" being under YHWH contextually describes foreign nations joining into one commonwealth, as is evident in ***Zechariah 2:11-12; "Many nations shall be joined to YHWH, in that day, and they shall become Ami (My people): And I will dwell in the midst of you, and you shall know that YHWH tzevaoth (of Hosts) has sent Me to you. And YHWH shall inherit Yahudau as His portion in the kadosh (set-apart) land, and shall choose Yahrushalayim again."*** The Christian mindset is that the Jew strayed from YHWH and Yahshua came to bring about a new faith based in the Gentile camp into which the Jew must adhere. But the truth is that there was never initially a division between Jew and Gentile. The Jews (but not all) gradually lost their way by adding to YHWH's Torah and observing it as a means of salvation in itself. The other tribes dissolved into obscurity by abandoning the Torah, but both houses through Yahshua have been given a re-entry point. Presently, because the church still preaches the abolition of the law the lost tribes are still lost, but are at least now in a state where the truth is not far away.

Chapter Three

Nazarene Israelites Explained

WHO ARE NAZARENE ISRAELITES? This is a fair question. The most alarming thing to reconcile is the reality that they are not Christians. This naturally and understandably causes immediate concern for a Christian. This concern will often cause a conditioned churchgoer to switch off at any subsequent explanation. If you haven't switched off please feel free to read on.

A Nazarene Israelite rejects the Greco-Roman interpretation of the Commandment altering Christ and accepts the reality of a Torah loving Hebrew Messiah. He believes that this Messiah is the visible expressed image of the Creator ***(Colossians 1:15; Hebrews 1:1-3)*** who was brought forth from the Father's bosom before creation ***(John 1:18, John 16:30, Micah 1:3)***. He believes that his name was and still is Yahshua, which means, "Yah is salvation" and that he is the Living Torah, the Word of Elohim made flesh ***(John 1:14)***. A Nazarene Israelite believes that ancient Israel looked forward to the coming Messiah as did key biblical figures such as Hava (Eve) ***(Genesis 3:15)***, Abraham ***(John 8:56)*** and King David ***(Psalms 16, 22, 31, 41, 41, 65, 68, 98)***. Indeed Orthodox Judaism, particularly Hasidic Judaism, acknowledges profusely that the Torah points to a Messiah.

The Nazarene Israelite also accepts that YHWH and Yahshua are one as opposed to three ***(John 10:30)*** and that this oneness exists in unity ***(John 17:20-23)*** and Yahshua has no authority accept what authority he receives from the Father. This is why he said in ***John 5:30-32; "I can by My own self do nothing: as I hear, I judge: and My mishpat (judgment) is righteous; because I seek not my own will, but the will of the Abba who has sent me. If I bear witness of Myself, My witness is not emet (true). There is another that bears witness of Me; and I know that the witness which He witnesses of Me is emet (true)."*** And in ***Mark 10:18,19; "And Yahshua said to him, 'Why do you call Me tov (good)? There is none tov but One, that is YHWH.'"***

The Nazarene Israelite also accepts that none of the Torah (law) has been abolished, but that it has been fulfilled through Messiah's death and resurrection. ***Matthew 5:17; "Think not that I have come to weaken, or destroy the Torah (law[1]), or the neviim (prophets): I have not come to weaken, or destroy, but to completely reveal it in its intended fullness."*** And in ***Matthew 5:18, "For truly I say to you, Until the current Shamayim (heaven) and earth pass away, not one yud (jot), or nekudah (tittle) shall by any means pass from the Torah, until all be fulfilled."*** A "yud" is the name for the smallest letter in the Hebrew language and a "nekudah" is a tiny Hebrew accent marking.

Question: But doesn't ***Romans 10:4*** say that Messiah put an end to the law? ***"For Christ is the end of the law for righteousness to everyone who believes." (New King James Version)***

Answer: Not at all. The word "end" was originally translated by a Christian (James Murdock) from the Aramaic word *saka*, which means "aim." That's why the passage continues with, ***"For Moses writes about the righteousness which is of the law, 'The man who does these things shall live by them.'" (Romans 10:5, New King James Version)*** The prophet Moshe never wrote about an end to the Torah, much less the law (another inaccurate word in the ***Romans 10:4*** passage). All the Torah always pointed to Yahshua.

1 Though the bracketed meaning "law" is used, it has been opted for to show the verse in context of its Christian understanding. In reality the word "Torah" means "counsel" or "teaching."

The Nazarene Israelite does not accept that Rabbi Sha'ul HaShliach advocated that the Torah was done away with. ***Romans 3:31; "Do we then make void the Torah through personal emunah (faith)? By no means: actually we establish the Torah."***

The Nazarene Israelite understands the importance of being separated from any religious organisation that is yoked together with pagan influence ***(Revelations 18:4)***. This includes all religious organisations and denominations that retain any ritual whose origin has been passed down from a pagan source. This includes Freemasonry and any other society (secret or otherwise) that practices recital of oaths of allegiance to an order whose full principles are not revealed to new initiates and whose rituals are blatantly drawn from a smorgasbord of pagan traditions.

Though Catholicism is chiefly cited as having pagan practices it is not fair to single it out as it draws attention away from the bigger picture. Rome is the mother of all forms of Christianity because every other accepted Christian organisation (even non-denominational groups and Sabbath keeping churches) still contain some ingredient of Catholicism and all possess historical evidence of minor or major withdrawals from its religious system at one time or another.

The Nazarene Israelite sees the majority of Jewish feasts, Sabbaths and festivals as shadow pictures of future events and as scriptural object lessons, which are to be upheld throughout all generations ***(Exodus 31:13)***.

Are Gentiles Excluded and without Hope?

A Nazarene recognises that they are members of the Commonwealth of Israel, OUTSIDE OF WHICH THERE IS NO SALVATION. ***Ephesians 2:12; "...at that time you were without Moshiach (Messiah) being excluded, aliens from the Commonwealth of Yisrael, as gerim (strangers) from the covenants of promise, having no tikvah (hope), and without Eloha in the olam hazeh (world)."*** because ***"Outside are the dogs, those who practice magic arts, the sexually immoral, the murderers, the idolaters and everyone who loves and practices falsehood" (Revelation 22:15).***

Clear your mind of the Greco-Roman Gentile spin you've received in church and look closer at the following verse: ***Ephesians 2:11-12; "Therefore remember, that you being in times past gentiles in the flesh, who are called The Uncircumcision by those called the Brit-Milah (circumcised) in the flesh made by hands; that at THAT TIME you were without Moshiach (Messiah), being EXCLUDED, aliens from the Commonwealth of Yisrael, as gerim (strangers) from the covenants of promise, having no tikvah (hope), and without Eloha (the Mighty One) in the olam hazeh (the world)."*** This verse clearly shows that to be identified as a Gentile, at the very least knowingly by one who understands this message, is to remain without hope.

Romans 1:16; "For I am not ashamed of the besorah (positive news) of Moshiach: for it is the power of YHWH for salvation to every one that believes; to the Yahudi (Jew) first, and also the Greek and Aramean." The seven congregations of Asia Minor (Modern-day Turkey), addressed in the Book of Revelations, were principally inhabited by descendants who came from massive influxes of Ephraimite migrants (descendants of the ten lost tribes) that pushed North. Interestingly this verse encourages sharing the positive news of Salvation through Messiah to the blinded Jew first and the foreigner second. This order is exhibited in the Book of Acts as thousands of Jews were first added to the ekklesia[2] ("called out and assembled citizens") in ***Acts 2:41***.

Who am I in Messiah?

The title we are to claim is neither Jew (which were just one of twelve tribes) nor Gentile (foreigners). It is Israel! But remember the Jews have the Torah and the teachers of the Torah sit in Moshe's seat. ***Matthew 23:1-3; "Then spoke Yahshua to the multitude, and to His Talmidim (students), Saying, the sophrim (scribes) and the Prushim (Pharisees) sit in Moshe's kesay (seat): All therefore that Moshe's kesay will invite you to observe, that observe and***

2 Ekklesia (ek-kaleo) means "an assembly of citizens summoned by (a) crier (or herald)… (a) legislative assembly." [R. Scott, and H.G. Liddell, A Greek-English Lexicon, p. 206.] "…an assembly of the people convened at the public place of council for the purpose of deliberating" [J. H. Thayer, A Greek-English Lexicon of the New Testament, p. 196]. "…the lawful assembly in a free Greek city of all those possessed of the rights of citizenship, for the transaction of public affairs" [R.C. Trench, Synonyms of the New Testament, 7th ed., pp. 1-2].

do;*"** Yahshua did not have a problem with what the Scribes and the Pharisees were teaching. He had a problem with how they were living. This is made clear in the next verse, ***"But do not do after their mitzvoth (love deeds): for they say, and do not." Notice Yahshua didn't say, "Those Pharisees and Scribes that reject me ignore and those that embrace me heed." I have found that it is folly to ever snub my nose at any Orthodox Jewish teaching without first investigating it thoroughly.

Making the Jews Jealous, not Angry

Salvation is not of the Gentiles, rather it is *available* to the Gentiles and is designed to provoke the Jews to jealousy so that they may be saved: ***(Romans 11:11; "salvation has come to the nations (gentiles) to make Yisrael envious."*** The Jew will never be jealous of a cross emblazoned church of any denomination, whether they keep Sunday or Sabbath. Because they know that the church is the *Temple of Circe*, a pagan Greco-Romanised amalgamation of Babylonian Mystery school teachings. There is no excuse for ignorance in this current technological age of information distribution and gathering. A rational individual knows it and YHWH knows it.

Worship without Knowledge is Dangerous

The Orthodox Jew knows and adheres to the Creator's unchanging view ***(Malachi 3:6,7)*** on marshalling customs and tools used in pagan worship to honour Him, which can be studied in the Golden Calf incident. ***Exodus 32:5; "So when Aaron saw it (the Golden Calf), he built an altar before it. And Aaron made a proclamation and said, "Tomorrow is a feast to YHWH."*** The calf was fashioned as a sincere icon to represent YHWH, but instead brought about abominable repercussions. This is why Sha'ul is concerned with the way people worship the Creator when he says, ***Romans 10:2; "For I bear them record that they have a zeal for YHWH but not according to da'at (knowledge)."*** And this is why. ***Hosea 4:6 says, "My people are destroyed for lack of da'at (knowledge): because you have rejected da'at, I will also reject you, that you shall not be a kohen (priest) to***

Me: seeing you have forgotten the Torah of your Elohim, I will also forget your children."

The Advantage of the Jew

The Commonwealth of Israel is defined by three major characteristics. They are:

- Keeping the Sabbaths ***(Isaiah 56:2; "Blessed is the man who does this, the man who holds it fast, who keeps the Shabbat.")***
- Loving the Name ***(Isaiah 56:6; "Also the sons of the ger (stranger), that join themselves to YHWH, to serve Him, and to love the name of YHWH…")***
- And holding fast to the covenants ***(Isaiah 56:6b; "...every person that guards the Shabbat from polluting it and takes hold of My brit [covenant].")***

Becoming a member of the Commonwealth of Israel is not defined by moving to Israel and taking up a secular citizenship there.

The above information clearly establishes the context of the following verses that you may have been glossing over for years in Bible study classes.

John 4:22; "You worship you know not what: we know what we worship: for salvation is from the Yahudim (Jews)." (Yahshua's very words) This is not referring to the Orthodox Judaism of today, it is referring to a walk that looks Jewish in almost every way accept it recognises Messiah Yahshua (Jesus) in his full capacity as our High Priest! Samaritans were loathed by the Jews, because they professed to worship the same El (Mighty One / God), but not according to the oracles of YHWH, which were first entrusted to Judah. ***Romans 3:2; "…because they (the Jews) were the first to be entrusted with the oracles of YHWH and the first to believe in His word."*** There is no excuse for those who have lost friends or relatives to Orthodox Judaism. Yes, they are in error, just as much as a Roman Catholic is in error, but this shouldn't cause one to delay investigating as to whether one should withdraw from the church and move into the Hebraic roots of the Nazarene Israelite faith. I'm not just talking about Rome, but the church in general!

Let's examine the above verse in greater context: ***Romans 3:1-2; "What advantage then has the Yahudi (Jew)? Or, what profit is there in brit-milah (circumcision)? Much in every way: because they (the Jews) were the first to be entrusted with the oracles of YHWH and the first to believe in His word."*** This verse clearly states that the Jews have an advantageous position in terms of their relationship with the Creator.

I recognise that some Christians may find this revelation problematic and difficult to reconcile, if for no other reason other than the locality of this statement in the Scriptures and the fact that Yahshua is recorded as saying it. But if Christians are not willing to depart from their canned Scripture and study from a Torah perspective, rather than a New Testament perspective, the Bible will remain largely unfathomable in so many areas. Rabbi Sha'ul warns those who embrace Messiah and boast against the Jews; ***"Boast not against the cultivated branches (The Jews). But if you boast, you better remember that you do not bear the Root, but the Root bears you." (Romans 11:18)***

Sect is Not a Four Letter Word

The Nazarene Israelite or Messianic movement has often been accused of being a sect. Those who have rejected such accusations, prepare for a shock. This faith is indeed a sect. There, I wrote it. A person's ignorance of the word's true definition gives this argument life. On the contrary, no one should make any apology for use of appropriate terminology. If anyone is weathering this accusation, take comfort in the knowledge that Rabbi Sha'ul was also accused as being ***"a ringleader of this*** (same) ***Nazarene sect..." (Acts 24:5)***

Consider the choice of language used in the following two verses (as they appear in most Bible translations): ***Acts 24:14: "But this I admit to you, that according to the Way which they call a heretical sect, I do serve the Elohim of our fathers, believing everything that is written in the Law and the Prophets." Acts 28:22: "But we desire to hear from you***

> ***what your views are. For concerning this heretical sect, it's known to us that it is spoken against everywhere."*** Notice the use of the description "heretical sect" by translators. A sect by definition is not sacrilegious unless it's branded as a "heretical sect." If this were not true the term "heretical sect" would be a grammatical tautology (i.e. a useless repetition of words that have the same meaning). The definition of sect is, "a separatist group characterized by loyalty to a certain school of thought and practice," a "sect, party, school." This is an accurate way of describing those who have followed "the way" for many generations. The Scriptures more affectionately refer to them (that's hopefully you too) as "the Remnant." There are three locations where the single term "sect" appears (on its own) in *The Book of Acts* (as it appears in most common English Bible translations). ***Acts 5:17: "But the High Priest rose up, along with all his associates (that is the sect of the Sadducees), and they were filled with jealousy." Acts 15:5: "But some of the sect of the Pharisees who had believed stood up, saying, 'It is necessary to circumcise them and to direct them to observe the Law of Moses.'" Acts 26:5: "since they have known about me for a long time, if they are willing to testify, that I lived as a Pharisee according to the strictest sect of our religion."***

A Jew to the Untrained Eye

For the most part, a Nazarene Israelite looks, acts, and thinks Jewish, but recognises Messiah Yahshua as his or her sovereign and saviour. This is because the Jews have been the only tribe to maintain Torah observance throughout their generations, though many Jews today, even in Israel, do not keep the covenants. The Torah observant Jew uses customs that are rooted in tradition (the majority of which are venerable), which teach crucial aspects of the one true faith in daily life.

The following is an extract from the writings of Epiphanius, a prominent early church father that clearly shows a negative view toward the Nazarene Israelite sect, but strangely enough also very accurately describes their practices and principles, of which there is no argument from me. So for this reason I think it only befitting to conclude this chapter with these sentiments (Also note the blatant reference to the Book of Matthew's original Hebrew written origin.):

> But these sectarians... did not call themselves Christians--but "Nazarenes," ...HOWEVER THEY ARE SIMPLY COMPLETE JEWS. THEY USE NOT ONLY THE NEW TESTAMENT BUT THE OLD TESTAMENT AS WELL, AS THE JEWS DO... THEY HAVE NO DIFFERENT IDEAS, BUT CONFESS EVERYTHING EXACTLY AS THE LAW PROCLAIMS IT AND IN THE JEWISH FASHION-- EXCEPT FOR THEIR BELIEF IN MESSIAH, IF YOU PLEASE! For they acknowledge both the resurrection of the dead and the divine creation of all things, and declare that G-d is one, and that his son is Y'shua the Messiah. They are trained to a nicety in Hebrew. For among them the entire Law, the Prophets, and the... Writings... are read in Hebrew, as they surely are by the Jews. They are different from the Jews, and different from Christians, only in the following. They disagree with Jews because they have come to faith in Messiah; but since they are still fettered by the Law--circumcision, the Sabbath, and the rest-- they are not in accord with Christians.... they are nothing but Jews.... They have the Goodnews according to Matthew in its entirety in Hebrew. For it is clear that they still preserve this, in the Hebrew alphabet, as it was originally written.
>
> (Epiphanius; Panarion 29)

Chapter Four

Torah and Tradition

SINCE ENTERING INTO a Nazarene Israelite walk, my wife and I have noted significant differences with a great many things pertaining to this faith and our former lives as Christians. Along the way, some people on the fringe of this movement have asked questions and made valid enquiries as to the origin of customs, rituals and liturgies involved in keeping Shabbat and aspects of worship services. There is also a natural curiosity about the significance of the Torah portions, lighting of candles, wearing of the tallit and reciting the Shema. Naturally the instinctive reaction when facing an unfamiliar religious custom is to ask the one hundred-thousand dollar question, "Is it Scripture?"

Firstly, it is worth pointing out that Scripture commands us to love YHWH (God) with all our hearts and with all our minds. ***Luke 10:27-28;"And he answering said, 'You shall love the Master YHWH your Eloha (Mighty One) with all your lev (heart), and with all your being, and with all your strength, and with all your mind; and your neighbour as yourself.'"*** Therefore, can anyone accuse another of not being Scriptural when a daily routine is structured in a manner that causes the Creator to be a central focus (provided that it does not go against, replace or hinder Torah)? For example, an Orthodox Jew will say a blessing upon arising from sleep, after a bowel evacuation, after showering and after donning his daily attire. In fact, by the time a religiously observant Jew leaves the front door he has prayed and spoken blessings over nearly every aspect of his morning routine, no matter how seemingly mundane or trivial. His day proceeds literally immersed in continual acknowledgement of the Creator, through various means outlined in the Scriptures, such as adhering to specific prayer times ***(Psalms 88:13, 69:13)*** and giving thanks to YHWH for anything that occurs, whether good or bad ***(Ephesians 5:20)***. To the average Christian this lifestyle comes across as time consuming and impractical. But, constant immersion in Torah will eventually lead to precisely this method of conduct.

Contrary to popular yet misinformed belief, particularly in religious circles, traditions are not only absolutely permissible, but encouraged in Scripture. Customs that first appear in the writings of the prophets such as facing toward Jerusalem in prayer ***(Daniel 6:11)***, the ordinance to avoid idle chatter on Shabbat ***(Isaiah 58:13)*** and citing righteous ancestors in prayer ***(Psalms 116:16)*** highlight traditions as being an acceptable part of correct halakha (Torah observant conduct) throughout the Biblical period.

Perhaps no other tradition is so authoritatively presented in Scripture than the festival of Purim, in which Mordechai charges his fellow Jews to annually observe a time of "feasting and gladness" in ***Esther 9:20-23***. The observance of Purim has been accepted by Jews as an official Biblical holiday since its institution.

Any type of ordinance or regular custom that is captured in Scripture that does not originally appear in the Torah shows a deeper aspect of spiritual service deciphered through intense study of the Torah itself. King David frequently refers to maintaining physically clean hands in relation to possessing a pure heart ***(Psalms 18;21,25, 24:4, 26:6)***, alluding to the value of the ritual washing of hands that according to a surface reading of Torah is only incumbent on the priesthood.

This chapter will delve into the concept of man-made tradition and highlight the differences between a good and bad tradition. Along the way it will show how some Judaic customs, assumed by many as poisonous hindrances to Torah, actually have strong Scriptural foundations.

Many people who have come out of false religious systems and had unbiblical practices thrust upon them, develop an "in-built" prejudice or suspicion toward man-made traditions in general. As a result the concept of traditions as a part of one's obligation in fulfilling YHWH's will can be hard to accept. For those who feel they fall into this category, this chapter will likely be a most valuable read.

The Hebrew word for "tradition" is *m'soret*, which literally means "to hand on" or "pass on" something. This word is only found once in the TaNaK (Old Testament) in ***Ezekiel 20:37; "And I will cause you to pass under the rod, and I will bring you into the bond of the brit (covenant)."*** The word "bond," sometimes translated as "obligations" is better translated as "tradition," therefore more accurately reading "...I will bring you into the tradition of the covenant."

Scriptures View of Traditions

Interestingly, all the instances of Yahshua's criticism of the traditions of the Pharisees are, if examined closely, primarily focused on the contrast between their obsession with manmade ordinances and their declining interest and in some cases total abandonment of some of YHWH's commandments. On the contrary, many rabbinical traditions set more workable platforms for the articulation of performing different kinds of mitzvoth (commandments). This is why ***2 Thessalonians 2:15*** says; ***"Therefore, Yisraelite brothers, stand fast, and hold on to the commandments and the traditions that you have been taught, whether by word or our letter."*** And this is why Rabbi Sha'ul boasts of traditions in ***Galatians 1:14; "And I progressed in Yahudim's religion above many of my equals in my own nation; above all I was especially zealous of the teachings of my ahvot (fathers)."*** Even the Scriptures speak affectionately about a tradition, which was started by Jeremiah in ***2 Chronicles 35:25; "And Yirmeyahu (Jeremiah) lamented for Yoshiyahu (Josiah) : and all the singing men and the singing women spoke of Yoshiyahu in their lamentations until this day, and made them an ordinance in Yisrael: and, see, they are written in the lamentations."*** Messiah Yahshua upholds a tradition in ***John 10:22*** when he enters the Temple to celebrate the festival of Chanukah. Would anyone dare accuse Yahshua of observing a manmade tradition? No, because there is nothing wrong with manmade traditions as long as they do not overshadow, impede, obstruct or contradict Scripture. ***2 Thessalonians 3:6*** speaks of following a tradition handed down by the Apostles. ***"Now we command you, Yisraelite brothers, in the name of our Master Yahshua ha Moshiach that you withdraw yourselves from every Yisraelite brother that has walked disorderly, and not after the tradition that he received from us."***

The Traditional View of Traditions Challenged

Let's look at the major passages and verses that are often cited when attacking traditions.

Matthew 15:2-6; "'Why do your talmidim (disciples) transgress the tradition of the Zechanim (elders)? For they do not wash their hands when they eat food?" But He answered and said to them, 'Why do you also transgress the commandment of YHWH by your tradition? For YHWH commanded, you saying, Honour your abba (father) and eema (mother): and, he that curses abba, or eema, let him die the death. But you say, Whoever shall say to his abba, or his eema, It is a gift by whatever you would have been profited by me; And does not honour his abba, or his eema, he shall be free. This is how you have made the commandment of YHWH of no effect by your tradition.'" Yahshua responds to criticism of his apparent failure to instruct his students to wash their hands before eating (in general). According to Judaism, the tradition of washing hands is only partaken upon arising, before prayer, handling set-apart objects, before eating bread during ritual service, after relieving one's self and before uttering specific blessings. Yahshua criticises the Pharisaic tradition of obligating a father and mother to forego direct financial benefit from offspring, thus impeding the commandment to honour parents. ***Mark 7:1-23*** also has a rendering of the above encounter with more initial detail. It is worth noting that one can actually break a commandment if the doing of it brings about evil, such as refraining from applying first aid to a person on Shabbat.

Colossians 2:8; "Let no man beguile you of your reward of a false humility and in the worshipping of heavenly malachim (kings) spiritually standing on things that he has not seen, empty handed things,

created by his fleshly mind." This verse warns Israel not to go after philosophies and concepts that are concocted from the carnal minds of men (i.e. Scientology, environment focused religions, secret societies). The entire nation of Israel beheld the cloud of YHWH at Mount Sinai. Therefore no other religion on earth can make the claim that all its original members witnessed its foundation by an audible and visual manifestation of their g-d.

1 Peter 1:18; "Knowing that you were not redeemed with corruptible things, like silver, or gold, from your futile spiritual conduct received by tradition from your ahvot (fathers)." Yahshua is reaffirming that traditional conduct and fancy objects have no power to bring about Salvation on their own. He is not addressing traditional conduct that is incidental in the observance of Torah. Nor is he saying that physical objects have no purpose in furthering the Divine Will. On the contrary, there are instances in Scripture where objects are used as conduits to enact YHWH's will. The staff of Aaron, the bronze serpent, the Ark of the Covenant and Yahshua's tzitzit are some divinely empowered objects found in Scripture. Even the mezuzah[1], a small Torah encapsulated cylinder affixed to the doorpost of the home, is likened to a guard box in which an angel can post himself to watch over a dwelling. A mezuzah may channel significant spiritual protection, but unlike a talisman it has no power of its own and is useless unless the occupants of the home are obedient to YHWH.

The above verse is not saying that traditional conduct or fancy objects are to be avoided. But such things are certainly worthless if seen as having isolated value in achieving redemption.

Mark 7:8; "Laying aside the commandments of YHWH, you guard the traditions of men, such as the washing of pots and cups; and many other such things you do." The Pharisees that Yahshua is addressing had ridded themselves of some of YHWH's mitzvoth (love deeds) for the sake of their own traditions. The Messiah is not condemning the fact that they had traditions. This verse is an extract from the same encounter in ***Matthew 15:2-6***.

1 The mezuzah contains the first two paragraphs of the "Shema" ***(Deut. 6:4-9 & Deut. 11:13-21)*** and is a reminder that whenever there is movement from one sphere of activity, to another, consciousness of Elohim must be renewed.

Mark 7:9; "And He said to them, 'Full well you do reject the mitzvoth (love deeds) of YHWH, that you may keep your own tradition.'" The concern here is the setting aside or abandoning of mitzvoth. As long as the tradition didn't inhibit, replace or contradict the performing of any mitzvoth, prayer or praise, it was never considered harmful in Yahshua's day or any other time within Scripture. For example a group may have a tradition of reciting a specific sequence of praise songs. The motivation for this might be because the songs lyrics and melodies are simply preferred. Either way it is not an issue as to whether this group is being Scriptural in following a particular recital of songs, but observing a repetitive action to enable the performing of praise and worship.

Michah 6:16; "For the chukim (statutes) of Omri are kept and all the works of Beit Achav (house of Ahab), and you have your halacha (ways) in their councils; that I should make you a desolation, and your inhabitants a hissing: therefore you shall bear the reproach of My people." This verse is talking about the observance of pagan practices, which are an abomination to YHWH and has nothing to do with the condemnation of traditions.

The Pharisees' Respect for Yahshua's Teachings

Scripture contains quite a bit of material that exhibits the Pharisees' respect for Yahshua's authority. Normally this demographic is portrayed as being enamoured with vain tradition, but close inspection reveals that many of them agreed with Messiah's teachings. Take for example Yahshua's verbal exchange with the teachers of the Torah in the book of Mark. Firstly, note the distinction that the Word makes between the Pharisees and Herod's henchmen when they came to try and catch him out. ***Mark 12:13; "And they sent to Him certain of the Prushim (Pharisees) and of the Herodians, to catch Him (Yahshua) in His words."*** Not all the Pharisees in Yahshua's day agreed with those on Herod's payroll, but they did none-the-less tolerate them, having no other alternative. This sometimes took the form of them tagging along to fulfil Herod's agenda. In the next verse note the opening remark, which would have offended the Herodians had they not falsely believed this was a lie to set Yahshua up. ***Mark 12:14; "And when they had come, they***

said to Him, 'Rabbi, we know that You are emet (truth), and are not concerned with man's opinion: for You regard not the person of men, but teach the way of Elohim in emet (truth).'" A little further on, one of the Scribes, having come later in the discussion, perceived that Yahshua was answering questions exceptionally well. ***Mark 12:28-33; "And one of the Sophrim (Scribes) came, and having heard them*** (Yahshua and the Pharisees) ***reasoning together, and perceiving that He had answered them well, asked Him, which is the first mitzvah (love deed) of all? And Yahshua answered him, The first of all the mitzvoth is, Shema (hear), Yisrael; the Master YHWH is our Elohim, the Master YHWH is Echad (One): And you shall love the Master YHWH your Elohim with all your lev (heart), and with all your being, and with all your mind, and with all your strength: this is the first mitzvah. And the second is like it, namely this; You shall love your neighbour as yourself. There are no other mitzvoth greater than these. <u>And the Sopher (Scribe) said to Him, Well, Rabbi, You have said the emet (truth)</u>: for there is One Elohim; and there is no other besides Him: And to love Him with all the lev (heart), and with all the binah (understanding), and with all the being, and with all the strength, and to love your neighbour as yourself, is more than all the burnt offerings and sacrifices."*** The Scribe, having ascertained that his agreement with Yahshua would have caused offence to some of the Herodian's, responded discreetly. Rather than this approach being met with rebuke for lacking courage to stand by Yahshua publicly, the Messiah confirmed his nearness to achieving his heavenly reward. ***Mark 12:34; "And when Yahshua saw that he answered discreetly, 'He said to him, You are not far from the malchut (kingdom) of YHWH.' And no man after that did ask Him any questions."*** This response by Yahshua was deliberate, allowing him to lay a pillar in a larger foundation that would enable his own brother Yakov (James) to receive enough support from such men like this Scribe to become head of the Sanhedrin after his death and resurrection.

Weighing the Value of a Tradition

It is the responsibility of each individual to carefully examine the nature of a tradition as it is handed down from one generation to the next. English playwright, W. Somerset Maugham, once wrote, "Let tradition be our guide, but not our jailer."

Some things you should ask yourself when faced with a tradition:

1. Is the practice originally adapted from a pagan ritual?
2. Does the practice or ritual hinder other mitzvoth or drown them out in some way?
3. Does it cause you to do and say things that contradict your knowledge of Scripture?
4. Does the practice replace an aspect of the Torah?
5. Does it help you focus your thoughts on YHWH?
6. Does it help, encourage and increase your ability and understanding of core Torah or Scriptural principles?
7. Does it provide a good framework to study, worship and interact with YHWH?
8. Does the practice establish a good foundation for performing mitzvoth?

Now let's look at some practices observed by Nazarene Israelites, which up until recently have almost exclusively been considered strictly Jewish customs.

The Weekly Shabbat

The Shabbat is a weekly rehearsal (*miqra*), which was not just given to the Jews, but to all twelve tribes of Israel and the strangers that dwelt among them. It is the first feast listed in Scripture ***(Leviticus 23)*** and is the head of all the set-apart days. It is a day that amplifies the blessings of all the other feasts and it is a glimpse of the restored kingdom of Israel. It is a delight to a believer, not a burden, but most of all it is a sign between the Creator and the believer throughout all their generations that they are truly His people ***(Exodus 31:13, 17, Ezekiel 9:4*** & ***Revelations 7:3)***.

The Messiah kept the Shabbat ***(Luke 4:16, 6:6, 13:10; Mark 1:21; 3:1-2; 6:2)*** as did early believers after His death and resurrection ***(Acts 15:21 & 16:13)***.

The Shabbat commences at sundown ***(Genesis 1:5)***. It is to be set-apart from other days and is therefore to be structured in a way that best vehicles rest, study and meeting together with other believers. The Shabbat is a set-apart (holy) convocation ***(Leviticus 23:4)***, which means believers should try and congregate together in a central location. A synagogue is preferable, but a house or a community hall is also acceptable. It is a day when a believer is to particularly focus and connect with YHWH. The Book of Acts records both Jews and Greeks attending a synagogue together. ***Acts 14:1; "And it came to pass in Ikoniom, that they went both together into the synagogue of the Yahudim, and so spoke, that a great multitude both of the Yahudim and also the Greeks believed."***

Since my wife and I first started keeping the Shabbat we have noticed an amazing change in our lives. The day has without a doubt become a most exciting event. We look with great expectation as the week draws to a close and the Shabbat nears. It's difficult to explain to a person who has never kept Shabbat before of the feeling of delight one gets from keeping it. Even with a Seventh Day Baptist background and attending church on the Saturday, my wife and I never really understood the uniqueness of the day until we began keeping it in the same manner as our Israelite ancestors. Unfortunately most Nazarene Israelites do not have an opportunity to attend a Messianic synagogue in their respective geographical areas. If possible it is advisable to affiliate oneself with a group that does, via internet correspondence.

Synagogue Attendance and the Torah Portion

The custom of meeting in a synagogue was observed by Yahshua ***(Mark 1:21, Luke 4:15, 16 & 13:10)***. This act was espoused from ***Leviticus 23:3 "...but the seventh day is a Shabbat-Shabbaton (Sabbath of solemn rest), a Migra Kodesh (Set-apart gathering)."*** The custom of reading a Torah portion in the synagogue is evident even in the Brit Chadashah[2] (New Testament). ***Acts 15:21*** describes that in them Moshe had been read ***"from old times."*** This included an accompanying selection from the books of the prophets (Halftarah) ***(Acts 13:15)***. The practice of reading Torah and Halftarah parshas (portions) was never practiced in any church that I have ever set foot in, yet according to Christian translations of the Brit Chadashah the *alleged* early church observed this practice.

The Lighting of the Candles

Traditional Judaism opens and closes the Shabbat with an *Erev* Shabbat Celebration and a *Havdalah* service. *Havdalah* is a Hebrew word, which means "division" or "distinction." The lighting of the candles for both the opening and the closing of the Sabbath symbolises many things and while it is not documented as a specific mitzvah the act represents core Scriptural principles. They symbolise the bride (Israel) who waits for her Husband (YHWH) and the light of the two houses, which are called Ephraim[3] and Judah.

It is up to the individual as to whether or not they pore over the Scriptures on the subject of the Shabbat or any other mitzvoth with a pretext of extracting the minimal requirements for their observance. Alternatively an individual may prefer to adopt the Scriptural principle of going the extra mile ***(Matthew 5:41)*** and see how they might be able to do the most they possibly can to set apart the Biblical festivals from other days of the week. In doing this, one's motivation should be to set a more receptive atmosphere to focus on YHWH and not compromise the Torah in anyway.

Different Messianic groups may have slight variations in their Shabbat service, as do seventh-day observant churches, which is an encouraging quality, because it makes them unique from each other, yet unifies them because of YHWH's key requirements.

Observing a group's order of service or liturgy and wondering whether some aspect of it is Scripture is fine, but if the motivation is because of a minimal requirement attitude, this can become

2 The term, "Chadashah" is derived from the Hebrew root, "hadash" and is understood to mean "new," but more accurately means "renewed" or "refreshed." It is for this reason that the New Testament is sometimes referred to as "The Renewed Covenant."

3 Ephraim is made up of ten Israelite tribes who departed from the Torah, but are now returning.

the seed of true legalism. In other words, it's like saying, "What is the least I can do to get into the kingdom of YHWH?" This type of outlook reflects a poor relationship with the Creator. Things we do for YHWH should not be motivated for fear of hell, but by progressing in stages of love and appreciation for Him as we learn and accept His will in our lives. If our attitude toward our partner was to do the absolute minimum to keep them happy it would turn into a legalistic going-through-the-motions exercise. But if we approach our relationship with our significant other with the attitude of going the extra mile whilst expecting nothing in return we begin to enact true unconditional love, the same type of love we hope to receive from YHWH.

The Kippah – Heavenly Head Gear

> ***Ezekiel 24:15; "Also the word of YHWH came to me, saying..."***
>
> ***Ezekiel 24:23a; "...your turbans shall be upon your heads..."***

In my experience, few other Hebraic practices have the potential to expose such obvious anti-semitic driven disdain within a Christian than the subject of the distinctive headwear that sits unobtrusively at the back of a Jewish or Messianic believer's head.

Why does a Jew come under such heavy fire for wearing a little hat, if it wasn't Biblical, when a Christian's "What would Jesus do?" wristband, which **definitely isn't** Biblical, yield comparatively minimal objection? In contrast, Judaism has adhered to the Creator's instruction to bind His Word on the arm ***(Deuteronomy 6:8)*** by literally wearing passages of Scripture since Sinai, as opposed to Christianity's late twentieth century invention of a slogan emblazoned fashion accessory. Why does the title "Rabbi" get singled out as a prohibited term when the titles, "teacher" and "father" in ***Matthew 23:8-10***[4] also apparently receive equal objection by the Messiah?

4 This verse sequence commences with the words, ***"But as for you <u>do not desire</u> to be called Rabbi..."*** and merely teaches that no man should desire this and other titles of authority for their own sake.

One has to be curious as to why distinctly Jewish things such as the kippah receive criticism when Christian men think nothing of praying whilst wearing conventional headwear, supposedly shameful according to Sha'ul, or why millions of qualified Christian educators go by the title "teacher" supposedly renounced by the Saviour?

The most common verse sequence used to attack the wearing of head coverings for covenant keeping men is found in ***1 Corinthians 11:4-7***. Sha'ul's initial address on the subject seems pretty straight forward in verse 4: ***"Every man praying or prophesying, having his head covered, brings shame to his Head…."*** It is then reconfirmed in verse 7***; "For a man indeed ought not to veil his Head"*** As amazingly as this may sound, Sha'ul was not suggesting that a head covering, much less a kippah, was dishonorable for a man to wear during intimate communication with the Father or during the delivery of a prophetic message to the masses. Let me explain.

The Head is Authority

The head being covered has a double meaning. It refers to a man wearing a woman's veil[5] and to Messiah, which should be the head of every man! ***1 Corinthians 11:3*** provides the context. ***"But I would have you know, <u>that the head of every man is Moshiach (Messiah)</u>; and the head of the woman is the man; and the head of Moshiach is YHWH"*** The second part of this verse reveals a deeper scope to ***Genesis 3:16; "…And your desire shall be to your husband, and he shall rule over you."*** A woman should only submit to a man (a woman's head) (as a man submits to Messiah) (a man's head) as Messiah submits to YHWH (Yahshua's head). This is reiterated by Peter who told covenant keeping women to ***"…be in subjection to your own husbands…" (1 Peter 3:1)***, and why a man is to honor his wife ***"as to the weaker vessel," (1 Peter 3:7)***. The order of human authority harks back to the order of creation. Adam was constructed from raw material by YHWH, but a woman was constructed by YHWH from the material of a man. Therefore in context "the head" signifies

5 This is specifically a woman's veil because even Moshe wore a veil to shield his glorified face before the children of Israel ***(Exodus 34:33-35)***.

"authority." A little bit further on in ***1 Corinthians 11:5,6*** it outlines a woman's optimum[6] form of worship apparel and code of conduct with yet another double meaning. ***"But every woman that makes tefillot (prayers), or prophesies with her head uncovered dishonours her head: For that is the same as if she were shaven[7]. For if the Woman does not have a head covering, let her also be shorn..."*** The double meaning refers to her head, which must be covered, and her husband who must be covered by Messiah.

The Plank in the Eye of an Uncovered Christian's Head

An interesting thing about the common ***1 Corinthians 11*** attack on head coverings for men is that it never seems to focus on Christian women who ritually pray with their heads uncovered. Some Christian men draw on this verse sequence to attack the wearing of a kippah and yet completely ignore taking the issue up with their wives who do not pray with head coverings, despite the verse clearly stating that praying without them is dishonorable to a woman. The kippah police are always poised ready to level an attack, yet a young man who prays whilst wearing a baseball cap or beanie at a church outreach function gets off scot-free. Can you imagine a soldier in Iraq crouching in a ditch under heavy gunfire unable to pray because he's wearing a helmet that if removed will increase his chances of never going home? I can just imagine him ducking bullets thinking to himself, "Father, I want to pray to you, but if I do with this life preserver on my head, I'll dishonour myself."

The Jew even tries to accommodate the Western tradition of removing headwear inside a building by reducing the size of the kippah to a ridiculously small dimension, but somehow this manages to draw out heavier criticism than a criminal wearing a Mexican sombrero in a police line up.

---

6 I say optimum because a woman who desires to pray may not have a garment available to cover her head and in such circumstances she brings no dishonour to herself. (Example: Consider the prayers offered up by thousands of Jewish women standing naked in gas chambers.)

7 ***Deuteronomy 21*** explains that it was a dishonor to shave a woman's hair.

God Cop, Bad Cop Theology

Christianity has so much trouble with the books of the Old Testament because their replacement theology portrays a schizophrenic Creator. On the one hand you've got YHWH requesting that all priests in the Temple, especially the high priest wear head coverings ***(Exodus 28:4, 28:36-38,40)*** and centuries later you have a devoted follower of this same Elohim saying that it's now shameful. The verses from ***Malachi 3:6; "I am YHWH I change not..."*** and ***Hebrews 13:8; "Yahshua is the same yesterday, today, and forever,"*** seem not to sink into the mind of the average Christian. The Old Testament is continually relegated as a book that depicts a vengeful and angry Creator. This is despite YHWH mercifully flooding mankind with water in the Old Testament and in the so-called grace garnished New Testament, raining down on the population with fire and brimstone and a rock called "Wormwood" that wipes out one-third of the earth's population in a single hit.

The only change according to Scriptural that happens is in the hearts of men. A head covering is a sign of a changed nature. It signifies a transformation from uncleanness to purity in Messiah. ***Zechariah 3:4,5; "And He answered and spoke to those that stood before Him, saying, 'Take away the filthy garments from him.' And to him He said, 'See, I have caused your iniquity to pass from you, and I will clothe you with a change of raiment (garments).' And I said; 'Let them set a clean turban upon his head.' So they set a clean turban upon his head, and clothed him with garments. And the heavenly malach (angels) of YHWH stood by."***

On Earth as it is in Heaven

The pure gold banded turban of the Kohen HaGadol's (High Priest's) vestments is one of the most distinguishing features of his attire ***(Exodus 28:36)***. Approaching YHWH without it would have been an extremely dangerous violation of Torah. ***Leviticus 8:9; "And he put the turban upon his head; also upon the turban, even upon its forefront, did he put the golden plate, the kadosh (set-apart) keter (crown), as YHWH commanded Moshe."*** The Kohen HaGadol could not preside in any part of the Temple, much less enter into the Set Apart Place (Holy of Holies) unless his head was covered at all times. He was even forbidden to remove any of his garments in mourning for the dead ***(Leviticus 21:10,11)***. A risen and glorified Yahshua, being our perfect High Priest after the order of Malkitzedek ***(Hebrews 5:5,6)***, who now ministers in the heavenly Temple, would not violate the Torah or be excluded from having a similar heavenly appearance to his mortal predecessors.

Just like the kohanim who performed sacred duties and worked together with the High Priest in the Temple, all believers are called to be priests, working in one accord under the headship of Messiah. ***1 Peter 2:5; "You also, as lively stones, are built up as a spiritual bayit (house), a kadosh (set-apart) priesthood, to offer up spiritual sacrifices, acceptable to YHWH by Yahshua ha Moshiach (The Messiah)."***

Scripture attests to Yahshua's own practice of wearing a head covering. ***Matthew 4:9; "And he (HaSatan) said to Him (Yahshua), all these things will I give you, if you will fall down and worship me and bare your head to me."*** If the kohanim were instructed to wear less distinctive headwear than the Kohen HaGadol, how much more should we cover our own heads as a nation of priests who are all part of one body whose High Priest is now a crowned and glorified Messiah?

Middle Eastern people wore head coverings from ancient times to the present day. The Scriptures never portray the Almighty commanding or requesting an Israelite to uncover his head. There are very few, if any, ancient depictions of Israelites with uncovered heads. Christianity even admits that their Jesus (the Greco-Romanised version of Yahshua) wore a garment (almost certainly a tallit) that was often pulled up over the back of his head. In fact it is absolutely reasonable to deduce that Sha'ul first wrote the statements in ***1 Corinthians 11*** whilst wearing a head covering, if for no other reason than the information I am about to present.

Sha'ul (Paul) the Little Tallit (Tent) Maker

Most Christians are understandably ignorant of the fact that Sha'ul did not make tents despite the verse in ***Acts 18:3*** that says; ***"because he was a tentmaker as they were, he stayed and worked with them."*** This is because the word, "tentmaker" has been mistranslated! Sha'ul actually made four-cornered garments called "tallitot" (plural), which functioned as prayer shawls. The tallit (singular) was literally used as a personal "prayer closet" that was pulled up over the head of an occupant when praying to prevent distraction and heighten concentration. The ignorance the church has as to the true nature of Sha'ul's profession most likely adds to their inability to see the significance of wearing tzitzit (tassels), which hang from a tallit (a four cornered garment).

The practice of wearing four cornered garments ***(Numbers 15:38)*** is ritually avoided within church despite YHWH specifically instructing all the tribes of Israel (not just Judah) to wear such garments throughout their generations.

Why would Sha'ul say that no man should cover his head when he sold garments that were used to do that very thing? The answer is Sha'ul was not talking about head coverings, but veils as worn by women.

YHWH not only commanded priests to wear head coverings, but all followers to wear them, even in exile. The disenfranchised Temple priest Ezekiel (Yehezkel), called by Elohim to be a prophet, was told to have the heads of all those who joined him in exile to wear turbans. ***Ezekiel 24:15; "Also the word of YHWH came to me, saying... (17) ...bind the turban of your head upon you... (23) And your turbans shall be upon your heads..."*** This was a direct command to wear a head covering written by a prophet that according to a cursory understanding of Sha'ul's writings is dishonorable.

As stated earlier, all Israel is a nation of priests ***(Revelations 1:6)*** and the wearing of a head covering by a Jew or Messianic believer is an outward sign of a believer's constant anticipation and readiness for the Bridegroom's return. ***Isaiah 61:10b; "He has clothed me with the garments of Yahshua, He has covered me with the robe of tzedakah (righteousness), as a bridegroom decks himself with ornaments, and as a bride adorns herself with her jewels."***

I've read many well researched papers on the tradition of head coverings and how they have no Biblical basis. Some of the most compelling studies that refute the wearing of kippah are actually written by fellow Nazarene Israelite believers. But at the end of the day, the final word has to come from the Scriptures themselves.

Half a Hill on Your Head

Depending on the source, the traditional appearance of the kippah has a variety of origins. Some sources cite its diminished size and shape as having evolved to make it easier to remove and hide from Greek or Roman soldiers. But the most reliable source for the shape of the head covering is provided in Scripture. The old English word "tires," which means "round," appears in the King James Version in ***Ezekiel 24:17, 23***. Interestingly the word "tires" also appears in ***Isaiah 3:18*** when referring to a round or domed shaped pendant. The Hebraic meaning of the head covering in ***Ezekiel 24*** literally means "half of a hill" or "dome," hence the domed shape of the kippah worn by the modern Jew today. The funny thing is that even the Vatican, the mother of all Christianity, holds to wearing head coverings. All Popes wear a kippah. But for some reason the Vatican hierarchy do not encourage their followers to do the same.

The Tallit

> ***Deuteronomy 22:12; "You shall make yourself twisted threads, on the four corners of your garment with which you cover yourself."***

The head covering is part of the tallit, which foreshadows the heavenly garment all members of the Commonwealth of Israel will receive in the New Kingdom. Adam and Eve were not naked before the fall, as we perceive someone to be naked today. They were clad in a heavenly covering that was not a foreign object, which is the definition of clothing in the true sense of the word. In a way, they were just like a crab or a bear that are technically naked, but clad in their own natural coverings.

The wearing of four tzitziot (tassels) that must hang from a four-cornered garment is a mitzvah (commandment). ***Numbers 15:38; "Speak to the children of Yisrael and you shall say to them that they shall make for themselves fringes on the corners of their garments, throughout their generations, and they shall affix a thread of blue (Hebrew: תכלת - tekhelet) on the fringe of each corner."***

The Shema – The Long and the Short of it

The Shema is a set-apart declaration of faith and a pledge of allegiance to the one El-Elyon (Most High Mighty One). It is taken from ***Deuteronomy 6:4-9***, ***11:13-21*** and ***15:37-41*** and is regarded as the most important prayer in Judaism. The word "Shema" means "hear" and commences the declaration. ***"Shema (hear) Yisrael: YHWH is our Elohim, YHWH is Echad (one): And you shall love YHWH your Elohim with all your lev (heart), and with all your being, and with all your might. And these words, which I command you this day, shall be in your lev (heart): And you shall teach them diligently to your children, and shall talk of them when you sit in your bayit (house), and when you walk by the way, and when you lie down, and when you rise up. And you shall bind them for an ot (sign) upon your hand, and they shall be as frontlets between your eyes. And you shall write them upon the posts of your bayit (house) and on your gates." (Deuteronomy 6:4-9)***

The Shema is said upon arising in the morning and upon going to sleep at night ***(Deuteronomy 6:7; "And you should speak about them when you... lie down and when you get up")***. It is also said when praising and beseeching YHWH. It is the first prayer that a Jewish child is taught to say and it is (if possible) the last words a Jew says prior to death. But the Shema is not exclusively for the tribe of Judah (the Jews). It is applicable to all who are members of the Commonwealth of Israel.

One of the most prominent rabbis in Jewish history, Rabbi Akiva, recited the Shema whilst Roman executioners stripped the flesh off his body with iron combs. When asked by his followers (who were nearby) how he managed to maintain his faith enough to recite it, he answered, *"All my life I have been troubled by this verse, 'You shall love G-d... with all your soul.' As I have explained its meaning: 'all your soul,' 'even if they take your life.' I have always wondered: will I ever have the privilege of fulfilling this mitzvah? And now that the opportunity has finally arrived - shall I not seize it?"* The Talmud records Rabbi Akiva's last word as a long and drawn out "echad" (YHWH is one).

Shema at Dawn and Evening

The Shema is more than just a preparatory act; it is primarily a spiritual elevation that requires considerable internalization when spoken. It is likened to a jewel in the crown of an Israelite's daily morning prayers and blessings. ***Psalms 5:3; "My voice shall You hear in the morning, O YHWH; in the morning will I direct my tefillah (prayers) to You, and will look up."*** It is also recited at one's bedside. ***Psalms 4: 4(5); "Stand in awe, and sin not: commune with your own lev (heart) upon your bed, and be still. Selah."*** The Jewish sages taught that it was to be recited twice before entering the world of sleep to allow a total of 248 words to be said, enabling a garment of protection to cover the body's entire 248 organs. As sleep is a state that constitutes 1/60th of death its recitation is likened to standing guard with a double edged sword at the ready throughout the entire night.

The Most Important Commandment

The sages also wrote that before Jacob was about to reveal the end of days to his children, he was concerned that one of them might be a non-believer. His sons reassured him immediately by crying out, "Shema Yisrael." Even the Torah records Moshe including the Shema in his farewell address to the children of Israel.

Yahshua quoted the Shema in the beginning of his discourse in ***Mark 12:29; "And Yahshua answered him, 'The first of all the mitzvah (love deeds) is, 'Shema (hear), O Yisrael; The Master YHWH is our Elohim, the Master YHWH is Echad (one).'"*** This statement was in response to the question, "What is the greatest of all the Commandments?"

Yahshua also referred to the Shema in ***John 10:30*** during Chanukah (Feast of Dedication) where some Jews asked him if he was the Messiah (the Anointed One). He answered them with the words ***"I and my Father are echad (one)."*** This was an allusion to the Shema, which the Jews immediately recognised, which prompted them to gather up stones to kill him.

Christianity Substitutes the Shema

In contrast the Christian declaration of faith is the "Apostle's Creed," which declares acknowledgement of a triune deity and a pledge of allegiance to the Catholic Church. This creed was principally derived from the council of Nicea, which was presided over by the pagan Roman emperor Constantine who went on to murder his wife and child.

Ultimately, if an act glorifies YHWH and does not dismiss, breach or cause the Torah to be curbed in any way it should never be a question of whether it was originally set down in Scripture (especially if the act supports performing a mitzvah). Questioning whether or not a perfectly acceptable act of worship is Scriptural astounds me. Invariably such a line of questioning exposes the enquirer as an individual who looks for the least that they have to do as opposed to the most they can do to please the Almighty. A person wouldn't normally have this attitude toward their spouse, so why should they have it toward their Creator? If a wife asks her husband for breakfast in bed and specifically asks for toast, eggs and juice, the husband, if he's devoted to her, will bring more than just the bare requirement of one egg and one piece of toast. He'll bring two eggs, two pieces of toast on a beautiful plate, with accompanying salt and pepper shakers, a large glass with his wife's preference of freshly squeezed juice and maybe even a rose, all neatly arrayed on a tray. Why should this desire to go the extra mile for one's own wife be any different from a desire to do the same for YHWH?

Traditions, provided they glorify YHWH in a manner that does not contravene His Torah, should not be rejected out-rightly for lacking an origin as obvious Scriptural commandments.

Chapter Five

Don't be Talmuddled

THE WORD "TALMUD" in Hebrew is *Lamud* and means "The Teaching" and is the name for a collection of volumes including revised and expanded volumes, which further expand and elaborate on another set of writings called "The Mishnah." The word "Mishnah" means "repetition," or more specifically, "repetition of the Torah." The Mishnah came from the written Torah of Moshe and from the Oral Torah[1] since Adam (though Judaism's definition of the Oral Torah's origin is not the same).

Depending on what theological camp you stand in the writings of the Mishnah and the Talmud are either a help or a hindrance to the study of Scripture.

1 The Oral Torah, though usually rejected by many Messianic believers, is in actuality constantly present in the Scriptures themselves, though it lacks a formal introduction unlike the Written Torah. The Oral Torah also goes by the name "Torah of your mother." This wording is present in ***Proverbs 1:8; "My son, hear the discipline of your abba (father), and forsake not the Torah of your eema (mother)."*** The beginning of the verse ***"My son, hear the discipline of you abba"*** in turn refers to the Written Torah.

The Plank in Christianity's Eye

The Jews view them as indispensable writings established by devoted scholars who wanted to preserve the sanctity of the Torah during threatening times. Christian scholars generally view them as a collection of additional burdens that undermine and misdirect the eternal authority of Scripture. This is despite Christianity retaining and promoting countless volumes of writings by early church fathers who largely teach a replacement faith severed from its Hebraic foundations. In addition, the current church, with assistance from the government, finances hundreds of bookstore franchises that sell millions of volumes of contemporary commentaries, discussions and studies, which promote grace garnished replacement theology with little or no emphasis on obedience to Torah. A simple search through a popular Christian bookstore to find anything that promotes Sabbath observance will invariably turn out to be an exercise in futility.

THIS IS A GOOD POINT!

March of the Rabbis

On the other side of the coin, prominent Jewish scholars who compiled much of the rabbinic literature we have today also effectively implemented their own type of replacement theology. What once started out as an historical, referential, and commentary based set of writings over time developed into a dominant teaching that began to overshadow the Torah. But if the climate that perpetuated this transition is not taken into consideration it can cause Rabbinic Judaism to be completely misunderstood and unnecessarily condemned by the Nazarene Israelite.

Over time the Kohanim HaGedolim (High Priesthood) and the Great Sanhedrin[2] absorbed a significant amount of unqualified men who were corruptly appointed by pagan authorities. As a consequence these two divinely appointed institutions slipped gradually into moral bankruptcy. Rabbinic Judaism evolved out of a strong social pressure that threatened to sever cultural identity and the continuous provision of suitably trained Torah scholars. Therefore, it is unfair to single out the rabbinic movement as the sole

2 Literally means, "sitting together."

instigator of bad doctrine particularly during the Diaspora (exile of Jews) without taking into account the consequences of a fallen second Temple and a foreign run judicial system.

Some Christian and Messianic groups accuse the very formation of rabbinical authority as an apostate regime, despite two of the most central individuals in Scripture (Yahshua HaMoshiach and Sha'ul HaShliach) retaining the title of "rabbi" throughout their ministries. Furthermore, the Scriptures are devoid of any criticism by them of the existence of rabbinic authority. On the contrary, by their own words they displayed familiarity with and respect for the rabbinic movement and the writings of the great sages.

The Origin & Meaning of the Title Rabbi

The first formal application of the title "rabbi" was applied in 46BCE to the Elder Gamliel. He was the president of the Sanhedrin and the son of Simon and the grandson of Hillel who were also renowned Elders but neither was known as rabbis. The title "rabbi" evolved from the term, "rabban," which means "our master." Over time the title shortened to "rabbi" and became associated with "teacher." Rabbi Sha'ul (Paul) studied at the foot of Gamliel and made no bones about pointing this out to the Jews ***(Acts 22:3)***.

Of course there were rabbis who taught and recorded error, making the Mishnah and the Talmud theological minefields to the untrained eye. But this is no grounds for avoiding them anymore than avoiding the writings of early church fathers who also recorded their share of error. Ironically, Talmud avoidance is almost an institution in Christian and Messianic circles, yet it is only the pen of the Early Church Father who wrote from a poisonous "Torah has been done away with" perspective.

When one studies the final collapse of the Temple Priesthood and the emergence of rabbinic authority there are often two angles to consider. One school of thought is that the rabbis dismantled the High Priesthood as a grab for power, which was driven by the shameless trafficking of manmade tradition with Talmudic literature as their guiding rule. Another school of thought is that the rabbis took authority over the Priesthood because it had become so corrupt and their writings were simply discussions and opinions expounded from the Torah.

The Appointment of Mini Moshes

Under YHWH's guidance Moshe formed the Tabernacle Kohanim HaGedolim (High Priesthood) and had authority over it, though he was not a kohen (priest) himself. Occasionally YHWH even allowed Israel to heed the wisdom of a Goy (Gentile). At the prompting of his pagan father-in-law ***(Exodus 18:17-27)*** Moshe appointed seventy elders to provide rulings over general matters ***(Numbers 11:16-30)***. The formation of rabbinic authority, which was a continuation of the Pharisees after the fall of the second Temple, was an attempt to re-establish this same type of delegation. This system was alive and well in Yahshua's day and was endorsed by him in ***Matthew 23:2*** when he said, "***...The Sophrim (Scribes) and Prushim (Pharisees) sit in Moshe's kesay (seat of authority): All therefore that Moshe's kesay (seat of authority) will invite you to observe, that observe and do...***" Though Yahshua was quick to point out the hypocrisy of the Pharisees and Scribes in the next verse ***(Matthew 23:3)***, he began his criticism by plainly establishing that he had no problem with their council or system of authority. And well he should not have, because the Torah plainly establishes Judah's authority, recognition and superiority over all other Israelite tribes even, the priestly family of Levi. ***Genesis 49:8-10; Yahudah, you are he whom your brothers shall hallel (praise): your hand shall be on the neck of your enemies; your abba's (father's) children shall bow down before you. Yahudah is a lion's whelp: from the prey, my son, you have gone up: he stooped down; he couched as a lion, and as an old lion; who shall rouse him up? The scepter shall not depart from Yahudah nor a lawgiver from between His feet, until Shiloh comes; to Him shall the gathering of the nations be.***" Other Messianic translations handle the last phrase in this manner, "***...and it is he whom the peoples will obey.***" Those who would seek to criticise the rabbinical movement and venerate the priesthood should bear in mind the above blessing bestowed on Judah and the blessing bestowed upon Levi's descendants. ***Genesis 49:6; "Shimeon and Lewi are brothers; instruments of cruelty are in their dwellings. O my being, come not into their secret; let not my honor, be united to their congregation: for in their anger they killed a man, and in their displeasure and selfwill they hamstrung an ox in pleasure. Cursed be their anger, for it was fierce; and their anger, for it was cruel: I will divide them in Yaakov, and scatter them in Yisrael."***

While the Messiah warns about the tradition of men ***(Mark 7:1-13)***, which is a direct reference to the Mishnah, which existed in oral form at that time, his rebuke is focused on how the Pharisee's reverence for it caused them to "let go" of the commandments of YHWH. The Pharisees and the Teachers of the Torah initiated this whole encounter and were abruptly silenced when Yahshua quoted the prophet Isaiah. Before long the accuracy of the prophets became so damaging to the Pharisees' position that they began to develop doctrine that elevated them over their authority. By the 12th century Moshe ben Maimon wrote this introduction to the Mishnah that neatly illustrated this view: *"If there are 1,000 prophets, all of them of the stature of Elijah and Elisha, giving a certain interpretation, and 1,001 rabbis giving the opposite interpretation, you shall incline after the majority (Exodus 23:2) and the law is according to the 1,001 rabbis, not according to the 1,000 venerable prophets... God did not permit us to learn from the prophets, only from the rabbis who are men of logic and reason."*

It is true that one who studies rabbinic writing is forced to weed out the good from the bad. Yahshua paralleled this process when he cleansed the Temple by sifting out the unrighteous High Priests from the righteous ones before his death and resurrection. Added to this there are those who dishonestly attack controversial, yet not necessarily wrong rabbinic writings. Take, for example, this quote:

> **Talmud Moed Kattan 17a.** "If a Jew is tempted to do evil he should go to a city where he is not known and do the evil there."

Here is how it really reads:

> **Talmud Moed Kattan 17a. Rabbi Ila'i said:** "If a person is tempted to do evil he should go to a city where he is not known, dress in black clothes, cover his head in black, and do what his heart desires so that G-d's name will not be desecrated."

Note how the term "Jew" is added and the sentence is shortened. In actuality the correct quotation aligns with Torah. Let me explain. The Scriptures warn emphatically about stark rebukes of those who are poor in spirit. ***(Proverbs 15:1; "A gentle answer turns away anger..." Galatians 6:1; "You who are spiritual ones restore him in the ruach of gentleness..." 2 Timothy 2:25; "In meekness instructing those that oppose him..." Hebrews 5:2; "He is the one who can humble Himself and have rachamim (mercy) on the ignorant who go astray."*** Rav Yochannan HaMatbil (John the immerser [Baptist]), Yahshua and Sha'ul only gave harsh rebukes to those who were wrapped in layers of pride and arrogance. Such people could not be impacted upon without harshness because they had seared their consciences with a hot iron. However, even when a righteous one rebukes harshly he still does so in meekness and with a spirit of gentleness because his awareness of YHWH's mercy is ever present.

If a person (not necessarily a Jew), is burning with sin and is abruptly commanded, "You can't do that!" they are not likely to be in the right state of mind to obey. On the contrary they might even lash out at such a sudden admonishment. This teaching causes the occupant to delay his intended actions by directing him to travel to a foreign city. Such a lengthy trip is designed to give the occupant time to cool off. Dressing in black garments also serves as a reminder that he is in darkness. This passage is actually an indirect rebuke to prevent sin. Aaron, though he was unsuccessful, tried something similar when he requested jewels to fashion the golden calf ***(Exodus 32:2)***. This was to discourage the women from going through with the construction of the idol by demanding they part with personal valuables. He also delayed the festival till the following day in the hopes that Moshe would return in the meantime ***(Exodus 32:5)***. YHWH knew this and still appointed him as High Priest though he appeared to be the ringleader of an act that brought about the deaths of many Israelites. Even Scripture contains instruction that if dissected out of context appears questionable. Take for example this verse that seems to encourage the drinking: ***Proverbs 31:6; "Give strong drink to him that is ready to perish, and wine to those who are of heavy of levim (hearts)."***

It is interesting to note that Nazarene Israelite and Messianic communities generally view the Mishnah and the Talmud with a cautious respect and as having varying degrees of merit whilst also containing misinterpretations and wrong teaching. It is not uncommon to hear a Messianic Rabbi every so often reference the Talmud with the same frequency as a Christian minister refers to the writings of the Ante-Nicene, Nicene and Post-Nicene Church Fathers.

But what would be the relevance of investigating Torah commentaries that were set down by Jewish rabbis, scholars, and sages who apparently did some of their own replacement theology and then went on to reject the Messiah?

Yahshua and Sha'ul Studied the Writings of the Great Sages

To fully comprehend Rabbi Sha'ul's writings it is advantageous to become familiar with his training to some degree, because of his continuous references to the Torah, the scrolls of the Prophets (Nevaim) and to Jewish learning. Here is how he introduces himself before the Sanhedrin in ***Acts 22:3; "I am indeed a man, a Yahudi (Jew) of Tarsus, a city in Cilikia, yet brought up in this city [Jerusalem] at the yeshiva (house of Torah study) of Gamliel, and taught according to the perfect manner of the Torah of the ahvot (fathers), and was zealous towards YHWH as you all are this day."*** Then he goes onto support the Torah by saying:

- ***Romans 3:31; "Do we then make void the Torah through personal emunah (faith)? By no means: actually we establish the Torah."***
- ***Romans 7:7; "What shall we say then? Is the Torah a sinful, or sin causing instrument? Let it not be! No, I had not known about sin, except by the Torah: for I had not known lust, except the Torah has said, You shall not covet."***

- ***Romans 7:12; "Therefore the Torah is kadosh (set-apart) and the mitzvoth (commandments) are kadosh, and just and tov (good)."***
- ***Romans 7:16; "If then I do that which I do not want to do, I consent to the Torah that is tov (good)."***

The writings of the Mishnah and the Talmud contained many teachings and discussions about Scripture that were often at the centre of many debates in Sha'ul and Yahshua's day. Consequently, ignoring these works inadvertently robs a student of the context in which the Messiah verbally wrestled with his critics.

Two famous rabbis, the liberal minded Hillel and the conservative Shamai lived a century before the time of Yahshua and were constantly a topic of discussion among the sages. Yahshua's teachings sometimes agreed with one or the other. Though many questions leveled at Yahshua were motivated to try and trap him, the Pharisees were often equally curious as to hear his genuine opinion, much as they would have been when he taught once as a twelve year old boy at the foot of the Temple stairs. The question about divorce asked in ***Mathew 19:3*** was an eager query as to see which school of thought Yahshua adhered to – Hillel who was for divorce or Shammai, who was very much against it. When Yahshua is asked, "***What is the greatest of all the commandments?***" he responds by saying, ***"You shall love your neighbour as yourself. On these two commandments hang all the Torah and the Naviim (prophets)" (Matthew 22:39, 40)***. This teaching followed in the spirit of Rabbi Hillel, who wrote, "What is hateful to you, do not to your neighbour. That is the Torah. All the rest is commentary."

Question: But don't the Scriptures say that Yahshua didn't study. ***John 7:15; "...How does this man know so much without having studied."*** *(The Complete Jewish Bible – David H. Stern)*

Answer: No, a more correct English rendering of this verse reads, ***"And the Yahudim (Jews) marvelled, saying, How does this man know how to read the scrolls, having never learned in a yeshiva (house of study)?" (John 7:15 [RSTNE])*** In Yahshua's day Jews attending a place of worship didn't arrive with their own kosher Torah scrolls to follow with in the synagogue. Yahshua was observing the mitzvoth (commandment) in ***Deuteronomy 31:10-13*** that required the entire Torah to be read at Sukkot in a sabbatical year. Yahshua's ability to do this without having attended a prominent house of study amazed the Jews.

The Mishnah – A Type of Early Biblical Encyclopaedia

The Mishnah is a written systematic codification of the Torah. It was written after the destruction of the Second Temple when there was concern that a specific style of interpretation of the Torah or the Oral Torah would be lost. Rabbi Jehuda was the first to consider the prospect of preserving the Oral Torah in written form. He compiled written lists and charts, which was called the *Sepher Mischnaioth* (Mishnah).

It consists of six major topics:

- Zeraim (Seeds) – Concerned with agriculture and prayer.
- Moed (Occasions) – Concerned with Shabbat, festivals, and fasts.
- Nashim (Women) – Concerned with infidelity, marriage, and divorce.
- Nezikin (Damages) – Concerned with civil and criminal law, the government, and ethics.
- Kedoshim (Holy Things) – Concerned with the Temple, sacrifices, and kashrut.
- Taharot (Purity Issues) – Concerned with laws of ritual purity and impurity, including menstruation.

The merit of this above arrangement meant that if a student desired to study the Sabbath, he could have done so without looking for isolated verses scattered through Exodus, Numbers and Leviticus.

While the majority of the Mishnah reads like a legal document, it is occasionally enlivened with teachings that expand on the Torah. The Mishnah is also heavily based on the Oral Torah, which is often questioned so the subject of the Oral Law or Oral Torah will now be examined.

The Oral Torah

> "The rabbis taught. A Gentile once came before Shamai and asked: 'How many laws have you?' 'Two laws: the written and the oral law,' answered Shamai. 'I believe thee as regards to the written law, but do not believe thee as to the oral law,' said the Gentile. 'I will be converted to Judaism on condition that thou teach me the written law." Shamai rebuked him and drove him away. He then came to Hillel with the same plea, and Hillel accepted him. He began teaching him the (Hebrew) alphabet in regular sequence. The next day he taught him the letters backward. 'You did not teach me so yesterday,' the man objected. 'Aye, aye, my son; must thou not repose confidence in me? Thou must likewise repose confidence in the oral law (which appears at first sight different from the written law).'" - *P.49 & 50 New Edition of the Babylonian Talmud (Translated by Michael Rodkinson / Revised and corrected by Rev. Dr. Isaac M. Wise)*

The Torah or the Word of YHWH was originally completely orally based. However, **this is not the same thing as the rabbinic view** of the "Oral Torah," which according to the Talmud has three principally, yet distinctly, different origins. They are:

1. That it was a separate revelation given to Moshe
2. That it was an extended elaboration and interpretation of the written Torah
3. That it was a protective fence that was later erected around the Torah

If option 1 is true there is no record in any of the Scriptures of additional rulings disseminated by Moshe to the children of Israel. If option 2 and 3 are correct then the (written) Torah predates it. This begs the question, which comes first, the hearing or recording of information? Of course information has to be heard or uttered before it is written down. It is the Ruach (Spirit) that quickens (gives life, instruction and power), not the viewing of physical shapes and markings on stone parchment or otherwise that represent spoken words, though the writing of words and letters have great instructional value.

The Amazing World of Paleo-Hebrew

There are synchronised layers of additional meaning contained in the elaborate pictographic form and arrangement of Paleo-Hebrew letters within the Torah. The link between this language and the subject matter of the Scriptures has remained intact even in Modern Hebrew and has been widely accepted as the closest written form of the pure Edenic language uttered by the first humans. These letters were the consequence of the Ruach (spirit) manifesting itself into physical form. The first Scriptural record of a written symbol occurs in ***Genesis 4:14-16*** when YHWH marks Qayin (Cain) after the murder of Hevel (Abel). Contrary to popular belief this mark was a good thing, at least for Cain, because it preserved his life.

The general rabbinic definition of the Oral Torah does not appear to refer to a pre-Sinai revelation. Yet, according to Scripture the Torah is eternal and therefore was in existence before the very foundation of the world. ***John 1:1; "Besesheeth (in the beginning) was the Torah, and the Torah was with YHWH, and the Torah was YHWH."*** But this is not to say that the first five books of the Bible where around before Moshe wrote them. The Torah both before and after it was formally given to the nation of Israel is YHWH's wisdom. It is how He considers Himself, considers us and considers all creation. It contains the full wisdom with which He creates and manages everything.

Adam was taught the Torah by YHWH. This is evident in the Scriptures when we see the prohibition against eating certain food ***(Genesis 2:15-17)*** and the commandment to be fruitful and multiply ***(Genesis 1:28)***. On another occasion after the fall, when the Creator sought them on foot ***(Genesis 3:8),*** He verbally identified Himself by calling out to avoid eavesdropping ***(Genesis 3:9)***. This is interesting, because HaSatan would have had to eavesdrop to set up his initial deception.

Even Cain and Abel display some knowledge of the Torah by presenting offerings before YHWH. In fact Noah, Abraham, Isaac and Jacob, all knew of a right ruling that was inseparable to the Creator. This is because it was originally in the hearts of all men, but over the generations it gradually diluted to a point where only eight humans retained obedience to it. How would Noah have known which animals were ritually pure (*tahor*) and what was Jacob studying in his tent if there was no formal knowledge of the Torah before Mount Sinai?

If a person does not accept that the Torah (in whatever capacity) was observed before Mount Sinai then ***Genesis 26:5,*** where YHWH tells Isaac that Abraham was obedient to His Mitzvoth (commandments), will remain a mystery.

The Oral Law Mentioned in Scripture

When reading chapter 7 of the Song of Songs (Solomon) in the *Stone Edition Tanach* one may notice a rendering of the text that is different from nearly all other Christian Bible translations, including the most popular Messianic Scriptures available today. This publication is one of the most accurate and literal translations of the Old Testament. Where any choices had to be made concerning word use its compilers chose devotion to the context over inaccurate simplicity.

The verse contains a reference to the Oral Law, a subject that is criticised by Christians and most non-Jewish Messianic believers as being unbiblical. It also correctly relates the subject matter to the reader. ***The Song of Songs 7:13; "Let us wake at dawn in the vineyards of prayer and study (Yeshivas). Let us see if students of Writ have budded, if students of Oral Law have blossomed, if ripened scholars have bloomed; there I will display my finest products (students) to You."*** I've added bracketed words to further help with the context of the passage. Now pick up just about any other

English copy of the Scriptures and try to find the same verse. You'll see there is a verse missing with some of its contents crammed into another. You'll also find that it just reads as if taking a stroll through a beautiful vineyard. No amount of studying this passage in a sanitised English Bible translation will ever reveal that it's actually talking about students of Torah studying in a Yeshiva and that it mentions the Oral Law!

Even before Israel reached Sinai they were given additional ordinances by Moshe from YHWH in ***Exodus 15:22-26.*** Note the underlined words in verse ***26; "And said, 'If you will diligently listen to the voice of YHWH your Elohim, and will do that which is right in His sight, and will give ear to His mitzvoth, and shomer (keep) all His chukim (statutes), I will put none of these diseases upon you, which I have brought upon the Mitzrim (Egyptians): for I am YHWH-Rophechah (your Healer).'"***

The first record within Scripture of a written Torah is concerned with Israel's successful victory over Amalek forces in the wilderness. ***Exodus 17:14; "Then YHWH said to Moshe, 'Write this for a memorial in a scroll, and rehearse it in the ears of Yahoshua (Joshua): for I will utterly put out the remembrance of Amalek from under shamayim (heaven).'"***

Question: How can it be that the Torah was around before Sinai if Scripture talks about the time of its introduction? ***Galatians 3:17; "...the Torah, that came four hundred and thirty years later, cannot nullify the Avrahamic brit (covenant), so that it should make the promise of no effect."*** IT DOESN'T.

Answer: At Mount Sinai certain mitzvoth (commandments) contained practices that were designed to recall specific events. Abraham would not have likely celebrated Passover, at least not in the form that it was given at Sinai, because it contained rituals designed to recall key moments in his future offspring's history. ***Deuteronomy 6:20-23; "And when your son asks you in times to come, saying, What do these testimonies, and chukim (statutes),***

***and mishpatim (judgements) mean, which YHWH our Elohim has commanded you? Then you shall say to your son, We were Pharaoh's avadim (slaves) in Mitzrayim (Egypt); and YHWH brought us out of Mitzrayim (Egypt) with a mighty hand: And YHWH showed signs and wonders, great and grievous, upon Mitzrayim (Egypt), upon Pharaoh, and upon his entire household, before our eyes: And He brought us out from there, that He might bring us in, to give us the land that He swore to our ahvot (fathers).*"** While Festivals, particularly Passover itself, embody rituals that foreshadow future events, it would have been "letting the cat out of the bag" if pre-Sinai Israelites were privy to a commandment with the above clarity.

The fact that Abraham was uncircumcised for the majority of his life also testifies to the likelihood that he did not observe Passover. ***Exodus 12:48; "…all his males must perform brit-milah (flesh circumcision), and then let him come near and shomer (hear) it; and he shall be as one that is born in the land: for no uncircumcised person shall eat of it.*"**It is interesting to note that Abraham's nephew Lot did hastily bake matzah bread for the angels who arrived at his home in Sodom, just like Israel was later instructed to do before leaving Egypt.

There are many layers of covenants given throughout Scripture in addition to the major covenant at Sinai. Each new covenant builds on the last and gives greater insight into YHWH's will. Their giving at different times throughout history should not imply that they were reactionary or made up on-the-spot statutes. On the contrary, the nature of their giving appears in event related tutorial form extracted from a pre-existent framework.

Marriage Sealed in Blood – The Biggest Wedding in all History

The Torah set down by Moshe was distinct from the Torah known by Israel's forefathers, because this Torah fit a demonstrative episodic model (i.e. a cohesive story). It reads like one long example of what happens when a nation chooses to abide in it or abandon it. It also contains the pattern for future events set out in Revelations.

However, there is one major distinction. It was eventually delivered to and accepted by the entire nation of Israel in a formal covenant ceremony, not all that dissimilar to a marriage. ***Exodus 24:3,4; "And Moshe came and told all the people all the words of YHWH, and all the mishpatim (right rulings): and all the people answered with kol echad (one voice), and said, all the words that YHWH has said we will do[3]. And Moshe wrote all the words of YHWH, and rose up early in the morning, and built an altar under the hill, and twelve pillars, according to the twelve tribes of Israel."*** Then the deal was sealed by young Israelite men who offered burnt offerings and sacrificed young bulls as a fellowship offering to YHWH. ***Exodus 24:6-8; "Moshe took half of the dahm (blood) and put it in basins; and half of the dahm he sprinkled on the altar. And he took the scroll of the brit (covenant) and read in the audience of the people: and they said, All that YHWH has said we will do and be obedient.' And Moshe took the dahm, and sprinkled it on the people and said, 'See the dahm of the brit that YHWH has made with you concerning these words.'"*** The nation of Israel had committed itself to the covenant in sacrificial blood, which Moshe had clearly written and read out in the presence of YHWH. After three hundred and fifty years[4] of merciless captivity in Egypt the largest single revelation of the Torah had finally been disseminated before a national body of chosen people who were to be set-apart as a nation of priests.

Not until forty years after Mount Sinai, prior to the death of Moshe and the Hebrews' entrance into the Promised Land, did the

3 Note the word "...all..." used in the affirmation "...we will do..." is reconfirmed in verse 7b and was declared by all twelve tribes of Israel and the sojourners who were among them. This means that the majority of those who took this oath were men and women whose descendants were later lead into captivity and spread to the forecorners of the globe. Those who are not blood descendants, but have a love for Israel are ripe converts who become grafted in. Hindsight shows us that this scattering of Israel was not a curse but a blessing so that the Name of YHWH might be spread throughout the earth.

4 The maximum possible time between Israel's move to Egypt and their Exodus can be estimated if we assume that Kohath had just been born at the commencement of Israel's captivity. Kohath lived to be 133 years old ***(Exodus 6:18)*** and Amram (Moshe's father) lived to be 137 years old ***(Exodus 6:20).*** If we further assume that Amram had Moshe in the last year of his life, these two life spans can be added to Moshe's age at the Exodus, which was 80 years. Kohath lived **133** years ***(Exodus 6:18),*** Amram lived **137** years ***(Exodus 6:20),*** Moshe's age at the Exodus was **80** ***(Exodus 7:7)*** TOTAL: 133 + 137 + 80 = **350**. ***Exodus 12:40,41*** refers to the three generations from Avraham to Jacob, which equals 430 years since their entry into Egypt, as opposed to their official enslavement to Pharaoh.

Torah (known as the Five Books of Moses) get completely written down and subsequently copied.

Better on Your Heart than on a Scroll

Until then an almost complete verbal recitation of Torah was the norm. It eliminated the fear of losing valuable scrolls and promoted phenomenal mental recall. Even an imprisoned Israelite could recite and ponder its infinite wisdom from the confines of an empty cell. The Oral Torah also enabled a student to ask questions and get immediate answers, thus minimising the pitfall of misinterpretation, a characteristic that plagues every kind of written religious instruction today.

Rabbi Aryeh Kaplan explains the value of the Oral Torah in his "Handbook of Jewish Thought" (Moznaim 1979):

> "The Oral Torah was originally meant to be transmitted by word of mouth. It was transmitted from master to student in such a manner that if the student had any question, he would be able to ask, and thus avoid ambiguity. A written text, on the other hand, no matter how perfect, is always subject to misinterpretation."
>
> "Furthermore, the Oral Torah was meant to cover the infinitude of cases which would arise in the course of time. It could never have been written in its entirety. It is thus written (Ecclesiastes 12:12), "Of making many books there is no end." God therefore gave Moshe a set of rules through which the Torah could be applied to every possible case."
>
> "If the entire Torah would have been given in writing, everyone would be able to interpret it as he desired. This would lead to division and discord among people who followed the Torah in different ways. The Oral Torah, on the other hand, would require a central authority to preserve it, thus assuring the unity of Israel..."

More to the Torah than First Meets the Eye

The Torah is not a set of religious guidelines that are adhered to by a believer. It is the national code of conduct for all members of the Commonwealth of Israel, whether they are descended from Abraham, grafted in, or living in or outside the land of Israel.

A cross reference of Torah and the rest of Scripture show that there were observances unique to the people of Israel before the revelation at Mount Sinai. These observances were not specifically reaffirmed at the giving of the Ten Commandments. For instance, the inclusion of the Sabbath in the Ten Commandments is clearly a central pillar, yet there is only an injunction against lighting fires, excessive travel, cutting down trees, ploughing and harvesting fields. But as one progresses from the Torah and into the books of the Prophets (Nevaim) and the Brit Chadashah (New Testament) additional rulings on the Sabbath become apparent. They include rulings for acquiring food if hungry, public Torah reading, meeting in groups, applying medical aid to the sick or injured and maintaining military duties during times of conflict.

Another thing that the Torah is silent on is the ritual of the marriage ceremony. Even though it encourages taking a wife ***(Genesis 2:24)*** it does not go into any detail on the wedding vow. My wife and I have been politely criticised by Christians for doing the Havdalah celebration ritual on the eve of Shabbat, because it is not in Scripture. But Christians will happily go through the recital of a wedding ceremony even though it too is not found in the Scriptures. A once in a lifetime wedding ceremony that is not based in Scripture seems to be a different story than a weekly Shabbat ceremony to the compartmentalised mind of the average Christian.

Without knowing the manner in which Israelites practiced Torah ordinances before the Mosaic Covenant was given at Sinai the context and interpretation of crucial aspects of the Torah are incomprehensible. For example circumcision, presenting offerings and tithing were already practiced among the tribes of Israel.

The famous quote, "an eye for an eye" [or in Hebrew, *ayin tachat ayin* ***(Exodus 21:24)***] would never be understood as referring to monetary compensation if we didn't know the ruling of "the value of an eye," which is found in the Oral Torah. This means that if someone damages the property of another (whether physical or material) they must pay the value of that property for an eye or an eye's worth. In no way does an eye for an eye literally mean one damaged organ for another or inflicting exactly the same punishment as issued by the offender. This is even in spite of the following passages that appear in Leviticus; ***"Anyone who maims another, what he inflicted will be done to him,"*** and ***"What injury he gave to another will be given to him."*** The first verse is paralleled in ***Judges 15:11*** by the mouth of Samson who answered to the Yahudim (Jews) after his Philistine wife was given to a former friend. He said, ***"As they did to me, so I have done to them."*** This did not mean that he had stolen all the wives of the Philistines. In actuality, he had burned their grain stocks and vineyards.

The Development of the Mishnah and Talmud

The principle motive for finally committing the Oral Torah to writing was out of fear that all the mouths that spoke it would be extinguished. Due to unprecedented losses of suitably trained scholars and teachers during the Great Revolt against Rome in 66CE and again in the Bar-Kokhba rebellion in 132-135CE the Oral Torah gradually became the domain of the scribe.

Around the year 200CE the Oral Torah was finally committed to parchment, though this act had been resisted for centuries by leading rabbis. The rabbis principally responsible for the content and the evolution of the Mishnah consist of:

First Generation: Rabban Yohanan ben Zakkai's generation (circa 40 BCE-80 CE).

Second Generation: Rabban Gamiel of Yavneh, Rabbi Eliezer and Rabbi Yehoshua's generation, the teachers of Rabbi Akiva.

Third Generation: The generation of Rabbi Akiva and his colleagues.

Fourth Generation: The generation of Rabbi Meir, Rabbi Yehuda and their colleagues.

Fifth Generation: Rabbi Judah HaNasi's generation.

The Mishnah was studied so meticulously by generations of Tannaim[5] rabbis that it eventually gave birth to volumes of commentaries and discussions which were called Gemara (meaning to "study" and "complete"). These writings were edited and formally compiled around 400CE and became known as the" Jerusalem Talmud." The most prominent rabbis between the Mishnah and the Talmud period consisted of rabbis Shimon ben Judah HaNasi and Yehoshua ben Levi.

Over a century later Babylonian rabbis expanded upon the Talmud by adding even more extensive discussions and deliberations. This became known as the "Babylonian Talmud." The format of the Talmud consists of laws from the Mishnah followed by deep deliberations on their meanings.

Rabbi Akiva ben Joseph - Model Scholar or Scheming Meddler?

The Mishnah was heavily revised by Rabbi Akiva, and then by Rabbi Meir. Finally, Judah HaNasi oversaw the writing down of the Mishnah (as it appears in its present form), in the academy at Yavneh.

Rabbi Akiva was chiefly responsible for changing the way the Torah was interpreted, which caused a comprehensive rabbinical religious framework to be erected that obscured and retarded the effectiveness of a perfectly divine teaching. While Rabbi Akiva may have helped preserve Jewish heritage and their unique awareness of Torah by erecting a type of "safeguard for the Scriptural Law" his intervention caused some damaging precedents that caused some fundamental departures from its teachings, which expanded like a ripple effect throughout the Jewish world and like Christianity caused it to shift considerably from its roots.

The most damaging of these precedents was the gradual abolishment of the tithe offering for the Levite priests. This action inadvertently instituted a transfer of the authority from the Tabernacle priesthood to an exclusive rabbinic authority. The priesthood eventually disbanded because they could no longer effectively

5 Means to "learn" and "repeat teachings."

survive without receiving the Torah ordained tithe offering from the people. However, this move may not have been without good reason because by this time most of the priests had become illegally appointed by Rome. This climate also accounted for the escalating death rate among high priests who insisted on entering the Holy of Holies chamber.

Rabbi Akiva's influence on the Mishnah was the most influential because he painstakingly attached significance to nearly every piece of text. It was and is still believed today by some Jews that he was able to gain insight into the Torah that even superseded Moshe. It is noteworthy to add that even Shlomo HaMelech (King Solomon) wrote explanations of every law of the Torah in hundreds of different ways to attain maximum clarity.

Rabbi Akiva is perhaps best known by his critics for his influence in the ill-fated Bar Kokhba rebellion. He and his students threw their full support behind a Jewish leader known as Bar Kokhba who they were convinced was the Moshiach (Messiah). Other rabbis ridiculed him for this belief (the Talmud records another rabbi as saying, "Akiba, grass will grow in your cheeks and still the son of David will not have come.") Eventually Akiva was captured and tortured to death.

One of the biggest ironies within Orthodox Judaism is that they still revere Rabbi Akiva as one of the most eminent figures in rabbinic history even though he believed in a false Messiah. To this day Bar Kochba's messiahship is not accepted by anyone. But an Israelite who accepts Yahshua as Messiah is not recognised under the Jewish "law of return" and forbidden to legally make Aliyah (return and take up residence) in the land of Israel. A Jew who accepts Yahshua is not even eligible to join a Shule (Jewish congregation) in their local community, yet Jews who revere and study Rabbi Akiva (who essentially venerated a false Messiah) are still entitled to return to the Land.

To some, Rabbi Akiva was a saint who strengthened and brought great clarity to the understanding of Torah by introducing a profound interpretation that elevated him as a standout among his peers. But to others he was a wolf in sheep's clothing that came and instituted narrow interpretations and subtle changes that robbed teachers who came after of a once clear understanding of Torah.

Conclusion

While I do not discourage studying the Talmud or any other rabbinic writing, I do believe that such material should not be read in preference to or as frequently as the Torah or any other part of Scripture. In fact I would go so far as to encourage the reading of Pseudo-Scriptures such as the Book of Enoch, the Book of Jasher and the works of the Apocrypha over the Talmud. However, someone who frequently studies the Scriptures and also finds time to read popular magazines or fantasy novels might benefit by replacing this secular material with the study of Talmudic literature. Ultimately the Talmud can never be compared with the Torah, because it is largely full of discussion, debate, examples that show multiple interpretations and differing opinions that are seldom resolved within the text.

While Nazarene Israelites generally respect rabbinic writings as a source of man-originated religious thinking, they see no Scriptural basis for according them the same level of authority as the Torah.

Chapter Six

The "Call No Man Rabbi" Fiasco

"You call me 'Rabbi' and 'Lord,' and you are right, because I am." – John 13:13

Yahshua's words (Complete Jewish Bible – Translation by David H. Stern)

SOME FELLOW NAZARENE ISRAELITES that I have met, often those who are in self-imposed isolation from other covenant members, have come up with some of the most off the wall theologies that make even a Sunday worshipping Christian look good. Beneath this I have found the root of such bad doctrines being taught by maverick leaders who handle the faith of YHWH like Han Solo handles his *Millennium Falcon*. "...I've made a lot of special modifications myself." – (Star Wars 1977)

One such issue concerns the claim that Messiah Yahshua imposed a ban on the use of the titles, "rabbi," "father" and "teacher" in ***Matthew 23***. The teaching of this doctrine is almost exclusively driven by the prohibition of the title "rabbi" with at best the rejection of the titles "teacher" and "father" dragging along behind it with barely a mention.

Citing the title "rabbi" as forbidden espoused from Messiah's discourse is a blatant manifestation of anti-semitism that masquerades itself as doctrine. This is because the same person who corrects someone using the title "rabbi" fails to correct others or even themself with the same vigilance in the use of the titles "father" or "teacher." The prevalence of the titles "father" and "teacher" far exceed the prevalence of the title "rabbi" and yet the objection to the title "rabbi" is the only one you will ever consistently hear. Imagine the "call no man rabbi" police trying to introduce their father to someone without using such a title or equivalent term. Using an equivalent title is no solution because it plunges Messiah's teaching into a pet dislike of particular words.

Here is the Scripture that apparently forbids the use of the titles rabbi, father and teacher as it appears in the 1995 Edition of the *New American Standard Bible (NASB)*; ***Matthew 23:8-11 "But do not be called Rabbi; for One is your Teacher, and you are all brothers. Do not call anyone on earth your father; for One is your Father, He who is in heaven. Do not be called leaders; for One is your Leader[1], that is, Christ. But the greatest among you shall be your servant."***

Without exerting any degree of study and isolating the above verse from the rest of the text is self explanatory. No man is to address another by the three titles, rabbi (one who has great understanding [master teacher]), abba (meaning father) or teacher. The absurdity of this conclusion from the text is mind-blowing in light of the amount of other Scripture that has to be ignored for it to work. In addition one should consider reading the teaching from a translation that recognises and restores a Hebraic perspective to the Scriptures. ***Matthew 23:8-11; "But as for you do not desire to be called Rabbi: For one is your Rabbi, even the Moshiach; and all you are Yisraelite brothers. And call no man abba (father) upon the earth: for one is your Abba, who is in the shamayim (heavens). Neither be called teachers: for one is your Teacher, even the Moshiach. But he that is greatest among you shall be your eved (servant)."[2] (RSTNE - Restoration Scriptures True Name Edition)***

1 Depending on the version the term "leader," "master," "instructor" or "teacher" can be found in verse 23:10.

2 This is from the Hebrew Shem Tov manuscript of Matthew. The word *tirzu*, which means desire, puts a whole different inflection on the text. Even early church father's attest to the book of Matthew's original Hebrew origin. "They have the Good news according to Matthew in its entirety in Hebrew. For it is clear that they still preserve this, in the Hebrew alphabet, as it was originally written." (Epiphanius; Panarion 29)

Yahshua taught according to Torah, never departing from it by so much as one yud or one nekudah (smallest letter and smallest marking in the Hebrew alphabet). If he forbade calling any man father he negated the very Torah that he came to proclaim by disallowing men to address Abraham as the forefather of Israel. It would have, from that point onward, caused all those who believed him to skim over Torah that refers to fathers and teachers. It would have also called into question many verses in the Torah and many future epistles that became part of Scripture. Take for example ***James 3:1; "My Yisraelite brothers, not many should be rabbis, knowing that we shall receive a stronger mishpat (judgment)."*** And ***1 Timothy 5:17; "The elders who rule well are to be considered worthy of double honour, especially those who work hard at preaching and teaching."***

Look carefully at the beginning of verse 8 to see what Messiah is really saying, ***"But as for you <u>do not desire</u> to be called Rabbi..."*** Judaism has had an ancient tradition that when a leader is appointed to the Sanhedrin, he declines the post three times. In fact it is unheard of within Judaism for a Jew to work ambitiously toward any spiritual leadership role with the aim of making a name for himself. In the light of the "stricter judgement" that is placed on teachers in ***James 3:1*** it can be said that Orthodox Jews (without realising it) follow this aspect of the Brit Chadashah (New Testament) very faithfully.

Messiah Yahshua is stating that no one should seek titles (in particular rabbi) to gratify his own selfish desire. Such a man receives openly the praise of men and in so doing becomes disqualified from a reward in the World to Come. ***Matthew 6:2; "Therefore when you perform your mitzvoth (love deed), do not sound a shofar before you, as the hypocrites do in the synagogues and in the streets, that they may have tifereth (praise) from men. Truly I say to you, They have their reward. So when you perform mitzvoth, let not your left hand know what your right hand does."***

The Messiah was teaching that all titles, which denote mastery of a profession should not be used to make one a master over another or allow one to view another as being more important. Torah teaches that the greatest person is the one who serves and attends to the needs of others vigilantly. For example Moshe, the meekest of all men, was called a "servant of Elohim" though he confronted Pharaoh, served as a chief intermediary between YHWH and Israel and had superiority over the priesthood. This is why ***Matthew 23:11*** continues in verse 12 saying, "***And whoever shall exalt himself shall be humbled; and he that shall humble himself shall be exalted.***"

In context Messiah's whole discourse also serves as a warning to a believer not to allow anyone to make himself an exclusive spiritual source of supply over the One who is the true Master and source of supply - YHWH.

Ceasing to acknowledge and use titles unleashes confusion into the body and nullifies its effectiveness to hear and act in an ordered chain of command. Prophets would no longer be prophets, priests would no longer be priests, judges would no longer be judges and kings would no longer be kings. YHWH raises men and women up for particular roles and commands that they be acknowledged accordingly. This is to maintain order within the body and allow people to know who's who. He has always used a defined order of authority to rule His Kingdom and his subjects. ***Deuteronomy 16:18; "Shophtim (judges) and officers shall you appoint in all your gates, which YHWH your Elohim gives you, throughout your tribes: and they shall judge the people with just mishpat (jugdement).***"

Consider ***Ephesians 4:11; "And He gave some, shlichim (Sent ones/Apostles); and some, neviim (prophets); and some, proclaimers; and some, roehim (shepherds) and morim (teachers); For the perfecting of the Yisraelite kidushim (saints), for the mitzvoth (love deeds) of service, for the rebuilding of the body of Moshiach.***"

Those who teach the "call no man rabbi" doctrine should consider this: If each individual will be called to account for every word they have uttered, then certainly every written word about the Heavenly Father will be judged with greater scrutiny. ***Matthew 12:36-37; "But I say to you, That every idle word that men shall speak, they shall give account of it on the Yom HaDin (Day of Judgement). For by your words you shall be declared tzadik (righteous), and by your words you shall be condemned.***" Furthermore if the accounting system in the heavens retains detailed documentation on each individual strand of hair that has ever grown on the head of every human being that has ever existed, how much more would potential misguidance, whether transmitted verbally or in writing be remembered on the Day of Judgement? ***Luke 12:7; "But even the very hairs of your head are all numbered...."*** It is for this reason that the Scriptures place great emphasis on believers at no matter what level of understanding to remain teachable and to love correction. ***Proverbs 12:1; "Whoever loves discipline loves da'at (knowledge): but he that hates correction is stupid."***

I appeal to all rabbis and teachers within the Nazarene Israelite community to unify and prepare the flock and step up to the task that you have been appointed. Natsarim (Offshoot Branch Watchmen) congregations are not to be fashioned with a pretext to compete with other congregations or used as opportunities to build personal empires. Such conduct has already occurred and scattered the flock and caused many to refrain from meeting together. Israelites (whether Jews or Ephraimites), as a people, are to meet YHWH in unity according to His prescribed method, not according to the traditions of men. This is done through preparing teachers, judges and rulers who shepherd different segments of the multitude. But how can this occur when wolves have come in and obscured these roles by denying frames of reference? ***Exodus 18:21-22; "Moreover you shall provide out of all the people able men, such as fear Elohim, men of emet (truth), hating covetousness; and place such over them, to be rulers of thousands, and rulers of hundreds, rulers of fifties, and rulers of tens: And let them judge the people at all seasons: and it shall be, that every great matter they shall bring to you, but every small matter they shall judge: so shall it be easier for yourself, and they shall bear the burden with you."***

My Rebbe has often said, "If there is a King there is a kingdom and if there is a kingdom there is a rule and if there is a rule there is a ruler and He's not kidding."

Chapter Seven

The Rapture Lie – Truth Left Behind

MILLIONS OF CHRISTIANS sincerely await a future rapture event that will zap them out of the midst of a great tribulation. To this lukewarm generation comes the warning: ***"Woe to you that desire the Yom (day of) YHWH*[1] *To what end is it for you? The Yom (day of) YHWH is darkness, and not light."*** *(Amos 5:18)*

When Messiah returns it will be as a warrior appearing in the clouds within a dense object in the shape of a millstone[2]. The image of an airborne chariot is also frequently used by the prophets to describe the appearance of YHWH and His heavenly host. The word chariot as it appears in Scripture is derived from the Hebrew word *rekeb {reh'-keb}*, which can mean "vehicle, cavalry or (upper)

1 The name YHWH or Yod Hay Vov Hay is the name of the God of the Hebrews, which was omitted over a thousand times and replaced by the words, "God" or "Lord" by translators in both the Old and New Testaments. Some ancient Greek New Testament manuscripts still carried the Paleo Hebrew rendering of His name even though some translators had no clue how the name was to be pronounced.

2 Due to the complete absence of technological understanding, ancient records from any cultural background carry an array of names for aerial anomalies not often picked up on by the modern reader. Some terms include: Thrones, chariots, fiery stones, dragons, cherubim, clouds, flying scrolls, spirits, wheels, shields, Vimanas, carpets and tempests to name a few. The gods of all the worlds' religions are depicted mounted on or seated within airborne transportation. The God that is portrayed in Christianity, Islam and Judaism is no different.

millstone." The millstone is a thick disc-shaped rock, similar to the current generally perceived appearance of a UFO.

Author, Jeff A. Benner makes a very interesting observation in his book, *His Name is One*, when he examines the Hebrew root of the word "Spirit" as it appears in ***Genesis 1:2; "And the Ruach (Spirit) of YHWH moved (or hovered) upon the face of the mayim (waters)."*** He notes that the same parent root of this word also resides in the Hebrew words, "moon," "traveler," and "millstone," which he concludes all carry the common characteristic of a prescribed path. In addition to this observation I have also noted that each individual word describes a specific characteristic. For example the moon describes a bright "glow," the traveler describes a "purpose," and the millstone describes a "shape."

On the day of YHWH this shape will resemble a lenticular cloud mass and hover at the head of a great armada of similar aerial craft. ***Matthew 24:30b; "They will see the Ben Adam (Son of Man) coming on the clouds of the shamayim (sky), and with power and great tifereth (glory)." Psalms 68:17: "The Mirkavot (chariots) of Elohim (God) are twenty thousand, even thousands of heavenly malachim (angels). YHWH is among them as in Senai, in the Kadosh (Holy) Place.***

The above verses clearly establish a link to the manner in which YHWH chose to reveal Himself to all Israel at Mount Sinai. ***Exodus 19:16; "On the morning of the third day there was thunder and lightening, with a thick cloud over the mountain (Senai)…"***

Through various forms of long-term conditioning YHWH's return may appear to the majority of the last generation as a hostile alien invasion. An arrival of a superior completely foreign air power will overwhelm and strike many people with fear and anguish. ***Matthew 24:30a; "And then shall appear the sign of Ben Adam (Son of Man) in the shamayim (sky): and then shall all the tribes (or nations) of the land mourn…"*** A precursor to this public reaction can be studied on a smaller scale with the H.G. Wells *War of the Worlds* radio drama aired in the 1930s.

Every eye will watch this event unfold physically or on televised media as a battle formation assembles in the sky amid flashes of lightening and cracks of thunder. ***Revelations 1:7a; "See, He comes with clouds; and every eye shall see Him…"*** All the dead pure blood humans from Adam will resurrect. ***Revelations 1:7b; ", and those also who pierced Him: <u>and all the tribes of the olam (earth) shall wail because of Him</u>. Even so. Amein."*** There was a foreshadowing of this event in ***Matthew 27:53*** when some saints rose from their graves.

A loud horn blast will emanate from a chief vehicle, which will have a distinct sound of a multitude of rams' horns (shofars). This will wake the dead – literally. ***1 Thessalonians 4:16; "For the Master Himself shall descend from the shamayim (sky) with a shout, with the voice of the chief heavenly malach (angel) and with His shofar (ram's horn) and with the tekiyah-ge-dolah (loud and long shofar blast) of YHWH: <u>and the dead in Moshiach shall rise first:</u>"***

When YHWH delivered His people through the midst of the Red Sea it was described by the Psalmist this way: ***"The voice of Your <u>thunder was in the shamayim (sky) the lightning lightened the olam</u> (world): the earth trembled and shook." (Psalms 77:18)*** Elsewhere in the Psalms His visitations are described as causing atmospheric and geological disturbances: ***"Our Elohim shall come...and it <u>shall be very stormy around Him.</u>" (Psalms 50:3)***. And ***"...come down: touch the mountain and <u>they shall smoke</u>."(Psalms 144:5)***.

Before YHWH revealed Himself to Israel He said, ***"...See <u>I am come to you in a thick cloud</u>..," (Exodus 19:9)***. He then descended in a cloud and proclaimed His Name ***(Exodus 34:5)***.

Major entertainment networks, education, political, and religious systems have been conditioning you and the entire public on various levels for nearly a century. Mankind is just about ripe for a deception that could even deceive the very elect of YHWH ***(Matthew 24:24, Mark 13:24)***.

On the Mount of Olives Yahshua spoke of the visible manner of his return: ***Matthew 24:27; "<u>For as the lightening comes out</u> of the east, and shines even to the west, so shall also the coming of the Ben Adam (Son of Man) be."*** And in ***Matthew 26:4; "...After this you shall see the Ben Adam (Son of man) sitting at the right hand of YHWH, and <u>coming in the clouds of the shamayim</u>."***

The word "rapture" does not make a single appearance in the Scriptures. The whole concept of a rapture that separates the people of YHWH from the trials that are increasing on the earth is an absolute fable. A fable that millions of "what would Jesus do" Christians have accepted like a lame animal accepts a fatal injection.

Here is a range of principle verses that Christians refer to when supporting the rapture doctrine. ***Acts 8:39, 2 Corinthians 12:2-4, Revelations 4:1-2, Colossians 1:13, Ephesians 2:5-6, 1 Thessalonians 4:17, Matthew 24:40-42, Revelations 4:1-2, 3:21 & 12:5***. Let's examine each verse in turn to see if any support a rapture. By rapture I mean a mass supernatural ascension of faithful believers (whether in secret or otherwise) before a major cataclysm.

Acts 8:39; "And when they came out of the mayim (water), the Ruach of the Master YHWH caught Phillip away to another place, so that the faithful believer saw him no more..." This verse has nothing whatsoever to do with a pre-, mid- or post- tribulation rapture. YHWH would on occasion transport or take individual followers by air to another earth location or up to His throne room to receive a briefing. Ezekiel was taken up by a lock of his hair ***(Ezekiel 8:3)***, John was taken up from the Isle of Patmos to receive a vision ***(Revelations 1:10)*** and Enoch was taken and did not return ***(Genesis 5:24)***. It is also argued that Yahshua was taken into the wilderness by some other means than simply walking ***(Mark 1:12)***. HaSatan also has the ability to be taken up by his own means and approach YHWH's throne room ***(Job 1:7)***.

2 Corinthians 12:2-4; "I knew a man in Moshiach about fourteen years ago – whether in the body, I cannot tell; or whether out of the body, I cannot tell: YHWH knows – such a one was caught up to the third shamayim (heaven). And I knew such a man – whether in the body, or out of the body, I cannot tell: YHWH knows – How he was caught up into Paradise, and heard unspeakable words, which is not lawful for a man to utter." This is Sha'ul talking in the first person of how he was taken up into the third heaven, though he is unable to tell whether he went physically or spiritually. He witnessed a confidential exchange of words between the Father, Son and their angels. This encounter has absolutely nothing to do with an end of days rapture.

Revelations 4:1-2; "After this I looked and see, a door was opened in the shamayim (heavens): and the first voice which I heard was like a shofar talking to me; which said, 'Come up here, and I will show you things that must be after this.' And immediately I was in the Ruach; and see, a kesay (throne) was set in the shamayim, and One sat on the kesay (throne)." Here's John being taken up and about to witness the events we read about in Revelations. Again, there is nothing here to support a mass ascension of followers to avoid a coming series of catastrophes.

Colossians 1:13; "Who has delivered us from the power of darkness, and has translated us into the malchut (kingdom) of His dear Son:" Halleluiah, He has delivered us indeed! Isolating this passage to support a snatching away of the faithful to avoid a cataclysm or tribulation is adding meaning that just isn't there. This is like using Yahshua's name, which means, "Yah is our Salvation" to support the rapture.

Ephesians 2:5-6; "Even when we were dead in our sins, (YHWH) has made us alive together with Moshiach – by unmerited favour you are saved – And has raised us up together, and made us sit together in the heavenly places in Moshiach Yahshua:" How can this verse be used in any capacity to support an end-time rapture? Separating the portion of this Scripture that refers to a simultaneous rising up of people as confirmation of a specifically timed mass rescue ignores its context. Without considering context countless passages may be extracted from the Scriptures and used to support any wild idea or concept. That is why from the mouth of two or three witnesses all truth shall be established ***(2 Corinthians 13:1)***.

1 Thessalonians 4:17; "Then we who are alive and remain at His return shall be caught up together with them into the clouds, to meet the Master in the air, and so shall we ever be with Master." Note the words ***"we who are alive and remain at His return."*** This verse refers to meeting YHWH in the atmosphere as opposed to heaven. This is the first resurrection and it occurs in the air AFTER the great tribulation while the earth is being reformed for the 1000 year Sabbatical millennial reign of Messiah.

Matthew 24:40-42; "Then shall two be in the field; one shall be taken, and the other left. Two women shall be grinding at the mill; one shall be taken, and the other left, because the malachim (angels) at the end of the age will remove the stumbling blocks from the world and will separate the good ones from the wicked. Watch therefore; for you know not what hour your Master is coming." Those left behind are saved and those taken, like in the days of Noah, will drink from the wine of the wrath of YHWH. The church has been thoroughly conditioned to accept the opposite of this teaching thanks in part to the global success of *The Left Behind* book, comic and television series. Those who are members of the Commonwealth of Israel and have been birthed from above (born again) will be left "in the field" and "grinding at the mill." The "stumbling blocks" will be removed.

The chief characteristics of a Remnant Israelite is a love of the name YHWH ***(Isaiah 56:6a)***, observance of His Sabbaths ***(Isaiah 56:6b)***, and holding fast to His Covenants ***(Isaiah 56: 6c)***.

Though I am sympathetic to a future mass ascension of an elect or remnant, I must clarify that the Scriptures do not portray it as a pre-, mid- or post-tribulation rescue, despite many Bible commentaries and church views to the contrary. Certainly if one interprets the term "rapture" to mean an event that is associated with a type of rescue then such a concept has no biblical basis whatsoever. The concept of a "post-tribulation rapture" is a misnomer because it describes a rescue after a trial has passed.

The truth is that there was no significant teaching on a rapture of the church before the 1800's. A Jesuit by the name of Emmanuel Lacunza, writing under the alias of a Rabbi first proposed this concept in his book, *The Coming of Messiah in Glory and Majesty*. This book compounded by the prophesying of a fifteen-year old Catholic girl ignited the appealing idea of "the rapture" which, centuries on has given birth to a series of books that continue to deceive millions to this very day. The Messiah taught in his parable of the wheat and tares that the righteous and the unrighteous would be together until the very end ***(Matthew 13:24-32)***.

Scripture teaches that followers will be led to Israel in the last days and be on or near Mount Moriah (Beit HaMikdash) upon seeing the "abomination of desolation." From there they will flee to a place called "Sela," which is now known as modern day "Petra"***(Isaiah 16:1-5, 42:11, Mathew 24:15-16, Revelation 12:6,14,)***. Like the early Hebrews who were present during the unfolding of the plagues in Egypt their latter day descendants will endure a similar situation before reaching the Promised Land.

Consider the following information carefully in light of a rapture doctrine.***John 17:15; "I request not that You should take them*** (believers) ***out of the olam hazeh (this world), but that You should keep them from the evil."*** Yahshua does not pray that all believers be removed from the earth, but that they remain protected in the days ahead!

Chapter Eight

A Faith Worth Losing Your Head Over

FOR MOST WESTERN PEOPLE, religious or secular, the subject of prophecy, particularly Bible Prophecy is a weighty issue and best left alone or at the very least at a distance. This is likely because the subject is usually portrayed by the media as the dangerous obsession of fanatical religious cults or the backdrop to a fictitious plotline of a dark paperback thriller or film.

Is reading and interpreting Bible Prophecy for everyone, or is it reserved for a select few who are either "nut jobs" or YHWH's elite of the elite? Posing this question is like asking if the Scriptures are for everyone. Provided a person's obedience to Torah is equal to their level of familiarity with it, the study of Bible Prophecy is open to anyone.

The correct manner to apply ourselves to studying this subject is best summed up by the prophet Isaiah. ***Isaiah 28:10; "For precept must be upon precept, precept upon precept; line upon line, line upon line; here a little, and there a little.."*** This piece-by-piece method of study avoids finding meanings that depart from the context and maintains a message's unity to the Scripture's foundational text – The Torah.

Anyone who is familiar with Scripture and spent any time in the Book of Revelations will remember a reference to the souls of those who suffered (or rather have yet to suffer) beheading at the hands of a ruler known as "the Beast" ***(Revelations 20:4)***. This title "beast" comes from the Greek word *therion*, which means, "dangerous animal."

Move Over Rome

One of the chief pillars used to support that Islam is the major end time beast according to the Messianic Scriptures (New Testament) is their continued practice of beheading. This is cited because of a future climate described in ***Revelations 20:4; "And I saw thrones and they sat upon them, and mishpat (judgement) was given to them; Then I saw the beings of those who had been beheaded for their witness to Yahshua and for the word of YHWH, who had not worshipped the beast or his image, and had not received his mark on their foreheads or on their hands..."*** Of late I have read some compelling material backed up by solid Scriptural foundations and historical evidence that support the teaching that the Islamic world will give rise to the beast of Revelations.

History tells us that Muhammad had as many as 400 Jews beheaded for not accepting his new brand of Judaism, which we now call Islam and today Islam remains the only religion in the world that still practices this form of execution.

However, pinpointing Islam based on their religious law of beheading as a critical sign of the end time beast is problematic for certain reasons, which I will outline in this chapter. Along the way I will touch on some other subjects that may be of some interest.

Horrific and Humane

The Western world is quickly growing accustomed to the fact that beheading by guillotine (that is mechanised apparatus) is the most effective, efficient and humane way to end massive numbers of lives. But what is beheading and why is the guillotine so efficient and unusually referred to as humane?

The definition of behead is "to cut off the head of someone, usually as a form of capital punishment." Its Etymology has an Anglo-Saxon root, which is *beheafdian*, from *be-* off or away + *heafod* head.

A Pro-lifer Invented the Guillotine

Doctor Joseph Ignace Guillotin was a member of a small political reform movement that wanted to completely banish the death penalty. He lobbied for a form of execution that would be equal for all classes and introduced an apparatus based method of beheading as an interim measure.

Beheadings in Scripture

Until this time mechanised beheading devices had only been used in Germany, Italy, Scotland and Persia, and as yet such methods of execution had never been adopted on a large scale. However, beheading as a form of execution is evident in almost every culture, nation and religion that has ever existed, including Judaism (see Noahide Laws), but was usually carried out with a manually swung or sawn bladed implement. The Sanhedrin (Assembly of Torah compliant elders) occasionally had prophets sawn in half. The prophet Isaiah was cut in two with a wooden saw as was the prophet Zachariah. Though he was not an official member of the Sanhedrin, Herod, the corrupt Roman client-king of Judaea also had John the Immerser beheaded at the request of a dancing girl's mother ***(Matthew 14:10)***. King David beheaded and amputated the hands and feet of some of his own men ***(2 Samuel 4:12)*** after they killed and beheaded Ish-Bosheth the son of Saul ***(2 Samuel 4:7)*** and the most famous beheading in Scripture was the decapitation of Goliath by David as a shepherd boy in ***1 Samuel 17:51***. A heifer is beheaded as a sin offering in ***Deuteronomy 21:6***.

Islam and Judaism's laws that pertain to capital punishment are very similar. But in their strictest form they are rarely utilised. The laws are so stringent that even if witnesses (willing to testify) see a man enter a cave followed by another man with a knife and they later see the second man emerge with blood on it and find the first man dead, capital punishment under no circumstances can be implemented.

Tired of Swinging

Decapitation without the use of a Guillotine is extremely dangerous and tedious. Even the simple act of chopping wood requires a level of skill and a well crafted and maintained implement to perform successfully. In contrast, the formal execution of a live and fully conscious individual with a swung axe into their neck region would take a level of physical and mental skill that would be beyond the average person's ability to comprehend. On the other hand, the clamped guillotine cuts through (no pun intended) this problem. Provided the victim can be secured, a lever is pulled and the blade does the work. The executioner may even be situated behind a curtain whilst operating the machine.

The *Guillotine Takes Shape and Lives*

Doctor Joseph Guillotin teamed up with a German engineer and built a prototype for the ideal guillotine machine. Later the diagonal blade was introduced and the spring system after that, until it evolved into the popular image we see today.

A civilian assembly in France rewrote the penal code to say, "Every person condemned to the death penalty shall have his head severed." From then on all classes of people would now meet a common fate. The first execution occurred on April 25, 1792, when Nicolas Jacques Pelletie was guillotined at Place de Grève and the last took place in Marseilles, France on September 10, 1977 (five years after this author was born).

Guillotine Facts

- Total weight of a guillotine is about 1278 lbs
- The guillotine metal blade weighs about 88.2 lbs

- The height of guillotine posts average about 14 feet
- The falling blade has a rate of speed of about 21 feet/second
- Just the actual beheading takes 2/100 of a second
- The time for the guillotine blade to fall down to where it stops takes a 70th of a second.

Beheading in Islam & Judaism

As pointed out earlier, both Islam and Judaism (in their most free forms) advocate execution by decapitation in rare circumstances.

Islam & the Koran

References in the Koran to beheading are vague. In book 47, verse 4 of the Koran, it says, "Therefore, when ye meet the unbelievers in fight [or jihad], **smite at their necks at length**; when ye have thoroughly subdued them, bind a bond firmly on them. Thereafter is the time for either generosity or ransom until the war lays down its burdens." Mr. Sam Hamod, former director of the Islamic Research Centre responded to this verse by saying that the "smite at their necks" wording "doesn't mean to kill somebody." He then went onto say that "any Islamic capital punishment must be handed down by a panel of judges plus there must be four credible witnesses of an extreme crime committed by the person to be executed. Beheading as an execution option remains a part of the criminal legal code in Saudi Arabia, Yemen, Iran and Qatar. Only Saudi Arabia continues the practice." - Christy Oglesby, CNN, Thursday, July 22, 2004. Despite every country listed being predominantly Islamic, the above article does not speak for independent or quasi-independent Islamic insurgent forces, gangs, militias or mentally detached commanders of small military units in any part of the world who partake in any type of crime that involves human decapitation.

Judaism, Torah, Prophetic & Messianic Writings and & the Talmud

Jews do not currently adhere to the practice of beheading because there is no officially formed Sanhedrin or Temple priesthood. There is a Sanhedrin and high priests alive today but the current political climate in Israel does not support their function or authority.

In the Torah there is no specification for this type of execution except for the heifer sin offering in ***Deuteronomy 21:16***, and the Scriptures are not specific on beheadings by Jews of "People of the Way." The Talmudic writings (diverse Jewish Torah commentaries) contain beheading as a form of execution against the act of murder in the Seven Noahide laws. These laws were given to Noah by YHWH after the waters of the flood began to subside. These Seven Noahide laws are evident in the Torah, though not found consecutively or specifically named.

The Noahide Laws and their Scriptural Foundations

1. Prohibition against Sexual Immorality ***(Genesis 2:24 "A man... shall cling to his wife...and they shall become one flesh...")***
2. Prohibition against Murder ***(Genesis 9:6 "...whoever sheds the blood of a man, by man shall his blood be shed...")***
3. Prohibition against Blasphemy ***(Leviticus 24:10-23 "...Bring him forth that has cursed...and...stone him.")***
4. Prohibition against Robbery ***(Leviticus 19:11-13 "You shall not steal...")***
5. Prohibition against Idolatry ***(Leviticus 19:4 "Turn not to idols...")***
6. Prohibition against Removing and Eating the Limb or Blood of a Living Animal ***(Genesis 9:3-4 "Flesh with blood in it you shall not eat.")***
7. Commandment to Establish Courts of law ***(Leviticus 19:16 "Do not stand by while your neighbour's blood is shed.")***

An Interesting Fact

The Seven Noahide laws incorporate 66 aspects of the 613 mitzvoth of the Torah. It is further interesting to note that while there is no Temple in Jerusalem only 271 mitzvoth of the Torah can be performed.

Covenants Galore - A Complete Covenant Takes Shape

The Scriptures show that YHWH always builds or reestablishes His perfect Covenant with men as each generation progresses or transgresses His Torah. This is evident with His Adamic Covenant ***(Genesis 3:14-23)***, Noahide Covenant ***(Genesis 9:1-17)***, Abrahamic Covenant ***(Genesis 17:1-27)***, Sinai Covenant ***(Exodus 19:1-31:18)***, Mosaic Covenant at Moab ***(Deuteronomy 29-30 & Leviticus 26)***, Davidic Covenant ***(2 Samuel 7:5-19 & 1 Chronicles 17:4-15)*** and the New Covenant ***(Jeremiah 31:31-34 & 32:40-44)*** and also hinted at in ***(Deuteronomy 10:16)***. None of these Covenants cancel out or replace each other. They all form a complete picture, which hang on a single act (Yahshua's death and resurrection). Their fulfillment is to be completely motivated by love and a longing to gain closer intimacy with the Father. Loving your neighbour as yourself is the blueprint for this action.

The Similarity of the Statutes Listed in Acts 15:20 & the Noahide Laws

Acts 15:20 says that those returning to YHWH are to have no initial burdens placed upon them other than to abstain from idols, fornication, eating the flesh of strangled animals and drinking blood. This is because these observances set an acceptable environment for the Jew to enter into the home of a Gentile to share the good news of the Torah. The above list of statutes would have not been a completely foreign request to a Gentile as they are directly taken from the Noahide Covenant, which was given to the first humans after the deluge (flood). Most humans would have been aware of these laws and observed them to a greater or lesser extent.

NoaHiding in the American Constitution (or what's left of it)

The Noahide Laws served as the backbone for the establishment of America's Constitution. Scholars have written extensively on John Adams and Thomas Jefferson's knowledge of the Talmud and the influence the Noahide Laws had on the Constitution.

The 1991 U.S. Congress passed a law that recognised the "ethical values and principles" of the Noahide Laws and how they formed "the bedrock of society from the dawn of creation."

Heads Will Roll

Please consider the following piece of information. As of 1996 a new legislation in the State of Georgia was proposed to have execution by guillotine be offered as an alternative form of capital punishment for inmates on death row. It did not pass, at least not yet. Here are some of the details of what happened.

Guillotine Proposed As Means of Execution in Georgia

Georgia lawmaker Doug Teper (Democrat, 61st Dist.) has proposed a bill to replace the state's electric chair with the guillotine. Teper's reasoning? It would allow for death row inmates as organ donors, he says, since the "blade makes a clean cut and leaves vital organs intact."

For decades there has been trouble associated with lethal injection and electrocution. Prisoners have died excruciating deaths and in some cases withstood initial administering of dosages and electricity, causing witnesses trauma and gathering the attention of human rights organisations that threaten lawsuits and abolition of capital punishment. Procedures as they stand require large teams of very highly paid trained personnel and even without hiccups is clumsy and time consuming. If a single crewmember is unable to perform his duties, this can cause delays that drag on for days, weeks, or even months. Here's how the plan to introduce the guillotine appears to look. I've broken it down into a 5-step program.

Five Steps to the Guillotine

Step 1. Clinton Administration sets up capital punishment for anyone who ATTACKS a Federal Building or Personnel in the wake of the Oklahoma City bombing.

Step 2. Have a Senator explain that Guillotine is the ONLY FORM OF EXECUTION that does not DAMAGE THEIR ORGANS...and have him add that these ORGANS could be used to save lives.

Step 3. Introduce specially televised executions that show the current forms of capital punishment.

Step 4. Show an execution by ELECTRIC CHAIR that goes horrifically wrong.

Step 5. Air radio broadcasts and run newspaper reports that show new initiatives/laws ready to go into effect in both Georgia and Florida...to USE GUILLOTINES AS AN ALTERNATE FORM OF CAPITAL PUNISHMENT

Islam is the only dominant religion to continue the practice of stoning, hanging and beheading. But in an Orthodox Jewish Torah observant climate, all of these practices would also be observed. The only thing holding the Orthodox Jewish world back is the absence of a Temple and a tattered priesthood. The Orthodox Jew is a Nazarene Israelite's brother, but history shows that they have persecuted the remnant of YHWH before. People who are entering into the original faith of the Apostles must be warned not to run blindly into the arms of mainstream Judaism. Persecution of Nazarenes or "People of the Way" was Sha'ul HaShliach's former profession, and the Natsarim have been viewed as a detestable people by the Jewish community for centuries. Historically Nazarene Israelites are not welcome to join Orthodox synagogues or get involved in Jewish communities. Does this mean that we should not support Israel? Absolutely not, we should watch and learn from the Jew and assist them to whatever degree possible, as long as it does not cause us to compromise our faith in Messiah Yahshua.

Was Yahshua Against the Death Penalty?

There is much more to the well-known story of the adulterous woman than the average Christian realises ***(John 8:3-4)***. The most horrendous interpretation is that Yahshua instituted a new ruling against the death penalty by sending the sinful Pharisees and Scribes away. What do the Scriptures say? According to Torah an adulterous woman would have been brought into the court of the Temple to partake in the ritual of the bitter cup. ***Numbers 5:27-8; "And when he has made her drink the mayim (water), then it shall come to pass, that, if she is defiled and has done trespass against her husband, that the mayim that causes the curse shall enter into her, and becomes bitter, and her belly shall swell and her thigh shall rot; and the woman shall be a curse among her people. But if the woman has not defiled herself and is pure, she shall be free and shall conceive zera (seed)."*** If the accused was found guilty she would be taken outside the city and stoned.

Christians are all familiar with the motives of the woman's accusers and how they sought to test Yahshua. Neither is it a secret that a stoning did not ensue because of each man's spiritual condition ***(John 8:5)***, but something far more intriguing, yet seldom realised is revealed in this incident. The Pharisees confront Yahshua with the following question, "Now Moshe in the Torah commanded, that such (an adulterous woman) should be stoned; but what are you saying?" Yahshua responds by writing something in the dirt. We know that it was due to this action that the accusers dispersed because they responded to his writing and not his famous words, "He who is without sin cast the first stone." Whether it was because each man recognised his own sins written on the ground or that Yahshua was performing a prophetic assignment, the Scriptures are not specific, but they depart in great shame as ***Jeremiah 17:13*** foretells, ***"O YHWH, the mikvah (immersion) of Yisrael, all that forsake You shall be ashamed; and they that depart from Me shall be written in the earth..."***

Yahshua then asks the woman, "Where are your accusers?" She responds by saying, "There are none Adonai (master)." According to the Torah of Moshe a woman cannot be stoned for adultery without witnesses. No witnesses, no accusers, no bitter cup, no stoning. All above board and all Torah.

"In both the Koran and the Torah, when a woman was found in adultery, she would be stoned. In the Koran there needed to be four male witnesses, and only the woman was punished. Also in the Koran, if two men were found together, they would be given the chance to repent. If they did not repent, they would be mildly punished. In the Torah, if adultery was discovered, both the woman and the man were to be stoned. According to the Torah, if two men were caught in improper relations, both were to be stoned." – "The Torah and the Koran" (Comparative Essay) by Rit Nosotro.

The Catholic Church, the Crusades and the Inquisition

Roman Emperor Diocletian had supporters of the Manichaeans (Ancient Iranian religion) beheaded. During the Crusades many who did not convert to Catholicism lost their heads. The Inquisition wasn't that big on beheading because it was a poor form of torture and they did not generally perform acts that caused bloodletting. Nonetheless beheading on mass is evident throughout its history.

Interestingly the infrastructure to vehicle an inquisition is still present in the Vatican's extensive and multi-layered network of offices today. 'The Holy Office' is the preferred name of the same organisation that once went by the title, 'Inquisition.'

Conclusion

We must remember that if an Easterner decapitates his enemy with a blunt butter-knife and the Westerner does the same thing with a sanitised, humane and efficient guillotine the end result is still ultimately the same. Both therefore still have the potential to provide this characteristic of the beast of the Book of Revelations. Though there is new evidence that has come to light to show that Islam has the potential to be the initiator of this beast, I encourage all Watchmen to keep an eye on all three organisations – Islam, Judaism[1], high Orthodox Catholicism and low Catholicism (Churchianity).

Matthew 10:28; "Do not be afraid of those who kill the body but cannot kill the being. Rather, be afraid of the One who can destroy both being and body in Gei-Hinnom (hell)."

1 I must make it clear that Judaism is not a religion that should be lumped in with Islam and Christianity in the negative sense that some may perceive by my closing comment. I am simply saying that in the days ahead there will likely be dangerous opponents among the Jews who will threaten the Natsarim; much like the Chassidic community was threatened when it first emerged.

Chapter Nine

Early Church Fathers – The Foundation of Western Anti-Semitism

RABBI YAHUSHUA BEN YOSEPH Ha Nazaret[1] (the Messiah) and Rabbi Sha'ul HaShaliach (the Apostle Paul) never instructed Jewish believers (or newly converted Gentiles) to avoid attending synagogues on Sabbath and gather in churches on the first day of the week. In their day the church was a sun-centered religion known as the Temple of Circe[2]. Followers of Circe worshipped around Asherah poles (now called Christmas trees) on "Yule day[3]" (now called Christmas), celebrated a yearly fertility rite (now called Easter), and met in buildings fitted with spires and steeples[4] (now called churches). Circe was not the name of congregations who followed Messiah Yahshua, but the name of those who worshipped the goddess-daughter of the Sun-deity Helios. The likelihood that Messiah would have encouraged believers to cease attending

1 This was Messiah's full earthly name as it would have been formerly spoken. *Ben* means "son of." Though he would have been addressed as "son of Joseph" his biological Father was the One Living Elohim. Yahushua (Yah'ooshua) is the long form pronunciation of his name.

2 "Circe" (Kirke) is an old English form of the word "church." It was originally the name of the daughter of the sun god Helios.

3 "Yule" is an ancient Chaldeen word that means child. The word "mass" in Christmas means "sacrifice."

4 Steeples and spires on churches are of pagan origin, representing the male phallus and perform the function of capturing natural light for sun worship.

synagogues and commence meeting in Temples of Circe would be akin to a modern-day pastor encouraging Christians to leave churches and attend Satanic Covens.

The Creator's unchanging view ***(Malachi 3:6-7)*** on superimposing foreign terminology ***(Joshua 23:7b)***, marshalling alien customs and using pagan objects to worship and honour Him can be studied in the Golden Calf incident. In particular take note of ***Exodus 32:5; "So when Aaron saw it (the Golden Calf), he built an altar before it. And Aaron made a proclamation and said, "Tomorrow is a feast to YHWH."***

Though the word church, which signifies a particular religious group, appears many times in modern Bibles, it replaces nonspecific terminology such as "congregation," "assembly," or "gathering." Early English translator, William Tyndale even used the word "churches" to describe heathen temples in ***Acts 19:37; For you have brought here these men, who are neither robbers of Churches (Temples), nor blasphemers of your female mighty One (Circe).*** The only difference between temple goers of Circe in biblical times and churches goers today is the level of ignorance of what is being truly worshipped. In Yahshua's day the Samaritans believed they worshipped YHWH, but not according to the custom of the Jews. This is why Yahshua says to the Samaritan woman in ***John 4:22, "You (Samaritans) worship what you do not know; we know what we worship, for salvation is of the Jews."***

The church was principally constructed to replace YHWH's chosen people (Israel). To this day it is viewed as an entity completely separate from the Jews despite ***Isaiah 56:3***'s declaration, ***"Do not let the son of the foreigner who has joined himself to YHWH speak saying, 'YHWH has utterly separated me from his people (Israel).'"***

Now let's take a peek into the mindset of the Early Church Fathers and in their own words read their views on the people that Yahshua said Salvation is of ***(John 4:22)*** and Sha'ul said have much advantage ***(Romans 3:1-2)***.

St. John Chrysostom (344-407AD)

"Many, I know, respect the Jews and think that their present way of life is a venerable one. This is why I hasten to uproot

> and tear out this deadly opinion. I said that the synagogue is no better than a theatre...the synagogue is not only a brothel and a theatre; it also is a den of robbers and a lodging for wild beasts..."

Response: As pointed out, nowhere in Scripture was there ever a teaching to cease meeting together in a synagogue and commence meeting in a pagan "Temple of Circe" (Church). Temple prostitution was a characteristic of pagan temple worship and was never tolerated within a synagogue where male and female occupants are segregated anyway. Yahshua and Sha'ul never attended a church or gave instruction to cease meeting in the same manner as in their day!

Ignatius, Bishop of Antioch (98-117AD)

> "For if we are still practicing Judaism, we admit that we have not received God's favour...it is wrong to talk about Jesus Christ and live like Jews. For Christianity did not believe in Judaism, but Judaism in Christianity."

Response: The Scriptures say ***in Romans 11:18; "do not boast against the branches. But if you do boast, remember that you do not support the root, but the root supports you."*** This is another reason why Yahshua says, "salvation is of the Jews." ***(John 4:22)*** NOWHERE, and I mean NOWHERE in Scripture do you find the phrase, 'salvation is of the Gentiles!'

Justin Martyr (135-161AD)

> "We too, would observe your circumcision of the flesh, your Sabbath days, and in a word, all your festivals, if we were not aware of the reason why they were imposed upon you, namely, because of your sins and the hardness of heart. The custom of circumcising the flesh, handed down from Abraham, was given to you as a distinguishing mark, to set you off from other nations and from us Christians. The purpose of this was that you and only you might suffer the afflictions that are now justly yours..."

Response: *(Regarding circumcision of the flesh)* The circumcision of the heart is a Torah teaching that originally appeared in ***Deuteronomy 10:16; "Therefore circumcise the foreskin of your heart, and be stiff-necked no longer."*** The circumcision of the heart is not a New Testament teaching that replaced flesh circumcision. Sha'ul disputed the teaching of the flesh circumcision because it sent fear into the heart of the Gentiles and obscured the heart felt motive that should initiate it. Indeed circumcision, on its own, is worth nothing ***(1 Corinthians 7:19)*** without the circumcision of the heart that must precede it. Never is the act of circumcision described as an affliction, nor is it ever specifically required just for Jews. In fact circumcision is a seal of righteousness! ***Romans 4:11; "And he (Abraham) received the sign of circumcision, a seal of righteousness of the faith..."*** Sha'ul also describes physical circumcision as profitable if the recipient keeps the law (Torah) and as unprofitable if the recipient abandons the law (Torah) ***(Romans 2:25)***.

(Regarding Sabbaths) Nowhere in the Scriptures are any Sabbaths given as a burden. On the contrary, they were given as rehearsals and object lessons, which are to be a believer's delight ***(Isaiah 58:13)***! The Commandment to keep the Sabbath throughout all generations ***(Exodus 31:13)*** was given to the Hebrews and the foreigners (Egyptians) who dwelt among them at Mount Sinai. ***Leviticus 18:26; "You shall therefore keep My statutes and My judgments, and shall not commit any of these abominations, either any of your own nation or any stranger who dwells among you."*** Watch a Sunday keeping Christian try and explain their way out of this one the next time you hear them say that the Commandments were just for the Jews. As a final note apply ***Isaiah 56:3b***, which says, ***"To the eunuchs who keep My Sabbaths and choose what pleases Me."*** And then ***Isaiah 56:6***, which says, ***"Also the sons of the foreigner who join themselves to the Lord (YHWH), to serve Him, and...Everyone who keeps from defiling the Sabbath."***

Origen of Alexandria (185-254AD)

"We may thus assert in utter confidence that the Jews will not return to their earlier situations for they have committed the most abominable of crimes, in forming this conspiracy

> against the Saviour of the human race…hence the city where Jesus suffered was necessarily destroyed, the Jewish nation was driven from its country, and another people was called by God to the Blessed election."

Response: ***Romans 11:1-2a; "I say then, did YHWH cast away His people? By no means! For I also am a Yisraelite, of the zera (seed) of Avraham, of the tribe of Benjamin. YHWH has not cast away His people whom he NEW AND CHOSE BEFORE HAND."*** YHWH never once speaks of a newly chosen people that have replaced the former ones. Surely neither the Gentile nor the Samaritan could be these "other people" when we read statements from Yahshua like this one in ***Matthew 10:5b; "…Go not the way of the gentiles by staying away from pagan practices, and into any city of the Shomronim (Samaritans)."*** Any foreigners or strangers who follow YHWH (through the example of Yahshua) are "grafted in" or "joined" to Israel. ***Isaiah 56:3; "Neither let the son of the ger (foreigner) that has joined himself to YHWH speak in this manner, saying, "YHWH has utterly separated me from His people…"*** Origen's statement is a perfect example of the emergence of "replacement" or "supersessionist" theology. Sha'ul who was an Israelite ***(Romans 11:1)*** and a lover of the law (Torah) ***(Romans 7:22)*** only identifies with the Gentile for the purpose of provoking his own people to jealousy, because of their acceptance of Yahshua as Messiah ***(Romans 11:13,14)***.

Saint Augustine (354-430AD)

> "How hateful to me are the enemies of your Scripture! How I wish that you would slay them (the Jews) with your two-edged sword, so that there should be none to oppose your word! Gladly would I have them die to themselves and live to you!"

Response: As this above statement does not address anything scriptural I am at a loss to apply the bandage of Scripture to it.

Saint Augustine also wrote:

> "The true image of the Hebrew is Judas Iscariot, who sells the Lord for silver. The Jew can never understand the Scriptures and forever will bear the guilt for the death of Jesus."

Response: This is statement is very odd, considering that the Jews wrote every word of the Scriptures and that without a Hebraic understanding it cannot be fully realised.

Let's have a look at some memorable words from the great protestant reformer, Martin Luther (1483-1536): "In sum, they (the Jews) are the devil's children, damned to hell...The Jews got what they deserved."

The Scriptures say that Gentile acceptance of Messiah will provoke the Jew to jealously ***(Romans 11:13,14)***, but this is because the Gentiles will also embrace the Torah that he came to fulfill.

The Early Church Fathers, having abandoned, outlawed, suppressed and replaced YHWH's chosen people, and the modern church that still stubbornly follows and proclaims their lawless replacement theology will have no part in the world to come.

The biggest stumbling block to Greco-Roman replacement theology is the following verse sequence: ***Matthew 23:1-4; "Then Yahshua spoke to the multitude, and to his talmidim (disciples), Saying, The sophrim (scribes) and the Prushim (Pharisees) sit in Moshe's kesay (seat of authority): All therefore that Moshe's kesay will invite you to observe, that observe and do; but do not do after their mitzvoth: for they say, and do not. For they bind heavy burdens too grievous to bear, and lay them on men's shoulders; but they themselves will not move them with one of their fingers."***

Yahshua didn't have a problem with the scribes or the Pharisee's instructions. And well he shouldn't have, because their teaching lined up with the Torah as found in ***Deuteronomy 17:11; "According to the sentence of the Torah that they shall teach you, and according to the mishpat (judgment) that they shall tell you, you shall do: you shall not decline from the ruling which they shall show you, to the right hand, nor to the left."*** The problem was with the way these teachers conducted their own lives. They would instruct righteously, but they themselves failed to live according to their own instructions. To them and anyone who teaches with authority the warning is made loud and clear in ***James 3:1; "My Yisraelite brothers, not many should be rabbis (masters of Torah), knowing that we shall receive a stronger mishpat (judgment)."***

The framework for teaching, instructing and ruling as YHWH intended was set down in the days of Moshe ***(Deuteronomy 16:18***

& ***17:9,10)***. A subsequent climate of hypocritical representations of this framework did not give pagan priests and politicians the right to step in, chop up pieces of foreign religions and glue them together and call them the faith of YHWH. The Hebrews at the foot of Mount Sinai appropriated their own method of worshipping YHWH by building and bowing down to a golden calf and declaring it as a representation of their deliverer from Egypt ***(Exodus 32:5)***. This sincere act nearly cost the life of every Israelite man, woman and child.

Yes, YHWH is a gracious and Eternal King and He is longsuffering, but He does eventually reach a point where He says, "That's enough; I will no longer accept strange fire from these people!!" Look at the examples of the Tower of Babel, Noah's flood, the twin cities of Sodom and Gomorrah and the cleansing of Revelations.

If nothing else, this work is a call for serious Christians everywhere to lend an ear to the Jew. I'm not saying become a Jew. I'm just saying that they have the covenants, Sabbaths and Festivals and they have insight into the Scriptures that we can all draw on and learn from.

Let the very words from the pen of the Early Church Fathers expose the inner dark recesses of their own hearts and in turn shine light on the rotten foundation of the now widespread multi-denominational Temple Cult of Circe (the church).

The Deeper Origin of Anti-Semitism

Anti-semitism was never born with the Nazi Regime. In fact a lot of what the Nazis did to the Jew had already been done by Christians. In 535 The Synod of Claremont passed a law that denied Jews the right to hold public office. In 1227 the Synod of Narbonne decreed that all Jews wear an oval badge as a mark of identification. In 1236 Pope Gregory ordered all church leaders to confiscate all Jewish books on the first Saturday of Lent. In 1555 a special charter was issued by the Pope that required all Jews to be confined to ghettos. Hitler merely adopted methods to deal with the Jews that had been carried out centuries before, but with the aid of technological means achieved unprecedented results.

The actual term "anti-semitism" was first used in 1873 in a pamphlet by Wilhelm Marr called *Jewry's Victory over Teutonism*. His intention was to replace the German word Judenhass (Jew-hatred) with a more politically correct and less offensive term.

Anti-semitism goes as far back as ancient Egypt, when Pharaoh feared that the children of Israel would outnumber his own people. He initiated segregated living conditions (ghettos), hard labour (slavery) and infanticide (murder of all newborn males). Persecution and eradication of the only remaining Torah keeping tribe continued to flow throughout history. Textbook anti-semitism is described in the ***Book of Ester 3:8; "And Hamman said, There is a people scattered abroad and dispersed among the nation in all the provinces of your malchut (kingdom); and their laws are diverse from all peoples; neither do they keep the melech's (King's) laws: therefore it is not for the melech's benefit to let them remain alive."*** Adolph Hitler clearly understood the roots of anti-semitism when one examines this true statement in his book, *Mein Kampf*, "The anti-semitism of the new [Christian Social] movement[5] was based on religious ideas instead of racial knowledge." The deeper reality is that Hitler and the Nazis were Christians. Adopting their no tolerance stance toward Jews simply followed the faithful roots and past practices of the Church. One can easily see disturbing similarities with Hitler's Nazi Youth and today's Catholic Youth League.

5 In context Hitler was referring to the Christian Social Party whose ideals appealed to his own ideology. Hitler used Christian based anti-semitist thought to propagate the destruction of the Jewish people.

Chapter Ten

Genesis Re-Revisited

A Stage-by-Stage Breakdown of the Cosmic Struggle

ONE THING THAT HAS really intrigued me, in terms of mankind's role within YHWH's plan, is the bigger picture. Believers at no matter what level of revelation can sometimes forget that there is a far larger and complex cosmic history that took place well before mankind's appearance that is well documented within the Scriptures. By having an understanding and appreciation of the things that transpired before Adam's creation, one can achieve a stronger realisation of his or her place in not only the present world, but in the world to come.

For example, how often does a believer contemplate his future role in judging rebel angels ***(1 Corinthians 6:3)*** or grasp the notion that he is a fellow Mighty One (El) in the eyes of YHWH and all His host ***(John 10:34)***?

In an effort to provoke independent investigation and open up new perspectives to the reality of the world to come, I have compiled a series of entries that document what transpired before and after the creation of men.

The following is a breakdown of the initial struggle between Heilel ben-Schahar (aka HaSatan) and YHWH (aka God). I have arranged each major turning point into fourteen simple stage-by-stage entries. There is still much that occurred, which is documented, particularly in the book of Enoch, that has been left out for the sake of clarity.

The Book of Enoch

The book of Enoch was accepted as Scripture until it fell out of favour with Post-Nicene church fathers and denounced as heresy. Nearly all copies were fed to the flames and it all but disappeared from history for a thousand years. In 1821 Hebrew professor, Dr Richard Laurence, produced the first English translation from a copy that was found by Scottish explorer James Bruce in Ethiopia. As prophesied within the work itself, the book disappeared and resurfaced for a distant generation. ***Enoch 1:2; "...but it was not for this generation, but for a remote one which is to come."***

I remember completely flipping out Christian author and member of the Christian *Answers in Genesis* community, Garry Bates when I forwarded him an early draft of this chapter via e-mail. At the time I thought we may have been on the same page as he had just released a work that dealt with the subject of Ufology from a Scriptural perspective. Unfortunately, his work dealt with Ufology from a Christian perspective, which is very different.

During the course of my research, it has become apparent that there is a wide gap between the study régime of the average Christian and the study régime of the average Orthodox Jew. So wide is the gap that it is like comparing a fourth year student studying rocket science to a first year high school student studying basic math. A sound grasp of correct theology is indirectly dependant on a clear understanding of the correct sequence, nature and implication of all Biblical events. Most Christians do not have the capacity to argue against basic biblical criticism because they do not consider valuable insights from the Jews.

No matter how outlandish some of the following information may appear, it does not contravene the Scriptures in any way.

Stage 1

Heilel ben-Schahar (His Latin name being Lucifer) serves in the Temple of YHWH as a guardian (Cheruv) high priest[1] ***(Ezekiel[2] 28:13,14)***. He is the most beautiful and beloved Elohim[3] of the entire heavenly host. Over time, growing self-centeredness corrupts and retards his wisdom. He perceives himself as "the light" rather than a bearer of light. This manifests itself in the actions of misdirecting incoming praise (meant for YHWH), the building of independent resources and defiling sanctuaries (i.e., misusing resources on terra formations [planets]) ***(Ezekiel 28:18)***. He then attempts to elevate himself above the Most High ***(Isaiah 14:13)*** by rallying one-third of the heavenly host to join in a rebellion ***(Revelation 12:4)***. A civil war ensues in the heavenly realms. The battle goes badly for the rebel host ***(Revelations 12:7-9)*** as they are cast down from heaven ***(Luke 10:18, Isaiah 14:12[4])*** to a sanctuary (planet) that was formerly under Heilel ben-Schahar's stewardship. The planet is known in our tongue today as "Earth." At this time mankind is pre-known by YHWH, but not yet created.

1 Verses 13 and 14 of ***Ezekiel 28*** describe the stones in the high priest's breast plate, which were built into Heilel's original form.

2 Though the opening verse in Ezekiel 28 refers to the prince of Tyre and later in verse 11, the king of Tyre, and in verse 20, the inhabitants of Zidon, it is clear by verse 13 that the text is actually speaking about the events that led to the downfall of the spirit behind them - Heilel ben-Schahar (the prince of the rebel host and the chief accuser of the brethren). Note the direct reference to the Garden of Eden by verse 13 and the sheltering Cheruv (Guardian One) in verse 14. The popular rabbinical view of this text isolates the context of the whole chapter, drowning out the former role and tragic events that led to the defecting of Elohim's most beloved angel. However, in comparison, Psalm 45, which mentions the daughter of the King of Tyre (verse 13), is ironically accepted as a chapter that describes the splendour of the coming Messianic age.

3 As the word "angel" is derived from the Hebrew word "Māl'ak," meaning "messenger," (only a job title), I address angels as 'Elohim,' 'sons of Elohim,' 'fallen sons of Elohim' or 'righteous sons of Elohim.' Elohim means "Mighty Ones of Renown." Some Elohim were appointed as Watchers (another job title).

4 Some rabbinical sources state that this verse is referring to the Babylonian King, Nebuchadnezzar. While this is true it is also synonymous with Heilel ben-Schahar (Satan).

Stage 2

Heilel ben-Schahar and his surviving armies (sons of Elohim) begin building immense military compounds[5] and merge their DNA with a range of earth animals in an attempt to physically replenish their numbers.[6] The result of this action sees the conception of a collection of beasts now relegated to human mythology, some of which include "centaurs," "satyrs," "elephant-headed gods" and "multiple-limbed humanoids."

Major land to air defenses consisting of enormous predominantly stone tired three faceted structures are set up in specific locations around the world. The remains of these structures are a global archeological phenomenon known as Pyramids.[7] The largest of them still exists near Xian in the province of Shensi in China and is more than twice the size of the Great Pyramid[8] of Giza in Egypt. "Obelisks" are also fashioned and fixed in positions that correspond with the "world grid"[9] to enable the use of energy efficient anti-gravity and allow the provision of crucial protective shielding technology. Rival factions within this society emerge which inevitably leads to internal conflicts and minor wars. These battles are recorded in great detail in Indian Sanskrit texts.

---

5 Joseph P. Farrel, author of the book, *The Giza Death Star*, draws an astonishing comparison to the oldest structural remains that surround the Giza Pyramid and the layout of a modern military compound.

6 Contrary to popular belief angels can die like men ***(Psalms 82:7)***.

7 Author and engineer, Christopher Dunn and physicist, Joseph P. Farrel both postulate in their books, *The Giza Power Plant* (Dunn) and *The Giza Death Star* (Farrel), that the internal construction of the Great Pyramid contains evidence of once housing acoustical wave technology (working on a principle Ferrel calls "Paleophysics"). This technology could have enabled a great concentration of energy to be expelled, much like a huge power generator. This energy could have been used to support a super-weapon or teleportation device. They further hypothesize that ancient Egyptians primarily venerated the structure as a sacred royal tomb because it once belonged to a superior race. As testimony to this the Great Pyramid is devoid of a single hieroglyph inside and out.

8 See Appendix for further notes on the Great Pyramid of Giza.

9 For information on the world grid see *Anti-gravity & the World Gird* by David Hatcher Childress. Though I recommend this work I do not endorse all of the conclusions held by the author or other authors and researchers cited by him.

Stage 3

YHWH and His heavenly host conduct several diplomatic missions in the hopes of attempting peaceful negotiations and put an end to all hostilities. Their offers are completely rejected.

Stage 4

YHWH and His heavenly host unleash multiple cataclysms and wipe out all earth structures and crossbred animal and angelic forces. This is recorded in New Age and some secular historical sources as the "Fall of Atlantis." This assault culminates in a pre-human global flood that leaves the earth void and without form ***(Jeremiah 4:23[10])***.

Stage 5

Heilel ben-Schahar and a host of temporarily pacified sons of Elohim survive and retreat to another inhabitable Sanctuary[11], possibly Mars and later Sirius.[12]

Stage 6

YHWH and His heavenly host re-terraform[13] the earth within a seven day period. During this time a new sentient species is taken out of the land and created to assume stewardship over it. They are

---

10 If studied carefully the flood account in ***Jeremiah 4*** does not refer to Noah's flood, but a previous flood where ***"there was no man,"*** ***"birds of the heavens...fled"*** and ***"all the cities thereof were broken down."***

11 There is support in Torah for intelligent life on other planets. In the Book of ***Judges 5:23*** the prophetess, Devorah, sings about Barak's victory over Sisera. In her song, she says, ***"Cursed be Meroz! Cursed, cursed be its inhabitants, says the angel of Elohim!"*** The Talmud gives two explanations of where Meroz is and who inhabits it. One explanation is that Meroz is a star or planet. Devorah also states one verse prior that members of the heavenly bodies had come to help Israel. ***("From the heavens they fought, the stars from their orbits...")*** The inhabitants of Meroz, the dominant star of Sisera, did not come to Israel's aid and were therefore cursed.

12 *Cydonia: The Secret Chronicles of Mars* by David Flynn.

13 This includes a full and diverse complement of all types of vegetation and animal life.

called *Adama*[14], Hebrew for "mankind." Their new habitation in a previously existing earth explains why the first humans, Adam and Hava, are instructed to ***"replenish the earth" (Genesis 1:28)*** and why King David describes them as being created to ***"renew the face of the earth"*** in ***Psalms 104:30***. They are given coverings like an outer mantle (cloak, robe or garment of light) that acts as protection, assists with endurance and increases strength "to till the land." YHWH visits and interacts with men intermittently and declares their relationship a successful and harmonious one.

Stage 7

Heilel ben-Schahar's forces eventually return to earth after having their presence on another sanctuary threatened by the heavenly host. They re-evaluate the new situation and devise a way of hiding in the DNA of a certain native earth animal (This process is commonly understood in religious circles as possession).[15] They favour upright, limbed, two to three metre high reptiles[16] (a species of Dinosaur). The purpose of their concealment is to hide from YHWH and present themselves to men in a familiar native animal. They begin a steady interaction with the Adamic pair through limited social contact and communication.

---

14 Adam also means, "red," "ruddy," "ground," and "man of low degree." Anyone who is familiar with the requirements for the construction of a Gollum (Kabbalistic practice of making a man from the earth) knows that it must come from undisturbed deep red clay.

15 Anthropologist, Michael Harner writes of his experiences in the Peruvian Amazon in the early 1960s after drinking a third of an hallucinogen called "ayahuasca," and goes on to relate an experience that emanated from "giant reptilian creatures" that allegedly showed him scenes usually reserved for the dead or dying: "First they showed me the planet Earth as it was eons ago, before there was any life on it. I saw an ocean, barren land, and a bright blue sky. Then black specks dropped from the sky by the hundreds and landed in front of me on the barren landscape. I could see the specks were actually large, shiny, black creatures with stubby pterodactyl-like wings and huge whale-like bodies...They explained to me in a kind of thought language that they were fleeing something out in space. They had come to planet Earth to escape an enemy. The creatures then showed me how they had created life on the planet in order to hide within the multitudinous forms and thus disguise their presence." (Note how the account contains the truth mixed with a lie) Source: *The Cosmic Serpent – DNA and the Origins of Knowledge* by Jeremy Narby.

16 This species produces limbless offspring from ***Genesis 3:14*** onward. A Jewish oral teaching, called *The Haggadah*, describes the serpent as being as tall as a camel and possessing arms and legs that are later described as being "hacked off" during YHWH's judgment. The serpent's skin is also removed and prepared as clothing for Adam and Hava.

The Reality of the Talking Serpent

The Hebrew root for the word "serpent" (nawkawsh) is *nawkash*, meaning "one who hisses" or "whispers enchantments" and gives some indication of the serpent in the Garden of Eden's ability to form speech, perhaps not unlike a parrot or cockatoo. As a parrot is able to form sounds that mimic human speech, an animal of a bygone era that exhibited a similar trait could have been easily utilised through demonic influence to audibly emit intelligent conversation, as if it were speaking itself.

After a level of trust develops between the Adamic pair and serpent, one of them entices Hava (Eve) to receive an enhancement without YHWH's approval. By way of deception he convinces men to willingly go against a certain rule set down by YHWH in the hopes of causing another rebellion.

The plan appears to succeed as the humans fall out of favour with YHWH. However, Heilel ben-Schahar's greater plan of inducting them into his ranks as angels fails when the Creator bans them from partaking of the Tree of Life. The Adamic pair is stripped[17] of their mantles (garments of light), which causes them to now perceive their maker (YHWH) and their deceivers (Heilel ben-Schahar and the sons of Elohim) in forms that have a similar outward appearance to great serpents[18] ***(Genesis 3)***.

17 A portion from The Jewish *Haggadah* reads; "The first result was that Adam and Eve became naked. Before, their bodies had been overlaid with a HORNY SKIN and enveloped with the CLOUD OF GLORY. No sooner had they violated the command given them then the CLOUD OF GLORY and HORNY SKIN dropped from them, and they stood there in their nakedness…"

18 Though I do not support Gnosticism, a first century Christian Gnostic tract tackles the encounter in a way that aligns with the language of the *Haggadah*: "Now Eve believed the words of the serpent. She looked at the tree. She took some of its fruit and ate, and she gave to her husband also, and he ate too. Then their mind opened. For when they ate, the light of knowledge shone for them; they knew that they were naked with regard to knowledge. When they saw their makers, they loathed them since they were *beastly forms.* They understood very much."

Stage 8

YHWH's heart is broken at Adam and Hava's decision to go against His natural law. He passes judgment on all participants with an array of afflictions. By YHWH's mercy, roused by the involvement of an intellectually superior being, Adam and Hava are given the opportunity to repent, but have their celestial garments withdrawn and are cast out of a particularly fruitful region. This repentance takes the form of future obedience and an acceptance in a promised Moshiach (rescuer) who will come from the seed of Hava and cause the serpent (Heilel) to be destroyed. ***Genesis 3:15; "And I will put enmity between you and the woman, and between your zera (seed) and her Zera (seed); He shall crush your head, and you shall bruise His heel."*** This is the first official announcement of Yahshua and his mission.

Heilel ben-Schahar tries to use man's fall to challenge YHWH's methodology of creation and freewill. YHWH responds by giving Heilel ben-Schahar, which He renames as "The Accuser[19]," a short time to prove his case.

Stage 9

Humans begin to multiply over the face of the earth. Righteous Sons of Elohim (angels) are appointed as "Watchers" to observe mankind's progress and report[20] to YHWH. Meanwhile, the Accuser devises a counter measure to YHWH's plan. He commands his remaining forces (two hundred[21]), having now set up a staging post on a nearby planet, to descend to earth and present themselves as gods to various human communities. By way of setting up harems and engaging in mass sexual unions with the daughters of men, they commence a mass corruption of the human genetic line ***(Genesis 6:2)***. The motive here is to hinder this future Saviour's arrival by contaminating the human race with the rebellious biological nature

19 ***Revelations 12:10; "...the accuser of your Yisraelite brothers is cast down, who accused and slandered them before our Elohim day and night."***

20 ***Genesis 18:21*** is an example of YHWH responding to a report from His *Watchers*. They are also described as invisible witnesses in ***Hebrews12:1***.

21 Enoch 6:6; "And they were in all two hundred; who descended in the days of Jared."

of fallen Elohim ***(Genesis 6:2-4)***. Some righteous Watchers[22] are also tempted by the daughters of men and join the angelic rebellion. These unions are described in Scripture as ***"going after strange flesh," "keeping not their first estate," "having left their own habitation,"*** and ***"giving themselves over to fornication."*** The outcome of this event is described in ***Daniel 2:43; "And whereas you saw iron mixed with muddy clay, they shall mingle themselves with the zera (seed) of men: but they shall not cleave one to another, even as iron is not mixed with clay."***

Angels in a Nutshell

Angels are immortal beings whose primary role is to minister the will of YHWH. They were created as a set-apart host to serve and function in perfect unity with the Most High, much in the same way that the torso and members of a healthy working body serve the securely attached head of a sane and clear thinking human being. Angels at their core are incorporeal (spiritual) beings, which are able to assume physical organic forms.

The children of Israel's declaration of obedience at Mount Sinai in ***Exodus 24:7*** mirrored a unique characteristic found only among angels in the heavenly realms. All twelve tribes stood before Elohim and declared that they would do His mitzvoth (love deeds / commandments) first and listen to them second. This same seemingly unusual order of obedience is described as a trait found in the heavenly host. ***Psalms 103:20; "Bless YHWH, you His heavenly malachim (messengers), that excel in strength, that do His mitzvoth (love deeds), that listen to the voice of His Word."*** This doesn't mean that angels or human followers blindly follow YHWH, but that they observe YHWH's commandments even before they are specifically issued.

22 This group could alternatively be the two hundred referred to in the Book of Enoch.

Soon the sons of Elohim withdraw from the surface of the earth and leave their thrones to fearsome progeny known as "nephilim[23]." These hybrid half-human half-angelic tyrants begin to dominate and eradicate all pure blood humans. The most common trait of these brutes was their enormous physical stature, though some had other characteristics such as half-human and half-animal traits like the lion men of Moab ***(2 Samuel 23:20)***. 1st century Jewish historian, Flavius Josephus, wrote about their sheer enormity in his work, *Antiquity of the Jews*:

> "There were till then left the race of giants, who had bodies so large, and countenances so entirely different from other men, that they were surprising to the sight, and terrible to the hearing. The bones of these men are still shewn (on display) to this very day, unlike to any credible relations of other men."

As the nephilim multiplied, their dietary requirements began to exceed the general availability of food, which caused them to use forced human labour to provide additional quantities. Eventually the nephilim began to consume humans themselves, then one another.[24] Some ancient records postulate that male giants began to exceed female giants, which may account for why many resorted to sodomy. The depravity of these unsanctioned part angelic offspring knew no bounds.

Stage 10

Spiritual and physical corruption spreads to all households except one. A human known as "Noach" (Noah), his family and many pureblood[25] animals are spared as a second flood wipes out the rest

23 Nephil, (nephilim [plural]) means "proficient bully" or "tyrant." The Hebrew root of the word is *nephel,* which means, "untimely birth, abortion, or miscarriage." This is because their birth was an abomination to YHWH.

24 ***The Book of Enoch 7:3-6; "... Who consumed all the acquisitions of men. And when men could no longer sustain them, the giants turned against them and devoured mankind. And they began to sin against birds, and beasts, and reptiles, and fish, and to devour one another's flesh, and drink the blood. Then the earth laid accusation against the lawless ones."***

25 Pureblood is in reference to animals that have not been subject to genetic crossing with men or nephilim. This terminology is not to be confused with the kosher laws of clean or unclean animals.

of earth's land dependant inhabitants ***(Genesis 6:7,8)***. Genetic tampering is evident in this period of history and is a chief catalyst for the total erasure of terrestrial life.

Gene Manipulation in the Pre-flood or Antediluvian Age

Elohim's decree to wipe out all flesh that creeps on the land testifies to an array of irreversible spiritual and physical traits that had penetrated and thrown off the harmony of not only mankind, but the animal kingdom as well. YHWH knew that even without man's intervention, animals would not be able to return to their natural state. In other words, the earth's condition could not be mended by simply wiping out all mankind and nephilim alone. Even the land and vegetation it produced had to be cleansed. The inhabitants of that era had wrestled themselves into a state of self-destruction by meddling with the growth and reproduction of organic life in a non-Torah compliant manner. If YHWH had not intervened, the occupants of that time would have eventually destroyed themselves anyway. Much like today...

The *Book of Jubilees* and the *Book of Jasher*, two infamous lost books of the Bible, exhibit some very specific references to not only a corruption of man-flesh but also the flesh of beasts. The authority of these works looked down upon by the ill-informed, can be tested on the following strengths:

- The Book of Jubilees was regarded as an authoritative work by ante-Nicene church fathers. However, due to political reasons it was eventually deemed unfit for canonisation by Rome and all available copies were committed to the fire. The relevance and importance of this originally Jewish work did not surface again until its discovery among the Dead Sea Scrolls. Until that time the only known copies to exist was as a small Latin rendered fragment comprising only a quarter of the whole text and four complete 15th century Ethiopic manuscripts.

- The Book of Jasher's authority is supported by two solid references in Scripture. ***Joshua 10:13; "And the sun stood still, and the moon stayed in place, until the people had avenged themselves upon their enemies. Is it not written in the Sefer Yahshar (Book of Jasher)? So the sun stood still in the midst of the shamayim, and did not set for about a whole day."*** And ***2 Samuel 1:18; "Also he ordered The Bow to be taught to the children of Yahudah: see, it is written in Sefer Yahshar (Book of Jasher)."***

Before I cite these verses it must be made clear that the existence of genetic manipulation in Scripture is evident only to the reader who understands the use of "phenomenonological language." This language describes things as they appear as opposed to using scientific terminology. For example: If I was to say, "The sun sank in the horizon," we know that the sun's disappearance had nothing to do with it literally sinking.

The use of phenomenological language in many ancient texts is completely appropriate because it simplifies the narrative and allows writings to be understood throughout different technologically developed ages.

Consider the corruption of both man and animal flesh beyond the limited boundary of sexual misconduct as you read the following passages: ***Jubilees 5:2-4; "And lawlessness increased on the earth and all flesh corrupted its way, alike men and cattle and beasts and birds and everything that walks on the earth - all of them corrupted their ways and their orders, and they began to devour each other, and lawlessness increased on the earth and every imagination of the thoughts of all men (was) thus evil continually. And God looked upon the earth, and behold it was corrupt, and all flesh had corrupted its orders, and all that were upon the earth had wrought all manner of evil before His eyes. And He said that He would destroy man and all flesh upon the face of the earth which He had created."***

Jasher 4:18-19; "And their judges and rulers went to the daughters of men and took their wives by force from their husbands according to their choice, and the sons of men in those days took from the

cattle of the earth, the beasts of the field and the fowls of the air, and taught the mixture of animals of one species with the other, in order therewith to provoke the Lord; and God saw the whole earth and it was corrupt, for all flesh had corrupted its ways upon earth, all men and all animals. And the Lord said, I will blot out man that I created from the face of the earth, yea from man to the birds of the air, together with cattle and beasts that are in the field for I repent that I made them."

The second flood is initiated by gradual but consistent collapsing of a protective firmament of water (aka middle water) ***(Genesis 1:6)*** that continues over a period of forty days and forty nights ***(Genesis 7:4, 12, 17; 8:6)***. All other flesh that creeps, including the nephilim, bar one[26], are killed. After the flood Noach's family begins to repopulate the earth. The spirits of dead nephilim (having no place in the world to come) are left in disembodied states to wander the earth to cause mischief and contend with men.[27] Their appearances and activities are largely misinterpreted as spirits of deceased humans, commonly referred to as ghosts. ***1 Enoch 15:8-10; "But now the giants who are born from the (union of) the spirits and the flesh shall be called evil spirits upon the earth, because their dwelling shall be upon the earth and inside the earth. Evil spirits have come out of their bodies. Because from the day that they were created from the holy ones they became the Watchers; their first origin is the spiritual foundation. They will become evil upon the earth and shall be called evil spirits. The dwelling of the spiritual beings of heaven is heaven; but the dwelling of the spirits of the earth, which are born upon the earth, is in the earth. The spirits of the giants oppress each other, they will corrupt, fall, be excited, and fall upon the earth, and cause sorrow. They eat no food, nor become thirsty, nor find obstacles. And these spirits shall rise up against the children of the people and against the women, because they have proceeded forth (from them)."*** The fallen angels who begat these nephilim are cast into the lower most portion of Gehenna, called Tartarus ***(2 Peter 2:4)***.

26 According to ***Deuteronomy 3:11*** and ***Genesis 6:4***.

27 According to the Book of Jubilees.

Stage 11

A giant called Og[28] survives the flood ***(Deuteronomy 3:11; "For only Og melek [king] of Bashan remained of the remnant of the Rephayim [Giants]")*** but is later killed by the nation of Israel ***(Deuteronomy 1:4; 31:4)***. This is why Scripture speaks of these hybridised tyrants also existing after the flood. ***Genesis 6:4; "There were Nephilim in the earth in those days; and also after that…"*** Og procreates with human women, causing a second corruption of pureblood humans to again obstruct the descendants of "Adamah" (Adam). Before long man forms a community that flourishes into a bustling economy called "Babel," the likes of which is set to equip its inhabitants with enough knowledge and power to achieve any end ***(Genesis 11:6)***.

Stage 12

YHWH infuses multiple languages into the economy of Babel, forcing its inhabitants to disband and divide into smaller independent communities. These communities move off into different directions and commence building individual settlements ***(Genesis 11:8-9)***. Supremely powerful nephilim conspire to control and continue interbreeding with men by splitting up and presenting themselves to these various communities as godlike beings. These deceivers set up unique laws and customs that are the origin of differing global cultures we see throughout the world today. This is why when various cultures are examined and stripped back that certain commonalities in religious stories are always evident. To these deceivers the prophet Jeremiah relates "***This shall you say to them, The elohim that have not made the shamayim (heavens) and the earth, shall perish from the earth, and from under these shamayim." (Jeremiah 10:11)***

---

28 ***Genesis 13:14*** also mentions Og's status as a survivor, though he is not mentioned by name: ***"And there came one that had escaped, and told Avram the Ivri (Hebrew)…"*** "Escaped" refers to Og not only having escaped the battle of the kings but also death during the flood. His act of telling Abram about Lot granted him long life, though his motive was not honourable. This wrong motive was dealt with at his eventual defeat by Abram's descendants.

Stage 13

More disobedient Sons of Elohim interfere with mankind. Ancient communities described their arrival and departure as beings who came and went in fiery chariots[29]. Modern communities describe them as UFOs, though UFO activity can have a range of origins.

YHWH commands Israel to annihilate all nephilim by the sword ***(Deuteronomy 9:1-3).*** These assaults diminish the nephilim population to small isolated communities ***(Joshua 11:21-22).*** Their numbers keep dwindling over the next two centuries as records of encounters with giants roaming isolated wildernesses and remote islands appear in countless historical records all over the world (even to this very day[30]).

Stage 14

YHWH, by means of His unseen enabling force (Ruach HaKodesh / Holy Spirit), causes a righteous pureblooded woman to conceive the promised Saviour[31]. This individual comprises unique faculties that are in complete unity with YHWH. He is rejected by many influential so-called members of his own nation, but later embraced by many people from foolish foreign nations ***(Romans 10:19).*** The converts graft themselves to the remnant of YHWH's originally chosen nation. His flesh is voluntarily extinguished in an act that fulfills His Father's promise and seals the fate of the Accuser and his minions.

29 Though the Scriptures exclusively associate the appearance of aerial chariots with YHWH and His host, ancient Indian *Sanskrit* texts describe highly sophisticated flying machines called *Vimanas* (aerial cars) piloted by god-like beings who regularly abduct beautiful women.

30 Bigfoot aka Sasquatch as he is known to the North American Indian, Yeti to the Tibetan and Yowie to the Australian Aboriginal.

31 He is the flesh encapsulated representation or the primary manifestation of YHWH who was in existence before the foundation of the world. His origin is in YHWH, brought forth from the Father's very bosom. He is therefore referred to as the "only begotten Son." From the time he was brought forth, the ability to think and act independently manifested itself in him. Independent action was never explored as the Son remained in perfect alignment with his Father's complete will (to this very day).

Chapter Eleven

Passover – Pass it On

NOT UNTIL I BEGAN to enter into a Nazarene Israelite walk did I realise the significance and necessity for individual believers to celebrate the festivals of YHWH found in ***Leviticus 23***. The fact that every festival was meticulously constructed as a participatory object lesson to train and prepare believers for major prophetic events is barely hinted at within most churches today.

The festival of Passover ***(Exodus 12, Leviticus 23:5-8)*** is perhaps the most significant of them all, but at best is only studied by the average Christian, remaining frozen in the pages of Scripture like an ancient custom that ran its course with Messiah's fulfillment as the perfect sacrificial lamb.

I once believed that the act of acquiring ***(Exodus 12:3,4)***, roasting and eating a lamb with unleavened bread and bitter herbs ***(Exodus 12:8-10)*** was just an old antiquated custom still vainly held onto by the Orthodox Jew and paid significant homage by the vastly different Eucharist ritual, commonly referred to within wider Christianity as "The Lord's Supper." The celebration of Easter also served as a suitable distraction to the truth as I danced unknowingly to the beat of Mystery Babylon's colorful array of replacement pagan festivals.

Much to my surprise the so-called New Testament not only encourages the keeping of Passover by all post-resurrection believers, but that it be done so in its original Hebraic format[1]. ***1 Corinthians 5:7,8; "Clean out therefore the old chametz (leaven), that you may be a new lump, as you are unleavened. For even Moshiach (Messiah) our Pesach (Passover) was sacrificed for us: So then let us keep the moed (appointed time), not with old chametz (leaven), neither with the chametz (leaven) of malice and wickedness; but with the unleavened matzah (unleavened bread) of sincerity and emet (truth)."***

What Part of Forever Do You Not Understand?

The eternal observance of this feast should have come as no surprise to me had I actually read the initial ordinance as delivered in ***Exodus 12:24; "And you shall observe this word (Passover) as a mishpat (right ruling) for you, and your sons le-olam-va-ed (for ever)."*** But even if I had, I would have probably fallen for the lie that it was just for the Jews or that the church tradition of consuming a wafer and swallowing a shot glass of grape juice was sufficient. The just for Jews thing becomes a little problematic when the statutes for a sojourner (foreigner) who wishes to observe it is also outlined in ***Exodus 12:48; "And when a ger (stranger) shall sojourn with you, and desires to shomer (keep) the Pesach (Passover) to YHWH; all his males must perform brit milah (flesh circumcision), and then let them come near and shomer it; and he shall be as one that is born in the land: for no uncircumcised person shall eat it."*** This is all beside the stark fact that the Jews were just one of twelve Israelite tribes who received this festival along with six hundred and twelve other commandments at the base of Mount Sinai. One has to wonder if the above requirement to participate in the festival is one of the reasons why Sha'ul said that there is much advantage in being circumcised[2] ***(Romans 3:1,2)***.

---

1 This is evident by the verse's reference to the symbolic act of cleansing personal dwellings of all leaven (leaven representing sin). This ritual is most likely where the Western concept of "spring cleaning" originated.

2 Flesh circumcision is a sign of righteousness ***(Romans 4:11)*** and an outward physical manifestation of circumcision of the heart as first taught in ***Deuteronomy 10:16. 1 Corinthians 7:19*** merely points out that flesh circumcision on its own is worthless. Circumcision is a token of the Sinai Covenant.

The Long Road to Truth

During my Christian walk I consecutively attended five different churches and in that time I received no encouragement to study or keep any Appointed Time, much less the Passover, which was faithfully observed by Yahshua and his followers ***(Matthew 21:1, 9-12, 17-18, 23).*** The sad fact is that I was not only kept in the dark about the importance of these original customs, but I was encouraged to observe festivals of a completely pagan origin like Christmas and the aforementioned Easter. Eventually my journey took me from Sunday observance to Sabbath observance. I remained in a Sabbath keeping church for a while, but still felt that I was missing out on something. I began to realise that I had to withdraw from church completely, because I could foresee that there was always going to be some aspect of the Hebraic roots of the original faith that was neglected or rejected in places of official Christian worship. All churches, and I mean all churches, even Jehovah's Witness and Mormon congregations exhibit obvious evidence of having broken away from mother Rome.

Have you ever noticed how most mainstream church denominations appear to fall short after a major or a set of major revelations? For example:

- The Baptist churches received the revelation of full water immersion, but more or less stop there and continue to follow Rome.
- The Seventh Day Adventist churches received the revelation of the dietary laws and the Sabbath, but more or less stop there and continue to follow Rome.
- The Pentecostal movements received the revelation of tongues but more or less stop there and continue to follow Rome.
- The Jehovah's Witness (not normally associated with the church) received the revelation of the coming kingdom, but more or less stop there and continue to follow Rome.
- The Protestant movement received the revelation of Apostate Rome, but amazingly continue to follow her in so many respects.

For years I thought that the most authentic body of Bible adherent believers was only going to be found somewhere within a church denomination. I remember meeting a new face at one of the last churches I attended who told me that he was looking for the remnant. He stopped coming after a while and this really played on my nerves because he had obviously not found them at the church I was attending. I sometimes think of him and wonder if his journey is running in the same direction as mine.

Stepping out of the Comfort Zone

Having come out of Christianity and withdrawn from observing pagan holidays it took quite some time to realise that there were a whole set of original Appointed Times given by YHWH for all generations of believers to observe.

Consequently the best material available that examines the significance of Passover is not found within Christian writings, but in Rabbinic and Messianic literature. Passover, or "Pesach" as it is called in Hebrew, historically represents Israel's deliverance from the bondage of Mitzrayim (Egypt). Spiritually it represents the application of Yahshua's blood to the doorpost of a believer's heart and Salvation from the bondage of a sinful world. Pre-resurrection observers of Passover did it in reflection of their exit from slavery and in expectation of Messiah's future atonement and post-resurrection observers do it in remembrance of the same.

A Constant Ancestral Connection

Modern-day believers are to respond to YHWH as if they had been personally led out of Mitzrayim (Egypt) by Moshe himself. The commandment to eat the roasted lamb in haste ***(Exodus 12:11)*** illustrates the swiftness of Israel's departure from captivity ***(Exodus 12:34, 39)*** and reflects a sense of personal inclusion by way of reenactment. Observing Passover in such a manner causes a believer to claim a direct association to Israel's patriarchs as their personal forefathers and sends out an appeal to YHWH to maintain a believer's absorption into the promise of Abraham.

In addition I have also found that without studying crucial aspects of the Passover ritual and seeing its direct relation to Messiah and the historical context surrounding his first and second entry into Jerusalem at the close of his earthly manifestation, so much wonderful detail in the passion story is lost and will remain perpetually opaque to the mind of the casual churchgoer.

Yahshua's earthly cousin, Rav Yochannan HaMatbil (John the Immerser) immediately proclaimed the Messiah's eligibility as the perfect Passover Lamb when he saw him walking toward him in ***John 1:29***. Looking up through his wild mane and clutching his staff he stated, "***Behold, the Lamb of YHWH, who takes away the sin of the olam hazeh (world).***"

The Passion, This Time with Passion

Come with me, if you will, over two thousand years ago to the outskirts of Jerusalem as a band of men converge on a city in need of a King. Let me tell you a familiar story, but this time within the context of the social and political climate of the time and take you beyond the sanitised religious rendering of the lead up to the most pivotal moment in the history of all mankind.

Arrival of a Militant Prince of Peace

It is a warm day on the 9th of Abib. Messiah Yahshua is heading to Yahrushalayim (Jerusalem) and for the first time cautions his talmidim (disciples) to exercise extreme caution after word reaches him of the death of several Zealot patriots, who recently tried to secure the city's perimeter after a general uprising. The incident called for the use of battering rams, which soon toppled the strong tower of Siloam in the Kidron Valley resulting in eighteen deaths. But despite all this, the city continued to swell with people in preparation for Passover.

The Roman colonial occupation and the dominating Herodian rule caused great unemployment, and social division among the Yahudim (Jews), which gave birth to an emergence of a coalition of movements called Zealots who frequently engaged in armed confrontations against Rome, Herod and even amongst themselves.

This was the climate in which Yahshua's ministry evolved and his talmidim needed little coaxing to bear arms if their Master's life was threatened before his appointed time.

Some of the Messiah's closest followers were associated with the Zealot movements. Shimon (Simon), one of Yahshua's talmidim, was known as a Zealot ***(Luke 6:15)*** and Rabbi Shimon Kepha (Peter) was called a "Bar-jona" ***(Matthew 16:17)***, which means "outlaw" and was a common name for a Zealot. The term "Boanerges" another common Zealot reference means, "Sons of Thunder" and was applied to Yaakov (James) and Yochannan (John) in ***Mark 3:17***.

Before reaching Jerusalem Yahshua pauses at Bethpage and sends two of his talmidim ahead to fetch a "colt" and an "ass" so that ***Zechariah 9:9*** might be fulfilled.

Yahshua makes a highly visible entrance into Yahrushalayim (Jerusalem) as a new claimant to the throne of David ***(Matthew 21:9)***. Retribution to any aspirant to this title by the Romans was always swift, but the millions in attendance for Passover keep the occupying garrison of five hundred Roman soldiers at bay.

During Passover the Temple priests would lead a lamb into Yahrushalayim (Jerusalem) as an offering to be slain. These lambs, like Yahshua, were born and bred in Bethlehem. When the time came, they, like Yahshua, would be paraded through the city before being slain. This would culminate with the animal's throat being cut by the high priest who would utter the familiar words, "It is finished."

Restoring the Temple

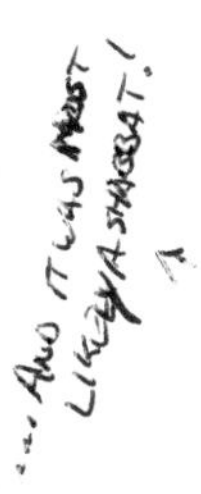

Yahshua goes to the Temple and with the help of his talmidim forcefully throws out the money exchangers, those selling sacrificial animals, and illegally appointed priests ***(John 2:11-17)***. He even commandeers a whip and uses it to drive out the animals from the Temple court. This is not a moment of uncontrolled rage, but a fulfilment of ***Jeremiah 7:11*** as he forcefully removes undesirables and reforms the illegal Edomite (Arab) priesthood.

By the time of Yahshua's ministry less than three out of the twenty-eight high priests that presided in the Temple were of

A'aronic descent. Because non-A'aronic priests were unable to sanctify themselves, the ordinance to sanctify the Temple on the 1ST of Abib ***(Ezekiel 45:18-20)*** was no longer observed. ***2 Chronicles 30:3; "For they could not keep it at that time, because the kohanim (priests) had not set themselves apart sufficiently..."*** Therefore Yahshua had to set the Temple apart in order for his death to be in accordance with the Torah and the writings of the prophets.

Yahshua and his most devoted followers marshal full control of the Temple compound. For two days, the sacrificial system is postponed as the priesthood is culled, restructured and the Temple cleansed. The entire priestly quarter of Yahrushalayim (Jerusalem) is in Yahshua's control. (Note: no aspect of the Passover ritual is cancelled at this time. If it were, he would have been perceived as the *Moshiach Neged* [negative Messiah / Anti-Christ] as mentioned in ***Daniel 9:27***) Yahshua proceeds to preach a message with an apocalyptic emphasis, heal people and enter into dialogue with the Pharisees, scribes and attorneys. With the high number of attendees for Passover, postponement of this duration threatens to be a major financial blow to the corrupt Pharisee and Sadducee authorities. However the corrupt high priest, Caiphas withholds sending in his Sadducean Temple guards and calling for Roman assistance because a substantial monetary loss was far better than a riot ***(Matthew 26:5)***.

Those Crazy Zealot Yahoos

Zealot patriots, knowing Yahshua's allegiance with the multitudes, his powers over nature and his ability to heal and raise the dead to life, take advantage of the political environment and this time successfully stage a coup and seal off the Temple Mount, the Kidron Valley and the Mount of Olives. Bara-abba (Barabbas) being one of the ringleaders is captured and detained for murder, but later released by Pilot ***(Luke 23:19; "Who for a certain uprising made in the city...")***. The Zealots completely expect Yahshua to lay full claim to the Messianic legacy by militant force! However, instead of engaging the Sadducean Temple guards and the Roman garrison stationed at the Antonia tower in battle, Yahshua heals the sick and ministers once the Temple is secured. This is a live demonstration of the true "Kingdom of YHWH."

On the first evening Yahshua leaves around seventy of his most trusted followers, most of them armed Zealots, to guard the Temple courts while he spends the night in Bethany ***(Matthew 21:17)***. Yahshua illustrates complete compliance to the Pharisaical and Zealot view of the militant aspect of the Davidic family by later personally encouraging his twelve talmidim to personally arm themselves in ***Luke 22:36-38***. These verses and their implications have been continually played down and glossed over by the church for centuries.

Yahshua goes with his twelve talmidim out to the Mount of Olives and settles there in the Garden of Gethsemane, which means, "the garden of the olive press." He acquaints his talmidim with the exact place where he will one day stand and split the earth before a great battle as prophesied in ***Zechariah 14:4***.

On the **10th of Abib** when the Passover lamb is normally set aside ***(Exodus 12:3)*** Yahshua heads out to Bethany and is anointed ***(John 12:3)***. This occurs on the Sabbath in the presence of Lazarus, Miriam (Mary), Martha ***(John 12:2)*** and Yahudah (Judas).

This is Not a Dress Rehearsal!

From Bethany, the same place where Passover lambs start their processional, Yahshua emerges on the **11th of Abib** for a second triumphant entry into the city. His followers clog the road to meet him, laying their tallitot (prayer shawls) and palm branches across his path as he enters ***(Mark 11:8)***. So great is the commotion over this man entering the city on a donkey ***(John 12:15)*** that it interferes with the commencement of the usual Passover ritual prompting the Pharisees to complain ***(Luke 19:39)***. They cry out to Yahshua, "Tell your talmidim and these people to be silent!" Their frustration reaches boiling point as the normal lamb processional is being held up and completely overshadowed by the One True Lamb that was announced by Abraham ***(Genesis 22:8)***.

The Pharisees have absolutely no idea that this day was the day that all their previous Passover rehearsals had pointed to. They were oblivious to the fact that this ritual, after being practiced for generations was finally unfolding right before their very eyes.

At this point, Yahshua's ministry reaches the peak of its earthly authority as the Jewish masses celebrate his every move. Despite functioning without an organised army he manages to successfully cleanse the Temple and preach from its courts without being apprehended. The Zealots who were largely made up of break-away Pharisees applauded his action in the Temple as being long overdue. Even the Temple guards began to recognise Yahshua as a lawful heir to the throne of David.

Key Events in King David's Life Forecast the Trials of Messiah

Yahshua spends each evening at the Mount of Olives, located about a mile east out of Jerusalem ***(Luke 21:37,38)***. It was at this same location where King David took refuge in times of trouble and where Ezekiel saw the fiery wheels of YHWH. Some similarities in King David's life uncannily parallel that of Messiah. Absalom, David's disillusioned son, managed to gain the support of his father's most trusted ally as a co-conspirator and launched an assault against him with the exchange of a kiss. David even ascended the Mount of Olives when he learned of his son's intention to attack Jerusalem and the betrayal of his chief councilor Ahithophel the Gilonite.

On the morning of the **12th of Abib,** whilst on his way to preach in the Temple, Yahshua stops at a fig tree to acquire food, but causes it to supernaturally wither after finding it has nothing to offer. This act demonstrates the judgment of one who bears no fruit as prophesied in ***Jeremiah 8:13***. Yahshua's talmidim look on in disbelief. He swiftly tells them that they possess the same potential even in the vicinity of altering major geographical locations at a single utterance. This is perhaps a snapshot of Yahshua's method of sculpting landmasses at the dawn of creation. On his arrival to the Temple he is forced to turn out more merchants ***(Mark 11:15,16)*** before resuming his teachings.

A War of Words

The following day on the **13th of Abib** the Pharisees ask him plainly, "...***By what authority are you doing these things? And who gave You this authority to do these things?" (Mark 11:28)***. Yahshua takes a deep breath and carefully responds with another question, deflecting the earnest back on them, "By what authority was Rav Yochannan's immersion ministry given? Was it by heaven or by men?" Reluctant to answer, Yahshua presses them further, "Tell Me!" Complete silence falls over the crowds who have assembled to hear him preach. They all know that if the Pharisees answer saying, "heaven," they will expose their unfounded prejudice toward Yahshua and if they answer saying, "men," they will incur the wrath of the Zealots. Finally, they reply. "We don't know." Then Yahshua concludes by stating: ***"Neither do I tell you by what I authority I am doing these things" (Mark 11:33)***.

The Watchmen in the Wilderness

Most of the rightful descendants to the Temple priesthood had been exiled to the Essene wilderness community of Qumran. This is why John the immerser was found ministering near this region and why Yahshua recognised his authority as a forerunner as is prophesied in ***Isaiah 40:3*** and reiterated in ***Matthew 3:3, Mark 1:3, Luke 3:4*** and ***John 1:23***. A close examination of the Scriptures will reveal that John the Immerser resided at a town called *Beth-Bara* located eight miles from Qumran ***(John 1:28)*** and like Yahshua had his own entourage of talmidim (disciples) ***(John 1:35)***. The Dead Sea Scrolls further validate John's association to this exiled settlement with the discovery that locusts were a part of the community's diet. ***Matthew 3:4*** and ***Mark 1:6*** confirm that John ate locusts, a food determined as Kosher in ***Leviticus 11:20-23***. Another indication of John's connection to Qumran is the emphasis placed on water immersion in his ministry and its great importance reflected in some of the community's discovered manuscripts. Having said this, there are some noteworthy differences with John and the general viewpoint of the Essene, which suggests that he may have formed a breakaway sect around the time of Yahshua's immersion. One major difference was the evangelical emphasis of John's ministry and the Essenes' blanket aversion to associating with men of ill repute (Man. Disc. Ix 21-26).

An Honest Question by a Pharisee

The verbal melee between Yahshua and his accusers continues to escalate in the Temple court. A sincere Sophrim (Scribe) perceives that the Messiah's handling of the Pharisees' questions is exceptional. This prompts him to ask the question, ***"Which is the most important mitzvah (love deed) of all?" (Mark 12:28)***. Yahshua answers straight out of the Torah when he says, ***"The first of all the mitzvoth is Shema (Hear), Yisrael; the Master YHWH is our Elohim, the Master YHWH is Echad (One): And you shall love the Master YHWH your Elohim with all your lev (heart), and with all your being, and with all your mind, and with all your strength [Deuteronomy 6:4,5]: this is the first mitzvah, And the second is like it, namely this; you shall love your neighbour as yourself [Leviticus 19:18]. There are no other mitzvoth greater than these." (Mark 12:29-31)***.

There is an unmistakable urgency to his teaching now. The apocalyptic emphasis of his message provokes more people to turn out earlier to hear him preach each day ***(Luke 21:37-38)***. His sayings at this time chiefly consist of predicting his own death, a great cataclysm that would befall the Jews and the destruction of the Temple by the Romans.

The Last Anointing

Matthew 26:1-5; "And it came to pass, when Yahshua had finished all these sayings, He said to His talmidim, You know that after two days is the moed (feast) of the Pesach (Passover), and the Ben (son of) Adam (man) is betrayed to be impaled."

Yahshua receives a second anointing out at Bethany, this time with all his talmidim present in the house of Shimon the jar merchant ***(Matthew 26:6)***. When a woman, moved by the Ruach, goes to apply pistachio ointment to him, his followers, like Judas, object, but are told, "...***Leave her alone; why do you trouble her? She has done a tov (good) mitzvah (love deed) for Me. For you have the poor***

with you always, and whenever you desire, you may do them tov: but Me you have not always. She has done what she could: she has come before the time to anoint My body for its burial." (Mark 14:6-8).

The Karaite (cariot) Movement

About the same time, Yahudah the Karaite (Judas Iscariot) secretly (though it was no secret to Messiah) met with the chief priests to negotiate a price for his Master's capture. Yahudah had become quietly disillusioned by Yahshua's interpretation of the Scriptures. The Karaites were a break-away sect of Sadducees who, like the Sadducees, did not believe in the resurrection or the existence of angels. They viewed private interpretation of the Torah as completely acceptable despite this philosophy going completely against Scripture ***(2 Peter 1:2)***. They did not follow after the teachings of the Pharisees or the Teachers of the Torah, but instead saw the rabbinical movement in general as an apostate régime. Neither did they believe that the Davidic King was to be sacrificed, but was to lead a great military victory before ushering in the New Kingdom. Yahudah still carried some of this baggage from his association with the Karaites and only a gentle nudge by HaSatan was needed to enable him to do the unthinkable. Yahudah rationalised his decision to have Yahshua apprehended by thinking that it would somehow provoke him and his followers to physically defend themselves and pave the way for a militant takeover. HaSatan operated, as he usually does, by suggesting that a forced confrontation might hasten the Nazarene's clemency to the Davidic throne, rather than instantly try to induce a complete about face in the mind of a trusted member of Yahshua's inner circle.

The Last Supper

Yahshua and his twelve most trusted followers assemble in a large fully furnished upper room of a volunteered temporary dwelling. It was arranged and acquired in the exact manner that the Messiah foretold ***(Mark 14:14)***.

Once settled, Yahshua almost immediately launches into a barrage of hard to swallow revelations. He reveals his betrayer, his imminent desertion, Peter's denial, servant-hood in the kingdo command to bear arms if need be, and the nearness of his own : fering and death.

The traditional manner of performing the Passover meal was formulated by the rabbis based on passages in the Torah. Interestingly Yahshua does not alter any rabbinical aspect of its practice and symbolism, but instead reveals yet another layer of meaning by showing its Messianic context ***(Matthew 26:27,28, Luke 22:19)***.

The last supper was a preparation meal, which, ironically is only practiced to this day within Orthodox Judaism[3], though some Messianic congregations are catching on.

The Passover meal took place just before or prior to the slaughter of the Passover lamb. Its absence from the last supper should be testimony enough that this was not the time when it was consumed. The preparation meal occurred at 5pm on the 14th of Abib while the Passover meal commenced on the night of the 15th. The Passover lambs were killed between 3-6pm on the 14th ***(Exodus 12:6)*** and are confirmed in ***Numbers 9:5*** as being consumed in the evening of the 15th. The lamb was to be completely disposed of before the angel of death swept through Goshen at midnight ***(Exodus 12:12)***. This took place before Israel's departure from Mitzrayim early in the morning on the same day as the Passover meal ***(Exodus 12:17)***. Remember, days according to Scripture are reckoned from sundown to sundown. The eating of the Passover lamb in haste ***(Exodus 12:11)*** confirms that there was no lag time between its consumption and Israel's departure from the land of bondage. The preparation meal or "meal of Messiah" took place on the 14th prior to the Passover slaughter followed by the Passover meal on the night of the 15th just prior to the Exodus.

Yahshua's Arrest

Having now narrowed his followers from seventy, to twelve and now three, Yahshua brings his most devoted into the Garden of

3 The Lubavitch movement (a respected sect within Orthodox Judaism) has always observed a prior Passover meal as a training lesson. In Yahshua's time it was seen as a preparation or rehearsal and treated with exactly the same respect as the Passover itself.

Gethsemane for a heavy concentrated effort of prayer. His followers pray so hard that they collapse from sorrow ***(Luke 22:45)***. Yahshua wakes them and is still speaking when the sound of many footsteps can be heard.

Yahudah the Karaite appears at the head of a large throng of armed men dispatched by the illegitimate Edomite high priest Caiphas. The mob consists of the high priest's servants, a detachment of soldiers and an array of officials. They carry swords, clubs and torches more suited to face off against a band of armed Zealots then an arrest of a single individual. Yahudah walks ahead and approaches the Messiah ***(Luke 22:47)***. He sarcastically greets him with the title "Rabbi," a term normally detested among Karaites ***(Mark 14:48)***. He then leans forward to kiss him, but Yahshua withdraws momentarily and asks, ***"Yahudah, do you betray the Ben Adam (son of man) with a kiss?" (Luke 22:48)*** Yahudah persists with his kiss and the Messiah responds with, ***"Beloved Chaver (friend), why have you come, what have you done?"***

Yahshua, perhaps sensing that Yahudah has just begun to realise what he has done, steps past him to face the waiting mob and asks, ***"Whom do you seek?" (John 18:4)*** They answer, "Yahshua Ha Natzaret."

When Yahshua utters the words, ***"I AM,"*** his captors recoil and shrink to the ground ***(John 18:6)***. This looks completely bizarre as a well armed group of men, most of them soldiers, instantly spin around and collapse in a heap by an unseen force.

Momentarily shocked and disorientated, they stagger to their feet, groping for their torches and weapons. Knowing full well the identity of Messiah due to Yahudah's kiss, but now afraid, they decide to save face and turn their attention to Yahshua's followers.

Yahshua again asks, ***"Whom do you seek?" (John 18:7)*** Bracing themselves for another fall, they hesitantly respond with the same answer, "Yahshua Ha Natzaret."

"I have told you that I am: if therefore you seek Me, are looking for me, let these (men) go their way." His very words flow with power as they compel his captors to fulfill the writings of the Prophets. They obediently change tactics and move towards him. Yahshua's talmidim quickly enquire as to whether they should now take arms.

But before he responds, Peter launches himself at one of the ants of the high priest. He swings his sword horizontally in a attempt to achieve a decapitation in the hopes of striking fear into the mob. His target reacts quickly and tilts his head to one side as the blade catches his ear, severing it completely ***(John 18:10)***. The Messiah instantly retrieves the detached ear and brings it up to the side of his head. Within seconds he withdraws his hand and the ear is restored.

Yahshua ministers sternly to Peter saying, ***"Put up again your sword into the sheath, for all those that take the sword shall perish with the sword. Do you not understand that I can meet My enemies and that I can now make tefillah (prayer) to my Abba, and He shall presently give Me more than twelve legions of heavenly malachim (angels)? But how then shall the Keetvay HaKadosh (the whole Scriptures) of the Tanach (all of the Old Testament) be fulfilled, that it has to be this way?" (Matthew 26:52-54)***. Not even Yahshua's own students are going to stop him from his appointment at the hangman's tree. He then turns to address the chief priests and officers, ***"Have you come out, like against a thief, with swords and staves? When I was daily with you in the Beit HaMikdash (the Temple), you did not even point your hands against Me: but this is your time, and the power of darkness."(Luke 22:52-53).***

All the way through this encounter there is a sense that Yahshua's sole concern is that it run according to prophecy and hence according to the Father's will. In some instances he is found virtually guiding his captors through the encounter. In the case of Yahudah's dialogue with Messiah it resonates like a bad school play when an actor stammers on a line and is carried by a fellow performer. From receiving his kiss to the final release of his last breath, Yahshua maintains complete control over each situation to see that every aspect of his capture beating and death occur in strict accordance with the Scriptures. Having prayed almost to the point of passing out ***(Luke 22:43–44)***, the Messiah's resolve and focus had now reached an all time high. He was thoroughly determined to be beaten, ridiculed and hung. He gave up his life willingly, and with joy he looked toward this brutal, yet pivotal phase of his ministry.

n to appointing and removing high priests as it saw
n it appointed a Sadducee named Annas who was
describes as being "haughty, audacious, and cruel."
been removed from office at the time of Yahshua's trial but still maintained control over the Temple by running it like a family business. He had five sons in the priesthood and Caiphas who was his son-in-law and the current Roman sanctioned high priest. Caiphas never made a move without first consulting Annas.

In Yahshua's day, the Sadducees from which the Karaite movement evolved, controlled much of the Sanhedrin and had formed an alliance with the Herodians. This association caused the Sanhedrin to reach new moral lows in the administration of judgments and rulings as they often made decisions based on outside political pressure and material gain.

The Sadducees

The Sadducees were a sect within Judaism who were closely affiliated with the Temple. Apparently little, if anything, has survived of their writings. Anything that can be gleaned from them is sourced primarily from the writings of their opponents. For anyone desperate to find something, a Karaite sage called Ya'akov al-Qirqisani has some surviving quotes from the *Sefer Zadok*, which can be found in a publication by Zvi Cahn called, *The Rise of the Karaite sect.*

Zadok is where the Hebrew name for the Sadducees (Tzedukim) allegedly originated. Zadok was the high priest who remained faithful to King David and anointed King Solomon. However, this origin is unlikely as the Sadducees do not appear as an official group until the Hasmonaean period, sometime after the Maccabean Revolt in 165BCE. The word Sadducee is more likely a Hebraisation of the Greek word, "sündikoi" ('syndics'), which is where we get the word "syndicate." The term has also been associated with the Hebrew word, "righteous."

> The Sadducees rejected the Pharisee's interpretation of the Torah and created new ones based on a literal understanding of isolated verses. For example the Sadducees believed that a physical eye should be removed from a person who took the eye of another, rather than the Pharisaic and overall Hebraic understanding that the monetary value of an eye be restored. The Sadducees, like their offspring, the Karaites, rejected rabbinic law despite rabbinic tradition stemming directly from the Sanhedrin's formation under the direction of Moshe the prophet (See the appointment of 70 Elders in ***Numbers 11:16***). The Sadducees are classically known for their rejection of angels, denial of the soul, and disbelief in full bodily resurrection. Fortunately they, like their writings, all but ceased to exist after the destruction of the second Temple in 70CE by the Romans. They were an apostate political regime who left a dark legacy that is still evident today in the rippling out effect of the Karaite movement that has made some inroads into the Nazarene Israelite sect.

The Sadducees did not generally accept the authority of the prophets, whose writings were held in high esteem by the Pharisees. They cast off many rabbinical interpretations of the Torah and they adhered to the Mosaic criminal justice system with a twisted inquisitional fervor. It was in this climate and with men of this disposition that Yahshua was tried.

Yahshua's Trial – Legal or Illegal?

Chapter Four of N.L. Kuehl's work, *A Book of Evidence*, declares Yahshua's trial to have been carried out legally due to the apparent ruling of *mesith* ("one who leads the nation astray"). He supports this claim with the following texts:

> "[the trial is the reversed]...*in the case of a Mesith, for the Divine Law states,* ***'Neither shalt thou spare, neither shalt thou conceal him' (Deuteronomy 13:8)****...Because such are more*

> *or less devoid of paternal tenderness [Tosef. Sanh. VII and X; Talmud, Sanhedrin 36b and 36b (6)]."* And, *"His case may be begun by day and finished by night; they may begin and end it on the same day, whether he be guilty or not; they may arrive at a verdict by a majority of one whether it be for conviction or acquittal;* ***all may plead for acquittal or all for conviction****; one who pleads for acquittal may retract and plead for conviction. The eunuch and the childless can act as judges, and, according to R. Jehuda,* ***even those who are biased in the direction of severity*** *[Tosefta, Sanhedrin X, 11]."* Furthermore, *"In capital cases they begin not with the case for prosecution, but with the case for the defence,* ***EXCEPT ONLY IN THE CASE OF A BEGUILER TO IDOLATRY*** *(Mesith), and, according to R. Jehoshua, the son of Karha,* ***THE CASE OF ONE WHO LEADS A TOWN ASTRAY*** *[Tosefta, Sanhedrin VII:2]."*

Despite the above claim and supporting data there are two major errors with this view. The first is that for the trial to be totally legal, Yahshua would be in violation of breaking Torah and would thus be disqualified as Messiah. The second is that there are aspects of his trial that are not conducted in direct reverse, but in an "ad hoc" fashion that unfold according to convenience. Not withstanding the argument for direct reversal of normal proceedings, here is a list of major events in his trial:

- The accused was beaten before any formal trial had commenced.
- The use of Yahudah the Karaite (Judas), who was Yahshua's former accomplice, in effecting an arrest and securing the accused was forbidden in ancient Hebraic law.
- An uncondemned man was not to be bound. **(*John 18:12-13*)**
- The arrest was not a legal summons, but a seizure and forced walkthrough of a theatrical legal proceeding.
- Capital cases began with the defense rather than prosecution. [Mishnah, Sanhedrin 4.1(e)]*
- The accused was not required to testify against himself. [Talmud pp.167-168].*

- Trials were not to take place on the eve of a Sabbath or festival day. [Mishnah, Sanhedrin 4:1 (k-l)]
- Yahshua was first tried by the high priest Caiaphas who sat as a single judge. This was a private examination without any witnesses, which took place a little after midnight. ***(John 18: 19-24)*** Arrests and trials that could potentially lead to capital punishment could not be held at night.*
- Yahshua was additionally tried by both Pontius Pilate and King Herod who both found no grounds to charge him.
- A unanimous verdict of guilty was not permitted by the Sanhedrin. [Mishnah, Sanhedrin 4:1 (f)]*
- False witnesses who were brought forward were not questioned according to the seven standard inquiries. [Mishnah Sanhedrin 5.1]
- According to ***Mark 14:55-59*** the witnesses could not agree. Even the high priest recognized this, so the first charge of sedition was abandoned. "Yet if they (any witnesses) contradict one another, whether during the inquiries or the cross-examination, their evidence becomes invalid." [Mishnah Sanhedrin 5.2]

(* = Can be argued to a greater or lesser extent as a legal process of trying a mespith)

Yahshua is taken bound before Annas who is curious to find out what he teaches and ascertain his number of followers. As he does so he deliberately asked vague questions in an attempt to extract incriminating information. Failure to inform the accused for the reason of his apprehension and performing a preliminary examination to establish a crime is illegal according to Torah. As Yahshua tells Annas to question those who heard him teach, he is met with a blow to the face from a senior guard. The Temple guards saw him as a leader of a Zealot movement and therefore looked for every opportunity to do him physical and psychological harm. Yahshua does not respond by turning the other cheek after being struck, but questions his assailant, proving that his teaching was meant as a figurative way to suitably handle insult according to ***Lamentations 3:30*** and not a literal blanket response to physical harm inflicted by an assailant.

The location of Yahshua's questioning before Annas being away from the Hall of Hewn Stones, where all accused were questioned, cannot be considered something for which the Sanhedrin could be held liable, as it was an independent decision of Caiphas to have him sent to his father-in-law first. No doubt this was done to show off, because Yahshua had caused considerable monetary loss to Annas by consecutively kicking out his merchants from the Temple court.

There is no doubt that Yahshua was processed illegally, but this was primarily due to the actions of Caiphas, and not the judiciary arm of the Sanhedrin, even if the implementation of a normal judicial protocol was to be reversed in the case of one who leads the nation astray.

So like a lamb to the slaughter (literally), Yahshua is swiftly moved on to the next phase of his atonement for mankind.

After witnessing Kepha (Peter) fulfill his prophecy by denying him three times in a nearby courtyard, Yahshua is then taken to the house of the high priest. While he waits for Caiphas and his acquaintances to arrive, he is blindfolded, beaten and sworn at by Temple guards. Being unable to see, he is unable to roll with the punches and each blow jars him severely.

Yahshua's Beatings

Caiphas knew that presenting Yahshua before Pontius Pilot on the Jewish charge of blasphemy would achieve little. So he emphasised the proclamation that he was King of the Jews. This would get the prefect's attention by exhibiting the Messiah as a potential threat to Roman authority. This is why Yahshua was executed according to the Roman custom of crucifixion as apposed to the Jewish custom of stoning for such a crime ***(Deuteronomy 13:10, John 10:33)***. Having Yahshua hung from a tree was also preferred by Caiphas and his cronies because it might be seen among Jews as a theological benefit based on ***Deuteronomy 21:23; "...He that is hanged will be cursed by Elohim..."*** However, their blindness prevented them from recalling Isaiah's words, ***"...yet we did reckon Him beaten, smitten of***

Elohim and afflicted (cursed)." (Isaiah 53:4) So like clever fools they strove to achieve their goal, unaware that they were fulfilling Messianic prophecy to the very letter.

Contrary to Mel Gibson's portrayal of a thoughtful and compassionate Pontius Pilot in his *Passion* film, history reveals the Roman prefect of Judea to be a cruel, inflexible and corrupt governor who had little concern for the welfare of Jews, much less Jewish trouble makers. The Hellenised Jewish philosopher, Philo, wrote that Pilate's stint as governor regularly consisted of "briberies, insults, robberies, outrages, wanton injustices, constantly repeated executions without trial, and ceaseless and grievous cruelty."

Pilot's disrespect for Jews was legendary. During his tenure he attempted to erect statues of Caesar in Jerusalem and successfully used Temple funds to build an aqueduct. Pilate's continued difficulty with Jews eventually caused him to be removed from office by the Syrian governor Vitellius. He was subsequently brought to Rome to face charges of excessive cruelty and later exiled to Vienna, France.

Yahshua's second round of questioning, this time before Pilot, has a reverse affect as it reveals something embarrassing about the Roman prefect. That is, his apparent failure to grasp the concept of truth ***(John 18:38)***. Whether he had a real struggle with this fundamental principle or he was just trying to sound intellectual, Pilot was not a complete idiot when it came to avoiding civil unrest. His reluctance to execute Messiah was not in any way driven by humanitarian concern, but that the Passover crowds might be appeased lest they cause a riot and turn on his garrison. Just days prior to Yahshua's audience with Pilot this man's entry into Yahrushalayim caused such a favourable commotion with the multitude that a decision to put him to death would be at best unwise. Despite his self-professed inability to identify truth, the Scriptures record that he eventually perceives that envy is the real reason for the Sadducees' eagerness to have Yahshua hung ***(Matthew 27:11)***.

After Pilot deems Messiah as being no threat, he is sent to King Herod ***(Luke 23:1-7)*** who seems more concerned about seeing him perform parlour tricks. Yahshua remains silent, quietly fulfilling ***Isaiah 53:7***. Disappointed, Herod mocks him, arrays him in an expensive robe and sends him back to Pilot ***(Luke 23:8-12)***.

The Roman Prefect sees no opportunity in flexing the muscle of his authority in executing a Jew who was so eagerly wanted dead by fellow Jews. Neither could he gain much satisfaction in harming a captive who would not verbally defend himself or put forward any objection to his treatment. He therefore offers to release him according to a goodwill custom that the Romans observed every Passover. Instead, this makes the gathering of no more than a hundred accusers that many have been led to believe were hundreds of Jews, become angry and they begin to show signs of rioting. Having already sensed that Pilot would use this custom as an avenue to have Yahshua released, certain chief priests went among the crowd and urged them to make an appeal to release Bara-abba (Barabbas), a vicious Jewish Zealot ***(Matthew 27:20)***. The crowds oblige and when Pilot asks, "What shall I do with Yahshua, who you call the Moshiach?" They respond with, "Let him be hanged!" Bara-abba is released and this act is a microscopic demonstration of Yahshua's goal as he takes the punishment that is deserved for a sinner.

In an act of complete hypocrisy, which is portrayed in Gibson's *Passion* film as noble, Pilot finds no charge against Yahshua, publicly absolves himself of the matter, but continues to punish and execute him under Roman law. Pilot did not surrender Yahshua over to Jewish judicial law, he surrendered him to Caiphas and the other Edomite priests who wanted him to be hung as opposed to stoned in hope that he would be cursed by YHWH!

He washes his hands and then has Messiah scourged with a cat-o-nine-tails that rips so much flesh off him that it exposes bone. This ordeal fulfils ***Isaiah 50:6***. Yahshua is then dragged away to the next stage of his atonement for mankind.

Romans soldiers were notorious for taking prisoners and administering the most brutal punishments imaginable. The Sanhedrin did not allow a man to be beaten or whipped more than 39 times. Romans recognised no such limit. If a prisoner collapsed they stood him back up and continued beating him. Many prisoners died during whippings that exceeded 39 lashes.

Roman soldiers hold Yahshua down while they squeeze a jagged ring of thorns onto his head signifying a crown ***(Matthew 27:29)***. They then adorn him in another robe and spit and mock him long enough for his lacerated flesh to congeal to the material before they tear if off. He is then humiliated further, bashed and re-clothed in his own garments. His tallit by this time is torn and soaked with his own blood, dirt and saliva.

Crucifixion

A detail of soldiers is sent to fetch two Jewish Zealots to join Yahshua. Pilot orders signs to be drawn up to exhibit the crimes of each condemned man. Much to the detriment of Caiphas and his buddies the sign above Messiah's head reads, "Yahshua the Nazarene, King of the Yahudim (Jews)." They had requested it read, "So-called king of the Jews."

The three men are given heavy cross-beams of olive wood, arranged in single file and led away. Yahshua's injuries cause the movement of the column to slow considerably. A mounted Roman centurion who is keeping an eye on the procession notices that Messiah is teetering on passing out. He quickly orders an onlooker, a pagan man by the name of Simon of Cyrene to take up the beam ***(Matthew 27:32)***. The procession resumes at a steady pace and continues to a place named Golgotha, also known as the "Place of Skulls."

As Yahshua drags his feet along the road, onlookers increase on all sides. Among them he sees a group of Jewish women weeping bitterly. To them he says the following words; ***"Daughters of Yahrushalayim, weep not for Me, but weep for yourselves, and for your children. For see the days are coming, in which they shall say, Blessed are the barren, and the wombs that never bore, and the breast that never nursed. Then shall they begin to say to the mountains, Fall on us; and to the hills, Cover us. For if they do these things in a green eytz (tree), what shall be done in the dry?"*** The green tree signifies Judah in the land and the dry tree is Judah in Exile. Forty years from this time those of these women who remained alive and their children would witness unspeakable horror as Yahrushalayim is laid siege to and razed to the ground.

Once at the correct location, the condemned are stripped naked and dressed in loin cloths in a token effort to respect Jewish law. Yahshua is hung first. An executioner clad in an apron steps forward with two centurions. They lay Yahshua along the vertical beam and straighten out one of his arms. One soldier rests his knee on the inside of Yahshua's elbow as the second soldier secures the forearm. The executioner places Messiah's hand at a specific point on the horizontal beam. The nail is pressed in the centre of the wrist and driven straight through the flesh to the wood with one very swift and well trained blow. It is then hammered in repeatedly until the flat head of the nail touches skin. Since ancient times anatomists saw the wrist as forming part of the hand. This process is repeated with the other hand. The feet are next. The right foot is placed over the left and another nail is driven clean through both limbs. The trunk, with Yahshua attached, is lifted up and fastened into the ground and the whole process is repeated with the two Zealots.

The duration of Yahshua's pain seems to linger, prompting him to echo the words of King David, ***"Eli-Yahuweh, Eli-Yahuweh, why are you keeping me?" (Matthew 27:46)***. Contrary to popular belief the Messiah did not say the Aramaic equivalent of the word "forsaken." The Book of Matthew was originally written in Hebrew as is attested to by the early church Father Epiphanius:

> "They (the Nazarenes) have the Goodnews according to Matthew in its entirety in Hebrew. For it is clear that <u>they still preserve this, in the Hebrew alphabet, as it was originally written</u>." Epiphanius; Panarion 29

Corrupt Greek translations preferred by Western scholars have birthed countless Christian apologetics concerning this verse of Scripture.

A soldier who is nearby hears Yahshua's call and takes a sponge filled with vinegar. He puts it on a long stick for him to drink, but it is not accepted. Then Yahshua speaks his last flesh incarnate words, "It is finished." He then breathes his last breath and goes on to the next phase of his ministry, beneath the earth.

Conclusion

Yahshua is the goal of all the Torah and the destination point of every aspect of the Passover ritual. YHWH declared Pesach (Passover) to be observed throughout every generation ***(Exodus***

12:2,6,13-14) for anyone who wishes to take a hold of the promises of Abraham. It was never presented as a custom to be reserved for a single tribe (Judah) or to be changed, postponed or done away with. Officially recognised religious teachers who do not teach it, teach against it or teach it in an alternate form will be judged. Ignorance is no excuse, because a formally trained teacher would have had to buy into the lie (taught within Christian seminary schools) that it was done away with or just for Jews, in order to receive permission to start an official church tour of duty. Ignorant lay preachers who do the same may be in circumstances where there are very few trained teachers available, and this will be between them and YHWH. Some third world countries at different times of the year have congregations who lose ministers to militia at a rate of one per week.

What am I Doing Passover for Again?

Passover is a demonstrative object lesson that reminds believers of Israel's deliverance from the bondage of Mitzrayim and the deliverance of each individual from the bondage of sin. It also reminds believers of the blood that was shed by Messiah and its application to the doorpost of the heart. It was to foreshadow a supernatural victory for all pre-resurrection believers and a memorial of the same event to post-resurrection believers.

How do I do It?

Passover is to commence at the beginning of months ***(Exodus 12:2).*** This occurs in the first month of Nisan on the Jewish calendar. You'll need to get a Jewish calendar or access one on the internet.

To celebrate Passover you'll need some lamb (if possible a first-born male). We usually have designated members of our congregation purchase some lamb from a Kosher butcher on the eve of Passover - usually enough so that it may be all eaten in the same night ***(Exodus 12:8).*** It must be eaten with unleavened bread ***(Exodus 12:8).*** Leaven represents sin. The lamb must be eaten with bitter herbs ***(Exodus 12:8).*** The bitter herbs represent the trials of Messiah and our own daily trials as we try to walk in perfection in a fallen world. The lamb must be eaten in haste ***(Exodus 12:11)***. This represents an eagerness to leave the influences of the world and run toward Messiah and on to true life ***(Luke 19:5-6)***. A staff must be in your hand ***(Exodus 12:11)***. A believer must have his walking staff on hand to leave quickly. A stick will suffice.

It is to be observed at the going down of the sun ***(Deuteronomy 16:2,6)***. It has to take place at a residence where YHWH's name is proclaimed ***(Deuteronomy 16:2,6)***. Not God or Lord, but YHWH! No bones in the lamb must be broken ***(Exodus 12:43-46)***. This represents Yahshua's bones remaining intact on the hangman's tree.

An uncircumcised man (whether Israelite or foreigner) is not permitted to participate in the sacrifice and eating of the sacrificial lamb ***(Exodus 12:48)***. Some translators make it sound like they are to have no part in the Seder whatsoever. The Talmud confirms the extent of their exclusion in b.Pesachim 96a noting that even an uncircumcised non-Jew is allowed to keep the Passover and the Feast of Unleavened Bread, but is forbidden to sacrifice and consume the lamb itself.

No laborious work is to be done during Passover and it must take place as a group experience (if possible) ***(Exodus 12:16)***. It is a time of singing and rejoicing ***(Exodus 15:1, 19-21)***. The essence of Passover is to inspire curiosity amongst the next generation of believers. Any children present are encouraged to inquire as to why the night is full of ritual and food. As they ask questions, they are told the story of the Exodus and relive their departure from bondage through being stimulated by hearing, seeing, feeling and eating.

For a detailed break down of a Passover Seder Service I recommend a book by Edward Chumney called *The Seven Festivals of the Messiah.* Passover Seders are available in various forms for free all over the internet. I recommend ones that refer to Messiah Yahshua, but also retain a degree of rabbinical structure. Yahshua had no problem with the Pharisees' teachings. He had a problem with the way they lived ***(Matthew 23:1-3)***. If you're not confident in holding a Passover Seder on your own I recommend finding a group who observe it.

Chapter Twelve

Super Grace Me

Would You Like Obedience with That?

THE GENERAL RELIGIOUS definition of the term "grace" is misleading. Its perception as being YHWH's longsuffering patience and its subtle use as a license to go on sinning unwittingly robs many believers of a relationship with their Heavenly Father. Grace is a transliteration of the Greek word "charis" (pronounced *Khar'-ece)* and is misunderstood by most Christians as meaning "unmerited favour." The true definition of grace is, "divine influence upon the heart and its reflection in life" (see *Strong's Concordance* [5485]) or, more specifically, it means, "unmerited power given by YHWH to enable man to do His will."

Translators have also superimposed the term "grace" over more specific words that mean "charm," "beauty," "lovely," and "well favoured." It appears seventy times in the TaNaK (Old Testament) as the Hebrew word "chen" (pronounced *khane*) and two hundred and thirty-three times in the Brit Chadasha (New Testament). The real word that means "unmerited favour" in Scripture is "mercy," and is transliterated as "chesed" (Hebrew) or "eleos" (Greek) and appears two-hundred and fifty times in the TaNaK and only fifty times in the Brit Chadasha. This means that "unmerited favour" ([mercy] what most Christians actually mean when they speak of grace) appears in the so-called Old Testament more frequently than in the New Testament.

The Same from the Very Beginning

The concept of grace (charis) and the descending of the Holy Spirit (Ruach Ha Kodesh) were not inventions cooked up as some crisis-reaction-solution-afterthought for a planet of people that couldn't cope with the rules of an overly demanding Creator! Nor is the concept of the New Covenant something that appears exclusively in the so-called New Testament as a band-aid replacement to an imperfect Sinai Covenant. YHWH did not go into crisis mode and elect Yahshua to die as a plan-B response to a strayed nation and nor were the Messiah's talmidim (disciples) the first followers to receive the tongues of fire[1] (aka Ruach Ha Kodesh).

Salvation[2] is the greatest concept a man can ever contemplate ***(Acts 16:30)***. The Scriptures refer to it as, ***"so great a Salvation" (Hebrews 2:3)***. Yet a man should not ask how will YHWH save him, but how will he respond in thought, word and deed to receive YHWH's salvation?

Many religious and non-religious Western people believe or quietly suspect that the Jewish Messiah Yahshua (most call him Jesus) is the true key to salvation, but many of these same people can't seem to agree on a unified response to his teachings. The major stumbling block to grasping the absolute truth of his message is the current generally accepted view of what grace is and how one receives it. Unfortunately there are many accumulated misconceptions on a set of other interrelated Scriptural subjects that need to be clearly defined first before grace can be properly explained so this analysis is quite extensive, but hopefully rewarding.

Please bear in mind that no matter how convincing any commentary may sound on any Scriptural subject or how compelling the sources it draws on may be, a reader will not be convicted by its message unless the Ruach (Spirit) moves on him or her to accept it.

---

1 "Tongues of fire" refers to the physical appearance of burning Hebrew letters.

2 That is being saved from a corrupt state and being brought into an eternal conscious existence under the headship of the Origin of all Things.

With this in mind a short prayer for a revelation of the truth is encouraged before reading any further.

News Flash - The Jews were One of Twelve Tribes!

For hundreds of years legions of people have believed that the majority of the 613 laws in the Old Testament were just for the Jews. Furthermore, it is widely believed that the Jews couldn't keep them and so became replaced by the church who ironically didn't have to keep them either. This view has been relentlessly administered through the teaching of selective verses that are espoused from a myriad of diluted Bible translations. How could the Sinai Covenant have been promised to the tribe of Judah only when eleven other Israelite tribes and droves of sojourners stood with them at the base of the mountain saying, ***"All that YHWH has said we will do, and be obedient"(Exodus 24:7)***? Over time, the Torah, grace, animal sacrifice, flesh circumcision, the New Covenant and the role of the Holy Spirit have all been misarranged in a neat little wall around the truth. This chapter will attempt to return a few of these concepts to their rightful place.

A Sore Subject

The phrase, ***"Perform brit-milah (circumcision) therefore on the foreskin of your lev (heart)..."*** or more commonly translated as, ***"You shall circumcise the foreskin of your heart"*** first appeared in the Torah (first five books of Moshe) in ***Deuteronomy 10:16*** and is <u>not a new teaching</u> by Messiah Yahshua. The pervasive thinking that physical circumcision has been completely replaced by a poetic circumcision of the heart comes apart at the seams when one studies the Book of Romans. Sha'ul says very clearly, ***"What advantage then has the Yahudi (Jew)? Or what profit is there in brit-milah (circumcision)? <u>Much in every way</u>: primarily, because they (The Jews) were the first to be entrusted with the oracles of YHWH and the first to believe His word" (Romans 3:1,2)***. Somehow the teaching in ***1 Corinthians 7:19*** that describes physical circumcision on its own as being worthless gradually morphed into circumcision PERIOD as being worthless. Rabbi Sha'ul states that it is a sign of righteousness in ***Romans 4:11*** as opposed to an affliction for "sins and the hardness of heart" as described by the anti-semite Church Father Justin Martyr (135-161CE). Circumcision of the heart has always been a prerequisite for physical circumcision (if the circumstances allow). If YHWH expected Abraham's herdsmen to be circumcised ***(Genesis 17:12)*** and was prepared to kill Moshe because his own son was not circumcised ***(Exodus 4:24,25)*** and persistently commanded all the men of Israel to be circumcised ***(Exodus 12:48, Leviticus 12:3, Joshua 5:3)*** then there is a good chance that physically uncircumcised male descendants will be expected to undergo the same ritual during the time of the second Exodus.

The Illusion of Dispensationalism

Like breaking the foreskin of the heart, the "that was then, this is now" dispensationalist view must also be broken. The half-understood message of circumcision is just one of several barriers that block the full messianic message of the Scriptures. The next barrier that I wish to dislodge is the false notion that "animal sacrifice" was for generations past.

To believe that right standing before the Creator was once attained by animal sacrifice and later changed by acknowledging a single miraculous event is to believe that there were two ways of salvation: the former way through presenting offerings to YHWH and the later way through an intellectual belief in Messiah's death and resurrection. In plain English this is what is being preached to a greater or lesser extent in nearly every church across the face of the earth for the past eighteen hundred years. To believe and subsequently preach that animal sacrifice **ever** atoned for man's sin is either a sign of unfamiliarity with the Scriptures or an act of willful heresy.

Animal Sacrifice was Never a Load of Bull

By the counsel of two or three witnesses all truth shall be established ***(2 Corinthians 13:1)***. So with this principle in mind let's look at the so-called Old Testament and see what it has to say about animal sacrifice.

King David writes in ***Psalms 51:16-17; "For You (YHWH) do not desire sacrifice, or else would I give it: You delight not in burnt offering."***

The prophets also write in ***Hosea 6:6; "For I desire rachamim (mercy), and not sacrifice; and da'at (knowledge) of Elohim more than burnt offerings."*** And in ***Isaiah 1:11; "'To what purpose is the multitude of your sacrifices to Me?' Says YHWH. 'I am full of burnt offerings of rams and the fat of fed cattle. I do not delight in the burnt offerings of rams, and the fat of fed beasts and I delight not in the dahm (blood) of bulls, or of lambs or of goats.'"*** Some Bibles exhibit the words, "had enough," which is not necessarily a mistranslation. It is important to realise that this verse is not insinuating that animal sacrifices were once acceptable, because in context it refers to YHWH's response to Israel's corrupted mindset that sin could continue provided that the quality and quota of sacrifices was regularly met.

And in ***Micah 6:6-8***; ***"With what shall I come before YHWH, and bow myself before El-Elyon (Most High) Elohim? Shall I come before Him with burnt offerings, with calves of a year old? Will YHWH be pleased with thousands of rams, or with ten thousands of rivers of oil? Shall I give my bachor (first born male) for my transgression, the fruit of my body for the sin of my being? He has shown you O ish (man) what is tov (good). What does YHWH require of you? But to do tzedakah (righteousness), and to love rachamim (mercy), and to have a humble halacha (walk) with your Elohim."***

Question: But what about the Book of Hebrews in the New Testament, doesn't that teach that we now give sacrifices of praise from our lips? ***Hebrews 13:15; "By Him therefore let us offer the sacrifice of tehilla (praise) to YHWH continually, that is, the fruit of our lips giving hodu (give thanks) to His Name."***

Answer: Well, the Book of Hosea, located in the so-called Old Testament, says the same thing in ***verse 14:2; "Take with you words of Torah, and make teshuvah (repentance) to YHWH: and say to Him, Take away all our iniquity, and receive us graciously: so will we render the bulls, the fruit of our lips."*** The reality is that the blood of an unblemished animal in and of itself never had any power to atone for sin. ***Hebrews 10:4; "For it is impossible that the dahm (blood) of bulls and goats can take away sins."*** The power was in the expectation of the one who brought it in the recognition of Messiah's future atoning sacrifice. These offerings were a demonstration to instill in those bringing them the cost of sin and evoked their mouths to praise YHWH. Sha'ul illustrated this by pointing out that Abraham was not justified by works (adhering to the ritual of sin offerings), but through faith in Messiah ***(Romans 4:1-5; Galatians 3:6-14)***. Yahshua rebuked the teachers of the Torah for their unbelief in the day that Abraham longed for ***(John 8:37-58)***, that is to see Messiah in the flesh. Even Moshe wrote plainly about Messiah ***(John 5:46)*** who the teachers of Torah professed to believe, but through demonstration denied. Christianity preaches that the requirement changed as YHWH gave more revelation. This causes most church goers to think that prior to Messiah's crucifixion at "the place of the skull" (Gulgoleth), salvation was attained through works, or by faith in YHWH as opposed to faith in the coming Messiah. Scripture clearly demonstrates that nothing has really changed; just that some believers existed in a state of looking forward to Messiah and other believers existed in a state of looking back to Messiah. Salvation has always been conditional to faith in Messiah. In other words pre-Gulgoleth believers looked ahead and post-Gulgoleth believers look back.

Ultimately Scripture interprets itself. Sha'ul demonstrated this by using Abraham and David to show his audience that their faith alone was always sufficient for eternal life ***(Romans 4:1-8)***. But if YHWH wills it, characteristics such as works and circumcision may eventually manifest themselves as physical evidence of righteousness in those who proceed in His ways. This is why unmerited power (grace) and unmerited favour (mercy) can be evident in the uncircumcised and circumcised alike ***(Romans 4:9-11)***.

Question: 'If the above is true, are animal sacrifices acceptable today and if so, why don't we still do them?'

Answer: The correct understanding of what a living sacrifice is must be defined before a simple yes or no answer can be delivered.

What is a Sacrifice?

Amazing as this may sound, the Western or secular definition of a sacrifice and the Biblical definition is not necessarily the same thing. When most people hear of a blood sacrifice they normally think of barbaric occult practices or an old form of worship required by the Creator in a primitive era for a primitive people. Pagans were the first to write down their rituals, though most of the modern scholarly world believes the opposite to be true. Just because something was written first doesn't mean it was practiced first! An instruction has to be made airborne (i.e. oral) before it is written down. Israel resisted making records of their ways for as long as they could. This was because learning by real-time verbal instruction was less likely to be misinterpreted than reading written instruction alone.

According to Webster's Dictionary, "sacrifice" means: (1) an act of offering something precious to a deity; specific: the offering of an immolated victim (2) something offered in sacrifice (3a) destruction or surrender of something for the sake of something else (3b) something given up for lost. ... {the sacrifice made by parents} LOSS, DEPRIVATION

The Hebrew word "korban" (le-hakriv), which is translated "sacrifice," is from the same Hebrew root as "to come near," to "approach" or to "become close." This is the essence of what happens when an offering is accepted as a sacrifice by YHWH. No word in the English language adequately renders the Biblical meaning of the Hebrew word "korban."

To a Hebrew the commandment to present offerings was like a life-line, and if an offering was accepted as a sacrifice, this was a blessing. Noah built an altar as soon as he hit dry land to see if YHWH's anger had subdued and if his family would continue to be blessed ***(Genesis 8:20,21)***. Acceptable offerings consisted of clean and unblemished animals or the finest grain or wine offerings. Animal or blood sacrifices were divided into three types. They were burnt offerings (where the whole animal would be burned) or guilt offerings and peace offerings (where only part of the animal was burnt and the other part was consumed by the High Priests). The prophets point out that if an offering was made without a suitable feeling of inner morality and goodness, it would be unacceptable as a sacrifice (see Cain's attitude in ***Genesis 4:3-8*** & ***1 John 3:12***). Yahshua also preached on this in ***Matthew 5:23,24***, but more on Yahshua's view of offerings will be discussed shortly.

Did Human Sacrifice Originate from YHWH?

Deuteronomy 12:31; "...for every abomination to YHWH, that He hates, have they done to their elohim; for even their sons and their daughters they have burned in the fire to their elohim."

Jeremiah 32:35; "And they built high places of Ba'al, which are in the Valley of the Son of Hinnom, to cause their sons and their daughters to pass through the fire to Molech; which I commanded them not to do, neither came it into my mind, that they should do this abomination, to cause Yahudah (Judah) to sin."

It is widely known and accepted in the heavens that firstborn male sacrifice is the highest act of servitude by a mortal. With this in mind, the dark forces ministered to men a twisted version of firstborn animal sacrifice to include the routine immolation of human infants as an attempt to outdo YHWH.

YHWH considers human infant sacrifice, firstborn or otherwise, as an abomination. Unnecessary adult human sacrifice without a victim's consent and not according to YHWH's will is also forbidden. His testing of Abraham, the acceptance of Jephthah's vow[3] and the willful offering of his only Son were all particular cases and not part of a routine ordinance. Jephthah's sacrifice of his daughter is an interesting case that has weathered much debate over the centuries. Some commentators (mainly Christian) even suggest that his vow was fulfilled by his daughter remaining a virgin, but even Jewish historian Josephus writes that his promise was literal and was faithfully carried out.

The Torah delves into great detail on taking vows because they are promises to YHWH that can run contrary to His Word. For example, if a man was to make an acceptable vow before the Almighty that he will never dwell in a booth (sukkah), his vow was

3 To give glory to YHWH for his victory against the Ammonites Jephath vowed to offer up as a holocaust (burnt offering) whatever emerged first from his dwelling ***(Judges 11:31)***. His oath was not a premeditated human sacrifice, but a potential offering of something he personally cherished. Most Jewish sages do not state that his vow was rashly made and nor does the narrative of the text itself imply that his vow was made in haste.

not expected to be broken even during the festival of Sukkoth. So too is the case with Jephthah who kept to his word and sacrificed his daughter, which would normally not be acceptable to YHWH. Honouring his word is like YHWH keeping his promise to us by sacrificing His only Son for our sins.

The Almighty even accepted the sacrifice of a Moabite king's own firstborn male by allowing him not to be defeated by Israel in battle ***(2 Kings 3:27).*** On this occasion the king's faith in his false elohim exceeded Israel's faith in their true Elohim and therefore his sacrifice caused YHWH to deny Israel victory.

It is important to realise two things when considering the Almighty's view on infant sacrifice: they are that Isaac, Adah (Jephthah's daughter) and Messiah Yahshua were not infants. And they were all willing to give up their lives. The Scriptures record no objection by Isaac, Adah or Yahshua to being offered up. In fact the Chumash, quoting from Midrashic teachings, reveals a more detailed account of Isaac's willingness:

> Isaac said: "Father, I am a vigorous young man and you are old. I fear that when I see the slaughtering knife in your hand I will instinctively jerk and possibly injure you. I might also injure myself and thus become unfit for the sacrifice. Or an involuntary movement by me might prevent you from performing the ritual slaughter properly."

The following verses in ***John 10:15*** & ***17,18*** not only emphasises Yahshua's deep resolve in his mission, but his complete control of the situation even after his capture and impaling. ***"As the Abba (Father) knows Me, even so I know the Abba (Father), and I lay down my chayim (life) for the sheep....Therefore does my Abba (Father) love me, because I lay down My chayim (life) that I might take it again. No man takes it from Me, but I lay it down myself. I have power to lay it down, and I have power to take it again. This commandment I have received from my Abba (Father)."***

Believers never ever brought sacrifices to YHWH. They brought offerings that were to be a foreshadowing or object lesson of the perfect sacrifice that was offered up before the very foundation of the world – Yahshua. Only if an offering was accepted by YHWH was it then considered a sacrifice.

One should not look on YHWH as being the author of human sacrifice but the author of *love* - The ultimate act of love being to give up one's life to save another. ***John 15:13; "Greater ahava (love) has no man than this that a man to lay down his chayim (life) for His chaverim (friends)."***

Is the Sacrifice of Animals a Cruel Concept?

But what of animals, is it cruel to offer them up to YHWH on our behalf? At least a human, sacrificed against his will knows of his fate. Is Judaism inhumane?

Judaism's most prominent forefathers Jacob, Moshe and King David were all at one time shepherds for a significant period of their lives. The Talmud relates that one of the reasons Moshe was chosen by YHWH was because of his skill in caring for animals. It was no coincidence that he received forty years of training as a shepherd before spending forty years in the desert leading his people.

Firstly, the sacrifice of animals as part of a larger process that assists a person to gain intimacy with the Creator is as equally important as slaughtering an animal for food to provide nutrients to the body. Yahshua demonstrates that meat is a perfectly permissible food by catching, requesting and eating it on several occasions ***(Luke 24:42, Matthew 15:37, John 21:10)***. Vegetarianism on the grounds that an individual dislikes the taste of meat or if it makes them ill is perfectly acceptable. But vegetarianism looked upon as a form of attaining superior righteousness is a doctrine of devils.

Kosher Slaughter for a Romantic Candlelit Dinner with the Creator

One evening I was browsing through some paintings depicting an offering in the Temple and I noted that many of the priests seemed to be dressed like chefs. This got me thinking. Much of their duties seemed to consist of carefully preparing types of foods similar to the atmosphere in a kitchen of a top class restaurant. Even down to the menorah in the entrance to the Holy of Holies setting the candlelit mood, added to this theme. Indeed, every service was approached with the same expectation as a lover preparing an intimate meal with his bride. In Judaism, teaching and instruction often revolves around food.

In Jewish law all animals, whether to be consumed as food or presented as an offering, are killed humanely. The practice of animal slaughter whether for food or offering purposes is part of the kashrut laws, which comes from the Hebrew root *Kaf-Shin-Resh*, meaning "fit," "proper" or "correct." This word shares the same Hebrew root as the word "kosher," which describes food that meets a certain level of purity.

Kosher Laws emphasize the sharpness of the slaughterer's knife, accuracy, precision and skill to slit the jugular vein of an animal with an absolute minimum of pain and suffering. Unnecessary suffering by an animal corrupts the meat and disqualifies it from being kosher. Also making the animal unconscious by anesthesia or any other means increases the risk of damaging the quality of the meat. In Judaism the optimum method of kosher slaughter is performed by holding the animal, praying softly into its ear and gently massaging the jugular vein before cutting. Finally the animal's blood is to be completely drained and returned to the earth. It must be noted that there was a much publicised incident in the US where a major kosher slaughter-house was exposed for not adhering to this practice. (See "PETA verses AgriProcessors.")

Judaism has been criticised by animal rights organisations as being inhumane despite secular slaughter houses retaining the use of batons for smashing the hind legs of pigs to get them to ascend ramps and killing cattle by firing a violent bolt into the brain or by electric shock to the head. More detailed information is available in Gail A. Eisnitz's book, *Slaughterhouse: The Shocking Story of Greed, Neglect, and Inhumane Treatment Inside the U.S. Meat Industry*. Know this, if you are not eating Kosher meat or growing and preparing livestock yourself you are exposed to an industry where virtually every piece of meat available within a supermarket with or without a safety stamp has not been inspected for feces, urine, pus, mucus, hair, dirt, grease, rat droppings or blood clots. Contamination control only extends to examining organs for gross malformations.

Yahshua was in Full Support of the Sacrificial System

Yaakov (James), Sha'ul and Yahshua were all in full support of animal sacrifice and never taught against it. Their endorsement of offerings is demonstrated in the following examples:

Yahshua taught on the correct attitude and resolution method for disputes concerning fellow covenant members who wished to present offerings. ***Matthew 5:23,24; "Therefore if you bring your gift to the altar, and there remember that your brother has anything against you; Leave your gift before the altar, and go your way; first be reconciled to your brother, and then come and offer your gift."*** He also instructed a man who he had just healed to present an offering in ***Matthew 8:4; "...go your way, show yourself to the kohen (priest), and offer the gift that Moshe commanded, for a testimony to them."***

Even after Yahshua's ascension, animal sacrifices continued to be endorsed by supporters of the Messiah. Yaakov (James) was attempting to rectify rumours that Sha'ul had taught against the Torah by asking him to assist some men who were about to conclude their Nazarite vows, which involved making offerings.

Acts 21:18-24, 26; "And the day following went in with us to Yaakov (James); and all the Zechanim (elders of the nation) were present. And when he greeted them, he declared particularly what things YHWH had done among the nations by his service. And when they heard it, they gave tehilla (praise) to YHWH, and said to him, 'You see, brother, how many tens of thousands there are who believe among Yahudim (Jews); and they are all zealous for the Torah: And they are wrongly informed about you, that you teach all the Yahudim who are among the nations to forsake Moshe's Torah, saying that they should not brit milah (circumcise) their children, neither walk after the halacha (way) of Torah. What is this therefore? The multitudes will hear that you have come. So do what we tell you: We have four men who have a nazarite vow on the: Take them, and cleanse yourself with them, and pay their expenses, that they may shave their heads: and then all will know that those things, of which they were informed about you, are false and nothing; but that you yourself also have your halacha orderly, guarding all the Torah... Then Sha'ul (Paul) took the men, and the next day cleansed himself with them and entered into Brit HaMikdash (Set-apart place), to signify the completion of

the days of their separation, UNTIL THE OFFERING SHOULD BE GIVEN FOR EVERYONE OF THEM.'" The details of what is involved in a Nazirite vow very clearly involve a burnt offering ***(Numbers 6:13-18)***.

The earth shattering reality is that if animal sacrifice was done away with as most Christians believe, then Yahshua, Yaakov and Sha'ul were not aware of it. But the reality is that animal sacrifices were never done away with.

What were Animal Sacrifices for?

The average Christian is educated to believe that nearly every time someone sinned in the Old Testament an animal sacrifice was required. The fact is that few sins required offerings brought by an individual. If this was the case, the Temple Priesthood would have had to work a twenty-four hour pit crew and Israel would have very quickly run out of animals. There was a single blood atonement made on Yom Kippur (Day of Atonement) by the High Priest, which would corporately atone for all the intentional sins of Israel for that past year ***(Leviticus 16)***. Each individual Israelite (and sojourner within their dwellings) was still required to seek constant *teshuvah* throughout the year and certainly also on Yom Kippur. According to the prophets, forgiveness for intentional sins was only atoned for through *teshuvah* (returning) rather than through the blood of animals ***(Psalms 32:5, 51:16-19)***. But the value of an offering was also a form of outward physical evidence of an inner departure from sin and a return to observance by the individual or the High Priest who offered it on behalf of the whole nation. Most people are surprised to learn that the most consistent type of animal sacrifice was principally designed for unintentional sin ***(Leviticus 4:2, 13, 22, 27; 5:5, 15 and Numbers 15:30)***. The only offering that was brought for intentional sin (aside from on Yom Kippur by the High Priest) was if an individual, accused of theft, had sworn falsely in an effort to acquit himself ***(Leviticus 5:24-26)***. The accompanying emphasis on *teshuvah* with animal sacrifice in the Old Testament further rattles the dispensationalist view of a new verbalised praise form of sacrifice.

Why Did Animal Sacrifices Stop?

In ***Deuteronomy 12:4-6*** YHWH states emphatically that offerings are to only take place in one location – the Temple Mount or Mount Moriah region in Jerusalem. ***Deuteronomy 12:13-14*** further warns against making offerings in any other geographical location. ***I Kings 8:46-50*** describes King Solomon obeying this ordinance by requesting prayer (as opposed to animal sacrifice) from those who could not make a pilgrimage to his newly completed Temple.

There were altogether built and re-built, three Temples on the same location, however only the First and Second Temples are acknowledged. The first was built by King Solomon and the second was built by returning Jews who came back from the Persian Exile, led by the prophets Ezra, Nechemiah and Zerubavel. The third Temple was more of a renovation by King Herod. Josephus does record that a Temple was attempted at Leontopolis in Egypt, but it was closed by Rome in 74CE. There is some speculation of a Tabernacle[4] at Qumran but this evidence is not reliable. There was an aborted Temple under Roman emperor Julian who planned to restore local religious cults as part of a program to strengthen his empire. The leading rabbis of the day were concerned with Gentile involvement in the Temple's construction and its ultimate function if it was built.

Sacrifices, the Land and the Temple – All One Living Organism

The last Temple was destroyed and plundered by Roman soldiers in 70CE. The Jews were driven from the site and did not reclaim it again until 1967 when Brigadier General Shlomo Goren exclaimed, "The Temple Mount is in our hands! Repeat, the Temple Mount is in our hands! All forces stop firing!" During the Six Day War Israeli defence forces had liberated the Old City of Jerusalem and the Temple Mount from enemy Arab forces after nearly 1900 years of exile. The Jews then turned over 97% of the Temple Mount back to the Arabs. This trend of trying to "out-mercy" the Creator continued as the IDF (Israeli Defence Forces) withdrew from much of

4 Portable Temple only permitted before Israel entered into the land.

their conquered territories in exchange for vain peace settlements that continue to this very day.

Animal sacrifices, the geographical location of Mount Moriah and the Temple structure itself were are all interdependent of one another. The Temple was not constructed for YHWH's benefit (as in a house for Him to dwell), but for the benefit of mankind. ***Ezekiel 37:26-28*** clearly establishes that there will be a Temple during the millennial reign of Yahshua and thus offerings will resume as in ancient days.

Today Jewish prayer services parallel the former sacrificial practices. For example on Shabbat (Sabbath) they add an extra service to parallel the Shabbat offering. All Orthodox prayer services contain prayers for the Temple's restoration and there is constant recitation of the order of the day's sacrifices in the daily readings of the psalms, which would have been sung by the Levites. Animal sacrifices were never introduced to man as an exclusive means of obtaining forgiveness, and they were never in and of themselves meant to do so. The only reason they do not occur today is because there is no Temple on Mount Moriah and as such their absence is not a supporting pillar to prove dispensationalism. Yahshua and Sha'ul never taught that animal sacrifice was to be done away with in their day or in the future.

New Testament, New Covenant – What's the Difference?

The concept of a New Testament (novum testamentum) and the selection of books that encompass it were invented by Early Church Father Tertullian around the 2nd century. In addition, the so-called "grace theology" of the New Testament (more accurately referred to as the *brit chadashah* or "new[5] covenant") can be found in the Torah ***(Deuteronomy 10:16)***, the Prophets ***(Jeremiah 31:31–32[6])*** and later in nearly every book after ***Malachi***. This clearly shows an

5 It is worth noting that the term "new," as it pertains to the New Covenant is a blanket translation over the Greek word "kainos" and the Hebrew equivalent "hadash," which are more accurately rendered as "renewed" or "refreshed."

6 Jeremiah 31 is not the first place to mention the concept of a New Covenant though the term "New Covenant" is used for the first time here. It's kind of like the phrase, "born again." Though Yahshua said one has to be "born again," it was not a new concept, though his method of describing it certainly was.

equally measured application of mercy and grace (unmerited power) extended by YHWH toward man that runs the entirety of Scripture, rather than confined to a latter super-grace golden era.

The extent of the average Christian's familiarity with the concept of the New Covenant can be testified to by asking them to flick to the introduction of the New Covenant in their Bibles. Invariably they will go to the first book behind the introduction page entitled, "The New Testament."

James Hastings, in his *Dictionary of the Bible* states that the earliest compilation of the New Testament was over a century after the Messiah's death. The first written reference to a collection of New Testament books was compiled by the Heretic Marion, who issued a canon of Scriptures consisting of a gospel of Luke and the epistles of Sha'ul in about 140 A.D. (p. 123). However a further canonisation of additional books and a solid definition of the New Testament didn't occur until 1546 at the Council of Trent.

Question: Why does it matter that the Scriptures were divided into two parts?

Answer: Actually, the Scriptures were divided into many parts. They consist of The Torah, Writings of the Prophets, Books of Wisdom, Major Prophets, Minor Prophets, Writings, The Gospels, The History (Acts), Pauline Epistles, General Epistles and The Apocalypse (Revelations). The problem is if you divide this set of teachings into two distinct parts and call the first part "old" and the latter part "new" an implication that the latter part holds precedence or superiority over the former is set in motion. In actual fact the so-called Old Testament is very important because it serves as a strong foundation and reference point to interpret the writings of the so-called "New Testament." If you meld the dogmatic use of the name, "New Testament," with a belief in its Greco-Roman interpretation of a Torah breaking Messiah, you are perpetuating two key ingredients that have helped keep alive one of the greatest deceptions in the history of mankind. Mainstream Christianity's general lack of interest in the Old Testament is evident when one listens to an average Christian's attitude toward it. I recall attending a Bible study class where it was seriously debated as to whether there was any merit in studying the Old Testament at all – I kid you not! Using terminology that consists of "old" and "new" sets a premise for students to develop a false dispensationalist view of the Scriptures. In its full grown state this reckoning leads to all kinds of theological mayhem such as belief in the trinity, New Testament confined grace and the Rapture.

The Power and Presence of the Ruach HaKodesh

The manifestation of the Ruach HaKodesh (Holy Spirit) in chapter 2 of The Book of Acts has been so frequently and unashamedly used as a catalyst to support the authenticity of the Church that its many prior manifestations in Scripture have been all but forgotten. Its prior descent on the 70 elders in ***Numbers 11:17 & 29*** is overlooked and its aforementioned descent on the talmidim (disciples) in the Har HaBayit[7] ***(Acts 2:1-4)*** and its exact timing with Israel's deliverance from Egypt that ended at the giving of the Torah in ***Exodus 19:10-16*** is unknown or has little significance to the average Christian.

The Ruach's identity as a man, woman or ghost and its attachment to a pagan triune godhead (trinity) concept has further served to alienate its origin, purpose and meaning from a Hebrew context. There is no Scripture that supports a gender specific Holy Ghost that is divine in and unto itself and there is no description of it as an extract from a triune body. YHWH and any aspect of His kingdom is one, not three.

The Ruach would descend and fill men to varying degrees to achieve specific purposes such as comforting, ministering, prophesying, teaching, praying, fighting, protecting and articulating an individual or mass of individuals in any way seen fit to achieve the Father's purpose. One of the earliest manifestations recorded in an individual is found in Exodus. The architect and builder Betzal-EL from the tribe of Judah (Yahudah) was selected and filled with the Ruach HaKodesh in ***Shemot (Exodus) 35:31*** to build the Tabernacle.

7 Mountain of the House, (name for the Temple Mount) as apposed to an "upper room" of a house evident in most modern translations.

All the books of Tehillim (Psalms) were compiled under degrees of the Ruach HaKodesh's abiding presence as was every Word of Scripture that came from the pens of its original scribes.

Twelfth century Jewish Scholar Moshe ben Maimon or Maimonides who wrote *The Guide to the Perplexed* lists the Ruach HaKodesh as delivering degrees of prophecy and as a certain thing that descends upon an individual, "so that he talks in wise sayings, in words of praise, in useful admonitory dicta, or concerning governmental or divine matters - and all this while he is awake and his senses function as usual."

According to Tosefta, Sotah 13:2; Sanhedrin 11a, the Ruach HaKodesh departed Yisrael (for a time) with the passing of the last three prophets Chaggai, Zechariah and Malachi and states that all subsequent revelations were given by "a mysterious heavenly voice."

When the Ruach abandons an individual it causes great grief and anguish. It is not usually recognised as gone until a grave sin is uncovered or if a crucial situation such as a battle goes poorly. King David cries out for its return in ***Psalms 51:11,12; "Cast me not away from Your shechinah (divine presence); and take not Your Ruach HaKodesh from me. Restore to me the simcha (joy) of your Yahshua (YHWH style Salvation); and uphold me with Your free Ruach."***

The Many Movements of the Ruach HaKodesh

The following is a short list of unusual and outstanding abilities that are manifested from the outpouring of the Ruach HaKodesh. This is not a closed-ended list of its powers. The Ruach of YHWH has no limitations and can cause such wonders as flesh, soul and spirit to reconstitute over dry bones, melt a mountain like wax down to sea level, impregnate a virgin or enable a woman well advanced in years to produce a perfectly healthy child.

<u>The Ruach enhances and guides combat efficiency</u> - ***Judges 3:10; "The Ruach (Spirit) of YHWH came upon Othni-El, and He gave mishpat (judgement) to Yisrael, and went out to war: and YHWH delivered Khushan-Rishathayim melech (king) of Aram-***

Naharayim (Mesopotamia) into his hand; and his hand prevailed against Khushan-Rishathayim."

The Ruach enables greater lung capacity - *Judges 6:34; "But the Ruach of YHWH came upon Gidyon, and he blew a Shofar; and Ave-Ezer was gathered to him."*

The Ruach increases physical strength - *Judges 14:6; "And the Ruach of YHWH came mightily upon him, and he tore him as he would have torn a young goat, and he had nothing in his hand; but he told not his abba (father), or his eema (mother) what he had done."*

The Ruach enables foretelling and alters molecular structure - *1 Samuel 10:6; "The Ruach of the YHWH will come upon you, and you shall prophesy with them; and shall be turned into another man."*

The Ruach elevates King David to a new spiritual level - *1 Samuel 16:13; "Then Schumel (Samuel) took the horn of oil, and anointed him in the midst of his brothers, and the Ruach of YHWH came upon Dawid (David) from that day forward. So Shumel rose up, and went to Ramah."*

The Ruach enables 100% accurate Extra Sensory Perception (ESP) - *Ezekiel 11:5; "And the Ruach of YHWH fell upon me, and said to me, Speak; 'this says YHWH; This have you said O Beit (House of) Yisrael: for I know the things that come into your mind, every one of them.'"*

The Ruach enables mass discernment on physical and corresponding spiritual matters - *Numbers 11:16; "And I will come down and talk with you there: and I will take of the Ruach which is upon you, and will put it upon them; and they shall bear the burden of the people with you, that you bear it not yourself alone."*

The Ruach enables mass prophecies - *Numbers 11:25; "And YHWH came down in a cloud, and spoke to him (Moshe) and took of the Ruach that was upon him, and gave it to the seventy Zechanim: and it came to pass, that, when the Ruach rested upon them, they prophesied, and did not cease."*

The Ruach enables aerial transportation or levitation – *Ezekiel 37:1; "The hand of YHWH was upon me, and carried me out in the Ruach HaKodesh of YHWH, and set me down in the midst of the valley which was full of bones…"*

The Ruach HaKodesh is Not a Person!

Orthodox Christianity teaches that the Ruach HaKodesh is a third divine person[8] of a triune or Trinitarian entity. The Biblical support of this view comes from the following verses: It can be resisted ***(Acts 7:51)***, grieved ***(Ephesians 4:30)*** and lied to ***(Acts 5:3)***. It speaks ***(Acts 21:11)***, teaches ***(Luke 12:12)*** and thinks ***(Acts 15:28)***. It is all powerful ***(Luke 1:35-37)***, eternal ***(Hebrews 9:14)***, all knowing ***(1 Corinthians 2:10,11)*** and it was involved in creation ***(Genesis 1:2, Job 33:4)***. It brings new birth ***(John 3:5)***, resurrected Messiah ***(Romans 8:11)*** and caused the Scriptures to be YHWH breathed ***(2 Peter 1:20,21)***.

Because the attributes of mind, will and emotion are covered in some of the above verses this is supposedly a secure enough premise to support a case for the Ruach's personage. Let's have a closer look.

Describing something that has an intricate response mechanism, performs highly sophisticated miraculous functions and is able to negotiate infinite situations is no more a qualifier for a self-conscious being than describing the latest artificially intelligent simulation program used by NASA.

With the extensive list of credentials displayed in the above verse references, it should make a rational person wonder what YHWH and Yahshua are left to do with this mysterious Holy Ghost running around covering the whole spectrum of divine acts. The truth is that none of the above verses define the Ruach as a person! I've never read a verse that reads, "The Holy Person filled the Tabernacle," and there is no record of it being worshipped like the Father and the Son anywhere in Scripture. In fact the doctrine of the Ruach as a person causes some denominations to have to deal with the annoying question as to whether or not it should be worshipped. This becomes a case of a misappropriated doctrine eroding away one sound teaching and contaminating another by way of natural deductive reasoning (i.e., If the Holy Spirit is a person, why then can it not receive worship?). Pretty soon one superimposed

---

8 Josh McDowell and Don Stewart's *Handbook of Today's Religions*, under the heading of Orthodox Christianity reads, "The Doctrine that the Holy Spirit is a person is clearly taught in Scripture...(p39)"

doctrine falls away from another and the Scriptures appear to collapse like a house of cards and the faith it promotes becomes easy prey to the well prepared atheist.

Question: What about the verses that seem to give the Ruach a mouth and gender?

Answer: Consider the language used in the following verses in terms of a mouth emitting speech to justify a person attached to it: ***1 Corinthians 12:15,16; "If the foot shall say, Because I am not the hand, I am not of the body; is it therefore not the body? And if the ear shall say, Because I am not the eye, I am not of the body; is it therefore not the body?"*** And ***Psalms 96:11,12; "Let the shamayim (heavens) gilah (rejoice), and let the earth be in simcha (gladness); let the sea roar, and the fullness of it. Let the field be full of simcha, all that is in it: then shall all the eytzim (trees) of wood gilah..."*** For further examples read ***Isaiah 55:12*** for singing mountains and hand-clapping trees.

A masculine gender reference attributed to the Ruach as evidence to support a self-conscious entity is as sane as suggesting a sailing ship is a woman based on a constant feminine gender reference.

The Ruach - Don't Leave Home without It!

The Ruach HaKodesh is a power that proceeds out from YHWH and perfectly articulates His will. It can respond to direct instruction by Him or any being that works in (or is faithfully working toward) perfect unity with Him to potentially achieve any objective, no matter how great or small (as long as it aligns with the flawless will of the Father). The Spirit can quicken or give actuated life through the verbal resonance of a command. It simultaneously manifests itself, to different degrees, for different purposes and at different times in the lives of believers from all walks of life. It is prophesied in ***Joel 2:28*** to be poured out onto all Yisraelite flesh (see context ***Acts 2:16***) in the Messianic era. Yahshua became the first flesh and blood example of a constantly Ruach filled vessel from the time of his water immersion ***(John 1:33)***.

The Ruach is the Father's life-giving breath. It is the aspect of Him that is truly omnipresent ***(Psalm 139:7-10, 1 Corinthians 2:10-11)*** and manifest as a guide and comforter to all who are beneath the shadow of the Father's merciful and protective wings. Angels are appointed as Watchers of creation, as silent observers, intercessors, ministers, messengers, transporters or full blown combatants. This is why YHWH responds to an angelic report of anguish not unlike a police chief responds to an incident after being informed by his subordinates in ***Genesis 18:21; "I will go down now, and see whether they have done altogether according to the cry of it, which is come to Me, and if not I will know."*** This opens up the question of YHWH's omnipresence as viewed by general Christianity and is discussed in my first book.

The bottom line in considering whether the Ruach HaKodesh is a person or not is this: If the Ruach is a person then Yahshua is the Son of the Ruach HaKodesh, not the Son of YHWH, and this view walks a fine line in suggesting the most uncomfortable thought imaginable; that the Ruach as a person entered Miriam's bedchamber and conventionally laid with her. Think about it. If one views the Ruach as a person and someone else tries to suggest the above scenario, how could you blame them?

The Ruach HaKodesh cannot be rationally cited from Scripture as a person.

Grace Wonderland

Now that flesh circumcision, animal sacrifice, the new covenant and the workings of the Ruach HaKodesh have been discussed and their place within the greater plan of YHWH outlined, the reader should be primed enough to consider the role of the Creator's mercy and unmerited power in the post-resurrection phase of the great struggle between the forces of good and evil, without the baggage of Christian theology getting in the way.

Have you ever heard the comment, "Now we are under grace," as to suggest believers prior to Yahshua were under something else? I have, and it is endemic within the church. There are two predominant schools of thought regarding mercy (which most Christians actually mean when they say "grace") in the Old Testament held by Christianity. They are that it was either not evident before the resurrection or that it was, but it was misunderstood by the Jews. Both these views are completely false, but are supremely important in maintaining the church's authority and identity. The church does not want you to bridge the dispensationalist gap between the teachings in the Old Testament and the teaching in the New Testament.

Through my own experience, most of Christianity teaches that working out of one's salvation is the responsibility of YHWH and a believer's role is primarily passive. This stands in complete opposition to ***Philippians 2:12*** where it clearly describes salvation as something that should be worked out ***"with fear and trembling."*** Have you ever heard the phrase "Salvation is by grace alone, faith alone, and Christ alone?" This view places the emphasis on YHWH to do something, rather than man to do anything apart from having intellectual belief and acceptance of a single miraculous event. This phrase has no focus on love or obedience to YHWH's will. In contrast, Yahshua's advice is, ***"If you love me, keep my Commandments." (John 14:15)***

The Father's Favour in Action

YHWH's mercy and equipping of man to do His will (grace) is evident from the first fall. Even Early Church Fathers believed that Adam received grace. "What then? Did not Adam have the grace of God? Yes, truly, he had it largely..." - AURELIUS AUGUSTIN (426CE) Abraham received YHWH's grace as Sha'ul points out in ***Romans 4:1-5; "What shall we say then about Avraham our abba (father), who lived in the flesh before Eloah (Elohim) called him? For if Avraham were justified by mitzvoth (love deeds) alone, he has something to boast about; but not before YHWH. For what says the Katuv (scriptures)? Avraham believed YHWH, and it was counted to him for tzedakah (righteousness). Now to him that performs mitzvoth (love deeds) alone is the reward not given as...*** **charis[9] (divine influence on the heart)...,** ***but as a debt. But to him that works not, but believeth on Him that makes tzedakah (righteousness) the***

9 The RSTNE interprets the word here to mean "unmerited favour."

unrighteous, his emunah (faith) is counted as tzedakah (righteousness)." Noah and his family found grace ***(Genesis 6:8)***, Joseph found grace ***(Genesis 39:4)***, Moshe found grace ***(Exodus 33:12)***, Jacob appealed to YHWH and received His grace ***(Genesis 33:10)***, Shechem, having raped Jacob's daughter, appealed for grace and was granted it in accordance with YHWH ***(Genesis 34:11)*** despite later falling by the sword of dissenters. Whenever an Israelite committed an offence and was given the opportunity to right that offence it was considered merciful. King David received unmerited favour (mercy) and unmerited power (grace) even though his transgressions where greater than Saul's, because he earnestly sought YHWH. When Saul got into trouble he sought the counsel of a witch. The ***Book of Ester*** mentions a favourable attitude (grace) in the eyes of YHWH six times. ***Proverbs 1:8*** encourages the wearing of an ornament on the head as a reminder of grace whilst heeding instruction and contemplating the Torah.

Bad Grace?

Proverbs 31:30 describes grace (in this instance referring to favour) as ***"deceitful"*** and beauty as ***"vain."*** This verse is referring to a woman who has been favoured by YHWH with exceptional physical beauty and how this favour is vain without the fear of YHWH. The Talmud contains various opinions on the meaning of this verse that are worth presenting:

> Babylonian Talmud: Tractate Sanhedrin Folio 20a - "'Grace is deceitful' refers to [the trial of] Joseph; 'and beauty is vain', to Boaz; while 'and a woman that feareth the Lord, she shall be praised', to the case of Palti son of Layish. Another interpretation is: 'Grace is deceitful', refers to the generation of Moses; 'and beauty is vain' to that of Joshua; 'and she that feareth the Lord shall be praised,' to that of Hezekiah. Others Say: 'Grace is deceitful,' refers to the generations of Moses and Joshua; 'and beauty is vain,' to the generation of Hezekiah; while 'she that feareth the Lord shall be praised.' refers to the generation of R. Judah son of R. Ila'i, of whose time it was said that [though the poverty was so great that]

six of his disciples had to cover themselves with one garment between them, yet they studied the Torah."

Yahshua Never Preached on Grace

Amazingly as this sounds, Yahshua never preached specifically on grace. In fact, in most modern Bible translations he only uses the term "favour" twice and never in a promotional sense like we hear preachers speak about it today. As a side note Yahshua spoke more about hell than he talked about heaven, he sometimes made statements to people who came to him for help like, "*...**you have little faith...***" and he also occasionally added comments like, "*...**how long will I have to put up with you?***" *(Matthew 17:17)* and he professed to come as a man of war to bring about division as opposed to a man of peace to bring about unity in ***Luke 12:49-51.***

Yahshua teaches that if believers are only good to those who are good to them, they will be found without favour. ***Luke 6:32; "For if ye love them which love you, what thank (or grace) have ye? for sinners also love those that love them."***

Luke17:9; "Doth he thank (give grace to / have a favourable attitude to) that servant because he did the things that were commanded him?" This verse highlights why going the extra mile is important.

Sha'ul (Paul) Graces the Stage

In apparent total contrast to Yahshua, Sha'ul mentions grace around 97 times in the Nazarene phase of his ministry. Having been given mercy and power so undeservingly by YHWH, Sha'ul was so permanently marked by an overwhelming awareness and appreciation for the Creator's grace, that it permeated his teaching.

Believe it or not, at the time of Sha'ul the Jews believed that the Torah was completely compatible with grace. It wasn't until a breakaway movement of Natsarim (offshoot branch watchmen) started gathering non-Jewish converts that a division grew. Torah observant believers and non-Torah observant believers began to clash as pagan customs seeped into various congregations. A sincere attempt at appealing to wider audiences by many groups caused the

Torah to be gradually discarded. The issue wasn't law versus grace; it was Torah versus no Torah. Grace began to be used as a mechanism to cause disillusionment in the Torah. The rabbis were concerned that Sha'ul's message fuelled this perception, but careful study of his teachings proves that he was a man with zealous love for the Torah.

The Torah by definition is grace. In essence it is a counsellor, a teacher, a right ruling of measure, a light that reveals error and directs us into all truth. It is YHWH's gift for humanity. The Torah cannot correctly operate without grace. Obedience to Torah and the desire to happily perform mitzvoth gets YHWH's attention; not continually cradling the abundance of His grace in order to avoid exerting any energy to attain mastery over the Evil Inclination.

Conclusion

Today, since Yahshua's death and resurrection, nothing has changed. The only thing that has changed is the absence of any Torah ordinance that is contingent on the Temple, but even this climate will cease shortly at its restoration. The faults of the first covenant were with Israel ***(Hebrews 8:8; "For finding fault with them ...")***, not YHWH; therefore, it is through their transgression (and ours today) that a second Covenant was necessary. The Torah appoints immortals without fault as High Priests for service in the Set-apart place, so the formation of the Aaronic Priesthood being temporary (fulfilled by mortals ***(Hebrew 7:23; "...because they were prevented by death for continuing*** [i.e., died of old age]***...")*** was the former command which was ***"...set aside..." (Hebrews 7:18)*** and soon to be presided over by the immortal order of Malkitsedeq headed by the Sar (Lower Level Prince of Peace [no lesser power than YHWH insinuated]) Yahshua Ha Moshiach (Messiah).

The Torah was not nailed with Yahshua to the tree. It was the curse of the adulterous woman (Israel) who had gone astray that had been done away with, which is established by the law of return, provided Israel (and all those who wish to be grafted in with them) seek *teshuvah*. YHWH's grace is completely in harmony with the Torah and is not a new thing that allows a believer to get something for nothing. This is not a super grace age; this is an age of forgiveness held forth at the same degree from Adam, though it was not *formally* established until the age of Shem to now.

Remember, "grace" means "unmerited power given to man to do YHWH's will" and "mercy" actually means "unmerited favor." Now go and study it.

Chapter Thirteen

Sha'ul at Last

FOR MANY PEOPLE THERE are parts of Rabbi Sha'ul's letters that contain some challenging teachings. When sufficient study is not applied to these grey areas a believer can unconsciously open the door to theological error. Occasionally I encounter some Natsarim who have declared "no confidence" in Sha'ul's writings as "Yah-breathed" and it is in response to these encounters that I include this chapter. My desire as I'm sure is also the desire of my heavenly Father, is that "the body" be equipped with a sharper understanding of this extraordinary Apostle's teachings. Rabbi Sha'ul was an extremely intelligent, driven and adaptable Pharisee. He was denied sleep, starved, beaten, stoned, flogged, shipwrecked and imprisoned. Many of these travails came from bandits, his own countrymen, Gentiles and even fellow Natsarim. In the face of all this, his mind never loosened from the task at hand. From his first letter to his last, he remained a constant vessel for Elohim. The controversy surrounding some of his more intricate teachings should never be attributed to poor scholarship of the author, but a lack of spiritual maturity in the reader. - AS WELL AS TRANSLATION ERRORS DOWN THROUGH THE YEARS & INTERPOLATIONS/ADDITIONS.

Whatever was Sha'ul Going on About?

Sha'ul's expression '***...rightly dividing the Word of truth'*** in ***2 Timothy 2:15*** was relating to the three levels of understanding in the Scriptures called "PaRDeS." This word is an acronym for *pashat*, which means the "simple meaning of Torah," *remez*, which means "the implied meaning," *drash*, which means the "allegorical meaning" and *sod*, which means "the hidden meaning." This he learned in the school of Hillel. The Rabbi Hillel passed this practice of deciphering Torah on to his son Simeon, who later passed the mantle on to Gamaliel. Gamaliel was Sha'ul's teacher according to ***Acts 22:3***. Sha'ul's letters and sayings were delivered in a learned Hebraic form of communication often utilising *G'zerah Shavah*, which means "equivalence of expressions." This took the form of taking two beliefs with similar elements and presenting them in an analogy to make a point. To understand Sha'ul's writings it has to be done by considering complete context, rather than isolating statements. This is called *Davar hilmad me'anino*, which means "explanation obtained from context" stemming from one of the seven rules of Hillel. Christianity comes undone when it approaches Sha'ul's teachings by completely ignoring this fundamental method of understanding Scripture.

But even in Sha'ul's day and well before Christianity, some parts of his epistles were considered hard to understand, sometimes suffering from misinterpretations and even willful manipulation. ***2 Peter 15b-16; "...even as our beloved brother Shaul...has written to you; As also in all his letters, speaking in them of these things; <u>in which some things are hard to understand, which they that are unlearned and unstable twist, as they do also the other Keetvay HaKadosh (whole of the Scriptures), to their own destruction</u>."*** These unlearned and unstable people extracted so many different spins on Rabbi Sha'ul's writings that it gradually gave birth to sectarianism within the faith. ***1 Corinthians 1:12-13; "For it has been declared to me about you, my Yisraelite brothers, by those who are of beit (house of) Chloe, that there are contentions and disputes among you. Now this I say, because some among you say, I am of Shaul; and I am of Apollos; and I am of Kepha (Peter); and I am of Moshiach. Is Moshiach divided? Was Shaul impaled for you? Or, were you immersed in***

the name of Shaul?" Now centuries later, the climate described in these verses is still alive and well.

The extent of these theological divides finally dawned on me one Shabbat, when a young Mormon gentleman, who had just attended our service, asked me with Bible in hand, "What do you guys believe?" This question astounded me, because what other response would have been more acceptable than, "We believe the whole contents of the Scriptures"? Unfortunately this is an all too frequent question asked between people who have accepted the religious teaching of movements who have amplified certain verses and avoided others.

Most of the so-called Bible believing Christian world has gotten this man's national identity, religious affiliation, teaching and even his very name completely and utterly wrong. Who was this man that the world unwittingly calls a midget?

Let's start by examining his name. The word "Paul" is a transliteration of the Latin word *Paulos*, from the Greek, *paucus* meaning "little" or literally "midget." The name Paul was applied to him as a slur. It was not attributed to him around the time of his conversion nor was it given to him by the Almighty. It emerged after he had started preaching Yahshua as the Moshiach. Notice the inclusion of the phrase ***"also is called"*** in the first place this name appears in Scripture: ***"Then Sha'ul, who also is called Paul…" (Acts 13:9a)***. Grammatically we can tell that the initial name used in the sentence means that the majority of people still called him Sha'ul, but others commenced calling him Paulos. Many of his Jewish peers would have been angered by his conversion and the Natsarim were almost certainly weary of him due to his former role as their chief persecutor. ***"I persecuted this Way to the death, binding and delivering into prison both men and women" (Acts 22:3-4)***. Many people on both sides of the fence opposed him and the name "Little" reflected this disdain. There is no record of Rabbi Sha'ul's rejection of the name, perhaps preferring to regard himself as small (or humble) before Elohim. His real Hebrew name Sha'ul (Saul) means "desire" or "ask for" as in "ask for Elohim." There is little doubt that those who respected him would have not only continued to address him (after his conversion) as Sha'ul, but as Rabbi Sha'ul. Good Scripture translations now available continue to refer to him as Sha'ul even after Acts 13 and in other books of the Brit Chadashah (New Testament).

His Letters

Of the twenty-one letters that make up the Brit Chadashah, Rabbi Sha'ul is attributed to having written fourteen of them. Thirteen books bear his name and the fourteenth book, Hebrews, is also attributed to him. Seven of the letters are accepted among Hebrew Scholars as if having been initially penned by Sha'ul's own hand. The others are thought to have been written by his closest talmidim (disciples) who, as was the custom among all Torah students, recorded many aspects of their teacher's life. Interestingly Sha'ul predominantly wrote to people who were already believers and who had a certain grasp of the Torah already.

Rabbi Sha'ul's letters were compiled around the time of his second missionary journey. This is certainly true if we accept that he had to make contact with individual believers and communities before he wrote about them. His first letter was 1 Thessalonians, which is estimated to have been penned around 49 to 51CE and his latest letter is 2 Timothy, written around 67CE. 1&2 Timothy are believed to be his final letters for a number of reasons. They contain reference to his extensive travels, key events that occurred after the book of Acts and also tell of his own impending martyrdom. The wide array of books thought to be written by Sha'ul are: 1 & 2 Thessalonians, Galatians, 1 & 2 Corinthians, Romans, Hebrews, Philippians, Colossians, Philemon, Ephesians, Titus and 1 & 2 Timothy.

Over the centuries countless volumes of material about Rabbi Sha'ul have amassed. Commentaries on his letters, biographical writings and articles that give deeper insights into his teachings and character have come from a myriad of Biblical, apocryphal and historical sources. With the amount of information that's available one would think it impossible to be ignorant of what this man actually taught. But nothing can be further from the truth.

How His Letters Became Scripture

The ultra Orthodox ChaBaD movement preserves a tradition whereby a letter written by a Tzedek (Righteous One) to an individual or congregation is revered as sacred. Such a letter is usually placed in a special location with other sacred writings and reviewed regularly. This tradition, also observed by the early Natsarim Jews, played a large role in the preservation of Rabbi Sha'ul's letters, enabling them to eventually be regarded as Scripture among the assemblies of the early Nazarene sect.

The Grace View

There are two dominant views of Rabbi Sha'ul's ministry. The first view is that he taught salvation comes by grace alone ***(Ephesians 2:8-9)***. While this sounds true, it takes human effort to maintain obedience to YHWH's commandments in order for unmerited power (grace) to bring on salvation. The "grace only" crowd tends to view diligent observance of YHWH's commandments as an ongoing attempt to acquire salvation by human effort. Furthermore, this outlook encourages advocates to have a lukewarm attitude toward obedience because all sin is supposedly covered by grace. "The Paul taught grace" philosophy is also an anti-Torah teaching that is principally used to support replacement theology, which is a view that presents the "church" as a new and improved "spiritual" Israel. Advocates of this view consider commandment observance as legalism at best and Judaizing at worst, an act, considered by the church, as severing one's connection to Messiah. This grace-fixated obedient-deficient teaching has been vigorously enforced by the Catholic Church either by way of the mailed fist (physical force) or the velvet glove (subtle manipulation). Early church father Marcion, later excommunicated by the Catholic Church, was the first to wrestle Rabbi Sha'ul's letters completely away from truth by teaching that the Old Testament was superseded by the teachings of Jesus Christ and his only true Apostle - Paul. Marcion saw Christianity as being completely opposite to Judaism. He rejected the entire Old

Testament and declared its G-d as a lesser entity than the Messiah of the New Testament. To sum up: this is a completely untruthful and unacceptable view that is fundamentally anti-semitic and presents a schizophrenic Creator.

The Heretical View

The second view is that Sha'ul was just a plain old heretic. In Judaism this is called "one who leads the nation astray." The heretical view is usually held by Orthodox Judaism, although a Jew can hardly be blamed. Sha'ul is constantly represented by Christianity as a Torah-hating-grace-junkie who turned his back on the Jews and went to the Gentiles. Christianity, to a greater or lesser extent, teaches that Sha'ul actually became a Gentile after his conversion and subsequently went out to preach to Gentiles exclusively. He is described as having taught that flesh circumcision was done away with and that Torah observance was no longer a required mark of someone who possessed an upright relationship with the Creator. This is despite Sha'ul's declaration; ***"What advantage then has the Yahudi (Jew)? Or, what profit is there in brit-milah (circumcision)? Much in every way!" (Romans 3:1)*** and his general view toward circumcision in; ***Romans 4:11; "And he (Abraham) received the sign of circumcision, a seal of righteousness of the faith***... " Sha'ul only addresses an objection against adult male circumcision, and even then it was only objected to if an individual's heart was not already circumcised (i.e., if that individual saw the act of circumcision as being solely contingent to his salvation). Sha'ul didn't want masses of converts attempting to mutilate themselves; particularly the ones who could not easily receive circumcision. Circumcision was never meant as an instant accompaniment to conversion. If it ever occurred, it was determined in the Creator's time, not the individual's. After all, "circumcision of the heart" was a Torah teaching, not a so-called New Testament teaching ***(Deuteronomy 10:16).***

The Correct View

The less well known view of Sha'ul is that he taught perfectly in line with the Torah and Messiah Yahshua's words. Sure, most Christians will say that this is their view too, but upon questioning at length, you'll eventually get the guts of the first view coated in the skin of this one. I remember debating with a Christian whilst I was still in church about the law. We were in the book of Romans when he read this verse out loud: ***"For sin shall not have dominion over you, for you are not under the law but under grace" (Romans 6:14).*** There he ceased his reading and awaited my response. I looked down and noticed the Bible he and I had, had a break between verses 14 and 15. Between this break was the heading, "From Slaves of Sin to Slaves of God." This was unusual for two reasons. Firstly, the text broke in a section that wasn't the commencement of a new chapter as is painfully common in many modern Bible translations. Second, the next verse ***Romans 6:15*** read: ***What then? Shall we sin because we are not under law but under grace? Certainly not!*** The layout appeared to give the impression that verse 14 was the conclusion of the topic, yet the teaching continues straight on through to 15 and beyond. I then proceeded to read verse 15 to my Christian friend's total dismay.

Sha'ul's Background

Rabbi Sha'ul was born in Tarsus, a capital city of Asia Minor ***(Acts 22:3). "He was ...circumcised the eighth day, of the race of Am-Yisrael (the Nation of Israel), of the tribe of Benyamin, an Ivri (Hebrew), son of an Ivri (Hebrew); regarding Torah, a Prush (Pharisee) an Israelite of the tribe of Benjamin, circumcised on the eighth day" (Philippians 3:5).*** There is reference to him having a sister with her own son in ***Acts 23:16*** as well as other relatives in ***Romans 16:7, 11*** & ***12***. Sha'ul was a citizen of Rome ***(Acts 22:25 & Acts 27-28).*** Because Asia Minor was a province of Cilicia, a city declared free by Rome, all native born there were entitled to citizenship.

Sha'ul's Education

Rabbi Sha'ul's credentials were impeccable. He studied under the great Rabbi, Gamaliel. ***Acts 22:3; "I am indeed a man who am a Yahudi (Jew), born in Tarsus, a city in Cilikia (Cilicia), yet brought up in this city at the yeshiva of Gamliel, and taught according to the***

perfect manner of the Torah of the ahvot (fathers), and was zealous towards Elohim, as you all are this day."

Rav[1] Gamaliel was a very highly respected teacher of the Torah among the Jews. ***Acts 5:34; "Then stood up one in the Sanhedrin, a Prush (Pharisee), named Gamliel, an honored Torah teacher, held in the highest esteem among all the people of Yisrael, who commanded that the shlichim (apostles) be taken out of the chamber for a while."*** Rav Gamaliel had gone on record as supporting the Natsarim faith. This information is documented in the *Archko Volume*[2], which also details his investigation into a 26-year-old Yahshua and his parent's.

Natsarim Association with the Sanhedrin

Rav Yakkov HaTzaddik (James), Yahshua's own brother, eventually became the president of the Sanhedrin. If Yahshua, a rabbi himself, had a problem with the existence of the Sanhedrin and rabbis in general, he failed to mention it, much less warn his own brother about becoming its president.

Rabbi Sha'ul was a Pharisee, even after his conversion. ***Acts 23:6a; But when Shaul perceived that the one part were Tzadukim (Sadducee), and the other Prushim (Pharisees), he cried out in the Sanhedrin, Men and brothers, I am a Prush (Pharisee), the son of a Prush (Pharisee): because of my tikvah (hope) in the resurrection of the dead – the meechayai hamaytiim – I am being questioned."***

Who Were the Pharisees?

Pharisee means "separated" and was the title of a role that represented a major school of thought that was alive and well in Sha'ul's day. Many of Messiah Yahshua's teachings

---

1 Means "strong rabbi."

2 AKA "The Archaeological and the Historical Writings of the Sanhedrin and Talmuds of the Jews..."

were in line with Pharisaic thought. Yahshua's criticisms of certain Pharisees were principally leveled at hypocritical lifestyles, puffiness, and focus on manmade traditions over Torah observance.

Pharisaism emerged during the Babylonian captivity. The first clearly visible party appeared on the scene during the Maccabee Revolt against the Greeks.

Sha'ul's Profession

Rabbi Sha'ul's first appearance in Scripture is as a delighted overseer to the martyrdom of Stephanos (Stephen) ***(Acts 7:57). Acts 8:1; "Sha'ul was there, giving approval to his death."*** Stephanos whose Greek name means "crown," was not the first martyr for the faith. The first martyr was Abel, the son of Adam. To say that Stephanos was the first "Christian" martyr assumes that every generation of martyred believers before Yahshua (even heathen converts) did not believe in a coming Messiah.

Rabbi Sha'ul was a sworn enemy to all followers of the living Torah (Yahshua) and played a lead role in persecuting them. He was also a devout Yahudi (Jew) ***(Acts 23:6)*** because the tribe of Judah had long since absorbed all Benjamites into its fold. Rabbi Sha'ul was responsible for bringing believers in Yahshua to court, where many of them were subsequently condemned as heretics and stoned. ***Acts 9:1-2; "Meanwhile, Sha'ul, still breathing murderous threats against the YHWH's talmidim (disciples) went to the Cohen Hagadol (High Priest) and asked him for letters to the synagogues in Dammesek, authorizing him to arrest any people he might find, whether men or women, who belonged to the way, and bring them back to Yerushalayim."***

Acts 8:3 gives a good account of the vigorous manner in which he performed his duties. ***"As for Shaul, he made havoc of the congregation of Yisrael, entering into every bayit (house), and seizing men and women, throwing them into prison."***

Make no mistake; prior to his conversion, Rabbi Sha'ul was, to a believer in Yahshua, public enemy number one. But what happened?

Struck Down and Made Blind

1 Corinthians 3:18; "Let no man deceive himself. If any man among Yisrael seems to be wise in the olam hazeh (world), let him become a natural fool, that he may be spiritually wise."

On his way to Damascus Sha'ul underwent an extraordinarily terrifying experience. Like something out of an X-Files episode, he was enveloped by a bright aerial anomaly that struck him to the ground. In UFO circles his experience would have been registered as a close encounter of the third kind, sub-type F. This means Sha'ul witnessed a close range aerial phenomenon that delivered a completely comprehendible "intelligent communication." ***Acts 9:3-6; "And as he journeyed, he came near Dameshek: and suddenly there shone all around him a light from the shamayim (heavens)."*** There are three separate accounts of his conversion within the Scriptures. They are:

- His description in ***Acts 9:1-20***
- His account before the crowd in Yerushalaym ***(Acts 22:1-22)***
- The testimony before King Agrippa II ***(Acts 26:1-24)***.

After Sha'ul's encounter he was physically blinded. He remained in such a state for precisely three days, harking back to the duration of Jonah's confinement in the belly of a great fish and the duration of Messiah Yahshua's post crucifixion ministry in *Sheol*[3].

The Scriptural narrative of Sha'ul's conversion unfolds like this: And he fell to the ground, and heard a voice saying to him, ***"Shaul, Shaul, why are you persecuting Me? And he said, Who are You, Master? And He said, I am Yahshua whom you are persecuting: it is hard for you to offer against Me this worthless resistance. And he trembling and astonished said, Master, what will You have me to do? And Yahshua said to him, Arise, and go into the city, and it shall be told to you what you must do." (Acts 9:4-6)***

3 See Chapter 18 for more information on *Sheol.*

Torah Observant Both Before and After

One frequently mistaken belief about Sha'ul is that he traded a Torah obedient lifestyle for a singular intellectual belief in the risen Messiah. Some Natsarim even had this view during his ministry. Knowing this, Yaakov HaTzaddik (James the righteous [Yahshua's brother]), instructed him to assist with four men in the purification ritual of the Nazarite vow. Rabbi Sha'ul agreed to do this to show his fellow Jews of his devotion to Torah ***(Acts 21:20-24)***.

James was recognised as the leader of the Nazarenes who were both Torah observant and accepted Yahshua as Messiah. Early Church Father Jerome attests to their devotion to Torah in his own writings. "(They are) those who accept Messiah in such a way that they do not cease to observe the Old Law." *(Jerome; On. Is. 8:14)*.

Sha'ul's only major transformation was that he came to accept Yahshua as the living inseparable manifestation of the living Torah. This caused his ministry to swing completely in favour of his former enemies. Prior to this he worked with inquisitional precision to see that the Torah was upheld whilst remaining ignorant of its identity in Yahshua. His insatiable energy for persecuting supposed heretics was redirected into appealing vigorously to his peers and converts. In each role, though one was completely off the mark, Torah served as the blueprint for his actions.

Question: Didn't Sha'ul consider the Torah and all his training as "garbage" once he accepted Messiah? ***Philippians 5-9; "I was circumcised the eighth day, of the race of Am-Yisrael, of the tribe of Benyamin, an Ivri (Hebrew), son of an Ivri; regarding Torah, a Prush (Pharisee); Concerning zeal, persecuting the Renewed Yisraelite congregation; regarding the right conduct that is in the Torah, blameless. But what things were once gains for me; I counted lost for Moshiach. Yes doubtless, and I count all things to be lost for the better excellence of the chochmah (wisdom) of the Moshiach my Master: for whom I have suffered the loss of all things, and do count them as garbage, that I may gain more of Moshiach, And be found in Him, not having my own tzedakah (righteousness), which is from the Torah, but that which is through the emunah (faith) of Moshiach, the tzedakah (righteousness) that is from YHWH by emunah (faith)."***

Answer: No, he did not, but at the expense of losing his knowledge of Yahshua, yes he certainly did! To say otherwise means that following the letter of the law and his heritage was one means of salvation and accepting Yahshua was another.

After Sha'ul's encounter with Yahshua he was led completely helpless into Damascus by those who were with him and was visited by a believer in Yahshua called Ananias. Note carefully Rabbi Sha'ul's description of Ananias in ***Acts 22:12; "And one Chananyah (Ananias), a devout man following the Torah, having a tov (good) report among all the Yahudim (Jews) who dwelt there."***

Ananias heals Sha'ul's blindness and began ministering to him. ***Acts 22:14-16; "And he said, 'The Elohim of our ahvot (fathers) has chosen you, that you should know His will, and see that Tzadik-One (righteous-one), and should hear the voice from His mouth. For you shall be His witness to all men of what you have seen and heard. And now why do you delay? Arise, and be immersed, and wash away your sins, calling on the Name of YHWH.'"***

The New Ministry of a Natsari Pharisee

Rabbi Sha'ul later departs to Arabia and commences preaching in support of the way that he formerly persecuted in local synagogues ***(Galatians 1:17)***. This causes trouble, which leads to him vacating the city by means of a basket lowered over a wall ***(Acts 9:23)***.

Rabbi Sha'ul supported himself during his travels by his own means ***(1 Corinthians 9:13-15)***. His principle form of income was derived from making tallitot (little tents) out of goat's hair [aka prayer shawls ***(Acts 18:3)***].

Three years from the time of his conversion, Rabbi Sha'ul goes to Jerusalem and meets Yaakov (James) and Kepha (Peter) ***(Galatians 1:13-24)***. He requests to join them, but is only accepted when another talmidim called Barnabas intercedes on his behalf. Because of Sha'ul's reputation they were all understandably afraid of him ***(Acts 9:26-27)***.

Trouble seemed to follow him as he is sent back to Tarsus after having disputes with various goyim (gentiles). Fourteen years after his conversion, Sha'ul returns to Jerusalem, where Barnabas eventually finds him and has him brought to Antioch ***(Act 11:26)***. Antioch had become a refuge for believers after the death of Stephenos. One could only imagine the level of apprehension among believers there when they heard that Sha'ul was coming. It was here and at this time that followers were first called "cretins" (Christians).

Upon hearing of a famine in Judaea, Rabbi Sha'ul, Barnabas and another convert called Titus go there to render financial assistance from funds raised at Antioch.

Sha'ul testifies to have met a post-resurrected Yahshua, after Kepha (Cephus), the twelve (talmidim) and five hundred. ***1 Corinthians 15:8; "And last of all He was seen by me also, ignorant and imperfectly trained as I was."*** Of Yahshua's original twelve talmidim, he only met and took counsel with Ya'akov (James, Yahshua's brother) and Kepha (Peter).

Rabbi Sha'ul died in Rome during the time of Emperor Nero's persecution. He remains the most debated and disagreed upon individual in the Scriptures both among not only Jews and Christians, but among many rival Christian denominations as well. Some Christian sects even venerate Sha'ul's teachings above the Torah and say they follow him as if his teachings differ in some way. ***1 Corinthian 3:4-7; "For while one says, I am of Shaul; and another, I am of Apollos; are you not still worldly? Who then is Shaul, and who is Apollos, but avadim (servants) through whom you believed, even as the Master YHWH gave to every man? I have planted, Apollos gave mayim (water); but YHWH gave the increased growth. So then neither is he that plants anything, neither he that gives mayim (water) anything; but YHWH who gives the increase."***

Rabbi Sha'ul was a man of conviction who honoured the various degrees of knowledge that the Almighty imparted to him. There has been much written about him. Some writers have said he was a tortured man who committed a transgression in his youth and disciplined his Evil Inclination. Others say he was of very short physical stature. Whatever the case, the Scriptures attest that he was a content man regardless of circumstance. ***Philippians 4:10-13; "But I had gilah (Joy) in YHWH greatly, that now recently your care and concern for me has been revived again; though you were concerned in the past, but you lacked the means. Not that I speak in respect of*** *want: for I have learned, in whatever state I am in to be content. I know what it is to be poor, and I know what it is to be rich: I have gone through and experienced many things, both to be full and to be hungry, to have plenty and be in want. I have the strength to do all things through Moshiach who strengthens me."*

Who was Sha'ul? ***"…YHWH said…'for he is a chosen vessel to Me, to bear My Name before the nations, and melechim (kings), and the children of Yisrael.'" (Acts 9:15)***

Chapter Fourteen

Meditation – Mind Field or Minefield?

> "In Hebrew thought, to meditate upon the Scriptures is to quietly repeat them in a soft, droning sound, while utterly abandoning outside distractions. From this tradition comes a specialized type of Jewish prayer called "davening," that is, reciting texts (and) praying intense prayers....while bowing or rocking back and forth. Evidently this dynamic form of meditation-prayer goes back to David's time." – Footnote from *The Spirit Filled Life Bible* (Edited by Pastor Jack Hayford)

Philippians 4:8,9; "Finally, Yisraelite brothers, whatever things are emet (truth), whatever things are honest, whatever things are just, whatever things are pure, whatever things are lovely, whatever things are of tov (good) report; if there be any virtue, and if there be any tehilla (praise), think (or meditate) on these things. Those things, which you have both learned, and received, and heard, and seen in me, do: and the Elohim of Shalom shall be with you."

Christianity, Judaism and Islam are not normally associated as being meditative based religions. However many believers within all three Abrahamic faiths practice various forms of prayerful and contemplative states that can be classed as meditation. The most extreme meditation focused sects within these religions consist of Gnostics (Christianity), Sufis (Islam) and Hassidim (Judaism). These sects range from being rejected, tolerated or celebrated by the greater majority of their own religious community.

Orthodox Judaism largely questions any discipline that exclusively relies on a self-induced mental or physical technique to gain spiritual enlightenment. Those in disagreement with this view often cite the contemplative nature of Scripture and the mystical characteristics of Kabbalah as evidence that transcendental style meditation is rooted in the faith of YHWH. Another common defence for meditation is its constant reference in the Bible. Depending on the translation, it is mentioned approximately twenty times throughout Scripture. But many of these references come down to translator preference and are utilised to stress deep contemplative states that are strictly attached to prayer or directly espoused from absorbing the Word of YHWH. For example, most modern Bible translations handle ***Philippians 4:8*** with the conclusion, "***...meditate on these things***" which in context means to think. Grammatically the term "meditate" is perfectly legal in this context. The debate as to whether meditation is Scriptural has more to do with its generally perceived definition than the inclusion of the word in a Bible.

Firstly, what is meditation? According to the dictionary it is, "a practice of concentrated focus upon a sound, object, visualization, breath, movement, or attention itself in order to increase awareness of the present moment, reduce stress, promote relaxation, and enhance personal and spiritual growth."

Ancient Kabbalah and Hasidic writings do support a specific practice of gaining understanding through intense logical reflection that can technically be defined as meditation. But neither Judaism nor Kabbalah subscribe to any intense concentrated state as having the potential to achieve sudden spiritual enlightenment **in its own right**. Rather the view is that illumination must come from intense reflection on initial insights that have already been gleaned from the Torah. This can be likened to an animal that chews its own regurgitated food so as to digest it in a more complete manner.

The process that can be most likened to meditation is an ancient form of solitary prayer and reflection known as 'hidbodeidut.' The word "hidbodeidut" comes from the Hebrew word "boded," meaning "a state of being alone," and describes the process of making oneself understand through analytical study. The great Jewish sage Rambam (Maimonides) talks about this method of prayer in his code of Jewish law. He describes hidbodeidut as prayer as it was originally practised prior to the advent of a formal liturgy service (3rd century B.C.E. -- Rambam, *Mishneh Torah, Hilkhot Tefilah* 1:2-4). Prayer services were introduced by the Great Assembly (Great Synagogue) that commenced from the end of the time of the prophets and continued through to the development of Rabbinic Judaism. According to Sanhedrin Law, this original form of prayer is still considered as most beneficial.

Isaac Meditating or Manifesting? - Opening a Can of Worms

Genesis 24:63 is often cited as a support text for meditation. ***"And Yitzchak went out to meditate in the field in the evening: and he lifted up his eyes and saw, and, see the camels were coming."*** This verse is almost universally agreed upon as being evidence of meditative prayer and is even understood by many Jewish scholars as the earliest Scriptural account of hidbodeidut. However, the actual Hebrew word for meditation in this verse is *lasuach* and is not marshalled by translators to mean meditation, meditating or meditates anywhere else in Scripture. A look at the first entry under "meditate" in *The New Strong's Exhaustive Concordance* (page 693, 1990 Edition) will yield no corresponding reference number. Some authoritative Jewish commentators suggest that the word means "to speak," (as in to speak with YHWH in prayer) but they also admit that its meaning is not obvious. Others speculate that it means to "discuss," "enjoy" or "to supplicate."

Lasuach actually means "gathering" or "forming." Its root word is "siach," which means "growth." What was Isaac actually doing in the field and why are the rabbis so speculative about the meaning of a word that is commonly understood to mean meditation? The answer is that Isaac was actually physically resurrecting before the very eyes of Rivka (Rebecca) as she approached, causing her to fall off her camel. This is why she is prompted to say, *"What is this man who is walking in the field to meet us?"*

Question: Are you saying that Isaac was being raised from the dead? If so, how could this be?

Answer: Isaac becomes mysteriously absent from the Scriptures after his father Abraham binds him up as an offering. It is not until ***Genesis 24:62***, which describes him as coming ***"from the way of the well Lachai-Roei"*** and having dwelt formerly ***"in the south country"*** that he appears again in the narrative. The term "Lachai-Roei" literally means "the tunnel of light from which He (YHWH) sees me." When people have near death experiences, they nearly always describe themselves as travelling down a tunnel toward a bright light. The rabbis refer to this light at the end of the tunnel as "the eye of YHWH." The "south country" is a reference to "*Sheol*," the place of the dead.

Question: If this is true and *lasuach* does not mean meditating, but "forming," as in resurrecting, are you suggesting that Abraham actually killed Isaac even though the Scriptures say he didn't?

Answer: The answer is "yes" to the first part of the question and "no" to the second part. Let's go to Scripture and see if Abraham refrained from offering him up. Look at the verse regarding Abraham's sacrifice of Isaac in ***Hebrews 11:17-19; "By emunah (faith) Avraham, when he was tried, offered up Yitzchak: and he that had received the promises offered up his only brought-forth son, Of whom it was said, That in Yitzchak shall your zera (seed) be called: Accounting that YHWH was able to raise him up, even from the dead; from where also he received Him in a (paraboloa) figure."*** A better translation of the last word "figure" is "perfect type" because the Greek word used here is "paraboloa." The meaning of "para" is "alongside" and the meaning of "bola" is "to cast." This is the origin of the English word "parable," which means a story that figuratively explains a specific message. The message in this instance is the coming death and resurrection of Messiah. Isaac couldn't have been a figure, parable or perfect type of Yahshua unless he actually died and was raised.

When the messenger of YHWH told Abraham to cease offering Isaac it was not the killer thrust that was intervened, but the subsequent dissection and incineration of his son's body. In ***Genesis 22:13*** a ram caught in thorns (signifying Messiah) is placed on the altar to be burned instead of Isaac. It is debated in some circles as to whether Isaac's body was burned with the ram or removed and buried. This author subscribes to him being buried because later in ***Genesis 24:63*** he rises up from the earth into which he was planted. Therefore the verse should read, ***"Yitzchak went out to form ("lasuach") in the field towards evening."*** Whatever the case, Isaac was certainly not meditating at all.

Sifting Out False Meditative States

There are a million forms of meditation and variants thereof in the world today. Many of them, which are virtually impossible to categorise accurately, adopt a range of mental and physical exercises that run counter to the Word of YHWH. Meditation that is primarily aimed at focusing on physical or mental objects or actions, other than or in addition to the Torah is a subtle form of idolatry that has managed to creep into the practices of many sects from all three Abrahamic religions. As a result certain mental or physical postures can become the main focus or goal of an otherwise valid meditative state. The desire to move nearer to YHWH through prayer or reflection should not completely depend on or run second to perfecting a technique.

Meditation in its non-biblically prescribed form can most definitely provide physical and mental short and long-term benefits, but at the same time allows the dark forces to portray the spiritual realm in a slightly tilted manner that undermines certain foundational truths and has the potential to set a believer on a path to seek access to YHWH by another means. ***Matthew 7:13; "Enter in at the narrow gate: for wide is the gate, and broad is the way, that leads to destruction, and many there be who go in that gate."***

Forms of meditation that promote visualisation and uncontrolled or abandonment of thought can enhance a person's lifestyle, but ultimately leads to destruction. ***Proverbs 14:12; "There is a***

derech (way) that seems right to a man, but the ends of it are the ways of death." It is absolutely important to realise that hardship, injury or death toward all mankind is not a rule-of-thumb goal of HaSatan. On the contrary, the dark forces will provide comfort and support to an occupant if it has the benefit of solidifying a false view of a truth. ***2 Corinthians 11:14; "And no marvel: for s.a.tan himself is transformed into a malach (messenger) of light."*** A good example would be when a grieving person wishes to contact a deceased relative via participation in a séance. The dark forces will happily provide comfort to the bereaved by masquerading as the dead person's deceased loved one.

Religious or spiritually related meditation in its own right is not evil if done in a capacity that reflects, ponders or engages in contemplation of YHWH's word. ***Joshua 1:7-8; "Only be strong and very courageous, that you may shomer (observe) to do according to all Torah, which Moshe My eved (servant) commanded you: turn not from it to the right hand, or to the left, that you may prosper wherever you go. This scroll of the Torah shall not depart out of your mouth; but you shall meditate on it day and night, that you may shomer (observe) to do according to all that is written in it: for then you shall make your derech (way) prosperous, and then have tov (good) success."***

The term "meditate" can be applied to any situation. For example a businessman can say that he was meditating on the details of a financial account or a football coach can meditate on his team's match performance. As pointed out, most views toward meditation in certain Orthodox religious circles are primarily due to its generally perceived definition. If a believer was to simply say, "I was meditating," and left it at that, this would be as clear as giving the answer "food" to someone who has asked, "What's for dinner?" Meditation in the Scriptures is mostly related to contemplating the knowledge and nature of YHWH. This stated, it should come as no surprise that a number of references to meditation are found in the Psalms.

Psalms 1:1,2; "Blessed is the man that walks not in the counsel of the wicked, nor stands in the halacha (way) of sinners, nor sits in the seat of scoffers. But his delight is in the Torah of YHWH; and in His Torah does he meditate day and night."

Psalms 39:3; "My lev (heart) was hot within me, while I was meditating the fire burned; then I spoke with my tongue, YHWH make me know my end, and the measure of my days, what it is; that I may know what it is; that I may know how brief I really am."

Psalms 48:8; "We have thought of your loving chesed (kindness), O Elohim, in the midst of your Hekal (Temple)." (Most translations use the word "meditated" instead of the word "thought.")

Psalms 77:12; "I will meditate also on all Your work, and talk of Your doings."

Psalms 104:34; "My meditation on Him shall be sweet: I will be in simcha (Joy) in YHWH."

A Nazarene Israelite understands that true enlightenment can only come from a deep concentrated contemplation on Torah and that salvation can only come from obedience to it. This is because enlightenment is not the same thing as salvation. One can receive wisdom, but still fail to apply it. King Soloman (Shlomo Ha-Melech) is a primary example of what happens when a gap between enlightenment and obedience emerge. In a sense meditation in Judaism is not meditation as understood by practitioners of Hinduism, Buddhism, Yoga, Heychasm and so on, but rather meditation in its original form.

Various unscriptural meditative states include (Note that some of these states may be a by-product of hidbodeidut.):

- Upward meditation (Lifting consciousness out of body)
- Downward meditation (Heart rhythm based meditation designed to pull outside forces into the body and anchor with the heart)
- Mind-centred meditation (Evacuating the mind of all thoughts)
- Heart-centred meditation (Enhances or expands emotional capacity)
- Monastic meditation (Increase sensitivity to erase fear of death)
- In-life meditation (Exploration of humanism to increase compassion)

- Observer meditation (Focuses on thoughts and emotion, commonly used in Buddhism)
- Lover meditation (Nurtures feelings derived from physical touch or visual stimulus)
- Passive meditation (The occupant is to remain unfocused, neutral, making no judgments)
- Active meditation (Focusing the infinite into the finite. Remain in a constant self-induced meditative state)
- Fantasy-based meditation (Role-play based technique)
- Reality-based (Thoughts are limited to what the occupant knows to be absolutely true)
- Trance meditation (Mindless rhythmic chanting)
- Awakening meditation (Frequent changes in rhythmic chanting to provoke fresh enlightenment)
- Denial or Dualistic meditation (Concentration on positive thoughts)
- Inclusive meditation (Focuses on one defined reality. Goal is to focus on mortality as a opposed to immortality)

Meditation, as it is prescribed in the Scriptures, is completely acceptable. ***Psalms 19:14; "Let the words of my mouth, and the meditations of my lev (heart), be acceptable in Your sight, O YHWH, my strength, and My Redeemer."*** But learning the Scriptures by heart is the basic foundation to achieving any type of meditative state. ***Psalms 119:11*** speaks of storing YHWH's Word up in a believer's heart to avoid sinning. The Scriptures teach without exception that the Torah is the basis for all meditation. ***Psalms 119:97; "Oh how I love Your Torah! It is my meditation all the day."***

Making Sense of Kabbalah

The word Kabbalah means "to receive." It is the name for a supremely intimate or even technical understanding of the inner workings and nature of YHWH. The term itself first came into usage as early as the 10th century, though the practice has far earlier origins. Kabbalistic literature has gradually evolved from writings that come from a group of books known collectedly as *The Zohar*. These books were first published in Spain around the 13th century by Moshe ben Shem-Tov (Moshe De Leon). He based his writings on the work of his contemporaries, who in turn drew their writings from the teachings of Rabbi Simeon bar Yohai from a time preceding the destruction of the Second Temple (aka the Mishnaic period). The essence of The Zohar is that it is Torah-based commentaries and teachings on a mystical level that date back to Abraham that were passed on in a continuous chain from teacher to student until they reached the 13 hundreds.

Today, the practice of Kabbalah has been fragmented into three major disciplines. The first is called "theoretical Kabbalah," which consists of study and in-depth contemplative analysis of the Torah and scholars who were familiar with the Torah's implications on a metaphysical level. The second is called "meditative Kabbalah," which focuses on adopting physical techniques to achieve higher spiritual states. And the last is "practical Kabbalah," which predominantly takes the form of extracting aspects of Kabbalah to affect the physical and spiritual world in a completely autonomous way. This form of Kabbalah is blatant occultism and condemned according to Torah ***(Leviticus 19:31; 20 & 20:27)***. Not surprisingly, practical Kabbalah overlapped with some principles of the meditative path, is the most popular among the mainstream.

Ideally, theoretical Kabbalah should be the only method pursued by a student, because it has its basis in study, albeit on a mystical level, of YHWH's eternal Word. From this foundation, aspects of practical and meditative Kabbalah might spring forth or manifest at the Father's discretion. A servant should not work to gain access to the engine room of creation with a motive to alter any working part to suit his own end.

A true Kabbalist, as opposed to someone who dabbles or abuses Kabbalah, is a human being who has attained a constant spiritually aware union with the Creator. This same level of awareness is usually only experienced as a fleeting climax of a particularly intense prayer or encounter by most believers. A Jew who attains this level is called a tzedek which means, 'righteous person.' This does not mean that a tzedek is sinless, but that righteousness is a working principle that permeates his conduct. Righteousness according to Hebraic thought is a joyous and successful fulfillment of a demand within any given relationship, whether with man or Creator. A tzedek reaches such a high level of closeness with YHWH that he moves beyond the physical world even while he inhabits a human body. In other words a tzedek moves, speaks and acts in accordance to the movements, speeches and actions of the Father in any given situation. ***John 5:19; "...I say to you, the Son can do nothing by himself, but only what he sees the Abba (Father) doing, for the things He does, these also does the Son likewise."***

Many people steer well clear of Kabbalah for two major reasons. One is because it exhibits some facets that are reminiscent of occult practices and the other is its fad-like portrayal in popular culture, driven by the likes of Madonna and Britney Spears. Unfortunately many aspects of Kabbalah are often more familiar to people in the twisted counterpart form of astrology, tarot reading, and numerology. A lot of the arts contained in these disciplines are merely practices that have been disconnected from their roots and executed outside an ordered chain of authority that is normally facilitated by the heavenly host in full accordance with YHWH's will.

The Gospels contain the popular account of Magi utilising astrology to locate Bethlehem. But this is done in complete harmony with YHWH. Contrary to popular belief among scholars, these Magi or sorcerers where not strict Chaldean Zoroastrian priests, but a sect that had become influenced by the Jewish Diaspora in Babylon. This is supported by the prophet Daniel being made chief of the ***"wise men,"*** literally Magi, by the king of Babylon ***(Daniel 2:48)***. This means that some Magi would have most definitely been revealed the pure origins of their teachings by exiled Israelites. Further evidence can be seen in the tradition of the Merkavah whose teachings underpin the complex intricacies of Kabbalah, which was clearly inspired by the Babylonian exiled Temple priest-come-prophet Ezekiel. Ezekiel's major contribution to Kabbalah was his vision of the Merkavah, the mysterious chariot throne of YHWH. The significance of Ezekiel's vision has undergone enormous debate between scholars through the centuries, but one major revelation was that it showed that YHWH could manifest in a glorified state outside the confines of the Temple. This manifestation was a key event that is a central theme to the study and practice of Kabbalah. In short, Kabbalah is a completely acceptable discipline to study, but is rarely practiced in its fullest and most appropriate form. Many people today launch into it without having fully grasped the basics of Torah. As a consequence they build a comprehensive understanding of YHWH on a weak foundation and its collapse is inevitable. Some rabbis have written that overly intensive study of the book of Ezekiel can cause madness. Authorities in Nazarene Israelites circles have commentated that this could be because there are large quantities of materiel in Ezekiel that depict Messiah Yahshua.

Hypnotism - Delusion is the Cure

Any mental activity that encourages us to entirely clear and surrender our mind leaves us opened to potential demonic influence. This is because the process of completely erasing the mind of all things must by definition include surrendering a belief system as well. Intoxication, the aforementioned list of meditative practices, hypnotism, acupuncture and visualisation are all potential doorways for demonic influence and are all attempts at gaining enlightenment outside YHWH's will, which is set down in the Scriptures. Any teachings that cannot be espoused from Torah, especially practices that induce a person to empty or trick the mind can leave doorways open to uninvited spiritual forces that have long defected from serving as members of the heavenly host.

One thing that amazes me is the public's ever-growing fascination with hypnotism in the entertainment industry. The basic premise of most performances entails to varying degrees the interaction of audience members with the hypnotist on stage. There, under hypnosis they perform antics at the request of the performer to the amusement of the audience. The main thrust of these shows is to get people up on stage and to do things in front of a crowd that they would not normally do. There is an apparent controversy as to whether a person is doing something against his or her will. One side argues that there are fundamental dangers in an individual possessing an ability to have a subject perform actions against their will. The danger in that scenario is obvious. The other side (usually that of the hypnotists themselves) argues that, "the will cannot be violated." I have great difficulty with accepting this latter line of thought as it becomes quite clear that the main highlight of the shows is the expectations of normal people doing abnormal things (i.e., things they would not normally do) in front of a live audience. You wouldn't find it necessarily funny if old Uncle Bob danced around a stage like a chicken if that's what he normally did.

Hypnotists seem to display an ability to have subjects believe nearly anything they suggest during these performances, even to the degree of causing the occupants to hallucinate at their request. In effect a type of "trance logic" state takes over in the subject where normality can be whatever the hypnotist says it is. This practice has also become firmly entrenched in the medical fraternity, with people overcoming childhood disorders, nervousness during exams, smoking, confidence issues and so on by undergoing hypnotism. This author accepts the notion only too well that these methods of treatment, at least on the surface, appear to have a high success rate. It is not my desire to denounce this act as mere trickery. If it were such, I would not have included this topic in this work. My main concern is that the foundations of hypnotism bear strikingly close resemblances to spiritism and trance channeling. The specific danger of hypnotism is that by its very nature a state must be achieved that submerges normal evaluating abilities, heightens suggestibility, reduces rational restraint and leaves the subject's will at best in danger of being violated. Therefore if a patient's will is rerouted from a certain path that is causing them problems, the hypnotic process could also produce other negative shifts in perspective on certain issues and areas, that may not come to light for years down the track and in addition, expose a person to spiritual attack.

Posthypnotic suggestion takes the cake in terms of it being downright dangerous as it equips the hypnotist with an ability to cause a subject to do an action such as impersonate Elvis at a later time after exiting a trance. After the subject comes out of this state they act normally, then at a time previously specified by the hypnotist, the person starts "shak'n and a mov'n" like the King. The subject will be able to provide no explanation as to why they did it or be able to cease the activity unless told to do so by the hypnotist. I have been interested to read that this type of posthypnotic suggestion is evident in UFO and psychic encounters. In some cases a witness hears a beeping sound and lapses into a trance, later they awaken in a different location to a similar sound. Hours have passed in which they cannot recall any activities. In other cases witnesses see an approaching object, usually a craft of some kind, and begin to read a series of numbers clearly visible on it that immediately triggers the occupant to lapse into a trance. Months or years may pass until the correct set of numbers or letters appear again, possibly on the number plate of a passing car.

Hypnotism stems from an occult practice that is evident in many ancient cultures. Its primitive counterpart is called Shamanism, which involves inducement of a joint hallucination to achieve healing or attainment of an enlightened state. Dr. Cathy Burns, PhD, author of the publication *Hypnosis: Cure or Curse*; states that up until the late sixties, many hypnotists themselves referred to the procedure as a séance.

Chapter Fifteen

The Mechanics of Repentance

Part 1

"In the place where a repentant sinner stands, a thoroughly righteous person is not entitled to stand." – Babylonian Talmud, *Brakhot* 34b

Luke 18:9-14; "And He Spoke this parable to certain people who trusted in themselves that they were tzadik (righteous), and despised others: 'Two men went up into the Beit HaMikdash (the Temple) to make tefillah (prayer); the one a Prush (Pharisee), and the other a tax collector. The Prush (Pharisee) stood and made tefillah (prayer) within himself, 'Elohim, I thank You, that I am not as the other men are, extortionists, unjust, adulterers, or even as this tax collector. I fast twice in the week, I give tithes of all that I possess.' And the tax collector, standing far off, would not lift up so much as his eyes to the shamayim (heavens) but smote his breast, saying. 'Elohim be merciful to me a sinner.' I tell you, this man went down to his bayit (house) justified rather than the other: for everyone that exalts himself shall be humbled; and he that humbles himself shall be exalted.'"

One of the most crucial aspects of the Nazarene Israelite faith is one's ongoing spiritual condition before YHWH. The core principle that maintains a close relationship with the Father is the act of *teshuvah*, which means "to return" or "turn back." As in to "go back to" or "return to one's first love." Specifically it is a conscious return to the same pure and harmonic state that was once enjoyed by Adam and Hava. ***Hosea 14:1-2; "O Yisrael, make teshuvah (a return) to YHWH your Elohim; for you have fallen by your iniquity. Take with you words of Torah, and make teshuvah to YHWH: and say to Him, Take away all our iniquity, and receive us graciously: so will we render the bulls, the fruit of our lips."***

Most people think the word *teshuvah* means "repentance." But this view is not correct. The Hebrew word for repentance is *charatah*, which means "feeling remorse," "guilt" or "having a desire to rectify one's ways." A state of feeling repentant describes the spark that initiates *teshuvah*, but not the actual act itself.

Evil Perceived as Good

Repentance can also cause a person to cease doing good and choose evil. For example, there is an old Norse tale about a Viking who was captured by some farmers. Binding him to a tree, his captors decided to celebrate with wine, song and dance. They celebrated long into the night until all of them eventually collapsed into a drunken sleep. Meanwhile the Viking managed to get free and flee into the forest. As he ran his mind became clouded with guilt. So he returned and killed all the peasants in their sleep and departed again with a clear conscience.

Spiritual Candy

There is no shortage in the religious world of books that inspire and motivate. Literally thousands of books aimed at motivating believers through pure emotional stimulation are produced every year. Such literature administers spiritual candy and lacks any real meat to sustain a believer in a way that truly reflects a mind of someone who loves and fears YHWH with every thought, word and deed. There is nothing wrong with being inspired, but using inspiration to govern a daily walk leaves one's mental and physical conduct at the mercy of an external motivating force.

Many Christian living books are bereft of moment-by-moment instruction to help guide a believer in the routine application of the Word in daily life. Judaism tackles this dilemma head on by drawing no distinction between a person's religious and seemingly non-religious activities. Therefore studying the manner in which an Orthodox Jew conducts himself or herself on a daily basis has unparalleled value to one who desires to maintain a mindset that is constantly focused on YHWH. Within Judaism this is known as "halacha," which means "way of walking" or "conduct." This fundamental principle drives one of the two greatest commandments (mitzvoth), ***"...to love YHWH your Elohim with all your heart, soul and might" (Deuteronomy 6:5)***. Consider the following actions of an Orthodox Jew when he wakes from a night's sleep. He opens his eyes and says, *"Boruch ato Adonoy Elohaynu melech ho-olom pokay-ach ivrim"* (Blessed are you Master, our Elohim, King of the universe, who gives sight to the blind). He stretches his body and says, *"Boruch ato Adonoy Elohaynu melech ho-olom, zokayf k'fufim"* (Blessed are you Master, our Elohim, king of the universe, who straightens the bent). He climbs from his bed and stands saying, *"Boruch ato Adonoy Elohaynu melech ho-olom, roka ho-oretz al hamo-yim."* (Blessed are you Master, our Elohim, king of the universe, who spreads out the earth upon the waters). He clothes himself and says, *"Boruch ato Adonoy Elohaynu melech ho-olom malbish arumim."* (Blessed are you Master, our Elohim, king of the universe, who clothes the naked). He walks to the toilet, relieves himself and says *"Boruch ato Adonoy Elohaynu melech ho-olom, asher yotzar et ho-olom b'chochmo, u-voro vo n'kovim n'kovim, chalulim chalulim. Goluy v'yodu-a lifnay chisay ch'vodecho, she-im yiposay-ach echod mayhem, o yisosaym e-chod mayhem, i efshar l'hiska-yaym v'la-amod l'fonecho. Boruch ato Adonoy rofay chol bosor u-mafli la-atot."* (Blessed are You, Master, our Elohim, king of the universe, who fashioned man with wisdom and created within him many openings and many cavities. It is obvious and known before Your Throne of Glory that if but one of them were to be ruptured or but one of them were to be blocked it would be impossible to survive and to stand before You. Blessed are You, Master, who heals all flesh and acts wondrously.) As the Jew progresses through the day, from the time he wakes to the time he retires, he is constantly in a state of divine acknowledgment. This type of lifestyle severely encroaches upon the opportunity for sin to gain a strong foothold.

But what if sin does prevail? Most religious people know they must turn from an evil path, but they don't really comprehend what this entails. The most significant record of *teshuvah* in Scripture is found in the writings of King David (Tehillim [The Psalms]). Here are found some of the most profound words that deal with illness, strife, remorse, happiness, triumph and joy. The Psalms are a blueprint of the travail of every person. *Teshuvah* or the ability to attain right standing before the Almighty after transgression is one of the most precious gifts that mankind has been bestowed. I believe that most religious people today have yet to fully comprehend its splendour.

The Relationship Between the Human Heart and the Evil Inclination

A detailed investigation into the action of *teshuvah* cannot be fully appreciated and understood without defining the external and internal conflict that can provoke its beautiful emergence.

Psalms 109:22; "...my heart is wounded within me..."

An honest and in-depth scrutiny of one's own heart will likely expose a twisted and dark labyrinth of untold corruption and perversion that seems beyond cure. ***Jeremiah 7:19; "The lev (heart) is deceitful above all things, and desperately wicked: who can know it?" Matthew 15:19; "For out of the lev (heart) proceed evil thoughts, murders, adulteries, fornications, thefts, false witness, and blasphemies."*** Understandably there is no verse within any of the Scriptures that encourages inviting the Messiah into the foul depths of the human heart despite Christianity's popular slogan[1] to the contrary.

---

1 The catch-cry to "invite Jesus into the heart" is espoused from ***Revelations 3:20***. This verse (in context) is not a salvation directive but was aimed at existing believers to encourage greater intimacy with YHWH through Messiah. There is no verse in all of the Scriptures that describes inviting Yahshua into one's heart.

There is no goodness in a man's heart that is in exclusion to YHWH. Even the Messiah rebuked an address that stated that he was good. ***Mark 10:18[2]; "And Yahshua said to him, 'Why do you call me tov (good)? There is none tov (good) but One, that is YHWH.'"*** Man, left to his own devices and without YHWH's guidance, will always gravitate toward evil. Anything that is of one's self that is not of YHWH is inherently wicked. To overcome this natural inclination to think and do evil a believer is to strive to have YHWH's will "increase" or "invade" his heart, soul and mind, and have his own will "decrease" or "retreat" accordingly. ***John 3:30,31; "He must increase, but I must decrease. He that comes from above is above all. He that is of the earth is earthly and speaks of the earth: He that comes from the shamayim (heavens) is above all."***

Question: But even a wicked person gives good gifts to their children ***(Matthew 7:11)***. Surely this is a sign of some goodness even in one who is inherently evil?

Answer: No it is not! The motive for providing for family members, in particular one's own children can range from appeasing the conscience (the most common), to pride, to seeking the praise of others or for conditional reasons (i.e., as long as the kids remain appreciative). A person who walks in righteousness performs acts of kindness purely motivated by loving obedience to YHWH's Torah, without any desire for human reciprocity or recognition. Jewish wisdom teaches that all believers should "do good beyond reason" in direct opposition to evil beyond reason. If the Evil Inclination compels one to do evil in secret, the Good Inclination should dominate and compel one to do good in secret. There's nothing wrong with a secret life, as long as it's full of mitzvoth (love deeds).

An unbeliever's definition of what is good outside the Torah's definition of what is good is guided by a conscience that is driven by the desires of the heart, which blows like a leaf in different seasons. Imagine the hesitancy of an ancient Israelite soldier who has

---

2 There are two dominant schools of thought as to the meaning of Yahshua's statement. One is that he was referring to his period of temptation where his body tried unsuccessfully to betray him ***(Matthew 4:1)*** and the other is that he was clarifying that all goodness comes from the Father in whom there is only one. Yahshua refers to himself as ***"the good Shepherd"*** in ***John 10:11***, which illustrates his complete unity or oneness with the Father. Yahshua may have suspected that his questioner was singling him out as good in isolation from the Father.

to slay pagan women, children and babies under YHWH's directive in ***1 Samuel 15:3*** if he was relying on his own moral judgment. Or if Abraham relied on his own conscience and refused to bind and slaughter his only son. If a believer orders his life via his own conscience he inhibits himself in his service to the Eternal King of the Universe.

The human conscience is no refuge for measuring goodness because it may vary depending on many external factors. But knowledge and obedience (no matter how rudimentary) of YHWH's Word (the Torah) always meets or strives to meet an immovable morally set-apart standard. ***2 Peter 1:2,3; "Favour and shalom (peace) be multiplied to you through da'at (knowledge) of YHWH, and of Yahshua our Master, according as His divine power has given to use all things that pertain to chayim (life) and Shabbat-guarding piety, through the da'at (knowledge) of Him that has called us to tifereth (glory) and power."***

Obedience to YHWH without knowledge of the manner in which He wishes to be obeyed is at best counterproductive and at worse, dangerous. ***Romans 10:2; "For I bear them record that they have a zeal for YHWH, but not according to da'at (knowledge). For they being ignorant of YHWH's tzedakah (righteousness), go about to establish their own tzedakah (righteousness), have not submitted themselves to the tzedakah (righteousness) of YHWH."*** The golden calf incident ***(Exodus 32:9)*** and YHWH's reaction to Aaron's two sons' conduct in the Tabernacle are testimony ***(Leviticus 10:1,2)*** to this truth.

Noble acts motivated to atone for sin outside the Creator's eternally prescribed method are not only insufficient, but are equated "***...as an unclean thing...***"This is because "... ***all our tzedakah (charity or righteousness) are as filthy rags, and we all do fade as a leaf; and our iniquities, like the wind, have taken us away." (Isaiah 64:6)*** A Hebrew understanding of the term "filthy rag" strengthens the message, because it meant a used menstrual cloth.

The desire to do evil is present in a man's heart from a young age. ***Genesis 8:21,22; "and YHWH smelled a sweet fragrance; and YHWH said in His lev (heart), I will not again curse the ground any more for man's sake; for the imagination of man's lev (heart) is evil from his youth..."*** The great Jewish sages wrote that if any man argues that no mortal can avoid sin and therefore has justification to entertain it, the answer is:

> "How many things in the world are even less bearable and more bitter than the impulse to (do) evil, yet you manage to sweeten them. Nothing is more bitter than the lupine, and yet, in order to sweeten it, you carefully boil it in water seven times, until it becomes sweet. Now, if you sweeten for your need bitter things that I alone created, all the greater is your responsibility for the impulse to (avoid) evil, which was placed under your control." - Avot D'Rabbi Natan 16

In the Hebrew language the desire to commit evil is called the "yetzer harah" (the Evil Inclination). When this inclination is creatively explored it can eventually spread from one individual to another until, like wildfire, it reaches a cultural climate not unlike that described in Noah's day, as described in ***Genesis 6:5; "And Elohim saw that the wickedness of man was great in the earth...*** " Eventually one evil thought attracts another evil thought until the mind meditates perpetually on wickedness. "...***every imagination of the thoughts of his lev (heart) was only evil continually.*** " Furthermore, Scripture records that in the day of Messiah's return it will also be, ***"...as it was in the days of Noach (Noah)..." (Luke 17:26).***

When a believer begins to live out of the Evil Inclination and reject the Good Inclination YHWH withdraws His presence. Though this is often unnoticeable at first it causes spiritual sickness and physical grief and eventually death. In the meantime countless physical or mental side effects can manifest in ways that range from subtle to extreme.

But through *teshuvah* (return), which takes the form of an appeal to YHWH's mercy, an invoking of His promise to Abraham and embracing the precious blood of Messiah, the path to forgiveness and salvation is reawakened. As life is in the blood and the penalty for sin is death, blood acts as a substitute to the penalty of death which is brought about through sin. *Teshuvah* ever so gently edges the believer back into the presence of the Master.

When the Torah was formally given to the nation of Israel, the Renewed Covenant was also established, first in ***Deuteronomy 10:16*** and then in ***Jeremiah 31:31-34*** & ***32:40-44***. This solidified

Israel's opportunity to seek *teshuvah* or invoke the law of return after having transgressed.

Israel always recognised a future atoning work that would be accomplished by a Messiah. Acknowledging this Deliverer has always been a key factor in performing *teshuvah* for the Israelite then and the Orthodox Jew today. The manner in which this atoning work would be enacted was illustrated in Abraham's offering up of Isaac. To avoid all of Israel falling for false Messiahs, the manner in which he would arrive was uniquely recorded in ***Isaiah 7:14; "Therefore YHWH Himself shall give you an ot (sign); See, the virgin shall conceive, and bear a Son, and call His Name Emanu-El."*** Unfortunately this verse has not stopped prominent rabbis[3] from pursuing a false interpretation, which has ultimately led to disastrous consequences. It is supremely important to remember that Messiah's sacrifice and resurrection to bring about salvation was planned even before the creation of mankind.

The Mitzvah to love YHWH with all the heart is an appeal to reach out to Him with both the Good and Evil Inclination. Just as the neck is stiff, the human heart is hard and needs to be filled with the knowledge of Torah. YHWH notices when a person seeks Him diligently and over time provides them with a new heart ***(Jeremiah 24:7)***.

The Eye - The Primary Sense that Causes Sin

> ***"All things are wearisome; man is not satisfied with utterance: the eye is not satisfied with seeing, nor the ear filled with hearing." – Ecclesiastes 1:8***

The human eye is the most exquisite of all the body's organs. It is the only body part that can function at one hundred percent capacity without rest. The eye is also responsible for an average of eighty-five percent of a person's total knowledge and, aside from the brain, is the most complex organ in the human body. In an average lifetime the human eye will take in twenty-four million images.

3 Bar Kokhba's rebellion against the Roman Empire. The influential Rabbi Akiva convinced the Sanhedrin to support commander Simon Bar Kokhba as the Messiah. He cited the verse from ***Numbers 24:17: "There shall come a star out of Jacob"*** ("Bar Kokhba" means "son of a star" in Aramaic).

This all sounds impressive, but what really makes the eye unique above all the other senses is its ability to present constant complex visual stimulus to the viewer. Sight is the most vital sense a human being possesses, because it essentially enables a person to navigate their way through life in the manner that the Almighty intended.

It is not hard to see why Yahshua's acts of restoring sight commanded unequalled attention amongst the multitudes. The Scriptures do not list every recipient of this type of healing, but show a good cross section of standout cases. ***Mark 8:22-26*** [one man healed], ***Luke 18:42, Mark 10:46-52*** [blind beggar healed], ***Matthew 9:27-35*** [two blind men healed], ***Matthew 12:22-32*** [one blind, mute, demon possessed man healed], ***Matthew 15:29-31*** [multiple blind, maimed, mute and lame healed] ***Matthew 20:29-34*** [two blind men healed], ***Matthew 21:14*** [multiple blind in Temple healed], ***John 9*** [one blind man healed]). The value of sight being restored to a mortal is second only to the miracle of being resurrected. Though Orthodox Judaism points out that miracle working should not be regarded as validation for authenticity of a ministry it should be stated that Hasidic Jews (a sect within Judaism) have a long history of miracle working rabbis[4]. The correct view is that miracles ALONE should not be used as singular proof of divine authority.

The eye sees an image and the heart responds by adding emotional depth to it. The heart works in tandem with the eye. It associates a certain feeling or desire with what the eye sees. For example, a deployed soldier will find an amplified sense of comfort if he looks at a photograph of a precious loved one. But without the assistance of that image he would be unable to attain the same level of emotional recollection. The heart naturally associates emotional experiences with visual imagery. Once an image is beheld it reaches a threshold in provoking an emotional response. Moshe knew of Israel's adultery, but it wasn't until his eye saw it that he broke the tablets on which the Ten Commandments were etched. Anatomically the eye and the heart are far removed, but in the spirit realm

4 Hasidism believed that the *Ba'al Shem Tov* (Rabbi Yisrael ben Eliezer) and some of his talmidim performed miracles. Stories of their miracles are an integral part of Hasidic literature.

they are closely connected. This is why the eye and the heart are sometimes mentioned within Scripture as being in close proximity.

The human eye is the primary organ that causes sin to enter the heart. It is interesting to note that if all five senses were withdrawn every avenue for sin to enter the body would be completely obliterated. There is an ancient Jewish story that relates one man's determination to attain complete mastery over the Evil Inclination that concerns the eye.

> "...Rabbi Matia ben Heresh...was rich and feared Heaven and...sat all his days in the house of study occupying himself with Torah. Now, the splendor of his countenance shone like the radiance of the sun, and the beauty of his features resembled that of the ministering angels. It was said of him that never in his life had he raised his eyes upon a woman."
>
> "Once, Satan passed by and, seeing him, was overcome with envy as he said: Is it possible that there is a righteous man entirely without sin in the world? At once he went up to the height above, stood before the Holy One, and said, "Master of the universe, Matia ben Heresh: what sort of man is he in Your sight? God: 'He is utterly righteous.' Satan: 'Give me permission, and I will test him.' God: 'You will not prevail over him.' Satan: 'Nevertheless!' So God gave him permission."
>
> "Satan went and found R. Matia seated and occupied with Torah. So he appeared to him in the guise of a beautiful woman, the like of which there had not been in the world since the days of Naamah, Tubal-Cain's sister, on account of whom ministering angels went astray. Satan stood in front of R. Matia, who, upon seeing him, turned his back to him. Satan went around and again stood in front of R. Matia. When R. Matia turned his face to still another direction, Satan was once more in front of him. When R. Matia saw that Satan [in the woman's guise] turned up on all sides, he said to himself: I fear that the impulse to evil will gain mastery over me and cause me to sin. What did that righteous man do then? He summoned one of his disciples, who acted as his attendant, and said to him: My son, go and

bring me fire and nails. After he brought them, R. Matia passed the nails through the fire, then plunged them into his own eyes. When Satan saw this, he was shaken, all but knocked out, and left R. Matia. In that instant, the Holy One summoned Raphael, prince of healings, and said to him, 'Go and heal the eyes of Matia ben Heresh.'"

"When Raphael came and stood before him, Matia asked, 'Who are you?' Raphael answered, 'I am the angel Raphael, whom the Holy One had sent to heal your eyes.' Matia: 'Let me be. What happened has happened.' Raphael returned to the Holy One and reported to Him, 'Master of the universe, thus-and-thus did Matia ben Heresh answer me.' The Holy One said, 'Go and tell him: From this day and henceforth, fear not. I guarantee you in this matter that, throughout your days, the impulse to evil will have no sway over you.' When Matia ben Heresh heard God's guarantee from the angel, he was willing to accept the angel's healing and was healed." - Tanchuma

The above story of Rabbi Matia ben Heresh is a remarkable one because it exhibits such an extreme level of determination to triumph over the Evil Inclination. It also brings into context some of Yahshua's most difficult teachings.

Matthew 5:28,29; "And I say to you, That whoever looks on a woman to lust after her has committed adultery[5] with her already in his lev (heart). And if your right eye seduces you, pluck it out, and cast it from you: for it is better for you that one of your members should perish, than your whole body to be cast into Gei-Hinnon (Hell)." Matthew 18:9; "And if your eye offends you, pluck it out and cast it from you: it is better for you to enter into chayim (life) with one eye, rather than giving two eyes to be cast into GeiHinnom fire (hell)."

Popular teachings about Samson tend to focus on his strength and his hair, but the real heart of the story is to do with his eyes. Samson was a Nazarite from birth who dealt with the Philistines in a way that caused him to sin. He had been deceived after the

5 It is the same as adultery if the physical refrain from doing it is maintained only through lack of opportunity. Physically restraining oneself from an unlawful act that manifests in the heart is venerable. For example, the mitzvah (commandment) to refrain from murder is only fulfilled when the desire to do it is overcome.

manner of Hava in the Garden ***(Genesis 3:6)***, which led to his enemies taking away his sight and his freedom. It is worth noting that it wasn't until Samson's offending eye had been plucked out ***(Mark 9:47)*** that he obtained TOTAL victory over all his enemies ***(Judges 16:28)***. The Scriptures relate that "...***those who he killed at his death were more than those that he killed in his chayim (life).***" This is an amazing testimony because this was a man who had once personally slain a thousand men in a single encounter ***(Judges 15:15)***. The rabbis wrote that Samson was lame in both feet, but when the Ruach (Spirit) fell upon him he would have the strength of an entire army. Can you imagine someone trying to convince Samson, after having slain so many Philistines, that he would one day kill even more whilst blinded and in captivity?

YHWH doesn't want every believer who has ever been enticed away by the lust of his eye to physically remove them, but in rare cases it may be permissible. Certainly if an individual's loss of sight would cause hardship to dependents it wouldn't be acceptable. It must be noted that self-mutilation is against Torah, but in the case of following after the lust of the eye - removing them is an absolute last resort that requires careful counsel before YHWH. Matia ben Heresh's disciple is referred to as his "attendant" before his sight is removed. So his blind state would have added no significant burden to his students who already tended his every need.

Lustfully Speaking

The eye serves as an efficient tool to provoke the observer to become captivated. This captivation serves as an entry point for lust to enter the heart. From there lust eventually manifests into actions ranging from (but not limited to) gambling, alcoholism, drugs and sexual immoral activity. Some manifestations may even take the form of retail therapy (materialism) or even overeating (gluttony). Such actions cause a recipient to regularly seek temporal peaks of satisfaction. Because there is a void in every man's heart that can only be satisfactorily filled with the knowledge and love of YHWH, these peaks repetitively demand and slowly demand greater levels of input to maintain the same level of satisfaction. Eventually, this activity becomes an addiction as it governs the conduct of its host.

Immoral sexual activity is the most widespread manifestation of uncontrolled lust in present times. What is alarming about this is that it is barely addressed within most religious circles including the Messianic community.

The physical appearance of a beautiful woman generally sparks a strong emotional reaction in a male. Though such initial reactions feel intense and potentially long lasting, they are always short lived. Attaching one's thought process to the intellect rather than emotion shatters the illusion of a long term desire as the viewer realises that his longing for the woman is only fleeting. Frequent Torah study strengthens the desire for the mind to follow after the intellect and causes the occupant to seek wisdom rather than pursue emotional highs.

According to Merriam Webster's dictionary lust is "an intense longing; a strong wish for something; desire; appetite; craving; longing; passion; urge; compulsion; impulse; want or greed."

Lust is a natural urge that is primarily driven by the Evil Inclination. It is inherent in both men and women. According to one Midrash this desire has a necessary function. For "were it not for the yetzer hara (the evil urge), a man would not build a house, take a wife, beget children, or engage in commerce." Though lust is driven by the Evil Inclination it is essential for procreation and reinforcing marital relations. Taking pleasure in sexual activity within the context of a marriage is a mitzvah (commandment). Rabbi Joseph Telushkin writes in his book *Jewish Wisdom*, "...the Talmud never associated saintliness with a dormant libido." Therefore it is good for a man, even a sage, to take a wife so that he might be able to release any lustful urges upon her within the sanctity of the marriage bed. ***1 Corinthians 9; "But if you do not have self control, let them marry: for it is better to marry than to burn with passion."*** Lust between husband and wife is not only permissible, but Scriptural. In fact it is as important an emotion to exercise as the act of cherishing. Those few believers who are gifted as Sha'ul was with the ability to remain single are very fortunate because they are naturally able to channel their desires into the things of YHWH, thus serving Him with both the Good and Evil Inclination.

A man and a woman are obliged to passionately desire one another. Sexual desire is no more evil than hunger or thirst. The

Mitzvah that forbids coveting (longing for) a neighbour's wife by implication means that a husband should covet his own wife.

According to the sages, Moshe initially refused the donation of women's hand mirrors to be used for the priests' washing basin in the Tabernacle. This was because their former purpose was to increase marital lust. YHWH told Moshe that they were sacred because they strengthened the attachment between husband and wife. The Talmud frequently describes men as being particularly prone to lust and forbidden sexual desires. Women on the other hand are regarded as generally being less disposed to succumbing to lustful behaviour.

Complete failure to wrestle temptations into submission binds and poisons the heart. It deludes the mind and leads to ever increasing misguided courses of action. This in turn sets in motion a chain reaction of diminished returns as the appeasement of the craving increases in value to retain the same level of temporary satisfaction. This evolves into a repetitive action that consumes the individual. That individual turns into a slave to that desire not unlike a drug addict that loses the ability to comprehend any level of moral rationale.

Pornography

> ***"I have made a (brit) covenant with my eyes; why then should I think on a maid?" (Job 31:1)***

Pornography is a fifty-seven billion dollar ($57.0b) worldwide industry. The US makes up twelve billion dollars of this figure alone. The total revenue of the US porn industry is larger than all the combined revenues of its professional football, baseball and basketball franchises. The US accumulated two point eight four billion dollars ($2.84b) in revenue on porn sites alone in 2006. American porn exceeds the combined revenues of ABC, CBS, and NBC, which equals six point two billion dollars ($6.2b). According to the Family Safe Media Website, child pornography generates an annual revenue of three billion dollars.

On a daily basis the World Wide Web processes around sixty-eight million search engine requests for pornography. There were three hundred and seventy-two million porn sites on the web as of 2006. Eighty-nine percent of these were produced by the US. It is estimated that a child's first exposure to internet pornography occurs at around eleven years of age.

The word pornography comes from the Greek word "porneia," which covers all forms of sexual immorality. It literally means "to act the harlot" or "to partake in unlawful lust." Interestingly, lust in itself is not a sin, but a desire fuelled by the Evil Inclination that can be put to productive use between a husband and wife.

Pornography, that is the production and distribution of explicit sexual images, is a global epidemic that robs millions of people of healthy and fulfilling lives. It flourishes in all environments including religious ones. It is intrinsically soulless and devoid of obligation or promise. Pornography's ultimate effect is exhibited here in an extract from Ezekiel's writings with crystal clear clarity. ***Ezekiel 23:14-20; "And that she increased her whoring: for when she saw men portrayed upon the wall, the images of the Chaldeans portrayed in red, Girded with belts upon their loins, flowing turbans on their heads, all of them looking like leaders, after the manner of the Babylonians of Chaldea, the land of their birth: And as soon as she saw them with her eyes, she lusted upon them, and sent messengers to seek them into Chaldea. And the Babylonians came to her into her bed of ahava, and they defiled her with their whoring, and she was defiled with them, and her being was alienated from them in disgust. So she uncovered her whoring, and uncovered her nakedness: then My being was alienated from her, like my being was alienated from her sister. yet she multiplied her whoring, in calling to remembrance the days of her youth, in which she had played the harlot in the land of Mitzrayim (Egypt). For she lusted after her lovers, whose flesh is as the flesh of donkeys, and whose emission is like the emission of horses."***

The following verse is recommended to be displayed over all audio visual apparatus in a dwelling: ***"I will set no wicked thing before my eyes..." (Psalm 101:3)***

The Mechanics of Repentance Part 2

On the Same Page as a Demon

A Nazarene Israelite must learn to constantly look ahead to the coming age of Messiah, forget those things that are behind and press on toward the goal. ***Philippians 3:13-14; "...forgetting those things that are behind me...and strive for those things that are yet before me, I press on toward the goal for the prize of victory of the high calling of YHWH in Moshiach Yahshua."*** Like anything else, striving to maintain this focus takes practice.

Having belief alone is good, but it does not magically manifest an inexhaustible ability to overcome the Evil Inclination. Intellectual belief in the Scriptures merely introduces a person to the same fundamental level of understanding that is inherent in a demon. ***James 2:19; "You believe that there is Elohim Echad (One Elohim); you do well: <u>the shadim (demons) also believe, and tremble</u>."*** It is Torah obedience that sets a believer apart and enables the application of YHWH's unmerited power to take root ***(Romans 1:5)***. But an obedient walk can lack the characteristic of trembling that even demons can exhibit.

The Lack of Trembling and the Pride of Life

> ***Proverbs 8;13; "The Fear of YHWH is to hate evil: pride, and arrogance, and the evil derech (path), and the perverted mouth, that I do hate."***

Within the church and even some Messianic communities today there is a widespread lack of fear of YHWH. This climate has caused a 'pride of life syndrome' to flourish. Pride is something that affects a believer's whole perception of their actual spiritual state before the Almighty. Therefore it gets equal billing with the lust of the eye and the lust of the flesh within the Scriptures. ***I John 2:16;***

"For all that is in the olam hazeh (world); the lust of the flesh, lust of the eyes, and the pride of chayim (life); is not of Abba (Father) but is of the olam hazeh (world)."

Consider the following scenario: A believer comes to another believer in confidence and admits to having a problem with a particular sin and is responded to with, "Are you still having problems with that? Oh my, I overcame that sin years ago." On the rare occasion that such an encounter like this should occur, the person fulfilling ***James 5:16*** by confessing his sin, ***"one to another"*** is trodden mercilessly underfoot by the recipient's high and mighty response. Instead of looking to restore a fallen member of the Covenant with dignity and respect, the hearer predominantly sees the confession as an opportunity to elevate himself to new heights of self-righteousness.

Pride is the chief stumbling block to humility. Without humility, even an observant believer can be disqualified from receiving YHWH's favour. ***1 Peter 5:5; "Likewise, you younger Yisraelites, submit to the shamashim (elders). Yes, all of you are to be subject one to another, and be clothed with humility: for YHWH resists the proud, and gives favour to the humble."***

Pride opens the door to arrogance. Arrogance leads to exaggerating one's own self worth and downplaying the achievements of others, which ultimately affects a person's ability to maintain reasonable communication. Pride is often mentioned in close proximity to arrogance in the Scriptures ***(2 Chronicles 25:19, Psalm 31:18, Proverbs 21:24, Isaiah 9:9, Jeremiah 48:29, & Daniel 5:20)*** and is equated with idolatry in ***1 Samuel 15:23***. Believers shouldn't look to take pride in anything; instead they should 'take pleasure.'

Don't Look Back

It is very easy to get caught up in the sentimental recollection of past glory days; to sit and reflect with a heart that looks back fondly at the days of one's youth. Though such times may have overflowed with outward appeal, the thought of actually going back there without the knowledge one has acquired in maturity quickly drains these recollections of their lustre.

Lot's wife looked back at the forbidden world of Sodom with spellbound eyes just for a moment and was no more ***(Genesis 19:26)***. Her death was not simply due to disobeying an angel's instruction. It was the way she looked back, with eyes eager to catch one last glimpse of a way of life to which she had grown accustomed. When a believer takes his eyes off Messiah he begins to sink amid the waves as things that are contrary to the kingdom begin to pull him down ***(Mark 4:19)***.

When one comes across an image that causes lust, the reaction to turn away must be quick. Instinctively a man wants to look at a beautiful woman disrobing and bathing herself. Seeing such a sight causes the heart of a man to leap and there is pleasure in it for a time. If any man says that there is no instant pleasure in sexually related sin then he is a liar. But this sin produces only a temporary satisfaction that gradually poisons and corrupts heart and soul.

The ability to turn away and remove oneself from a compromising situation is crucial. ***1 Corinthians 6:18*** says ***"Flee!"*** YHWH wants us to make no bones about it. A man cannot negotiate a situation while his gaze is fixed on a scantily clad woman swinging around a fireman's pole. ***2 Timothy 2:22; "Flee also youthful lusts: but follow righteousness, emunah (faith), ahava (love), shalom (peace), with them that call on YHWH out of a pure lev (heart)."***

A fascinating aspect of YHWH's Torah is the commandment for wearing tzitziot. That is tekhelet blue and white threads or tassels that hang from a four cornered garment that is to be personally worn by all believers. The four cornered garment's purpose is to support the tzitziot which hang from it and constantly remind the wearer of YHWH's commandments. ***Numbers 15:38; "...they shall make for themselves fringes on the corners of their garments, throughout their generations, and they shall affix a thread of blue (Hebrew: תכלת - tekhelet) on the fringe of each corner."*** If an immoral sexual act is about to occur to one who is clothed in tzitziot, the tassels must be lifted up and in so doing physically remind the wearer of YHWH's Torah. ***Numbers 15:39; "They shall be to you for a tzitzit, that you may look upon it, and remember all the mitzvoth (love deed) of YHWH, and be kadosh (set-apart) to your Elohim."***

Habitual Sin

"The Evil Urge begins like a guest and proceeds like the host." - Isaac Nappaha, Genesis Rabbah 22.6

Habitual sin is a lifestyle plagued by chronic transgression. The power of this sin is chiefly derived from a nurtured repetitious action that, over time, has become deeply ingrained into the fabric of a person's behaviour. In other words, it is sin that has become customary. Sha'ul was acquainted with the heartache of bearing a repeated transgression. ***Romans 7:14-24; "For we know that the Torah is full of the Ruach (Spirit): but I am of the flesh, sold under sin. For I do not know what is going on: for what I purpose to do in obeying Torah, that I do not do; but what I hate in the olam hazeh (present world), that I wind up doing. If then I do that which I do not want to do, I consent to the Torah that is tov (good)."*** In his letter to the Ephesians Sha'ul likens habitual sin to an "old man" that is to be "put off." ***Ephesians 4:21-22; "If you have heard about Him, and have been taught by Him, as the emet (truth) is in Yahshua. That you put off concerning the former way of chayim (life) the old man, which is degenerated with deceitful lusts…"***

The Scriptures allow for a believer's inevitable stumbling as they emerge out of a habitual sinful lifestyle. ***Matthew 18:22 "Then came Kepha (Peter) to Him, and said, 'Master, how often shall my brother sin against me, and I forgive him? Up to seven times?' Yahshua said to him, 'I did not say to you, up to seven times: but, up to seventy times seven.'"*** Living a lifestyle that feeds the Evil Inclination can be directly reversed by feeding the Good Inclination. For example, a married man who is inclined to ring chat lines on a regular basis can reverse this cycle by making phone calls to a distant relative instead. This alternative phone use will also affect the depth of his *teshuvah*, as an object that was formerly used for evil is now used for good.[6]

---

6 This is illustrated in the actions of the Canaanite harlot Rahab who assisted the two spies sent by Joshua. ***Joshua 2:15*** relates how she lowered Caleb and Phinehas out of her window, which was located on the outer wall of the city. This rope was often used by her clients, but the Sages record her as making the following declaration as she lowered it for the last time, "Elohim, with this rope I sinned; let this rope be the vehicle for me to earn forgiveness!" - (Rashi) Among her descendants were the prophets Jeremiah and Ezekiel. Jeremiah was once cast into a pit and later pulled up uncomfortably by a rope. When he pleaded for a ladder Elohim answered him,"Just as your grandmother Rahab lowered the spies with a rope, so you will be saved by a rope." This illustrates the positive effect that teshuvah can have on generations to come, but that it is repaid measure for measure. – (Yalkut Shimoni 326)

This aspect of atonement is not always achieved by entirely avoiding a situation, object or person, but avoiding the pursuit of evil in a situation, misusing an object or mishandling a relationship.

Another example of effective atonement for someone who has led a secret life of sin is to instead lead a secret life of doing good deeds. If a person ceases a secret life of sin and also ceases to have a secret life, their atonement hasn't reached its maximum potential. If a man does good deeds in secret the Heavenly Father will certainly reward him openly ***(Matthew 6:4)***. This teaching is very prevalent within Orthodox Judaism and was not a new idea cooked up by the Messiah.

Now that both the internal and external climate of transgressive behaviour has been explored, the way of *teshuvah* as it is taught by YHWH should be carefully examined.

Teshuvah, Like Comedy, is All in the Timing

The Guardian of Israel chiefly relates to His people according to a specific cycle of time. He created the world, its landscape, the climate, the sea, the wind, the sun, the moon, the stars, the seasons and all living things within a distinct interrelated cohesive timeframe. He commanded the keeping of a day of rest to commemorate this event and the counting of days to keep seasons that are marked with a variety of special occasions usually referred to as "Appointed Times" (Moedim). These times were given to enable man to see snapshots of the Creator's unique character and acquaint us with His divine plan.

It amazes me when I hear teachers describe YHWH as existing outside of time when the Scriptures never portray Him in such a state. YHWH is the Supreme Mighty One of time eternal. In fact according to the most authoritative dictionaries the word "eternity" has nothing whatsoever to do with timelessness, but time without beginning or end. YHWH "inhabits" eternity ***(Isaiah 57:15)***. He does not literally inhabit timelessness. Literal timelessness by definition is an unmeasurable, intangible and completely lifeless domain. However, if the concept of timelessness is applied to YHWH in a poetic sense then this is quite different.

The Scriptures even describe the passing of time in heaven. ***Revelations 8:1; "And when He had opened the seventh seal, there was silence in the heavens for about half an hour."*** There was a time in heaven before HaSatan's fall and there is now a time in heaven after HaSatan's fall. There is a rich history in the heavenly realms that must follow a distinct timeline to enable key events like HaSatan's fall to be recorded. Within Scripture heavenly time is simply described as having a different scale. ***2 Peter 3:8; "...one day is with the Master YHWH as a thousand years, and a thousand years as one day."*** And ***Psalm 90:4-12; "For a thousand years in Your sight is but as yesterday when it is past, and as a watch in the night."*** YHWH's very name indicates a dimension of time. The name given to Moshe at the burning bush was "Eyeh ashur eyeh," which means both "I am who I am" (originator of present tense) and also "cause of all causes" (originator of future tense).

Rosh Hashanah – Rehearsal for the Day of Judgement

Every year, during the Hebrew month of Elul, *teshuvah* is regarded with particular significance by the Almighty. The word Elul means "search" and indicates the action of probing and cleansing the heart from all sin. Nazarene Israelites and Jews (both Messianic and Orthodox) accordingly engage in a special time of reflection and supplication. The Month of Elul is also called "The Month of Mercy" because YHWH's attribute of mercy becomes elevated as He judges us. This period culminates in a High Sabbath day known as Yom Teruah, meaning "day of blowing the shofar." This day is regarded as a high Sabbath and marks the first day of the next Hebrew month of Tishri. ***Leviticus 23:23-24; "And YHWH spoke to Moshe, saying, Speak to the children of Yisrael, saying, 'In the seventh month, on the first day of the month, you shall have a Shabbaton, a remembrance of blowing of the shofar blasts, a miqra kodesh (set-apart gathering).'"*** This day is also known as "Rosh Hashanah," which means, "head of the year" and is thought by many to be the Jewish New Year. Other sources refer to it as the creation of mankind, but there is no Biblical support for either of these views. In actuality the only similarity to Rosh Hashanah and the secular New Year is its atmosphere of optimism and resolution making.

The term "Rosh Hashanah" is first used in ***Ezekiel 40:1*** though it appears translated as "the beginning of the year" in most English Bibles.

Quite a few names for Hebrew months and holidays come from pagan words or even the names of pagan gods. This is because many names were developed during Israel's exile in Babylon. Before then months were strictly identified by numbers. One might consider returning to the use of numbers as identification. But in many instances pagan words such as the name of the Greek god "Adonis" ("Adonoy" in Hebrew, meaning "Lord."), were later borrowed by pagans from Hebrew words and used as personal names for their deities.

Rosh Hashanah is essentially a rehearsal for the day of judgement (Yom ha-Din). This may make it sound like a day that is to be met with fear and trepidation. On the contrary, it is a day that should be filled with joy and hopefulness as a believer anticipates his salvation as his *teshuvah* increases in intensity. Rabbinic literature describes the opening of three heavenly ledgers at this time; one book containing the names of the wicked, another, the righteous, and the third those pending a final decision. The Almighty may bring to a believer's mind certain conduct that might need more reflection and repentance. From this day a ten day cycle commences that allows believers to appeal to the Almighty for a better judgment. This time is called the "Days of Awe" (Yamim Noraim) and is referred to in ***Psalms 81:3-4; "Blow the shofar in the month, at full moon for the day of our chag (feasting). For this was a statute-chuk (a mysterious ordinance) for Israel, and a Torah-mishpat (judgement) of the Elohim of Yaakov."*** The ***"judgment of the Elohim of Jacob"*** means the nation of Jacob (Israel) is about to enter a final phase of judgement. The shofar is blasted to wake and rouse Israel to a higher level of repentance.

A noteworthy aspect of Yom Teruah is the tradition of Taslich throwing where believers symbolically cast their sins away by throwing bread into a river or stream. This is based on ***Micah 7:19*** where it describes YHWH casting a believer's sins into the sea. Casting bread into a river is a great way of demonstrating *teshuvah* as a physical object lesson to stimulate the mind.

Yom Kippur – The Day of Atonement

The "Days of Awe" all point to the jewel in the crown of the high holidays - Yom Kippur, which means, "Day of Atonement." This day is seen in Judaism as the most set-apart day of the whole year, because it was especially set aside by YHWH as a day of atonement and purification. ***Leviticus 16:30; "For on that day shall the kohen (priest) make keporah (atonement) for you, to cleanse you, that you may be clean from all your sins before YHWH."***

Yom Kippur is referred to in the Torah as, "achat bashanah," which literally means "the one of the year," as opposed to the more common interpretation, "once a year." The Hebrew word "Kippur" means to deflect or avert a severe judgment. A believer has a final opportunity at this time to overturn any harsh decree that may have been established on Rosh Hashanah. On the surface, traditional Judaism teaches that repentance, prayer and acts of charity merit forgiveness alone[7]. However, this is not the case on closer inspection. Acknowledging Messiah's atonement for mankind was always the focal point of attaining forgiveness. The only difference between ancient and modern Torah obedient Israel was the existence of a Tabernacle or Temple that enabled the giving of offerings. These offerings were symbolic illustrations of Messiah's future death and resurrection, demonstrated by the shed blood of bulls and goats ***(Leviticus 17:11)***. A Rabbi by the name of Yochanan Ben Zaki instituted the concept of atonement through acts of good deeds, prayer and repentance at the Council of Yavneh in 70CE. This ruling, while not without its merits, obscured the fact that all sin sacrifices pointed to the coming Messiah. The blood atonement of Messiah Yahshua has always been the only means by which one can attain forgiveness of sins. But this should not draw away from the value of good deeds, prayer and repentance. One who

7 As mentioned earlier, repentance (Hebrew *charatah* ["feeling remorse"]) is not actually an accurate transliteration of the word *teshuvah*, which means "return." Neither is *tefillah* and *tzedakah*, usually transliterated as "prayer" and "charity" accurate. Prayer in Hebrew is called *bakashah*, which means "to request." Tefillah, on the other hand, means "to attach." This is because an audience with the King of Kings should not be motivated by a request, but a desire to attach oneself to Him. The Hebrew word for charity is *chessed*. This word implies that the recipient of charity is not worthy to receive it. But *Tzedakah* means "righteousness" and refers to "a dutiful act" applied to anyone whether deserving or not. Due to the complexity of my analysis of *teshuvah* I have left the more familiar terms in the majority of the text to lessen confusion.

accepts Yahshua has only to appeal to YHWH that he or she will live in accordance to this belief by observing Torah. Rav Yochannan HaMatbil (John the Immerser [Baptist]) preached this same message in his address to the multitude. ***Luke 3:8a; "Bring forth therefore fruits worthy of Teshuvah..."*** Other translations read; ***"prove by the way you live that you have repented of your sins..."*** Even the so-called Old Testament teaches that the shed blood of animals was not what YHWH desired, but rather what it represented. ***Psalms 40:6; "Sacrifice and offering You did not desire....burnt offering and sin offering You did not require."*** An Orthodox Jew may well reject the Greco-Roman "buddy Christ" counterfeit when they seek *teshuvah*, but will acknowledge the role of a Moshiach (Messiah) in the greater plan of personal and corporate salvation nonetheless.

Carried Home

Yom Kippur is a unique time. According to the sages the intrinsic oneness of a believer rises to the surface to present itself before YHWH. At this time the dispersed fragments of the last three hundred and sixty-five days of a believer's life are allowed the unique capacity to unite with their source (YHWH) and point upward toward the goal of perfection. This time is in no way meant to retract from the need to seek *teshuvah* at any other time throughout the year. It is simply a time when the Almighty personally looks down and pulls a repentant believer up the final rung of the ladder of *teshuvah*. Like a prodigal son who collapses at the edge of his father's property after having returned from a long journey in a land where he committed much sin, the father, filled with joy, comes running out, picks up his son in both arms and carries him inside his house.

Why So Much Emphasis on Judaism?

It is important to realise why *teshuvah* and the high Sabbaths that chiefly articulate it are discussed with such a heavy emphasis on Judaism. The answer is simple. The Jews are the only people among the twelve tribes of Israel to have kept Torah, however legalistically, throughout the entire two thousand years of the Diaspora. Therefore they serve as the only model from which Nazarene Israelites can learn demonstrative examples of Torah observance. In many cases the Jews' (manmade) traditions helped to preserve Torah observance. Furthermore, their often critisised "walls around the Torah" can be argued as having Scriptural basis in light of the mandate to guard it as the apple of one's eye ***(Proverbs 7:2)***. Those who point fingers at perceived walls around commandments should acknowledge times in history were Torah was being specifically outlawed, which called for desperate measures to preserve it. The institution of peripheral rituals, for the most part, was to cushion and protect a most precious jewel. Messiah Yahshua's criticism of certain Scribes and Pharisees was aimed at their reverence to manmade traditions over the Torah. Some of their practices had cancelled out or inhibited the performance of the Father's eternal commandments. Yahshua never criticised or called into question the mere fact that they observed manmade traditions.

The *Mishnah tractate Yoma 8:1* lays out the five major traditions that are observed on the day of Yom Kippur to most effectively occupy a person's mind to increase an awareness of atonement and purification. They are:

1. No eating and drinking
2. No wearing of leather shoes
3. No bathing or washing
4. No use of anointing oil
5. No marital relations

It is important to note that fasting is forbidden if a person's health is put at risk. Example: Newborns, infants and some elderly are to be excluded from fasting.

Many Orthodox Jewish synagogues lock their doors at the close of the Day of Atonement to signify YHWH's final irrevocable judgment. This is yet another object lesson that foreshadows an event, illustrated in this parable: ***Matthew 25:10-12; "And while they went to buy, the Bridegroom came; and they that were ready went in with Him to the marriage: and the door was shut. Afterward came also other virgins, saying Master, Master, open to us. But He answer and said, Truly I say to you, I know you not."***

Mitzvoth (Love Deeds) – The Positive and the Negative

YHWH's commandments or mitzvoth (love deeds) that were established in the heavens and on the earth are an amazing set of statutes that form the blueprint for a perfectly harmonious existence. The Torah was intrinsically programmed into the hearts of the first humans. After the fall, as generations came and went on the earth, mankind gradually departed from it until only eight humans remembered its way.

After this, key individuals (patriarchs) began to receive pieces of it until it was formally given to an entire nation at Mount Sinai. The fullness of the Torah was then subsequently revealed when Messiah Yahshua came to rightly teach and fulfill it during his short earthly ministry.

The Torah was in existence before the very foundation of the earth, and its knowledge, albeit to a lesser extent among pre-Sinai believers, is evident in Scripture. This can plainly be seen in the examples of Cain, Abel, Noah, Abraham and even the entire nation of Israel adhering to certain rituals and conduct that predates the giving of the Torah at Sinai.

It is important to note that some mitzvoth were born from YHWH's interactions with men and were designed to remind believers of key events that occurred a long time after the likes of Noah[8], Abraham[9] and Jacob[10]. For example the commandment to

8 Genesis 8:20; "And Noach built an altar to YHWH; and took of every clean beast and of every clean fowl..."

9 Genesis 26:5; "Because Avraham obeyed My voice, and kept My charge, My mitzvoth, My chukim (statutes), and My Torot." "To point the way" (*l'horot in Hebrew)* means to establish a house of Torah study. See commentary by Rabbi Nehemiah in B'reisheit Rabbah 95:3.

10 Genesis 46:28; "And he sent Yahudah before him to Yoseph, to direct his face to Goshen..."

tie tefillin[11] upon the arm was principally designed to remind all the generations of Israel of their rescue from Egypt. Therefore this commandment would not likely have been observed by pre-Sinai Hebrews. However, it is evident in the Scriptures that YHWH does administer rituals that foreshadow future events. Rabbi Yeshaya Horowitz elaborates on the pre-Sinai existence of Torah in the following discourse based on the view of Rabbi Moshe ben Nachman:

> "As the Torah exists in the spiritual realms, it has more than one application. After all, the Torah is not just G-d's knowledge and wisdom -- it is His will and inner desire. How that desire meets this world depends on many things. If, for example, the Jewish people would not have tolerated worship of a golden calf in their midst forty days after having heard the Ten Commandments, there would have been no need for a Tabernacle. Each one of us would have been a perfect temple for the Shechinah (Divine presence) and G-dliness would have dwelt on earth in a much simpler way." *(Shnei Luchot HaBrit / The Covenants Two Tablets)*

The written Torah (the first five Books of Moshe) is merely a demonstrative episodic manifestation of the eternal wisdom of YHWH that was around before creation itself. If Israel had responded differently after their exodus, different training wheels would have been applied and other rituals may have been added or retracted.

YHWH's 613 commandments can be divided into 248 positive and 365 negative mitzvoth. These correspond to the 248 organs and the 365 sinews found in the human body. Each morning when a Jew or a Nazarene Israelite dons his prayer garment (tallit) a blessing is usually recited that acknowledges this truth.

The 248 positive commandments are best defined as actions that are to be carried out to maintain close relations with the Father. They can be broken down into eighteen categories, which are all founded on particular verses in the Torah.

---

11 Tefillin are hard leather cubes that contain passages of Scripture and are bound to the arm during morning prayers. Exodus 13:9, Exodus 13:16 and Deuteronomy 11:18 all carry the commandment for wearing tefillin.

These categories are:

- Relationship to YHWH
- Torah study
- Temple and Priesthood functions
- Sacrifices
- Vows
- Ritual purity
- Temple donations
- Sabbatical year observances
- Consumption of clean animals
- Festivals
- Community related rulings
- Destruction of idolatry
- Regulations during war
- Social rulings
- Family rulings
- Maintenance of judicial functions
- Laws pertaining to slaves
- Torts (laws related to civil wrongdoing)

The 365 negative commandments are best described as actions that are not to be carried out. They too can be broken down into thirteen categories. These are:

- Avoidance of idolatry and related practices
- Prohibitions resulting from past events
- Avoidance of blasphemy
- Not being lax with Tabernacle duties

- Sacrificial prohibitions
- Things forbidden to priests
- Consumption of food (dietary laws)
- Abstinence according to the Nazarite vow
- Agriculture
- Loans and the treatment of slaves
- Administration of Justice
- Forbidden relationships
- Monarchy

The Jewish sages teach that there are three types of atonement according to the degree of the transgression committed. A transgression committed out of ignorance has a different weight before the Almighty than a willful transgression. There are punishments that differ in magnitude that await either the willful or ignorant sinner ***(Matthew 10:15; 11:22*** and ***Luke 10:12, 14; 12:47, 48)***. ***1 John 5:16*** talks of a sin that leads to death and a sin that does not lead to death. ***1 Corinthians 6:18*** speaks of a sin that is committed inside the body as opposed to all other sins that are committed outside the body.

Basic *teshuvah* (ceasing the activity and confessing it before YHWH) is a key component of all degrees of atonement from sin. *Teshuvah* is to be sought as soon as a transgressor has become aware that a sin has been committed whether through action or inaction.

If a person fails to perform a positive commandment, such as avoiding Torah study or eating unclean food, but sincerely repents according the way that Elohim has made known to them by His Word, forgiveness can be instantly attained. If a negative commandment is broken, but repented of, forgiveness commences, but may not be fully realised in the heavens until repentance is engaged on the Day of Yom Kippur. This is not to say that one cannot receive a good judgment if they pass away before Yom Kippur after having transgressed a negative commandment. Judgment is YHWH's domain and He sees all a man's circumstances and ways from birth.

If on the other hand the day of Yom Kippur should pass and *teshuvah* for transgressions of negative commandments has not been sought a punishment may ensue. A harsh punishment or trial brought about by one's own transgression can be a blessing as it can allow atonement to be achieved before the Almighty.

Fast Repentance – The Role of Food

Despite YHWH's declaration in ***Joel 2:12; "...teshuvah (return) to Me...with fasting, and with weeping, and with mourning..."*** fasting is not an indispensable companion to *teshuvah*. The Scriptures do not advocate it as a rule-of-thumb aspect of a return even for a grave sin that brings about suffering. The act of confession and requesting forgiveness are the only two crucial functions that allow an annulment of a transgression before YHWH. They are even held in greater esteem than refraining from revisiting a transgression. This is because *teshuvah's* cleansing affect can have equal potency for one who dies immediately after confession or goes on to live without stumbling again in the same sin.

Confessing and requesting forgiveness dismantles the body and soul of a sin. A sin's action is its body, which is destroyed through confession and the pleasure derived from a sin is its soul, which is destroyed through seeking forgiveness. The fasting, weeping and mourning aspect of ***Joel 2:12*** refers to averting a harsh punishment whereas *teshuvah* itself involves returning to the correct path. The motive for Israel's fasting in ***Esther 4:3*** is clearly to annul King Haman's evil decree as opposed to an act of *teshuvah* from a communal transgression.

The purpose of fasting is not to cause self-inflicted suffering to achieve atonement. Allowing suffering to befall an individual or a community to achieve atonement remains the exclusive prerogative of the Creator. Fasting is principally designed to avoid, accelerate or diminish the magnitude of a heavenly decree. No other additional actions, aside from confession, requesting forgiveness and refraining from a sin can secure any more further atonement.

Teshuvah – It's All in the Name

The Hebrew word *teshuvah* is spelt with the Hebrew letters, *Taf, Shin Vav*, *Bet* and *Hei*. The first four letters, *Taf, Shin*, *Vav* and *Bet* form the word *tashuv*, which means "return." The addition of the *Hie* makes the word literally mean "returning the hei." What does this mean? The name of YHWH is spelt with a *Yod*, *Hei*, *Vav* and another *Hei*. True *teshuvah* has two significant stages as a person returns to their former state. Stage one returns the first *Hei* back to the name of YHWH and stage two returns the second *Hei*. So whenever someone enters into repentance they restore the name of YHWH back into their own lives. In Paleo-Hebrew the letter *Hei* was in the shape of a person with raised arms.

Conclusion

In closing, I cannot stress enough how valuable it is to carefully read through material concerning *teshuvah* from a Jewish perspective. The material presented in these two parts is a good start, but a Nazarene Israelite must look thoroughly at the writings of the great Jewish Sages who have written extensively on the subject. A person coming into this walk who has a church background faces a new choice. He or she can continue to read material on this topic from Christian commentators who write from a grace garnished "Torah has been nailed to the cross" standpoint or ancient commentaries by men who loved the Torah as Messiah Yahshua did. My Rebbe, Rabbi Robert O. Miller, once said, "no one accidentally trips and falls into hell. If anyone ends up in hell, they worked at it." I encourage all those that have read these two parts on repentance to make *teshuvah* a daily focus. Study the significance of the Month of Mercy and Yom Kippur and when they come, do what the rabbis instruct you to do. You prayed hard for these things to be revealed to you and YHWH has now honoured your persistent requests. Now it's time to get to work and study Torah like there's no tomorrow.

Chapter Sixteen

Original Sin, Original Lie

> **"Sin is no more a substance than friendliness, goodness, or virtue are substances. If sin is a substance that can be transmitted physically, then virtue also must be a substance that can be transmitted physically. And what would be the result if all this were true? Why, sinners would beget sinners, and saints, of course, would beget saints!" - A. T. Overstreet (Are Men Born Sinners?)**

WHAT IS SIN? ***1 John 3:4; "Anyone who commits sin violates Torah, for sin is the transgression of the Torah."*** Sin is usually defined as an action, but even the Talmud states, "Thoughts of sin are more grievous than sin itself." This is in harmony with Messiah Yahshua's teaching and is true because the accumulation of a multitude of sinful thoughts weighs a person down, usually culminating in the person eventually committing a physical sin. Judaism commonly refers to a sin as an *avera*. This word comes from the Hebrew root *ayin-bet-resh* and means "to pass over or cross over" or to literally "cross a boundary."

There are two Hebrew words in the TaNaK[1] that have been blanketed with the term "sin" by translators. They are *pasha* and *chatta'ah*. *Pasha* means "transgression," "rebellion" or "revolt" and Chatta'ah means "to miss the mark." Some sources also insist on an additional third Hebrew word that means sin. That word is *avon* and is sometimes translated as "iniquity." Note King David's plea to the Almighty and his inclusion of both sin and iniquity as separate issues in the following verse: ***Psalms 32:5; "I acknowledged my sin to You, and my iniquity I did not hide. I said, I will confess my transgressions to YHWH; and You forgave the iniquity of my sin. Selah."*** The grammar in this verse would be considered very poor if sin meant exactly the same thing as iniquity. The ignorance most believers have to the meaning of iniquity and how it differs from sin has caused many to accept the concept of "inherited sin" as acceptable Scriptural doctrine without even blinking. I will discuss iniquity shortly, but for now, let's look at the teaching of original sin.

The concept of original sin, that is sin which is genetically inherited from the fall of Adam and Hava, is the most sadistic and cruelest false doctrine that inhabits the theology of almost all so-called Bible based religions across the face of the earth. It manages to remain alive, even within some major Messianic movements, because of a range of key verses that have been spun very convincingly off kilter for so many centuries.

How often does the mind of an original sin advocate, defending his view, go immediately to the so-called proof text of ***Psalms 51:5*** yet remain blissfully ignorant to the implications of such a view in light of ***Psalms 22:9-10***? ***"But You are He that took Me out of the womb: You did make Me tikvah (trust in you) when I was upon My eema's (mother's) breasts, I was cast upon You from the womb: You are My El from My eema's (mother's) belly."***

1 TaNaK is an acronym ("T-N-K") for Torah (teaching) Nevi'im (Prophets) and K'tuvim (writings) and was given to the collection of books now referred to in Christianity as the Old Testament.

False Proof Texts Exposed

The complete list of so-called proof texts for original sin is as follows:

- ***Genesis 6:12; "And Elohim looked upon the earth, and, see, it was corrupt; for all flesh[2] had corrupted its way upon the earth."*** This says nothing about a sin that is passed on, but rather all flesh corrupting its way by generations exponentially. All having sinned does not mean all are born with sin as taught in ***Romans 3:23***. This teaching by Sha'ul was based off ***Ecclesiastes 7:20***; ***"For there is not a just man upon earth who does tov (good), and sins not."***

- ***Genesis 8:21; "And YHWH smelled a sweet fragrance; and YHWH said in His lev (heart), 'I will not again curse the ground any more for man's sake; for the imagination of man's lev (heart) is evil from his youth; neither will I again smite any more every living thing, as I have done.'"*** This says nothing about sin being passed on at the point of conception, but that it manifests in man during the days of his youth. A human being is only accountable for his own actions when he reaches a point of knowing right from wrong. At that point he becomes accountable.

- ***Deuteronomy 32:5; "They have corrupted themselves, they are blemished and are not His children: they are a perverse and crooked generation."*** This is a classic example of how the truth that all men have sinned is associated with the meaning that it is manifest at the point of conception.

- ***Psalms 14:1-3; "The fool has said in his lev (heart), 'There is no Elohim.' They are corrupt, they have done abominable works; there is none that does tov (good). YHWH looked down from the shamayim (heavens) upon the children of men, to see if there were any that did understand, and seek Elohim. They are all turned aside, they are all together become filthy: there is none that does***

---

2 Though this verse says "all flesh" we know that Noah and his family were not corrupt. Similarly we know that though *Genesis 7:4* says, ***"...every living substance that I have made I will destroy from off the face of the earth,"*** does not literally mean every living subst[illegible] for even the giant Og survived by clinging to the ark for forty days and nights acco[illegible] to *Deuteronomy 3:11* and *Genesis 6:4*.

tov (good), no, not one." Again this is guilt by association. "None that has done good" is the sugar that makes the poison go down as the original sin advocate automatically assumes it's addressing a concept of an inherited sin from the very first human.

- ***Ecclesiastics 7:29; "Behold, this only have I found, that Elohim has made man upright; but they have sought out many devices."*** If anything this verse supports the notion that YHWH makes men pure at the outset, rather than allowing them to be formed in impurity.

- ***Romans 3:23; "For all have sinned, and come short of the tifereth (glory) of YHWH."*** All have sinned, but none are condemned [punished in Gehenna] at the point of conception by a sin committed by someone else.

- ***Romans 7:17-22; "Now then it is no more I that do sinful deeds, but sin that dwells in my flesh. For I know that in me, that is, in my flesh, dwells no tov (good) thing: for the choice and desire to do the right thing is present with me; but how to perform that which is tov evades me. For the tov that I should do I do not: but the evil that I desire not, that I wind up doing. Now if I do what I should not do, it is no more I that do it, but sin that dwells in me. I find then an interesting Torah, that, when I would do tov by the Torah, evil is still present with me. For I delight in the Torah of YHWH after the inward man."*** Note the flesh is depraved but the inner man is not. If this section teaches inherited sin that can only be closed off by receiving Messiah, why does Sha'ul still have it? Be also mindful that the NIV wrongly interprets the word "flesh" as "sinful nature." This whole verse sequence teaches nothing about inherited sin or a release from it, but the ongoing war between the Good and the Evil Inclination.

- ***Exodus 20:5; "for I YHWH your Elohim am a jealous Elohim, visiting the iniquity of the ahvot (father) upon the children to the third and fourth generation of those that hate Me..."*** This verse speaks of those who hate YHWH and earthly trials as opposed to judgement, which only extends to a maximum of four generations. This verse can no more be used to support the argument of original sin than gasoline can be used to put out a bushfire.

- ***1 Corinthians 15: 21-23; "For since by man came death, by Man came also the resurrection of the dead. For as in Ahdahm all die, even so in Moshiach (Messiah) shall all be made alive. But every man in his own order: Moshiach the Bikkur (first fruit); afterwards they that are Moshiach's at His coming."*** Death is what we inherit from Adam, not sin, though all have sinned and fallen short.

- ***Ephesians 2:1-3; "And you has He made alive, who were dead in trespasses and sins; In which in times past you walked according to the course of this olam (world), according to the prince of*** the ***power of the air, the ruach (spirit) that now operates in Torah-breaking children."*** These verses speak of sins committed not inherited. Hence the wording "you walked…" as opposed to "you were born…"

- ***1 John 3:8; "He who sins is of s.a.tan (the Accuser), for s.a.tan has sinned from Beresheeth (the beginning). For this purpose the Son of YHWH was manifested, that He might destroy the works of s.a.tan."*** One would have to question how the opening words "He who sins…"fit in with a concept of automatic sin grafted to an individual.

And the award goes to:

- ***Psalms 51:5; "See, I was shaped in iniquity; and in sin did my eema (mother) conceive me."***(I have written a detailed analysis on this one as it's the most popular among the original sin fraternity. [See bordered text.])

The Holy Grail Verse of Original Sin Debunked

Psalms 51:5 is the perfect example of a verse that suffers from Christian theological spin. ***Psalms 51:5 "See, I was shaped in iniquity; and in sin did my eema (mother) conceive me."***

This is the Holy Grail text of original sin, yet if read carefully it has absolutely nothing whatsoever to do with inherited sin passed onto babies. The verse in question is written using Hebrew poetic parallelism. This means that the second line of the verse is saying the same thing as the first line, but in a slightly different manner. The first line, referring to David, is an idiom referring to the creation or origins. The verse is not at all referring to David's sinful nature at the point of birth, but the circumstances of his conception, being an act of sexual sin. The NIV handles the verse in a completely irresponsible manner, reinterpreting the meaning and reading as: ***"Surely I was sinful at birth, sinful from the time my mother conceived me."*** David was actually referring to his mother's state as opposed to his own at birth because according to Torah, she was considered 'defiled' by her previous relations with an Ammonite. ***Deuteronomy 23:3; "An Ammonite, or Moavite shall not enter into the congregation of YHWH; even to their tenth generation shall they not enter into the congregation of YHWH le-olam-va-ed (for all eternity)."*** Yet in Tehillim (Psalms) David refers to his mother as YHWH's handmaiden in verse ***86:16*** and ***116:16***, confirming that she had found favour in the eyes of Elohim. This issue is studied in further detail in an article called, *A Perspective on Psalm 51:5* by William P. Murray, Jr.

The Many Faced Definition of Original Sin

If many of those who say they support the notion of original sin thought through the implications of what this view means, they would flee from such an opinion like a vampire flees from a stake. So what does original sin mean and why am I labeling it as sadistic and cruel?

Original sin is the belief that a single wrong action by the first human put into effect a situation that caused all his offspring, at the point of conception, to be equally condemned for that same action. The follow-on result of this view means that if a human is unable to reach a state on an individual basis that enables him or her to accept Yahshua and repent of this sin; they are bound for Gehenna (Hell) to receive punishment for the first sin of breaking a koshrut (kosher) law. This is regardless of a person's developmental state, whether still a fetus, a newborn baby or disabled. Infant baptism, born directly from this doctrine, is no remedy to the situation because there is no Scriptural support to show that such a procedure was taught and practiced.

There are slightly varying definitions of original sin, all impressive, but all drastically wrong. They include:

- All mankind sinned in Adam when he sinned. Adam's will was the will of man, so all men sinned and rebelled with him when he sinned.
- Adam's sin corrupted human nature, so that now all men are born with a sinful nature.
- Adam set in motion an innate sinful nature that is the direct cause of all of man's sins. Man has sin in his nature from birth because of Adam.
- Because of Adam's transgression, all men are guilty, under the just "wrath and curse of G-d," and are liable to the "pains of hell forever."
- Even newborn babies open their eyes in this world under the "wrath and curse" of Elohim. They are guilty and condemned from the moment of their birth.

YHWH Himself Rejects Original Sin

In ancient Israel a fashionable proverb had begun to circulate throughout the people that angered the Almighty. The proverb spoke of how a father who eats sour grapes sets his children's teeth on edge. ***Ezekiel 18:1-3; "The word of YHWH came to me again, saying, 'What do you mean, when you use this mishle (proverb) concerning the land of Yisrael, saying, "The ahvot (fathers) have eaten sour grapes, and the children's teeth are blunted?" As I live, says the***

Master YHWH, you shall not have an occasion any more to use this mishle (proverb) in Yisrael.'" This proverb meant that the present generation inherited punishment of previous generations (i.e., children inherited the sins of their fathers). Note YHWH's response to this philosophy in verse 3. This is scripturally documented proof of an original sin philosophy creeping into the body and Elohim's complete rejection of it. He goes on to declare that men are personally responsible for their own actions in ***Ezekiel 18:20; "The being that sins, he shall die. The son shall not bear the iniquity of the abba (Father), neither shall the abba (father) bear the iniquity of the son..."***

The Scriptures state emphatically that a son will not suffer for the sins of his father. ***Deuteronomy 24:16; "The ahvot (father) shall not be put to death for the children, neither shall the children be put to death for the ahvot (father): every man shall be put to death for his own sin."***

The Brit Chadashah echoes the same sentiment. ***2 Corinthians 5:10; "For we must all appear before the bema seat (judgement seat) of Moshiach (Messiah); that every one may receive the things done with his body, according to what he has done, whether it be tov (good), or bad."***

Sin has no physical substance. ***1 John 3:4*** defines sin as a transgression of the Torah. Thus sin is a conscious choice not a genetically passed on disease. Sin is the character of an action and not a name of a physical substance. Trying to sell the idea of original sin is like trying to sell friendliness as a genetically inherited trait. If original sin were true then sinners would produce sinners and righteous people would produce righteous people. Think about it.

One Nature Divided into Two, Then Back into One

The phrase "original sin" does not appear in the Scriptures. Sha'ul HaShliach did not teach that all men were under the condemnation of an original sin committed by Adam and Hava. He merely points out that their fall initiated death and an increased tendency to sin. This is called iniquity and is manifest by the co-existence of the good and the Evil Inclination. We know this because Adam and Hava were created with one nature, but after the fall they developed two (knowing good and evil). As it was one man (Adam) who let sin enter the world, one man (Yahshua) causes its departure by freeing those who lay claim to the covering of his shed blood. ***Romans 5:12; "Therefore, as by one man sin entered into the olam hazeh (world), and death by sin; and so death passed upon all men, for all have sinned."*** Only one of three core natures is ever present in the heart of a human being. They are:

- The pure[3] nature, which we are all created with at birth.
- The sinful nature, manifest by committing a sin (breaking Torah), which causes a man to fall short of the glory of Elohim. This nature is voluntary (i.e., it is a consciously chosen path). It makes a man an enemy to YHWH. The sinful nature has many levels of descent. In Judaism one who perpetually lives out of the Evil Inclination is called a *Rasha*, meaning "wicked person."
- Being born again or receiving the birth from above. This is also a voluntary nature in which a man, by faith, becomes a partaker of the divine will. This was the typical state of righteous Israelites (usually Jews) even before Yahshua's arrival in the flesh! The sinful nature can still make inroads to a person in this state. In Kabbalah such a person is called a *beinoni*, meaning "intermediate one," and defines a person who has control over their Evil Inclination. Like the sinful nature, the good nature also has many levels, the highest being a tzaddik, meaning "righteous one." Messiah Yahshua displayed the highest possible degree of righteousness. The Chassidic movement refers to a person at this level of righteousness as a "perfected tzaddik." This means he has extinguished the Evil Inclination entirely (i.e., the door to the Evil Inclination has been removed entirely [though the passage is still present beyond a heavy wall[4]]).

---

3 This state is usually the domain of a newborn baby that is not yet guilty of committing any personal sin. The five senses; sight, hearing, touch, smell, and taste are all potential gateways for sin to enter the body. Personal sin has no way of manifesting until a human develops these senses. When Sha'ul said, ***"All have sinned and fallen short of the glory of YHWH," (Romans 3:23)*** he was referring to all who are accountable. A person born without the use of the primary senses of sight and hearing grows up absent from the sin these senses can draw in.

4 HaSatan would not have bothered to tempt Yahshua unless there was at least a covered entrance to a passage of unexplored sin present. Even the claim that HaSatan was just enticing Yahshua to reveal himself to the world as Messiah before the appointed time (as taught by some teachers) is still an invitation to sin.

What is Iniquity and How Does it Differ From Sin?

Iniquity is certainly related and co-dependant on sin. But it is not exactly the same thing as sin. Iniquity is what people are actually referring to when they speak of sin that is carried on through a generational line. But in reality it is simply an increased susceptibility that a family has to particular sin. The birth of an iniquity in a family is caused by an ancestor who commits a particular desire related sin and passes it to his children and his children's children through the ministry of "family" "liar" "spirits" (familiar spirits). King David's iniquity was polygamy, which was a practice that continued on in his sons. Though the Torah gives provisions for taking more than one wife, it forbids it. King David had victory over this iniquity as it is recorded in his last days when a young maiden is given to lie with him and provide warmth, yet he refrains from having relations with her ***(1 Kings 1:4)***. According to Strong's Concordance, "iniquity" means "perversity," "moral evil, "fault" or "mischief."

The False Dual Nature and God-Man Accusations

The coexistence of the Good and Evil Inclination is a condition that is manifest in all flesh. The avenue to go down either path is ever present in all human beings. I am not talking about double mindedness, but simply the presence of gateways to two paths. Certainly this presence of two paths is also evident even among the heavenly host as is illustrated by HaSatan's actions and one third of the heavenly host that defected with him. One thing that Adam, Hava and HaSatan had in common was that they sinned and yet were without so-called "original sin." The difference in the gateway to the evil path between man (since the fall) and the heavenly host is that its entrance is perceived as being figuratively decorated with neon signs and populated by seducing salesmen, whereas the same gateway for an angel stands unnoticed or appears like a fire or a gallows.

This truth may raise the question of Yahshua's nature, a topic that has been in the spotlight in regards to a new teaching that has arisen in certain Messianic circles. This teaching theorises that Messiah Yahshua's entire flesh, the egg and sperm, were completely prepared in the heavens and impregnated into Miriam reducing her to the status of a surrogate mother. This theology works quite impressively based on the doctrine of original sin, but if removed it deflates like an air balloon. The teaching claims to rectify the problem of a Messiah inheriting the sinful nature of his mother by giving full heavenly substance to his physical flesh form. A completely acceptable deduction provided the concept of original sin holds it together. Until now most criticisms of this teaching have been impressively silenced, but this is because its foundation, original sin, has been for the most part overlooked.

The rightful removal of original sin returns Yahshua to an acceptable state as our Passover lamb. Yahshua had no more physical faculties available to him than a normal healthy Hebrew male, though his conception was a combination of Miriam's egg and the Ruach HaKodesh. This is what Yahshua said about himself in regards to his capabilities: ***John 5:19; "...I say to you, the Son can do nothing by himself, but only what he sees the Abba (Father) doing, for the things He does, these also does the Son likewise."*** and again in verse ***30, "I can by My own self do nothing: as I hear, I judge: and My mishpat (judgement) is righteous; because I seek not My own will, but the will of the Abba (Father) who has sent Me."*** So he wasn't a G-d-Man as some may accuse me of advocating. Biologically Yahshua was just like you and I.

The Torah being at one time likened to a school master allowed the ongoing maintenance of the Good Inclination. Messiah Yahshua is the flesh manifestation of the Torah whose redemptive work allowed it to be completed at a specific point in time. Yahshua is not a shortcut to salvation that was only accessible by following a type of Torah obedient lifestyle that was any different before he arrived (not withstanding the observance of some traditions that were drowning out the Torah).

It must be made clear at this point that I am not advocating that Messiah had a dual nature in that he entertained both the Good and Evil Inclination at any time during his earthly life. On the contrary; Messiah Yahshua was without sin, meaning he never pursued the path of the Evil Inclination. This is not to say that he didn't have an Evil Inclination, just that he never entertained it in any capacity. Without a belief that Yahshua had an inactive Evil

Inclination present, is to believe in a Messiah that wasn't human, a Messiah that we can't identify with and who was equipped with superior faculties to fight the dark forces. Here's what he said in relation to this matter: ***John 14:12; "Amein, amein, I say to you, He that believes on Me, the works that I do shall he do also; and greater works than these shall he do; because I go to My Abba (Father)."***

Original Sin's Origin

> **"People will sometimes study and understand the implications of inherited sin. Instead of rejecting it as false doctrine, they continue to believe in hereditary depravity, but deny that babies are born destined for hell. When this happens they are not being honest and are usually suffering from a conflict between their heart and their head." - Anonymous**

One of the most prominent fathers of the Reformation, Augustine of Hippo came up with the idea of original sin around the fifteen hundreds. From this concept he then deduced that an infant who dies before baptism is bound for hell. This is a clockwork example of an unscriptural belief giving birth to an unscriptural doctrine. Apart from the Scriptures being devoid of infant baptism, a newborn or infant is completely ineligible for full water immersion (baptism/mikvah) because they do not have the intellectual capacity to believe ***(Mark 16:16, Acts 2:38)*** and repent ***(Acts 2:38)***.

According to Scripture, an infant who dies has a place in the *olam haba* (world to come). If the infant's parents are believers they will receive their child again running in with open arms from the borders of a new Israel. ***Jeremiah 31:15-16; "This says YHWH; 'A voice was heard in Ramah, lamentation, and bitter weeping; Rachel weeping for her children; refusing to be comforted for her children, because they were not found. This says YHWH; Refrain your voice from weeping, and your eyes from tears: for your work shall be rewarded, says YHWH; and they (your children) shall shuv (return) from the land of the enemy.'"***

Prior to Augustine's "infant goes to hell" brainwave, the Catholic Church taught that deceased infants inhabit a type of limbo realm.

This information is widely documented and there is no excuse for being ignorant to the origin of the original sin doctrine.

To believe in original sin is to believe that every human being from birth is condemned to hell by the sinful actions of Adam and Hava. This belief enforces the view that such a state is inescapable unless an infant is baptised, despite this process being completely absent from Scripture.

What we inherit from Adam is physical and spiritual mortality. A concept of eternal punishment for millions of infants based on the act of one individual is irrational. Logically if original sin were legitimate each new generation would come under an ever increasing weight of condemnation. Judging an individual for an ancestral, hereditary or original sin is absurd because it fails to take into account exponentially accumulated sin that increases with every generation after Adam. Most people who say they believe in original sin are unaware of what it actually means.

Judaism has never cradled a belief in original sin. Principally because the whole concept of a human core that is inherently corrupt disables a person's ability to seek effective repentance. "Repentance...can be mobilized only from an initially uncorrupt core." – The Kasirer Edition Rosh Hashanah Machzor (pg. xxvi [essays])

Chapter Seventeen

A Golem Truth

STUDYING THE EXODUS as a companion text to the Book of Revelation is a subject that tends to go under the radar for many who delve into the study of end time prophecy. This is a concern because the mayhem that unfolds in Egypt and Israel's conduct during the plagues is a model of what will eventually happen on a global scale. Added to this, there is a significant event that receives far less attention that must be addressed.

Anybody who professes to have an exceedingly high knowledge of eschatology (study of end time events) should know of the creation of a golem by the Navi Sheker (False Prophet) and the Moshiach Neged (Anti-Messiah) in the Book of Revelations. That is the bringing to life of an artificial person molded from raw red clay. Sadly, most religious leaders fail to address this issue in any of their teachings. On the contrary, many of them would likely view the creation of a golem as a concept originating from a science fiction novel rather than the sacred Scriptures.

While the community of Nazarene Israel is abuzz with new end time insights, such as the "Islamic Beast" teaching predominantly driven by *Your Arms to Israel Ministries*, I am dismayed at the lack of understanding regarding basic apocalyptic events within this movement. The persistent mention of the fabled "rapture" inhabiting conversations and writings of many Natsarim is testimony to large numbers of believers still clinging to the remaining fragments of a false belief system. The definition of rapture, a term used almost exclusively in religious circles, defines a complete snatching away *before* a coming strife, that is no more evident in Scripture than is the mention of Homer Simpson, though some who have read the *Bible Code* may disagree.

A Short History of the Golem

> ***"Who shall conceive the horrors of my secret toil, as I... tortured the living animal to animate the lifeless clay"*** **– Mary Shelley's Frankenstein**

Many are familiar with the story of *Frankenstein*, a novel written by Mary Shelley, which tells of a scientist who conducts a macabre experiment in which he uses electricity to bring an excessively powerful human being to life. However, centuries before an 18 year old British woman was challenged to write a ghost story, the legend of an artificial man, known as a golem, first emerged in Judaism.

Mary's influence of the golem is apparent in the tale's subtitle, *The Modern Prometheus*, which is a reference to Prometheus Plasticator, the lesser known of two Greek Mythological figures, who fashioned a man out of clay and brought him to life. The other myth tells of the titan, Prometheus Pyrphoros, who deceived the god Zeus by bringing fire to mankind.

The word "myth" at one time simply meant "ancient story" or "story of unclear origin." *The Oxford Dictionary of English Folklore* states: "Myths are stories about divine beings, generally arranged in a coherent system; they are revered as true and sacred; they are endorsed by rulers and priests; and closely linked to religion."

The Athenian philosopher Plato originally coined the word "mythologia," to distinguish between the accounts of gods and the accounts of men. This word later developed into a term that carried a distinction between imaginative accounts and factual accounts. While these fantastic stories may have evolved over the centuries they should never be dismissed as tales that originated completely from an individual's imagination. Greek myths were merely cross cultural stories of fallen angels who abandoned their posts as Watchers to procreate with earthly women according to ***Genesis 6:2***. Titans were the Greek equivalent of nephilim (tyrants) who usually grew larger than normal men as a result of human and angelic relations. The gods of myth did exist and the Scriptures make clear mention of such mighty beings. The myths and legends that the average Christian has been conditioned to dismiss as fiction are however loosely knit records of these "mighty men of renown."

The Golem of Prague

The most well known Jewish story of the golem concerns Rabbi Yehuda Bezalel Loew, the Marharal[1] of Prague (c. 1513[25] -1609), who wanted to protect his community from riots incited by blood libel accusations by a Jew hating priest. He created the golem solely for the purpose of protecting his people. There have been many versions of the story published in books and produced in films over the years.

Loew served as the chief rabbi of Moravia for twenty years before moving with his family to Prague in 1573. He was appointed as head of the Yeshiva at Klaus Synagogue and eventually appointed as chief rabbi of Prague in the late 1590s. His delay in this second appointment was perhaps due to his deeper interest in the more complex and weightier matters of the Torah known today as Kabbalah. This was evident in his frequent reference to a central work in Judaism called the *Zohar*. Whatever the delay for his second appointment, he was still considered within Central Europe as a leading Jewish scholar of his day, publishing many books expounding on the Torah.

1 An acronym for "Our teacher, the Master Rabbi Loew."

Though many sources play down Loew's actual creation of a golem, saying it was merely a legend that grew out of his exceedingly high knowledge of Kabbalah, a statue of him still stands outside Prague's city hall to this very day commemorating his protection of the local Jewish community. The Altneuschul[2] (old new) Synagogue in Prague still has Loew's chair on display, which no rabbi will sit in, and according to some a coffin containing the remains of his golem still resides in the building's attic so it can be summoned again if need be. Furthermore, there exists a letter written by the late Rabbi Menachem Mendel Schneersohn's father-in-law that tells of how he as young adult persuaded the caretaker of the Altneuschul synagogue to view the golem in the attic. Apparently his father was very displeased with him because Rabbi Loew of Prague had issued a *herem,* which was a formal decree to exile any Jew from the community who ventured up to see the remains of the golem.

The creation of a golem by Jewish sages is discussed during the Talmudic era prior to 500CE. Such literature describes the first human Adam as being a golem before having the breath of YHWH breathed into him to receive his *nefesh* (soul). Aside from this the earliest known story of a golem comes from the Babylonian Talmud, in Sanhedrin 65b:

Rava said: "If the righteous wished, they could create a world, for it is written: 'Your iniquities are a barrier between you and your G-d.'" For Rava created a man and sent him to R[abbi] Zeira. The rabbi spoke to him [the man] but he did not answer. Then he [Zeira] said: "You are from the pietists. Return to your dust." (Translation Moshe Idel)

The rabbis of this era studied the Torah to such an intense degree that they were able to unlock some of the secrets of creation. This level of study and commitment is now referred to as Kabbalah, which simply means "receive." Today Kabbalah has been mystified and is usually portrayed in popular media and esoteric publications in a way that resembles a strand of witchcraft rather than the study of Torah on a level that is seldom attained by the most committed

2 *Altneuschul* is a German word meaning, "old new Synagogue" and was the result of a new Synagogue that was built in Dusni Street on the site where an old one stood until it was demolished in the 1860s.

scholars. It is wise not to dismiss Kabbalah as an occult practice, but instead be mindful that its depiction in media and in most publications is false.

The reality of the golem in history and not just being confined to legend has been a source of debate among rabbis for centuries. Suffice to say that the more one studies the golem, the more one finds material that adds weight to its credibility and where there is smoke there is generally fire. Take for example, this story from the Second World War where a Holocaust survivor from Prague related a most unusual incident to a soldier:

> "The golem did not disappear and even in the time of war it went out of his hiding place in order to safeguard its synagogue. When the Germans occupied Prague, they decided to destroy the Altneuschul. They came to do it; suddenly, in the silence of the synagogue, the steps of a giant walking on the roof began to be heard. They saw a shadow of a giant hand falling from the window onto the floor... The Germans were terrified and they threw away their tools and fled away in panic."
>
> "I know that there is a rational explanation for everything; the synagogue is ancient and each and every slight knock generates an echo that reverberates many times, like the steps of thunder. Also the glasses of the windows are old, the window panes are crooked and they distort the shadows, forming strange shades on the floor. A bird's leg generates a shade of a giant hand on the floor... and nevertheless...there is something."
>
> Archives of Jewish Folklore, Haifa, No. 11383, 1945.

In current times the golem has been referred to in the popular X-Files series. In one episode a librarian tells Agent Mulder that the technique for creating a golem comes from a Jewish source called the *Sefer Yetzira (The Book of Creation)*. This work, whilst being a major source of creation study for the early sages, does not specifically single out the process for creating a golem and is a painful reminder of Hollywood's on-going fact fudging efforts to push entertaining story lines over correctly educating a potentially intelligent audience.

The Golem in the Brit Chadasha (New Testament)

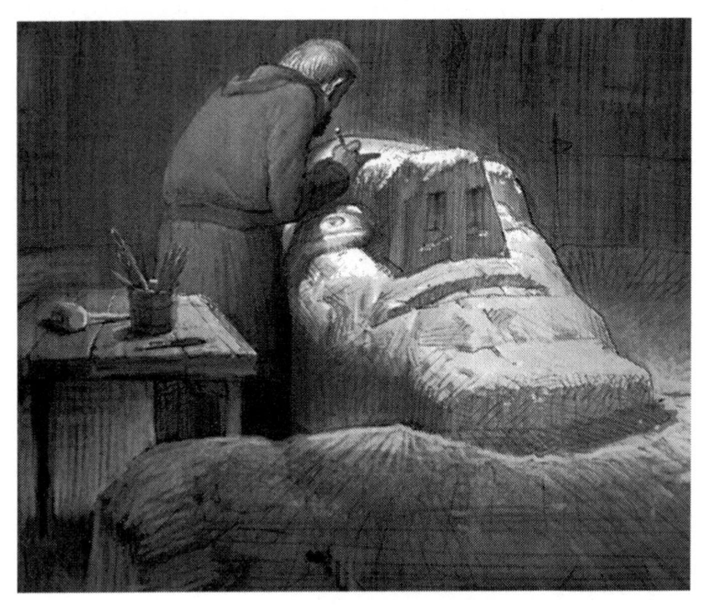

According to Scripture, the Moshiach Neged (Anti-Messiah) starts out righteous [like Yahudah the Karaite (Judas Iscariot)] and reinstitutes a full sacrificial service in the third Temple, but after a time he angers YHWH by bringing them to a halt. ***Daniel 9:27 "And he shall confirm the brit (covenant) with many for one week: and in the middle of the week he shall cause the sacrifice and the offering to cease, and on the wing/corner of abominations shall be the one who makes it desolate, even until the complete end of the olam hazeh (world to come), which has been determined and shall be poured upon the one who lays waste."*** Whilst this truth is often news to most Christian theologians the creation of a golem is even far less known, much less discussed or debated over within Christian eschatological commentary.

At a stage in history where unprecedented numbers of people are dying due to various plagues and diseases, the Navi Sheker (False Prophet) will devise a way to grab the world's absolute attention by co-creating a living person in the likeness of the Moshiach Neged who had already healed from a fatal wound to the head. ***Revelation 13:11-15; "And I looked and another beast came up out of the earth; and he had two horns like a lamb, and he spoke as a dragon.***

And he exercises all the power of the first beast before him, and causes the olam (world) and those who dwell in it to worship the first beast, whose deadly wound was healed. And he does great wonders, so that he makes fire come down from the shamayim into the olam in the sight of men, And deceives them that dwell in the olam by means of those nisim (miracles) which he had power to do in the sight of the beast; saying to those that dwell in the olam (world), that they should make an image to the beast, who had the wound by a sword, and did live. And he had power to give chayim (life) to the image of the beast, so that the image of the beast should both speak, and cause as many as would not worship the image of the beast to be killed."

According to ancient Jewish tradition, a golem is a manlike creature that is created by "kneading virgin soil (raw red clay) from the mountains (preferably the Temple Mount) with pure water[3]" into a 1:1 scale human form. The Hebrew word "golem" means "cocoon," from the root *gelem*, meaning "raw materials." The word appears once in ***Psalms 139:16*** where it is translated in English Bibles as "unformed substance." In context the verse refers to the raw material that YHWH used to form King David before he was born.

Outwardly a golem appears as a real person and remains perpetually in the same state that Adam was in before YHWH breathed into his nostrils. This leaves the golem devoid of a *nefesh* (soul) and without YHWH's ruach (breath). The word "EMET" (Hebrew for "truth") is carefully engraved into its forehead and the 72 letter name of YHWH is then whispered into its ear. This final act initiates animation in the form. Eyewitness accounts of such rare acts relate that the clay turns red hot as if being heated in a furnace.

The Navi Sheker's action of engraving a sign upon the head of the golem (aka: the abomination of desolation) to give it life will finally push the classic conspiracy theorist "Mark of the Beast" wary crowd over the edge in receiving a similar mark whether on or underneath the skin. Many people will already be in a weak state of mind after struggling through illnesses and being deemed unable to participate in the economy without such a mark. This will be compounded by some religious teachers who relate how Noah was 666 years of age at the time of the great flood and was spared.

3 From Eleazar of Worms Commentary on *Sefer Yetzira (Book of Creation).*

Revelations 13:16:18; "And he causes all, both small and great, rich and poor, free and bond, to receive a mark in their right hand, or in their foreheads: And that no man might buy, or sell, except he that had the mark, or the name of the beast, even the multitudes who have his name. Here is chochmah (wisdom). Let him that has binah (knowledge) consider the multitude (some translations use number) ***of the beast: for it is the multitude*** (some translations use number) ***of a man; and his multitude is encoded in 'chi, xi, sigma*** (666 according to many manuscripts).**'"**

Utterance of the Sacred Name to Activate the Golem

If a Nazarene Israelite maintains a consistent effort in his studies he will eventually find out that the Tetragrammaton[4] name of YHWH is the tip of the iceberg when it comes to the Sacred Name subject. While the Creator has many names, these are not to be confused with His many titles. Other significant names have been revealed from the pages of Scripture that were unlocked by devoted Sages who studied the deeper complexities of the Divine Text. Some of these names are very intricate and their study is to be pursued with caution for reasons that will become apparent shortly. The three most prominent names in relation to the animation of a golem are the Tetragrammaton, the 42 letter and 72 letter name (as previously mentioned).

A golem could not have been created by men any earlier than the time of Enoch[5] (Seth's firstborn son). The ancient Sages reasoned this according to Genesis, which says that when Enoch was born, ***"men began to call upon the name of YHWH" (Genesis 4:26).*** This was because all methods of activating a "human shaped" golem, hinged on the correct pronunciation of either a combination of the Tetragrammaton and 42 letter name or the 72 letter name of YHWH.

---

4 Greek word meaning, "four letters" (tetra means "four" and "gramma" means "letter." This is used as a reference to the four Hebrew letter name of the El of Israel, which appears in the TaNaK 6,800 times.

5 Not to be confused with the 7th born Enoch who walked with YHWH and is quoted in the Book of Jude.

Entering Abracadabra Territory

Some readers may accuse this author of entering Abracadabra[6] territory with presenting a heavy emphasis on what appears to be "name-magic" in relation to Torah. This is an understandable concern, especially if a reader has a strong traditional Christian mindset and a negative outlook toward Kabbalah. Most people's view of correct name pronunciation in relation to spiritual matters is chiefly dominated by an occult frame of reference due to various forms of media exposure. In reality the studious accumulation of multiple names of YHWH and their careful and respectful invocation for certain purposes by Jewish Sages has always been completely paralleled in pagan religions with their own false gods.

The occult borrows just about everything it teaches from the truth and twists it into a perverted replacement. Every false religious group from outwardly satanic cults to widely accepted Christian movements follow rituals that are directly reversed, parodied or subtly altered that originally stemmed from the one true faith of YHWH. The exhaustive array of religions spanning the entire globe simply evolved from a rebellious attempt at achieving a pleasurable state via an alternative avenue. ***John 10:1; "Amein, amein, I say to you, He that enters not by the door into the sheepfold, but climbs up some other derech (way), the same is a thief and a robber."***

Question: Aren't you in danger of placing far too much emphasis on the Creator's name over the Creator himself? Surely YHWH is much more than a name?

Answer: This question is born from the average Western mind's limited understanding of what a name is. And herein lies the problem. Scripture itself constantly emphasises focus on YHWH's name as opposed to YHWH himself. ***John 12:28; "Abba, bring tifereth (glory) to Your Name. Then there came a voice from the shamayim (heavens), saying, I have both esteemed it, and will esteem it again."*** A person might question why the text doesn't simply read, "Abba,

6 Possibly an Aramaic word (ab'ra k'dabra) that means, "I will create according to the word."

bring glory to Yourself?" or why other verses read ***"I have manifested your Name…" (John17:6)*** and ***"shomer (protect) through Your own Name those whom You have given Me…" (John 17:11).*** There is no line of demarcation between the power of YHWH and the power of His name or the divine letters that He spoke which wove all creation together. The opening of Genesis describes the creation process, which is entered into with utterances that bring things into being, therefore it is not often disputed as to whether one is saved by YHWH or saved by His name. They are one and the same. ***Acts 4:12; "Neither is there salvation in any other: for there is no other Name under the shamayim (heavens) given among men, whereby we must be saved."***

The 42 Letter Name

The exact pronunciation of the 42 Letter name is believed to be unknown. The letters of the name are derived from the 1st century prayer *Ana Bekoah* (Please with Might). This prayer was written by Rabbi Nehunia Ben Hakannah and was constructed using a seven letter sequence derived from the first 42 letters of Genesis. Reciting this prayer in a suitably prepared and highly meditative state is said to cause the immediate environment to become enveloped in the same uncorrupted energy that was present at the beginning of creation. This prayer is contained in the Jewish Shaharit (morning), Mincha (afternoon) and Shabbat prayers. The origin of the 42 letter name is also referred to in Talmudic literature, though the very influential Sage Rashi quotes that it "was not given to [us in the Torah]." Many of the more complex names of YHWH are frowned upon by less studious believers because they are not so obviously exhibited in the Torah itself. Despite this, it is important to note that the 22, 42, and 72 letter names are widely accepted within Judaism as being solidly rooted in Torah, whilst other names of YHWH can be more freely disputed as being the product of individual construction. The 42 letter name is read right to left. The "Tz" and "Kh" shown here in reverse are to be read as one letter.

NTSIRQzTTYGBA

GTzTRTB SKYDGN

QZPLGY INTDKhK

TYzTVKS

The 72 Letter or 72 Part Name

The 72 Letter name is considered to be the most powerful and the most potentially dangerous to use. It is composed of *a harmony of letters derived from* ***Exodus 14:19-21***. The name was said to be taught to Moshe at the burning bush and was used to part the Red Sea. The name can be used to heal, destroy, create and influence any part of creation. Use of this name by a person who is not in an appropriate state of physical and spiritual purity will cause instantaneous death. Such an end may also come about by mispronunciation.

The utterance of these complex names would come at the close of a highly detailed ritual. Though the process of creating a golem varied, it would likely have included an uninterrupted 36 hour stint of meditative breathing and concentration, preceded by purifying oneself from food, preparation of the golem's form in virgin soil, and painstakingly inscribing Hebrew letters on its forehead.

The late American Orthodox rabbi and physicist, Aryeh Kaplan, who was known for using his physics background to analyse Torah, describes the process of making a golem:

> "An initiate should not do it alone, but should always be accompanied by one or two colleagues. The Golem must be made of virgin soil, taken from a place where no man has ever dug. The soil must be kneaded with pure spring water, taken directly from the ground. If this water is placed in any kind of vessel, it can no longer be used. The people making the Golem must purify themselves totally before engaging in this activity, both physically and spiritually. While making

> the Golem, they must wear clean white vestments… One must not make any mistake or error in the pronunciation… no interruption whatsoever may occur…"

Misusing the Building Blocks of Creation

Fallen angels were the first beings to mishandle the creation and manipulation mechanics of YHWH's Torah. Their rebellion did not bring about an instant death or cause them to lose their ability to function as "mighty ones." A limited essence of YHWH still resides in them as it does all living things by virtue of life remaining in a vessel. Fallen angels directly and indirectly taught the misuse of the mechanical and technical aspects of Torah to men under the guise of different mystical paths. They also attempted to present a twisted form of Torah to new initiates. In this way Kabbalah has been used as a means to an end by many disillusioned people today. This is how the Moshiach Neged and Navi Sheker will be able to raise up a golem. Supernaturally affecting the environment in a manner that is not in accordance with YHWH has a track record of being unmanageable and ultimately brings about a person's own destruction. YHWH is not subject to the will of a fallen angel or a sinful man who studies the dark arts. On the contrary, nothing happens outside YHWH's complete control. Letting rebellious beings live can allow them time to repent, give immediate earthly rewards for any good they may have done or cause goodness in other beings to flourish as they repeal and endure their misdeeds.

Having said this, the question arises concerning the actions of Rabbi Yehuda Loew of Prague, who constructed a golem to save his community. After the golem had stood at the gates of the ghetto and so effectively repealed the mob, so much so that he caused those who remained alive to flee for their lives, Rabbi Loew finally saw that the creation of the golem was against the Divine Will. So later he ushered it up to the attic of his synagogue and took away its life-force.

The Origin of Wizards in Fantasy Literature

The classic image of the magician or wizard hunched over a pile of dusty books with chemicals bubbling away in the background originated from the appearance of the typical medieval Jewish Sage. Their flowing robe, long white beard, constant proximity to scrolls, ointments, incenses and trinkets, formed the basis of the popular look of such fantasy characters as *J.R.R. Tolkien's* Gandalf the Grey and *J.K. Rowling's* Wizard Headmaster Dumbledore.

In fact some of the most unlikely modern-day films and organisations exhibit very Orthodox Jewish themes. Take for example the movie *Pirates of the Caribbean - At World's End.* In the second last act of the film an impending war causes pirates from all over the known world to come together. To determine what should be done, two pirate elders, complete with long white beards and head coverings produce a sacred law book called "the Code." As they carry it out, a look of awe envelopes the faces of the roughest company of men on the high seas. Ironically there was actually a real series of Pirate Codes formulated in the 17th century by buccaneers who functioned under an agreement called the "Custom of the Coast" or "Jamaica Discipline." This code, though it varied between groups, eventually became known as the "Article of Agreement" or "Pirate's Code."

Outlaw motorcycle groups (bikey gangs) also observe some of the most complex rules and regulations. I was once told about two members of a particular gang who were both interested in the wife of a recently deceased member. They had to approach the club elder to get permission to even speak to the widow. Outlaw organisations have some of the strictest laws on the face of the earth. Take for example the following news report with statements by a senior detective and a Superintendent:

> In June 23, 2007, an article in *The Australian* called, "Bikies' Code Makes Them Hard to Crack," **stated the following, "THEY (bikey gangs) impose strict discipline, operate under rigid rules, demand fanatical loyalty, live by a code of honour and deal ruthlessly with outside threats.** They are, in the words of one senior detective, 'frighteningly like the police, except their motives are different. It is the

military-style structures of outlaw motorcycle gangs – a legacy from their establishment in the US following World War II by ex-servicemen looking for the sort of camaraderie they had in the armed services. It is what makes them so effective and so hard for law enforcement authorities to penetrate. 'It is frightening when you look at the way they operate, their hierarchical structure, their constitutions and their rules,' says the head of Western Australia's organised crime division, Superintendent Kim Porter." - Written by Gary Hughes

The oriental mafia group known as the *Triads* often implement injurious and at times fatal beatings to members who fail to observe their customs. This reality confirms my belief that even the most dangerous individuals and organisations crave law and order within their own communities. This is because true freedom cannot be enjoyed without some measure of law present, even among thieves.

The Origin of the Pointy Hat

The distinctive pointy hat seen in the typical depiction of a Wizard or Mage came about with the Jews. In 1215 at the conclusion of the Fourth Lateran Council, presided over by Pop Innocent III, a decree went out invoking the command that all Jews wear particular clothing. Part of this clothing consisted of a *Judenhat* (a pointed Jewish hat). Some Jews at this time, usually scholars, already had the custom of wearing them (probably due to former edicts enforced on them by other foreign powers).

Pointed headwear appears to have been worn by Babylonian (Persian) Jews as early as 245CE according to the wall reliefs of the Dura-Europa synagogue[7] of upper Mesopotamia (Syria). This immediately shatters the commonly held view that Jews adopted headwear as a custom in the early modern era. There are also sixth-century pottery figurines from China that depict Jewish merchants wearing distinctive pointed headwear. The style of pointed

7 The *Dura-Europa Synagogue* is one of the oldest and most well preserved synagogues in the world. It has a large volume of pictorial art on its walls, challenging the widely held belief that Jews prohibited the use of visual images.

hat, depending on the era and cultural setting, varied. Some consisted of a soft cap with a floppy peak and some of a hard material with a pointed peak. The Persian hat worn by the Jew was soft brimmed and ended in a vertical conical point.

Saint Joseph is shown wearing a *Judenhat* in a 12th century German nativity scene, whilst Jesus' is shown in one on the road to Emmaus ***(Luke 24:13-32)*** in quite a few etchings and paintings from the same era. A 5th century painting in a Roman catacomb also shows Jesus using a wand to raise Lazarus from the dead.

The Origin of the Wizard's Staff

The rod or staff is a symbol of great power in many cultures. Perhaps the most famous staff in history is Aaron's rod. Rabbinical literature identifies this staff as originally being used by Jacob when he crossed the Jordan and then by Judah who gave it to his daughter-in-law Tamar. From here it found its way to Moshe and Aaron, who both used it to performed wonders. King David is said to have possessed it and passed it on to his son Solomon. After this it remained in use as a scepter until the destruction of the Temple at which time it disappeared from history. It is believed to have been made of sapphire and inscribed with a Hebrew abbreviation of the Ten Plagues of Egypt.

The rod was apparently created by YHWH at the close of the sixth day of creation and given to Adam when he was driven from Gan Eden (paradise). From here it moved to Shem, Enoch, Methuselah, Noah, Abraham, Isaac, Jacob and finally Joseph. Egyptian nobles stole the staff after Joseph's death, but it miraculously found its way to Moshe's future father-in-law Jethro, who planted the rod in the ground. There it stayed, unable to be removed by anyone until Moshe withdrew it many years later. The Midrash describes its miraculous removal by Moshe from Jethro's garden. YHWH showed Moshe the significance of the rod he carried in his encounter at the burning bush. ***Exodus 4:17; "And you shall take this rod in your hand, with which you shall do the signs."*** The story of the rod eventually gave rise to the popular Arthurian legend of *Excalibur*. The staff's journey also bears a striking similarity to J.R.R. Tolkien's *One Ring* in the literary classic, *The Lord of the Rings*.

The Authority of a Sage

The act of employing specific sacred texts to produce a supernatural effect is not the domain of pagans nor was it a practice that originally took root with them. The longing to discern the outcome of a future event or to manipulate nature in times of distress are not by definition characteristics of someone who practices the dark arts. But the fact that most people who try to achieve such results use twisted and unhinged methods to do so has conditioned most people to think otherwise. There is a story of the founder of the ChaBaD movement, Rabbi Shneur Zalman (aka The Alter Rebbe) who was arrested in the Russian town of Liozna in 1798. It was known among his community that he could perform miracles, but the occasions for which he chose to do them were very rare. He was taken away on Friday morning in a special wagon called the "Black Mary," which was reserved for rebels who faced capital sentence for crimes against the Czarist regime. Along the way he humbly asked his captors for permission for the wagon to cease its journey for the duration of the Shabbat. The officer in charge ignored his request. Not long into the journey the axels of the Black Mary broke. They stopped and repaired it (which took quite some time) and eventually continued on. A little while later one of the horses pulling the wagon suddenly died. Eventually his captors agreed to stop traveling. They asked the Alter Rebbe if he could allow them to at least make it to the next village. The Rebbe refused, but agreed to allow the carriage to be taken to a nearby field. So the Rebbe spent his first Shabbat in captivity, but in full control of the situation. He achieved this end through supernatural means, but not through bold control over his captors' wills or nature itself, but through subtle ways until he received approval from his captors to rest on the Shabbat. It was important that the carriage at least be moved by his captors to a nearby field because it is not good to perform a mitzvah directly through a miracle. Messiah Yahshua acted the same way during his capture, arrest and eventual execution. He is found almost coaching Yahudah the Karaite (Judas Iscariot) through his betrayal and allowing his captors to return to their feet after knocking them down supernaturally with a verbal response to a question.

There are two texts within rabbinical literature that outline the use of the Torah and the Psalms to achieve specific results. These texts though they appear esoteric, encapsulate this idea. They are known as the *Shimmushei Torah* and the *Shimmushei Tehillim (Psalms)*. The word Shimmushei means "practical use of." These texts are known to reveal YHWH's Names and passages of the Psalms that, upon utterance, allow the achievement of particular supernatural feats. I have included a background to each of these works in the appendix of this book.

Final Note and Warning

To anyone who has read this and now feels inspired to go off and research the subject for the purpose of creating a golem, forget it. With the onset of the internet (a researcher's dream in the form of the effortless *Google* search) the formula for constructing a golem appears to have crept into the public domain, however, the exact method of creating one requires far more than studying the *Sefer Yetzira* and following the faithful directions of Eleazar of Worms due to several reasons. One is that some phases in the golem's construction are deliberately withheld in all authoritative texts and passed down only in oral form from teacher to student. Another reason is that thorough knowledge of the spiritual manifestation of each letter of the Hebrew Alphabet (a principle requirement in creating a golem) is believed to be lacking even amongst the most knowledgeable of Kabbalists alive today. And yet another reason is the level of spiritual and physical endurance that is required to complete the task (extreme fasting and long periods of intense meditative prayer). Finally, the Torah mandates that nothing be fashioned in the likeness of anything above, on or beneath the earth. The purpose of this chapter is to merely shed light on a key action by the Navi Sheker and the Moshiach Neged that enables them to place the jewel in the crown of their final deception. Now go and study it...

Chapter Eighteen

The Origin of Familiar Spirits

THE FAMOUS ***Ghosts of SS Watertown*** photograph is an intriguing image, if for no other reason than the story that surrounds it. In 1924 seamen aboard the *SS Watertown* began spotting the recognisable heads of their recently deceased shipmates in the waters of the Pacific. The slightly larger heads would appear roughly ten feet apart and no closer than 40 feet from the boat. Their appearance would fade in and out, lasting no more than 10 seconds at a time. Upon entering port, the captain purchased a camera (at the shipping company's request) and managed to snap six pictures of the strange phenomenon that continued for a further two voyages. Once the photos were developed, five of them showed nothing, except the one on page 283.

The credibility of this account is solidified by multiple witnesses, its repeated occurrence and the negative having undergone checks for fakery by a detective agency. On the downside, the image was not released to the public until 1934, and by the time the story gained enough momentum to warrant further investigation, the photographer had died. To add to this, the remainder of the crew were extremely difficult to locate and the original photograph was officially lost.

According to Hebrew thought the sea covers a place where the dead are gathered. This place is called *Sheol*. *Sheol* means, "abode of the dead," and is a place that is located geographically straight down according to ***Genesis 37:35, 42:38, 44:29, 44:31, Numbers 16:30, 16:33*** and ***Ezekiel 31:15-17***. *The King James Bible* uses the word *Sheol* 31 times as "hell[1]," 31 times as "grave" and 3 times as "pit."

The slightly exaggerated size of the deceased shipmates' heads floating in the waters by the *SS Watertown* is interesting in light of the following verse: ***Job 26:5,6; "Raphaim are formed from under the waters, and the inhabitants thereof. Sheol is naked before them."*** (These verses literally mean: Disembodied spirits of deceased giants roam in the waters above Sheol [the place of the human dead].) Raphaim (plural) contains the Hebrew root *rafa*, **which means "spirit"** ***(Genesis 14:5)*** **and is why most common Bible translations start the verse with "the dead" or "spirits of the dead."** But what does this mean?

The majority of giants (offspring of unlawful relations between Sons of Elohim and human women ***[Genesis 6:1-4, Jude 5-7]***) were killed by drowning and starvation during the great deluge ***(Genesis 6:17)***. After this time, their spirits being unable to partake in the resurrection, began to roam the earth. ***Isaiah 26:14; "[They are] dead, they shall not live; [they are] deceased, they shall not rise [resurrect]: therefore I (YHWH) have visited and destroyed them."*** These

1 The word "hell" is derived from the old Germanic Anglo word *helan*, which means "concealed" or "covered." If this is true the only relationship this term has with a place for the dead is with the word "sea," which according to Scripture covers *Sheol*.

deceased disembodied spirits drifted to-and-fro on the land, finding all places, except humans, too dry to inhabit. ***Matthew 12:43; "When the unclean spirit is gone out of a man, he walk through dry places, seeking rest, and finds none."*** The modern-day discovery of the similarities between the cardiovascular system of a pig and a human could reveal why legions of evil spirits requested to be sent into a herd of pigs after they were cast from a man by Yahshua in the country of Gadarenes ***(Mark 5:1-20).***

Sheol at a Glance

Sheol is the most common place for the dead[2]. Other locations include the surface of the earth[3], the heavens and a place in the heavens called the "Golden Altar" ***(Revelations 6:9-11).*** Only a handful of righteous men have been taken into the heavens alive[4]. They

---

2 In Scripture, the word *Gehenna* is sometimes used interchangeably with *Sheol.* This is because *Gehenna* was also a physical refuse tip located outside Jerusalem that continually burned. Its location was a place where Canaanites sacrificed their children to Moloch ***(2 Chronicles 28:3, 34:4-5, 36:6).*** *Ge Hinnom* means "valley of Hinnom's son." Hinnom means "lamentation." The place is first mentioned in The ***Book of Joshua (15:8; 18:16).*** King Solomon eventually erected "high places" to Moloch there in ***1 Kings 11:7*** allowing some measure of pagan worship to return to the site during his time. Though the Word says King Solomon worshiped idols in his latter years ***(1 Kings 11:7),*** he did not do so physically, but his tolerance and sanctioning of building idols for his wives who did made him liable. A wicked leader of Israel, Ahaz later returned the valley to its former abominable use by making children ***"pass through the fire"*** there in ***2 Kings 16:3*** and ***2 Chronicles 28:3; 33:6.***

3 This locality is applicable only to deceased nephilim and fallen angels. ***Isaiah 13:21*** & ***34:14*** refers to demons ("satyrs" [goat-demons] and "screech owls" aka "night creatures" [lilith or sucubi]) dwelling in ruins or in the wilderness or places where the living do not frequent. These references are thought to support the reality of ghosts who inhabit haunted houses. "The Hebrew word in these verses is 'sa`iyr' (Strong's #8163, pronounced saw-eer'), and due to the similarity in pronunciation, maybe where the Greek derived 'saturos' (pronounced saw-toor'-os), leading to the English 'satyr'. The Hebrew word occurs 59 times in the Old Testament, and the KJV has translated it thus: 'kid' (ie., young goat) 28 times, 'goat' 24 times, 'devil' 2 times, 'satyr' 2 times, 'hairy' 2 times, 'rough' (goat) 1 time...In fact, right after the 'satyr' in ***Isa 34:14*** it mentions the 'screech owl' ('night creatures' in NIV, 'night monster' in 1611 KJV marginal note), which in the Hebrew is "lilith" (see also NRSV) - a female night demon according to Jewish and pagan tradition" Source - *Mythological and Mysterious Creatures in the KJV* (http://www.kjv-only.com/satyr.html)

4 Judaism teaches that seven men were taken into heaven alive. Interestingly they acknowledge that one of these seven was none other than Yahshua's disciple Yochannan (John). According to another rabbinic opinion there were "nine worthies who (attained) paradise without tasting death: Enoch, Elijah, the Messiah, Hiram, Ebed Melech, Batya, Jaabez, Joshua ben Levi and Serach bat Asher." – *The Encyclopedia of Jewish Myth, Magic and Mysticisim* by Rabbi Geoffrey W. Dennis. Note that this last view refers to "Paradise," which is often confused with the Heavens.

were Enoch ***(Genesis 5:24)***, Elijah ***(2 Kings 2:11)*** Yochannan (John) ***[John 21:23[5]]***, and Messiah Yahshua ***(Acts 1:9)***. This is despite Yahshua's declaration in ***John 3:13; "And no man has ascended up to the shamayim (heavens), but He that came down from the shamayim (heavens), even the Ben Ahdahm (son of Adam [Yahshua]) who is in the shamayim."*** This refers to any human passing into heaven after death before Yahshua's crucifixion and resurrection. Enoch and Elijah were snatched living from the earth. Similarly unrighteous men have been taken into *Sheol* alive (such as Korach and his dissenters in ***Numbers 16:33***). *Sheol* contains separated chambers, one of which is referred to by Messiah himself when he comforted the Zealot (thief) who was crucified with him ***(Luke 23:43)***. The place he refers to is transliterated as "paradise[6]," which comes from the word *Pardes*[7] ("orchard"). This location is also referred to as "Abraham's Bosom" ***(Luke 16:22-23)*** and is a place that was set aside for the righteous dead before the resurrection of Messiah Yahshua. At Yahshua's ascension all the righteous dead of "Abraham's Bosom" or "Paradise" were moved to the "Golden Altar[8]." Other compartments of *Sheol* are "The Pit or Abaddon[9]," "The Abyss" (aka "Bottomless Pit") and "Tartarus." Tartarus is a place where the original conspiring angels who mingled with human women are held in chains ***(2 Peter 2:4)***.

---

5 ***John 21:23; "Then this saying went out around among the Yisraelite brothers, that this talmid (student [John]) would not die: yet Yahshua said not to him, you shall not die, but if I choose that he remains alive until I come, what is that to you?"***

6 This word is of Persian origin (*Pardis*). It evolved into the Latin, *paradisus* and then into the French *paradis* before finally being rendered in English as "Paradise." It means "walled" or "partitioned garden." This reference to a walled off place testifies to its locality among other walled off locations in *Sheol.*

7 This word is also an acronym for the four methods of Torah interpretation, *pashat* (plain meaning), *remez* (allegorical meaning), *d'rash* (homiletic meaning) and *sod* (esoteric meaning). According to rabbinic thought this signifies that those who enter the "orchard" are ones who have penetrated the depths of the Torah.

8 Before ascending to the Golden Alter these righteous dead emerged physically from their graves according to ***Matthew 27:53***.

9 *Abaddon* is a Hebrew word that means "place" or "realm of destruction." This place is mentioned in ***Job 26:6*** and ***Proverbs 15:11***. It is one of seven compartments in *Gehenna.* The Angel that presides over this compartment is mentioned in ***Revelations 9:7-11***. He has the same name (Abaddon) but it is rendered as *Apollyon* in Greek, which means "destroyer." After his death, the Prophet Moshe is said to have visited there according to *The Legends of the Jews*, Volume II: From Joseph to Exodus. 1909, by Lewis Ginzberg.

Even Demons Study Torah

According to Ashkenazi rabbi, Judah He-Chasid (aka Judah ben Samuel), demons also study and adhere to Torah so they know when they may attack a victim who has transgressed it.

Sheol was designed to temporarily or eternally detain, punish or even entirely destroy rebellious angelic host[10]. Humans can also be sent there, but according to an almost unanimous rabbinic understanding, the longest most souls are there is approximately 12 months. It is perhaps a common misconception that an eternal punishment awaits wicked mortals who live temporal lives. The Hebrew view of *Abaddon* is likened to a spiritual forge where all imperfections in the soul are purged so that it may pass onto *Gan Eden* (place of delight), which can be either *Pardes*[11] or the Golden Altar. Exceptionally wicked mortals may suffer in *Abaddon* for a longer period of time or even become completely destroyed. This destruction is so powerful that it burns away the very memory of them.

The Rabbis Did (on Occasion) Cast Out Spirits

Messiah Yahshua's first Scriptural example of exerting authority over an evil spirit ***(Mark 1:24)*** and then passing this authority on to his talmidim (disciples) ***(Matthew 10:1)*** certainly supports an argument that such a practice was not previously known. However, it is important to acknowledge that rabbinic literature does contain accounts of rabbis removing *dybbukim* (spiritual attachments). One approach for removing a *dybbuk* involves a *minian* (10 men) who represent the 10 Kabbalistic *sephirot* (10 attributes of YHWH). They encircle the individual and recite ***Psalms 91*** three times. At the conclusion of this a shofar (ram's horn) is blown. The sound of the shofar is said to cause confusion in the dark forces and prompt

10 ***Psalms 82:7*** speaks of some rebel angels dying like men.

11 *Pardes* is predominantly being refilled with Torah observant believers who do not recognise Yahshua as Messiah (Note the use of the word recognise as opposed to the word "reject"). Yahshua proclaimed his victory before the spirits in prison (another compartment of *Sheol*) after *Pardes* emptied ***(1 Peter 3:18-22)***.

them to flee an area. The rabbi leading the ritual will usually enter into dialogue with the *dybbuk*. Whatever the case, this type of authority was exhibited well after the time of Noah and well before the Catholic Church's rite of exorcism.

Most people who believe they are experiencing an evil spirit are simply going through a psychological episode and simply wish to externalise their problem to a foreign entity. There is a story that dates back to the eighteenth century where a woman took her daughter to a local rabbi after suspecting she was being influenced by a *dybbuk*. The rabbi found that she exhibited no real signs of a *dybbuk*, but noted that the girl and her mother were so convinced that he instructed them to take home an alarm clock and at 4:30pm the *dybbuk* will leave the girl. Hours after they arrived home the alarm clock rang and the mother and daughter were completely convinced that it had gone by the mere shock of hearing the bell of the alarm clock go off precisely at the time the rabbi predicted.

Another view that developed after the flood was that human figures seemingly walking on air and striding through walls were that of spirits, as is evident in Yahshua's very own talmidim who mistaken him for a ghost on at least two occasions ***(Matthew 14:26*** & ***Luke 24:36-37)***. By the absence of the said methods of spiritual authority and a belief in ghosts prior to the flood we can safely say that a dispensation of disembodied genetically mixed spirits plaguing living men is evident in Scripture.

The first mention of evil spirits occurs in the Book of Leviticus. Israel is warned not to associate with those who have tried to cultivate a livelihood out of contact with evil spirits. ***Leviticus 19:31; "Regard not those who are mediums, neither seek after spiritists, to be defiled by them: I am YHWH your Elohim."*** The actual appearance of the first evil spirit is mentioned as being sent out by YHWH in ***Judges 9:23; "Then Elohim sent an evil ruach between Avimelech and the men of Shechem; and the men of Shechem dealt treacherously against Avimelech..."***

An evil spirit also plagues King Sha'ul (Saul) after the king had become angered by a popular song in Israel that celebrated David's success in battle to a higher degree than his own. Here again is an evil spirit being sent forth by YHWH, which immediately challenges most popular spiritual warfare teachings. ***1 Samuel 18:10;***

"And it came to pass the next day, that the evil ruach (spirit) from Elohim came upon Shaul, and he prophesied evil in the midst of the bayit (house): and Dawid played the harp with his hand, as at other times: and there was a javelin in Shaul's hand. And Shaul cast the javelin; for he said, 'I will smite Dawid even to the wall with it.' And Dawid withdrew from his presence twice."

For many believers, particularly Christians, the phenomenon of ghosts and how it is dealt with from the pages of Scripture, remains an enigma that through lack of knowledge is either compartmentalised away as tomfoolery or as a blanket belief of fallen angels masquerading as the dead. The Book of Enoch, a text deliberately withheld from accepted Scripture until the last days, explains in further detail the origin of familiar spirits. ***1 Enoch 15; "But now the giants who are born from the (union of) the spirits and the flesh shall be called evil spirits upon the earth, because their dwelling shall be upon the earth and inside the earth. Evil spirits have come out of their bodies. Because from the day that they were created from the holy ones they became the Watchers; their first origin is the spiritual foundation. They will become evil upon the earth and shall be called evil spirits. The dwelling of the spiritual beings of heaven is heaven; but the dwelling of the spirits of the earth, which are born upon the earth, is in the earth. The spirits of the giants oppress each other, they will corrupt, fall, be excited, and fall upon the earth, and cause sorrow. They eat no food, nor become thirsty, nor find obstacles. And these spirits shall rise up against the children of the people and against the women, because they have proceeded forth (from them)."***

Flavius Josephus elaborates further in his *Legends of the Jews*: "...And the spirits of the giants will devour, oppress, destroy, attack, and do battle and cause destruction on the earth and work affliction. They will be invisible, and these spirits shall raise up against the children of men and against women, because they have proceeded from them, thus they will destroy until the day when the consummation of the great world will be consumed."

The range of familiar spirits described in Scripture consists of the following:

Spirit of jealousy ***(Numbers 5:14)***

Familiar spirit ***(I Samuel 28:7)***

A spirit *(Job 4:15)*
Spirit of deep sleep *(Isaiah 29:10)*
Spirit of whoredoms *(Hosea 4:12)*
Unclean spirit *(Luke 8:29)*
Spirit of infirmity *(Luke 13:11)*
Spirit of divination *(Acts 16:16)*
Spirit of bondage *(Romans 8:15)*
Enticing spirit *(2 Chronicles 18:20)*
Spirit of devils *(Revelation 16:14)*
Spirits of false prophecy *(I John 4:1)*
Seducing spirits *(I Timothy 4:1)*
Evil spirits *(Acts 19:13)*
Spirit of fear *(2 Timothy 1:7)*
Spirit of error *(I John 4:6)*
Foul spirit *(Revelation 18:2)*
Another spirit *(2 Corinthians 11:4)*
Spirit of the world *(I Corinthians 2:12)*
Unclean devil *(Luke 4:33)*
Dumb spirit *(Mark 9:17)*
A lying spirit *(2 Chronicles 18:22)*
Spirit of heaviness *(Isaiah 61:3)*
Perverse spirit *(Isaiah 19:14)*
Spirit of travail and vexation *(Ecclesiastes 4:6)*
A haughty spirit *(Proverbs 16:18)*
Hasty spirit *(Proverbs 14:29)*

The spiritual world, which all the above spirits manifest from is what the non-religious generally call the supernatural realm. The term **supernatural** means "above the natural," but is somewhat of a misnomer because it is generally understood as a power beyond nature, in that it cannot be explained from the laws of the natural world. One has to wonder about the application of the term "tomfoolery" when there is no exact definition of what "natural" is, or where the limits of naturalism end. Man's foundational scientific knowledge is never final. It is ever expanding and causes technological boundaries to increase exponentially. Take this extract from Richard Milton's book *Alternative Science* for example. It contains views by men who believed they stood near the maximum ceiling of a scientific capability.

> "But despite scores of public demonstrations, affidavits from local dignitaries, and photographs of themselves flying, the claims of Wilbur and Orville Wright were derided and dismissed as a hoax by *Scientific American*, the *New York Herald*, the US Army and most American scientists. Experts were so convinced, on purely scientific grounds, that heavier than air flight was impossible that they rejected the Wright brothers' claims without troubling to examine the evidence...only weeks before the Wrights first flew at Kittyhawk, North Carolina, the professor of mathematics and astronomy at Johns Hopkins University, Simon Newcomb, had published an article in The Independent which showed scientifically that powered human flight was 'utterly impossible.' Powered flight, Newcomb believed, would require the discovery of some new unsuspected force in nature. Only a year earlier, Rear-Admiral George Melville, chief engineer of the US Navy, wrote in the North American Review that attempting to fly was 'absurd'. It was armed with such eminent authorities as these that Scientific American and the New York Herald scoffed at the Wrights as a pair of hoaxers."

An interesting aspect to this extract is that it addressed a view that something unknown was needed to achieve simple air travel, which is the same line of argument carried on by some sceptics of anti-gravity technology today. Science is a perpetual field of discovery that has no static boundary. ***Genesis 11:6; "And YHWH said, See, the people are echad (one), and they all have one language; and this they begin to do: and now nothing will be restrained from them, which they have imagined to do."***

Technological advancement without regard to Divine accountability is an inevitable path of man and many things previously unimaginable are now firmly within the grasp of companies and corporations worldwide. The holocaust was unprecedented in its efficient harnessing of technological means to orderly dispose of millions of human beings. The climate that led to its occurrence is following the same trajectory today.

A Nazarene Israelite should focus on standing fast and maintaining their faith with white knuckles. This doesn't mean you have to project confidence all the time in everything you do, but when your confidence is shot, hold onto faith and ride it through. Currently we have an opportunity to train and hone skills to prepare for the future. In part this is what Sukkoth is all about, spending a week in temporary dwellings and communing with YHWH in a wilderness environment.

Situations may soon arise and unusual things may occur, which could cause us some serious concern. But take heart. Evil men and even familiar spirits who sometimes influence them have no power to harm or confuse anyone beyond that which YHWH allows – **period**. HaSatan can only move against man, both individually and collectively by the permission that he is granted by the Almighty ***(Job 1:12; Job 2:6; Matthew 8:31-32)***. This should also be evident in the first Scriptural record of YHWH's sending out of an evil spirit.

Rest assured that YHWH uses HaSatan and the dark forces to lift up the integrity and love of His people. The trials of Job illustrate his integrity and deep loyalty to YHWH. Rabbi Sha'ul's (Paul's) affliction in ***2 Corinthians 12:7*** was in place to prevent pride from manifesting in him. Even Yahshua's rejection of HaSatan provided a platform to exhibit his loyalty to his own Father.

> "(YHWH) employs the wicked as his instruments of chastisement to purify the righteous after their task is accomplished, however, the wicked, themselves will perish in their own fire." – *(R'Hirsch) Pg 55 Tehillim* ***(Psalms 21:10)*** *The Seif Edition Artscroll Transliterated Linear Tehillim / Psalms*

A believer should focus his attention toward YHWH like a lover focuses his attention on his bride. If He be our desire we needn't fear anything else ***(Psalm 27:1)***.

If you are unfamiliar with the Scripture's take on familiar spirits, study it…You might be surprised what you find.

Chapter Nineteen

Prophet
A Most Dangerous Office

"I will raise them up a Navi (Prophet) from among their brothers, like you, and will put My words in His mouth; and He shall speak to them all that I shall command Him."(Deuteronomy 18:18)

WITHOUT REALISING IT, many believers can take prophecy for granted, faithfully scouring the Scriptures without ever considering the birthing process of the very words they're reading or the background of the men and women who first uttered them. As a consequence, a general lack of awareness into the origin and evolution of the phenomenon of prophecy has caused millions, if not trillions, of sincere people to accept and nurture false belief systems right to the grave. Messiah Yahshua warned that in the last days thousands will be deceived ***(Matthew 24:11)*** by lawless people who will prophesy, cast out demons and perform many wonders in his name ***(Matthew 7:22-23)***. It's time to pull the antique subject of prophecy from the shelf, blow off the dust, and take a fresh look at the most dangerous office in the army of YHWH.

What is Prophecy?

The concept of prophecy was meticulously examined by the 12th century rabbinic scholar Maimonides[1] (Rambam) who wrote:

> "Prophecy is, in truth and reality, an emanation sent forth by the Divine Being through the medium of the active intellect, in the first instance to man's rational faculty, and then to his imaginative faculty." - *The Guide for the Perplexed*

In other words, prophecy is a communication by YHWH packaged in the form of a personal encounter, vision, dream or sign for the benefit of the recipient or another individual, group or community. Prophecy first took the form of a direct communication by YHWH to Adam and Hava in the Garden of Eden. After the fall it withdrew in this capacity and gradually reemerged in certain forms until it noticeably evolved into the format of a divine warning.

Some prophecies included promises or blessing, but they most notably come in the form of warnings in the TaNaK. This was perhaps not a bad thing, because according to Jewish wisdom, "It is more blessed to have a bad dream than a good dream, because a bad dream can provoke one to repentance." Such is the benefit of a prophetic warning.

There are many levels of prophecy, from the highest such as was experienced by the Prophet Moshe who was able to apprehend, reason and relate the Divine Will, to Noah who could only apprehend it. The rabbis teach that each prophet metaphorically beheld the Divine Image in the reflection of a certain number of mirrors or filters. The more minor the prophet or prophecy the larger the number of mirrors that obscured YHWH's image. It is said that Moshe beheld the Divine Glory of YHWH with only one mirror. "He (Moshe) beheld truth as if it were reflected by a clear mirror; all others, as by a dull glass." (Yeb. 49b)

1 Rambam, often criticised as denying Messiah Yahshua, wrote an interesting conclusion to his discourse on the credentials of the true Messiah. "[If the person legitimately fulfills part of the prophecies] but is killed before completing the restoration of the Temple…he is to be considered as 'all the other proper and complete kings of the Davidic dynasty who died.'"

Who is a Prophet?

> "For the laws of Nature demand that every one should be a prophet, who has a proper physical constitution, and has been duly prepared as regards to education and training." – *The Guide for the Perplexed*

Though this view is correct in light of Adam and Hava's spiritually attuned state before the fall, it does not mean that everyone's potential for prophecy will or should be realised to the degree of the major and minor prophets in the TaNaK. All members of the body should not look to divinely rebuke, warn, advise or interpret dreams for individuals or communities as a goal per se. ***1 Corinthians 12:18-20; "But now has Elohim set the members every one of them in the body, as it has pleased Him. And if they were all the same member, where would the body be? But now there are indeed many members, yet just one body."*** 1 Corinthians 12 states further in verse 29 that not all are given the gift of prophecy and ***Ephesians 4:11*** says that YHWH only ***"...gave some to be neviim (prophets)..."*** Rambam is referring to a type of prophetic awareness in matters, whether mundane or otherwise, arrived at by conventional inquiry based on Torah study. In other words those who arrive at spiritual insights in the course of their labour for knowledge and understanding without dreaming dreams, hearing utterances or seeing visions, are in a sense also considered prophets[2]. However, they are never to be confused with the prophets mentioned in Scripture who received messages via supernatural visitations. Nor are they to be confused with some of these who received the Divine Will, but did not preach it to their own generation. For example, Daniel was given the gift of prophecy yet never spoke directly with YHWH, and he was not mandated to verbally transmit his revelations as a warning to his own generation. So a person seeking to define Daniel's function by measuring it against the actions of the prophet Moshe would not consider him a prophet in the classical sense of the word.

2 The fruits of such insight are usually held privately to enrich self development.

Use of Symbology

The language used by the prophets had a very distinct flavour. Though the use of diction varied according to each individual, metaphors were commonly employed giving rise to expressions like, "the sun will be ashamed" when describing a nation's impending judgement or "the light of the sun has increased" when describing national prosperity. The uses of particular metaphors equip the prophet's sayings with additional information. For example "the dimming of the sun" not only refers to strife, but also a nationwide lack of discernment. Reference to Abraham's descendants being as "numerous as the sands of the sea" describes not only great multitudes, but unity as sand is hard to separate.

Much of Daniel's prophecies contained symbolic imagery. Prophecy in this form affected a great portion of the world's population and reached far into the future, spanning many generations. Symbology assisted in protecting the text's meaning and kept it aligned with the language of former prophetic writings over long periods of time. This interlocking use of symbology guarded against private interpretation. Though private interpretations of Scripture still abound, a student familiar with a Hebraic understanding of the Scriptures as a whole is able to discern false views easily.

Symbolic images in prophecy, though cryptic, were still time dependant and 100% accurate after the symbols of the message were decoded[3]. This decoding was done by applying other passages of Scripture to find exact meaning. No symbolism used by the prophets of Israel was meant to be understood in a loose or open-ended manner (i.e., their words could not share a range of completely different interpretations).

Prophets did not operate like clairvoyants who depended on external assistance from the subject that the prophetic word was going to affect. All true prophecy, whether cloaked in symbolism or not, was 100% accurate, because YHWH was always 100% accurate. This includes prophecy in metaphoric or parable form, because though its delivery came in a cushioning simile, it still contained solid meaning. Prophecy can take ten different forms. They are:

3 The decoding of cryptic imagery in Scripture can only be accurately done by marshalling other Scripture to illuminate its meaning. ***Isaiah 28:10; "For precept must be laid upon precept, precept upon precept; line upon line, line upon line; here a little, and there a little."***

vision, pronouncement, parable, speech, metaphor, riddle, dream, command, prophecy and saying. Of these there are four key subjects. They are: general prophecy (concerning people and places), eschatology (end time events), millennialism (the thousand year reign of Messiah), Israelology (prophecy directly concerning Israel) and messianic prophecy (prophecy concerning Messiah). These key subjects overlap each other to varying degrees.

A Nation of Prophets

There were times when many of the children of Israel reached extremely high levels of prophetic awareness. For example, all the Hebrew women began to sing prophetically after witnessing the collapse of the Red Sea on the Egyptian army. Then later all of the Children of Israel were regarded as prophets when they stood at the foot of Mount Sinai. The Spirit also fell on the 70 appointed elders causing them to prophesy in ***Numbers 11:25*** and future widespread prophetic states are attested to in ***Joel 2:28; "…I will pour out my Ruach (Spirit) upon all flesh and your sons and your daughters shall prophesy…"*** Prophecy is also described among the heathen in reference to "the prophets of Baal" and "Asherah." One can also argue the level of prophetic revelation made known to Balaam's donkey. But again, these types of prophets are never to be confused with the prophets or prophetesses of Israel.

Prophecy in its classic form was always a rare phenomenon. It was a strange gift that was never meant to be defined as a paid profession. No true prophet or prophetess of Israel boasted of being one. Those who heard and observed the real deal did this for them. When Yahshua spoke to the Samaritan woman at Jacob's well she responded with, ***"Master, I perceive that You are a Navi" (John 4:19)***. *Navi* is the Hebrew word for prophet and means "spokesperson" or literally "mouthpiece." One of the surviving sons of Korach writes in ***Tehillim 45:2b, "My tongue is like a pen of a skillful scribe"***[4] The term Navi describes what someone does as apposed to what someone is. In ***Ephesians 4:11***, Rabbi Sha'ul describes prophecy as one of

4 Stones Edition Tanach.

the five ministerial duties that are designed to equip believers with the necessary skills to edify and unify the body of Messiah.

The Scriptures describe periods in Israel's history where prophecy was extremely scarce ***(1 Samuel 3:11)***. During this time the few prophets that did exist would only perform seemingly mundane functions like helping King Saul find his father's lost donkeys. During this time prophets were called "seers." It can be argued that YHWH is pleased with the world when there are few prophets in the land, because He has little need to send them out to rebuke nations.

Ultimately the nature of prophecy evolved to suit the requirements of a given era. *The Jewish Encyclopedia*, citing Sanh. 11a; Ber. 57a; Suk. 28a; B. B. 134a, describes prophecy as being "...sometimes contingent upon the character of the generation among whom the potential prophet lived."

There are ten types of prophets described in Scripture. They are: men of Elohim, men of faith, servants, messengers, seers, visionaries, sentinels, envoys, spokesmen and angels. In addition, there are twelve modes of prophecy. They are:

1. Divinely directed action
2. Divinely directed speech
3. Revelation by correct interpretation of a dreamt allegorical message
4. Auditory revelation within the confines of a dream
5. Audiovisual revelation within the confines of a dream by a human speaker
6. Audiovisual revelation within the confines of a dream by an angelic speaker
7. Audiovisual revelations within the confines of a dream by the Expressed Image of YHWH (pre- or post-incarnate Yahshua)
8. A fully conscious vision of an allegorical nature
9. A fully conscious auditory revelation

10. A fully conscious audiovisual waking revelation by a human speaker
11. A fully conscious audiovisual waking revelation by an angelic speaker
12. A fully conscious audiovisual waking revelation by the Expressed Image of YHWH (pre- or post-incarnate Yahshua)

A Prophet's Core Credentials

Put simply, a prophet can be someone who forecasts information (whether verbally or in writing), works or exhibits miracles, interprets signs, or warns and rebukes individuals or multiples of individuals.

Very few people according to Scripture become prophets. The credentials of a true prophet of YHWH consist of nothing less than the following (chances are that many people have never even met one):

- He must be a scholar in Torah (Messiah Yahshua was the living Torah exhibiting profound understanding at age 12 as he began to awaken to his identity and mission.)
- Powerful in character
- Have exceedingly reliable, great or vast wisdom
- Have full mastery over his Evil Inclination (His intellectual understanding of the goodness of YHWH's commandments always conquers his temporal desires)

Only fifty-five prophets' writings are recorded throughout the entirety of the TaNaK (Old Testament) constituting what scholars refer to as "needed prophecy for future generations."

> "The Rabbis taught: **Forty-eight** prophets and **seven** prophetesses prophesied in Israel, and they did not detract from or add to that which is written in the Torah, except for instituting the reading of the Megillah [on Purim] ...It is taught: Many prophets arose for Israel – twice as many as those who left Egypt – however [only a] prophecy

needed for future generations was recorded [in twenty-four books of Scripture] and that which was not needed was not recorded (Megillah 14a)."

The Mind of a Prophet

Articulating a prophetic warning or rebuke demanded extraordinary levels of fortitude and courage, because such efforts often resulted in ridicule or death. Even Messiah was almost thrown from a cliff by his local community in response to his prophetic words in ***Luke 4:29***. But it is in the writings of the Prophet Jeremiah where we get some of the most intimate autobiographical insights into the struggles and travails of this office. ***Jeremiah 20:7b-9; "...I have been ridiculed daily, everyone mocks me. For when I speak, I cry out, declaring violence and plunder; because the word of YHWH has become a reproach to me, and a derision, daily. Then I said I will not make mention of Him, nor speak any more in His Name. But His word was in my lev (heart) as a burning fire shut up in my bones, and I was weary with holding back and I could not stop."*** Though Jeremiah struggled with his calling, the drive of his active intellect to serve the will of his Master allowed him to overcome temporal emotional doubts and push onward toward the goal. When YHWH's Word is described as residing in a man's heart, which is usually the seat of his wayward desires, it means that his walk is governed by an impenetrable intellectual resolve, rather than a penetrable emotional resolve alterable by circumstance. Jeremiah's intellect was carefully nurtured and perfected in his upbringing in Torah, but its predisposition to allow prophecy effectively stemmed from a pre-programmed state. ***Jeremiah 1:5; "Before I formed you in the belly I knew you; and before you came forth out of the womb I set you apart, and I ordained you as a navi (prophet) to the nations."***

At the commencement of their Divine missions YHWH eliminated moments of doubt in the greatest of prophets with statements like, ***"I will be with you" (Exodus 3:12)***, ***"Don't be afraid of them." (Jeremiah 1:8)*** and ***"Do not fear them, neither be afraid of their words" (Ezekiel 2:6)***.

The Most Successful Prophet

Moshe, the greatest of all prophets, was disbelieved by many of his own beloved people in his day, causing thousands of unbelieving Israelites to die in the wilderness. Jonah, the most disobedient of all prophets, **convinced all** who heard him, causing all the occupants of Nineveh (who he hated) to repent and be saved.

The Blueprint Prophet

Moshe ben Amram (Moses), is considered the most unique of all the prophets in the TaNaK. This view is not based on the great miracles he performed, but his dual role as civil and religious leader of the nation of Israel. Among his duties, he provided the climate that allowed Israel to leave Egypt in an organised and orderly manner and re-established their identity by administering a formal worship service to YHWH. This service continued to be held together to a greater or lesser extent by the prophets who followed after him. He was not a priest, yet he established and had authority over them according to YHWH's direction. He assembled and trained Israel's military force and formed a governmental and judicial system, which enabled the nation to grow beyond a simplistic tribal society. He was Israel's lawgiver, teacher and even saviour (pleading with YHWH after the Golden Calf). But in all these things he acted as a humble conduit for the Almighty. Moshe's writings set the direction that all the generations of prophets would adhere to, even Messiah Yahshua.

Elijah - The First Prophetic Reformer

The prophet *Eliyahu ha-Navi* (Elijah) exhibited the first political qualities in the office of prophet by publicly opposing a king and orchestrating an open confrontation ***(1 Kings 17-21)***. Like Moshe, he played a pivotal role motivated to bring about a return to the high ethical standards inherent in YHWH's people in the midst of uncertain times. His bold introduction onto the pages of Scripture with the following words attests to his authority "*...**As YHWH Elohim of Yisrael lives, before whom I stand, there shall not be dew nor rain these years, without my word" (1 Kings 17:1)***. Having no stated ancestry, Elijah appeared to come from nowhere shaking spiritual and physical foundations wherever he went. Is it any wonder that he was carried from earth in a fiery chariot ***(2 Kings 2)*** to await his future role as leader of the second exodus? At this time it is believed that he will again bring about a prophetic reform and a return of Israel to the golden age of prophecy. His lack of stated ancestry in Biblical narrative and his unique exit from earth has been a point of speculation among many Hebrew scholars as some claim that he was an angel who took on human form.

Checking Messiah Against Moshe, Not the Other Way Round

When someone interprets and reproduces data from a document, that document is considered a master. Messiah Yahshua's words and actions underwent close scrutiny to see if they lined up with the writings of Moshe and the prophets. Therefore, the prophet's words, which came directly from the Father, were a type of master over Messiah. By orchestrating this, the greater Master allowed Himself (through the work of His Son) to have lowly men act as intermediaries to prove His promise.

The School of Prophets

In Samuel's day schools of prophets had begun to emerge. Though the nature of prophecy was spontaneous, institutions of men who were ministers and companions of leading national deliverers had grown to warrant a structured formal training environment. These schools came into being after a long period of Philistine oppression had ended (around the time of Elijah and Elisha) and were the result of a recognised need for an organised body of seers and diviners that exclusively represented the faith of YHWH. By King David's time prophets mainly served advisory roles to kings and nobles, desiring that the will of YHWH was secure in the hearts and minds of Israel's leaders.

False Prophecy

YHWH knew from the very beginning that false prophets would rise up and cause His Chosen People to go astray. These deceivers would try to ride on the heel of Israel's blessings, capitalising on a legitimate office to fulfill their own desires. But they could only ever go so far before meeting calamity. When Pharaoh and his army rode out after Israel into the divided waters of the Red Sea, they knew that YHWH had enabled their enemies to cross. With this knowledge they capitalised on the situation by making a fast pursuit. YHWH allowed them to achieve a certain distance ("gathering them up like stones") before smashing them to pieces by thousands of tons of water. Under a Spirit-driven Torah-abiding government a similar inescapable plight awaits the false prophet who cannot withdraw his time-based decree after he declared it. He looks around in stark panic as the passing of time causes truth to collapse on unfulfilled words just like the Egyptians who began to panic as walls of water came crashing around them.

Law of the False Prophet

Deuteronomy13:1-3, 5, 8; "If there arises among you a navi (prophet), or a dreamer of dreams, and gives you an ot (a sign), or a wonder, And the ot (a sign), or the wonders come to pass, of which he spoke to you, saying, 'Let us go after other elohim, which you have not known, and let us serve them;' You shall not listen to the words of that navi (prophet), or that dreamer of dreams: for YHWH your Elohim tests you, to know whether you love YHWH your Elohim with all your lev (heart) and with all your being...And that navi (prophet), or that dreamer of dreams, shall be put to death; because he has spoken to turn you away from YHWH your Elohim..." You shall not agree with him, or listen to him; neither shall your eye pity him, neither shall you spare, neither shall you conceal him..." The use of the Hebrew word translated as "wonder" is significant in this passage because a sceptic who is only convinced when he sees a wonder still retains a measure of doubt because he still ponders if it was fabricated. The Children of Israel did not believe Moshe because of the miracles he performed, but through Pharaoh's eventual wearing down and resolve in letting them leave with an abundance of riches. Moshe's miracles were all necessity driven. Even his miracles before Pharaoh were not considered wonders to entertain or entreat, but motivated to allow Israel to leave and worship YHWH. Even the spectacular manner in which Israel crossed the Red Sea was necessary to enable the Egyptian solders to be drowned.

The death penalty for false prophecy will be reinstituted when a Torah compliant judicial system is completely restored during the millennial reign of Messiah Yahshua.

Question: Isn't this advocating putting people back under the law?

Answer: No, not at all. The phrase "under the law" means "under indictment of the law." The laws of the Torah governed by the Spirit through the implementation of the Sanhedrin and appointed judges are a mirror of the order and harmony kept in the heavenly realms. The daily standing Amidah prayer contains a blessing for the restoration of a judicial system that contains the death penalty. If believers question the morality of the death penalty in a so-called grace era or the coming Messianic age, consider the decree against Ananias and Sapphira in ***Acts 9:10-16***. Once we get organised as a people, ready to make our second Exodus toward Israel, YHWH is not going to tolerate a great many things that He's turning a blind eye to now.

If a person asks, "are you pro-capital punishment?' I say, "It doesn't matter what I am. YHWH is, so that settles it." Messiah Yahshua respected one of the Torah's processes for administering capital punishment so much that he didn't want the death penalty for the law of the adulterous woman defiled by unsuitable judges ***(John 8:3-4)***. With no suitable witnesses, a guilty woman was not eligible to be stoned according to Torah. Every one of her accusers was put to shame according to ***Jeremiah 17:13; "…All that forsake You shall be ashamed; and they that depart from Me shall be written in the earth*** (literally 'the dirt'). "It doesn't matter how repentant she was, and she was certainly repentant, the trial of drinking the bitter cup would have ensued.

YHWH should be presented with the right measure of His attribute of justice tempered against His attribute of mercy. YHWH is not afraid to institute a "scorched earth policy" on a city or nation if the need arises. The destruction of Hiroshima and Nagasaki pale in comparison to Sodom and Gomorrah. The same Set-apart Spirit that blesses is the same Set-apart Spirit that kills and makes alive.

Discerning a True Prophet

Legions of gullible people flock to hyped prophecy services to see the spectacle of men and women strut their stuff amid light and music shows that put David Copperfield to shame. During these performances audiences are pushed to a point of euphoric intoxication, as they ride an emotional rollercoaster of praise and worship, intermitted with snappy motivational speeches delivered with an almost theatrical zeal. So great is the desire to hear the words of a prophet that many people allow themselves to be drawn in and snared by the glitz and glamour of the laying on of hands and the miraculous conveyor belt healings.

The problem with prophets who earn an income from it is as soon as they start delivering bad news and rebuking their clients, they lose money.

Question: But how does someone know if a true prophet has spoken?

Answer: Well, straight away: they'd have to be well acquainted with Torah. Most, if not all, Christian "prophetic speakers" believe the Torah has been done away with so this fact alone instantly disqualifies them. A short-range prophecy has to unfold as the prophet forewarned. ***Ezekiel 33:33; "And when this comes to pass – see, it will come – then shall they know that a navi (prophet) has been among them."***

"And if you say in your heart, 'How may we know the word that YHWH has not spoken?' - when a prophet speaks in the name of YHWH, if the word does not come to pass or come true, that is a word that YHWH has not spoken; the prophet has spoken it presumptuously" (Deuteronomy 18:21-22a)

A long-range prophecy is a little more dangerous, because a prophet has to deliver the message and hope that his listeners accept it. Otherwise he flees. This was an option for a range of prominent prophets who shared long-range revelations. Another fear for a prophet was that a warning to a community would get heeded and a harsh decree overturned. This would cause quite a few recipients to disbelieve that their community was ever in danger and thus influence them to call into question a prophet's legitimacy.

False Founder - False Movement

When Jehovah's Witnesses pay me an unsolicited visit I always mention the founder of their faith, Mr. Charles Taze Russell. Under a merciful Torah system of government this faith would have never gotten off the ground and caused so many people to be drawn so drastically away from truth. After Mr. Russell's first false end of the world prophecy, that would have been the end of him according to the law of the false prophet. The birth and growth of false religious movements across the globe is the result of governments that do not handle the founders of these movements with the right measure of accountability. Some would call this present state of affairs freedom; others would call it freedom to ruin lives.

In this environment individuals like the founder of the Jehovah's Witness Movement are not only able to get away with false prophecy and deceive the masses, but also enabled to make subsequent false prophecies even when proved false. After three monumental false prophetic blunders, followers of Mr. Russell's religion are still trying to make excuses for him. Yes, the Jehovah's Witness movement adopts some practices that are based in truth, which the Church doesn't, but for every such practice they observe, there are a mountain of other practices they ignore. Whenever I mention Mr. Russel to a J.W. Elder, the comment is either met with the procurement of a leather bound Jehovah's Witness Apologetic Manual and a carefully trained response or an overly defensive rebuttal that exhibits a basic ignorance about the movement's foundation.

Objection: But they were persecuted along with the Jews in the holocaust!

Response: Yes they were, but so were homosexuals. When people say this they risk validating that lifestyle by using this line of reasoning to defend a false religious system.

200 Jehovah's Witness men, known at the time as "International Bible Students" were executed by the Nazi government for refusing military service and a further 2,500 to 5,000 died within concentration camps. Jehovah's Witnesses were one of more than 40 banned religious movements at the time. Captured and detained members of the movement continued to seek converts within the camps right up to their liberation. My point is that these people were sincere in their belief even in the face of torture and death. But they were sincerely wrong! This doesn't mean that I have the authority to judge or condemn these people. YHWH deals with each person's exposure to different levels of truth and their actions toward it as He sees from His vantage point.

Whether a person realises it or not, whenever they speak on behalf of the Holy Spirit on an issue that concerns a prophetic word for another person or a community and it is not correct, they are practicing a form of armchair witchcraft that brings with it the penalty of death according to Torah. A person who thinks they have a minor gift of prophecy going on had better consider how their credentials and conduct stacks up against the examples of Prophets outlined in Scripture.

The TaNaK's 48 prophets and 7 prophetesses clearly show how they received, vetted, and shared their prophecies. In nearly all cases of my exposure to so-called prophetic words by maverick Christians I have never seen any who operate in a way that remotely resembles any of the prophets in Scripture.

The list of prophets and prophetesses in the TaNaK consist of:

1. Abraham
2. Isaac
3. Jacob
4. Moshe
5. Aaron
6. Joshua

7. Pinchas
8. Elkanah (father of Samuel)
9. Eli the High Priest
10. Samuel
11. Gad
12. Nathan
13. King David
14. King Solomon
15. Eido
16. Michiyahu ben Yimlah
17. Obadiah
18. Achiyah of Shiloh
19. Yahu ben Chanani
20. Azariah ben Oded
21. Chaziel ben Metaniah
22. Eliezer of Morisha
23. Hosea
24. Amos
25. Micah
26. Amos
27. Elijah
28. Elisha
29. Jonah
30. Isaiah
31. Joel
32. Nahum
33. Habakkuk
34. Zephaniah
35. Uriah
36. Jeremiah
37. Ezekiel
38. Shmaya
39. Baruch
40. Neriah
41. Seriah
42. Mechasiah
43. Haggai
44. Zechariah
45. Malachi
46. Mordechai
47. Chanani
48. Oded

Prophetesses:

49. Sarah (wife of Abraham, mother of all Jews)
50. Miriam (sister to Moshe)
51. Deborah
52. Chana (mother of Samuel)
53. Abigail
54. Chuldah
55. Esther

Have you ever encountered the following statement? It generally comes when a line of reasoning on a theological issue by someone is going badly. Here it is: "The Father has something he wishes to reveal to you, but you're not ready to receive it." To this I say, "LIAR!" This is akin to saying, "I know something that is going to affect you profoundly, but I'm not going to tell you what it is." One who has ever said these words should repent. Prophets (according to Scripture) who shared their revelations with others never delivered vague or mystical information.

Question: What about ***1 Corinthians 13:9***? It says, ***"For our knowledge is partial, and our prophecy partial..."*** *(Complete Jewish Bible)* Surely this supports the potential for vague prophetic messages.

Answer: This verse does not justify the delivery of cryptic messages by novice believers. It is simply stating that a prophet is not required to know the surrounding details of the information they are dispensing on behalf of the Almighty. Take for example, the advice given to Ariel Sharon by the Lubavitcher Rebbe of blessed memory after their meeting in the US. The Rebbe asks the former prime minister of Israel to avoid getting on the next plane home. He stays and the plane he would have boarded gets hijacked. When the Rebbe is later asked why he didn't warn the authorities of the plane's fate, he says, "I didn't know about the hijacking. I just knew Ariel Sharon could not get on that plane." His warning was clear and concise, but the bigger picture was unknown to him.

Conclusion

True prophets of YHWH always delivered truthful and precise forecasts. Whether deciphered from a cryptic dream or delivered with symbolic imagery, their prophetic utterances were always 100% accurate. True prophecies are time dependant and always came to pass as foretold. If a prophet's words did not appear to strictly align with Torah, they were killed without recourse. According to *Yerushalmi (Sanhedrin x.)*, the prophet Isaiah fled Manasseh the son of Hezekiah, because of an alleged heretical comment. Manasseh challenged Isaiah's statement, "I saw Elohim seated upon His throne" with a quote from the prophet Moshe, "no man shall see Elohim and live." Whilst being pursued, Isaiah hid inside a cedar-tree by uttering the 72 letter name of YHWH. On hearing the name, the tree opened its trunk and closed over him. Manasseh, on seeing the prophet's tzitzit dangling from the tree, gave orders for it to be sawn in half with the prophet still inside. Isaiah was certainly no false prophet, but he lived amid a time when relevant authorities upheld golden age Torah observance, which meant that penalties ranging from physical injury to death were faithfully carried out, even when these authorities had become blinded to the truth.

People who feel compelled to share a prophetic word might want to think about the consequences of misrepresenting (or appearing to misrepresent) YHWH in a Torah abiding society. Having stated this, it is also worth noting that there are harsh penalties according to Torah for suppressing prophecy. Sanhedrin 89a states, "…one who suppresses his prophecy…is liable for the death penalty at the hands of heaven." This halachic ruling is based off ***Jonah 1:4; "The YHWH cast a mighty wind toward the sea, and it became such a mighty tempest in the sea that the ship*** (carrying Jonah) ***threatened to be broken up."***

The fact that Orthodox Judaism has not officially recognised a true prophet of Israel since the 3rd Century BCE[5] should be enough proof that prophets don't grow on trees and that prophecy isn't something that people dabble in; it's serious stuff and indeed a potentially dangerous office.

Unlike soothsayers and diviners of pagan nations who attempt to discover the will of their false g-ds, true prophets serve as mere mouthpieces to the One Living Elohim.

5 Malachi is widely acknowledged as being the last prophet of Israel. This office is treated as a joke in mainstream Christianity who has so-called prophets appearing in nearly every form of ministry to this day.

Chapter Twenty

Judaism in the New Testament

THERE'S A SAYING WITHIN the Nazarene Israelite community that goes: "Just because it's Judaism, doesn't mean it's right." This statement is to instill in the hearer that though Judah (the Jews) were the only tribe to keep Torah throughout their generations, they concocted some manmade traditions that inhibited its very observance. The point being to establish that all teachings in Orthodox Judaism shouldn't be taken as gospel. While this is certainly true, I wish to discuss whether it is fair to brand obstructive manmade traditions as practices that are worthy of being classified as true "Judaism." In the course of doing this, I hope to show from Scripture, particularly the New Testament, how Judaism still fit with a range of traditions, but in a form that upholds belief in Messiah Yahshua was the correct religion practiced by true believers in Biblical times. Ultimately, I hope to present a clear case for why the true faith is actually Judaism in its original form.

Judaism Explained

But what is Judaism? *Merriam-Webster's Online Dictionary* defines Judaism as, "A religion developed among the ancient Hebrews and characterized by belief in one transcendent G-d who has revealed himself to Abraham, Moses, and the Hebrew prophets and by a religious life in accordance with Scriptures and rabbinic traditions."

Fair enough, but let's examine the actual word "Judaism" in a more faithful transliteration of the original word. Before a hard "jay" sound was superimposed over "yah" sounding words in Hebrew, Judaism was pronounced as "Yahudaism" and a single Jew was called a "Yahudi" (יהודי). Many Jews were called "Yahudim." There exists a debate on the sound of the first syllable of these words within the messianic movement. This subject was explained in chapter one of this work.

The Praise YHWH Tribe as Shock Troops

The plural name "Yahudim" (transliterated as Judeans depending on the translation) first appears in the Book of Kings when the nation of Israel separated into a north and south kingdom. ***2 Kings 16:5-6; "Then Rezin king of Aram and Pekah son of Remaliah king of Israel marched up to fight against Jerusalem and besieged Ahaz, but they could not overpower him. <u>At that time, Rezin king of Aram recovered Elath for Aram by driving out the men of Judah (Yahudim)</u>. Edomites then moved into Elath and have lived there to this day."***

A Yahudi, now commonly called 'a Jew,' was of course a person from the tribe of Yahuda. The evolution of the term Jew is: Yahudi > Jehudi > Judean > Jew. The name Yahuda was given to one of twelve sons and grandsons of Jacab (aka Israel) and was subsequently given as a collective name for that son's descendants, making up one of the twelve tribes of Israel (each tribe denoting a people with lineage from one of Jacob's twelve sons and grandsons).

"Yahuda" means "praise Yah" and the circumstances of its giving are found in ***Genesis 29:35; "She (Leah) conceived again, and when she gave birth to a son she said, 'This time I will praise YHWH.' So she named him Judah..."*** *The word* comes from the root, *yadah* which means, "an extension of the hand in adoration or acceptance" or "to throw or cast." Interestingly Yahuda is called upon to go up first into battle against the Canaanites ***(Judges 1:1-12)***. Therefore this can literally be understood as meaning, 'let praise go up to YHWH at the commencement of a trial.' We see this illustrated in Job's reaction to hearing the worst news he could possibly imagine in ***Job 1:21; "Naked I came out of my mother's womb, and naked shall I return: YHWH has given, and YHWH has taken away; blessed be the name of YHWH."***

Yahuda's unique blessing among Jacob's other sons and grandsons was to be "the chief lawgiver" ***(Isaiah 33:22)***, a post that would remain in his descendant's charge to this day.

Ultimately the name Yahudim is the prophetical and Biblical name of a Covenant People who were "first" entrusted with YHWH's oracles ***(Romans 3:1)*** and it was the exclusive name used by the prophets in the TaNaK ***(Zechariah 8:23)***.

It is important to acknowledge that the tribes of Levi and Benjamin also became absorbed into the tribe of Judah at a subsequent time. But from that time until the future reformation of the tribes, they were first regarded as Yahudim, before being regarded by their former tribal heritage. See ***Acts 21:39*** and ***Romans 11:1*** for Sha'ul's dual proclamation of being both a Jew and a Benjamite.

In Greco-Roman translations of the Brit Chadashah (New Testament) Judah, as in Judas Iscariot, is written as "Judas" to denote Yahshua's betrayer. Unfortunately false transliteration of names and places is a common practice evident in all Anglicised Bibles. The handling of the names "Yahoshua the son of Nun" and "Yahushua of Nazareth" are a prime example of this practice. Yahshua who led Israel into the Land retains the correct transliteration of "Joshua," while Yahshua the Messiah is relegated to the name Jesus, which means "the horse" in Hebrew.

Today the evolved word "Jew" is most commonly used as a slur. The Book of Deuteronomy foretells of the negative view many now have for the name in chapter 28, verse 7, ***"You shall become...a byword among all the Gentiles."*** In contrast, the word "Gentile" means, "confused," but at present is adopted as a name that instills pride in many Christians within the church today. Eventually the Gentile will hold onto the fringes or tzi-tzi-yot of a Yahudi, because they will eventually perceive that Elohim is with them ***(Zechariah***

8:23). And it is well that they do this in light of Messiah's words, ***"Salvation is of the Jews"*** in ***John 4:22***.

Manmade Traditianity

With the observance of the one true way dwindling down to one tribe, the faith itself began being called after that tribe's name – Yahudah > Yahudaism (Judaism). This tribal specific name for "the way" continued into the apostolic era. Rabbi Sha'ul was accused of being a ring leader of a heretical Nazarene branch or sect of Judaism ***(Acts 24:5)*** by men who in actuality followed a heretical version of it. Judaism or "the way" was always a Messianic faith. The prophet Moshe was instructed to build a tabernacle, and populate it with a priesthood to mimic the priesthood in the heavens, so even he knew there had to be a High Priest also interceding in the heavenly realms.

The most unique thing about the tribe of Judah is their unshakable tenacity in upholding Torah in spite of 3000 years of persecution, genocide and countless other creative forms of oppression administered by Egyptians, Babylonians, Assyrians, Persians, Romans, Muslims, Nazis and even Christians. Does a Messianic or Christian believer really comprehend the level of ignorance inherent in comments that ridicule Jews who built traditions that pointed to Torah when the very observance of it was being outlawed on point of death?

The Scriptures that the so-called "Bible only believer" claims to follow actually defines "the way" as a religious lifestyle that contains manmade or rabbinic traditions. To say otherwise would define a religious lifestyle that is not Biblical. The one true faith as delivered in its entirety at Mount Sinai, cannot be fulfilled without some framework of traditional activity linking it together. Without tradition, observance of YHWH's commandments would be like trying to transport water to someone who desired a drink without anything to carry it in.

Traditions inhabit all three of the Abrahamic faiths (Islam, Christianity and Judaism). The one religion out of these three that retain the least manmade traditions is Judaism. Ironically it gets bashed by the one faith that persistently refuses to use correct names, observe correct festivals, Sabbaths and so-called Jewish laws. The very faith whose entire anatomy is stuffed full of Babylonian mystery religion has always been the most vocal about the pitfalls of tradition.

Yahshua's criticism of traditions focused on the Pharisee's reverence for them over Torah. Some influential Pharisees had elevated their traditions to such a high level that they inevitably became detrimental to the authority of Scripture. They literally ended up neglecting some aspects of Torah to retain their "doctrines of men" ***(Isaiah 29:13)***. This is what the prophet Isaiah, and Yahshua who quoted him, was referring to. These Pharisees still followed more Torah than the average Christian does today, so if I was a Christian I would stop criticising the Pharisees. If the Scribes and the Pharisees were so wrong in their lifestyles and teachings why would Yahshua decide to use them as a benchmark for righteousness to have a place in the World to Come? ***Matthew 5:20; "For I say to you, Except your tzedakah (righteousness) shall exceed the tzedakah of the Sophrim (Scribes) and Prushim (Pharisees), you shall in no case enter into the malchut ha shamayim (the Kingdom of Heaven)."***

The Scriptures, particularly, the Brit Chadashah promotes the observance of manmade traditions, but not in exclusion of or in preference to the Torah. ***2 Thessalonians 2:15; "Therefore, Israelite brothers, stand fast, and hold on to the commandments and the traditions that you have been taught, whether by word or our letter."*** Note the separate mention of commandments and traditions in the verse. Clearly this verse encourages the keeping of traditions and commandments whether transmitted orally or expounded from the Word.

The TaNaK has its share of traditions that became customary practices, such as facing toward Jerusalem in prayer ***(Daniel 6:10)***, the building of and attendance in a Synagogue ***(Ezekiel 11:16)***, praying three times a day ***(Daniel 6:10)*** and the observance of the festival of Purim ***(Esther 9:17-22)***. ***2 Chronicles 35:25*** even speaks of how Jewish women started a tradition that became an ordinance.

How can a religious group who has core doctrines that have no place in Scripture, and additional traditions that fan out from these foreign foundations, criticise a religion whose core practices are completely Scriptural and whose traditions are largely the product of in-depth gleanings from the text itself? For example, Sunday mass is not a Biblical practice and the structure of its service is built in a way that detracts from any similarity to synagogue service in Yahshua's time.

In contrast, an Orthodox Jew observes Yom Kippur, which is mandated in Scripture to observe throughout all generations. On this day they will usually fast and wear white (simple) clothing to signify mercy and repentance, yet there is no ordinance in the Torah to do so. But if one reads the Book of Jonah they will find the king of Nineveh's decree to abstain from food and wear sackcloth to repent from their wicked ways. Another example is the tradition of a *minyan*, the presence of ten men as a minimum requirement for the recital of key prayers. This tradition was formed in response to YHWH's willingness to spare Sodom and Gomorrah from destruction if at least ten righteous people could be found within them.

A good tradition didn't impede Torah observance, but enabled the Torah to be kept more securely. Rabbi Sha'ul vigorously presents himself as a leading proponent of Judaism and also boasts of his zeal for the oral teachings of his fathers in ***Galatians 1:14; "And I progressed in Judaism's religion above many of my equals in my own nation; above all I was especially zealous of the teachings of my fathers."***

Fake Judaism

There is a very popular branch of Judaism called, "Reformed Judaism," which is characterised as a "progressive movement." This means that its teachings change and adapt to an ever evolving social environment. It promotes a form of Torah that tolerates a reactionary observance to an external factor rather than a proactive observance that remains anchored despite the onset of unstable social, economic and political climates. The biggest problem with Reformed Judaism is that in twenty years' time there is no telling what it will or won't accept. Though it is accepted as a form of Judaism by many, it is not true Judaism according to Scripture.

"The Way" Morphs into a Religion Named After a Tribe

Originally Adam and Hava (Eve) enjoyed a harmonious and pure walk with YHWH Elohim in a beautifully natural and perfectly acclimatised environment. These beings had the entire Torah of YHWH written on their hearts, though not in a form that was situation based as found in the first five books of the Bible. The breaking of a kashrut law led to a breach in their relationship with the Creator, causing them to experience (among other things) an awareness of two opposed inclinations.

They produced offspring, the majority of which become corrupt after many generations. Eight humans alone found favour (Noah and his family). The population of mankind literally came through a "bottleneck" as this family was spared and the earth was cleansed in a giant mikvah (immersion). Mankind multiplied again into many different nations. Eventually a Chaldean man called Abram also found favour with Elohim and received slightly more revelation of His will. Abram had a son called Isaac who through his lineage produced a nation of people that received the whole Torah by Divine appointment. During this period the lifestyle of people who were favoured by Elohim is never defined as Judaism until...

...the tribe of Levi and the tribe of Benjamin became absorbed into Judah and the remaining ten tribes abandoned Torah.

During the first and second dispersions of people across the earth, fallen angels, masquerading as g-ds, caused communities to develop other belief systems contrary to the one true way. These diverse belief systems received an all encompassing term that defined lifestyles that were dependant on pleasing the desire of a superior being. This word became known as "religion."

What is Religion?

According to the *Webster's Collegiate Dictionary* the word "religion" is derived from an old Latin word, "religio" and means, "taboo." A more thorough study reveals that it is made up of the prefix "re-," indicating a "return" to something. The Latin word "ligare," is where we get the word "ligament" and means, "to bond" or "bind." When the prefix "re-" is attached to the word "bond" it brings about the literal meaning, "return to bondage." This meaning was never originally inferred in the three to five places where we find the word "religion" in modern Bibles today. According to *Strong's Exhaustive Concordance* it appears in ***Acts 26:5, Galatians 1:13, 1:14 and James 1:26, 1:27.*** More accurate translations exhibit the following:

Acts 26:5 – This verse contains the word **"observance"** meaning, "the practice of adhering to a particular rule."

Galations 1:13, 1:14 – Both verses contain the word, **"Yehudaism"** meaning, "Judaism."

James 1:26, 1:27 – The verse contains the word **"service,"** meaning, "an act of assistance."

As you can see none of these words mean, "return to bondage," yet when the Brit Chadashah refers to a "return to bondage" or "slavery," as in ***Galatians 5:1***, the option to use the word "religion" is ignored. With this understanding, believers can confidently accept and sympathise with the phrase, "I don't like religion." However, on hearing this response from an unbeliever, one should be quick to enlighten the occupant of the fact that the term doesn't even appear in modern translations of Scripture in its correct context. Furthermore, its true meaning is not a concept that is endorsed in Torah. Bondage is not associated with what YHWH offers His people.

Word choice in Bible translations can often set linguistic trends that negatively affect aspects of a belief system that the source manuscripts promote. This occurs when scribes of differing philosophical backgrounds copy manuscripts. If written language is the vehicle for ferrying truth to a reader, a scribe, over time, may successfully blend this vehicle with falsehood to cause linguistic misguidance. A translator can successfully misguide a reader if their ability to examine word origins and contextual meaning is withdrawn or discouraged. This can be done by revealing a Bible translation to a foreign audience who is not familiar with its language of origin. Any curiosity of tracing a text's language of origin can be erased if its appearance in a former foreign language is denied (Greek and Hebrew New Testament Debate).

Conclusion

Do Christian ministers or any of the clergy that make up any denominational movement within any church profess to sit in Moses' seat ***(Matthew 23:1-3)***? Do they say that the Torah, which they call "the law," is still in effect ***(Matthew 5:17, 18)***? Do they teach the whole covenant? Do they keep the Sabbath? Do they proclaim the Name of YHWH? ***(Isaiah 56)***

The answer is no, no, no, no and no.

The Church will tell you that the Mosaic covenant was replaced by the New Covenant as taught by Jesus and that Israel is now replaced by the Holy Church. The Church says that they are a "new" or "spiritual" Israel. This is called "replacement theology." They have been teaching this since the Council of Nicea. The Roman Catholic Church is the mother of all other recognised church denominations across the globe (yes, even Sabbath keeping churches are easily traced back to Rome).

Imagine a prostitute who has children. These children grow up and resent their mother for denying them a father and exposing them to a lifestyle that causes them to lose their innocence. They leave their mother but also engage in less obvious forms of prostitution, the whole time saying that they are not prostitutes like their mother.

The blindness of the Jew to Messiah is temporary. Its perpetuation has been strengthened by the Church who wrongly exhibits the character and heritage of Yahshua as a lawless Greco-Roman crusader. Therefore we must be more patient with and mindful of this ancient people. They are our brothers together with us in the same covenant. ***"One Torah shall be to him that is home-born, and unto the stranger that sojourns among you." (Exodus 12:49)***

The word "Judaism," regarded with suspicion or at best caution among most Messianic believers today, essentially means "Praise YHWHism." The word should not be looked upon as the name of an enemy religion, but a name that has rightly been given to "the way" that for centuries signifies Yahudah's sole guardianship of it. As a Nazarene Israelite who observes Judaism in a form that completely accepts Messiah Yahshua as Sovereign, I am grateful that YHWH provided such courageous lawgivers. May Yahudah be blessed and continue to be blessed.

Perhaps instead of saying, "Just because it's Judaism, doesn't mean it's right," we might say, "Just because it's called Judaism, doesn't mean it is."

Chapter Twenty-One

Geography by Faith

"And I will give to you, and to your zera (seed) after you, the land in which you are a ger (sojourner), all the land of Kanaan, for an everlasting possession; and I will be their Elohim." (Genesis 17:8)

A WESTERN MIDDLE-CLASS family settles in for the evening as their favourite sitcom is rudely interrupted by a news report showing another eruption of violence in Israel. The man of the house makes a flippant comment before changing the channel to see what other escapism he can find until the correct program resumes. The average materialistic comfort-seeking Westerner is dumbfounded by what drives the Muslim and the Jew to continue fighting each other with no sign of reprieve on the horizon.

The unrelenting nature of the Middle East conflict is incomprehensible to the average Western person who has no vested interest in the historical, cultural and religious context of the situation. In other words, a person who sees himself as being insular from the crisis and therefore qualified to comment and discuss it with a premise to offer a solution, will find himself perpetually handicapped in anything he says that pertains to it. This is because a person without or disinterested in attaining knowledge of the deeper religious significance of the crisis runs the risk of offering a solution that appeals to a completely different mindset. The process is like offering a koala bear a bowl of water. Koalas primarily receive their water from the moisture of eucalyptus leaves and though they may accept water in small quantities during a drought, it is not the type of sustenance they naturally seek.

Even the trained journalist fails to comprehend the basic anatomy of the dispute because they persist in viewing it through the haze of current socioeconomic and political trends whilst ignoring its religious implications. The correct religious context even fails to be marshalled by many Christians because of the baggage of their dispensationalist and replacement theological interpretation. Most Christians remain inept at comprehending the crisis because they accept a false view that the Almighty abandoned His chosen people and abolished His Torah.

Even a noble act of providing medical aid to either Palestinians or Israelis (without the will to understand the deeper religious motivations that cause the casualties) gives rise to exploitation of such a person until either side's overall cultural and religious objectives are fully achieved. At the end of the day if either side's religious attitude prevails in full, they are both contrary to the philosophy of the West. In fact Islamic and Judaic religious laws are completely incompatible to the values and creeds of the religious and nonreligious Western world. Even despite the fact that 70% of Israelis are nonreligious, their participation to preserve Israel as a nation is the fulfillment of a scriptural mandate. If this mandate is successfully achieved it will enable the country to prosper and expand, which will inevitably allow its religious percentage to put YHWH's judicial and governmental will into action across the board.

Greater Israel and the Real Deal

According to Scripture the Land of Israel stretches from the Nile to the Euphrates River, encompassing all the Palestinian territories, including Lebanon, large parts of Syria, Jordan, Egypt, Iraq, Saudi Arabia and Turkey. The first mention of its geographical size is found in ***Genesis 15:18-21***. Descendants of Jacob (aka Israel) are scripturally mandated to remain unequivocally tied to the Promised Land, to the point that if they deserted it, the Almighty would force them back by whatever means necessary. The Holocaust is cited by many religious historians as being the essential catalyst that allowed Israel to be reborn as a nation.

If Israel actively tries to minimise portions of the Land whilst living in it, they historically receive grief. The relinquishment of the Gaza and the inevitable use of this land by *Hamas* as a staging post to fire rockets into deeper parts of Israel is a prime example of the result that follows the act of surrendering land. History shows that Israel's attempts to live peacefully by trying to appease and coexist with its enemies usually results in increased hardship. But when Israel moves aggressively against its enemies it frequently experiences prosperity. Having stated this, it is supremely important to point out that Israel is currently only made up of those from the tribe of Judah, Benjamites and Levites. Therefore it is virtually impossible to expect such a small nation to conquer, occupy and defend the entirety of the Land of Israel according to its Scriptural dimensions. However, should the Almighty will it, even this could happen.

The militant action in Lebanon against Hezbollah laboured because of Israel's failure to move with convicted aggression and thoroughness, which was brought on by the pressure of negative world press concerning the conflict. The nature of the media and its use as an effective propaganda tool against Israel will be examined shortly.

Torah is clear on Israel's correct course of action against its neighbouring enemies, and the result of not executing this task is clearly prophesied. ***"But if you will not drive out the inhabitants of the land from before you; then it shall come to pass, that those which you let remain shall be thorns in your eyes, and thorns in your sides, and shall distress you in the land in which you will dwell." (Numbers 33:55)*** At no time does the Word of YHWH Elohim deviate from the directive to "drive out" the heathen.

Punch and Judy on a Merry-go-Round

The main problem in modern-day Israel is the degrees of flawed logic exhibited by both sides.

Palestinian logic is this: Being delayed at a checkpoint and having a field bulldozed equals blowing up a bus full of civilians.

Israeli logic is this: If we give away this piece of land and add these concessions, our enemies will be happy and leave us alone. Oops, no they won't, we have to respond militarily. Bless Hashem, we prevailed. If we give them this piece of land and add these concessions, our enemies will be happy and leave us alone. Oops, no they won't, we have to respond militarily. Bless Hashem, we prevailed. If we give them this piece of land ...and so on ....

YHWH promised Israel victory over its oppressors in ancient times. ***"Then will YHWH drive out all these nations from before you, and you shall possess greater nations and mightier ones than yourselves." (Deuteronomy 11:23)*** And so too YHWH promises this same victory today.

Lashon Hara - The Mechanism that Keeps the Problem Airborne

In ***Psalms 120:2-6*** King David writes of a personal trouble that is startlingly similar to the trouble facing the whole nation of Israel today. Quite often the TaNaK exhibits happenings in the lives of the patriachs that foreshadow the experiences of Israel in general. In this instance David relates the problem of Lashon Hara (Evil Speech). ***"Deliver my being, O YHWH, from lying lips, and from a deceitful tongue. What shall be given to you? Or, what shall be done to you, you false tongue? Sharp arrows of the mighty; with coals of oak. Woe is me, that I sojourn in Mesech; that I dwell in the tents of Kedar! My being has long lived with him that hates shalom (peace)."*** With today's modern technology powering the media, deliberately slanderous exaggerations and lies about Israel have never been easier to circulate. King David's time amid the tents of Kedar is mimicked whenever Israel is forced to compromise with its enemies. Kedar were the most powerful Arab nation in David's time, comprising the descendants of the twelve sons of Ishmael. This was prophesied in ***Genesis 16:12*** where it says they will ***"dwell in the presence of their brethren."*** Today this attempt to compromise has brought with it some acceptance of slanderous teaching that is present in some Jewish schools who describe Israel's modern day existence as an occupation with apartheid elements.

Thorns Build Faith

The ancient land of Canaan sat in between many great eastern civilizations. Egypt was located to its southwest, Phoenicia and Syria were to the north, and Assyria and Babylonia resided in an easterly direction. Canaan's geographical location meant that its dwellers could not isolate themselves from these other nations. As a consequence settlers were forced to weather political, social and economic pressures from all sides. The placement of these kingdoms around Canaan, though chosen for a range of divine reasons, was to teach Israel (as a nation) to rely on YHWH by faith. Any surrounding nation that had a grievance with another kingdom would have to tread through Canaan to make war. Today Israel is faced with similar challenges. It is a nation that is smaller than California and is surrounded by twenty-two hostile Islamic dictatorships. Amazingly Israel still manages to exist whilst occupying only one-sixth of one percent of a land that is otherwise populated by diametrically opposed Islamic nations. ***"A thousand shall fall at your side, and ten thousand at your right hand; but it shall not come near you. Only with your eyes shall you observe and see the reward of the wicked. Because you have made YHWH, who is my refuge, even the most High, your dwelling place; There shall no evil befall you, neither shall any plague come near your dwelling." (Psalm 91)***

The Seven Canaanite Squatters

Think for a moment. Would you be angry if your husband built you a beautiful house, but before you moved in, it was being lived in by messy squatters? Accusing Israel of banditry by taking the Promised Land is the same as accusing a person who was promised a gift as having stolen it by the one who was not its intended recipient.

From the very outset YHWH makes it clear that he wants His people to possess and live in a specific geographical earth location. Much like the original Garden of Eden, the Land of Israel is a specific place with specific dimensions. It supports a special place that serves as a direct portal from heaven to earth that was recorded in a vision by Jacob ***(Genesis 28:10-22)***. Right from the Book of Genesis through to the Book of Revelations Scripture attests to Israel's spiritual connection and longing for the Holy Land. ***"If I forget you, O Yahrushalayim, let my right hand forget me." (Psalm 137:5)***

Question: But...... ***"The Canaanites were then in the land." (Genesis 12:6)***

Answer: Yes, that's right. The Torah attests that the Promised Land was already inhabited by a people. In fact it was teaming with foreign nations well before Israel settled there as a nation. ***"In the same day YHWH made a brit (covenant) with Avram, saying, 'To your zera (seed) have I given this land, from the river of Mitzrayim (Egypt) to the great river, the River Euphrates: The land of the Kenites, and the Kenizzites, and the Kadmonites, And the Hittites, and the Perizzites, and the Rephayim, And the Amorites, and the Kanaanites, and the Girgashites, and the Yevusites." (Genesis 15:18-21)***

Did Israel Rob the Land from Seven Canaanite Nations?

The first commentary of the entire Torah discusses the ownership of the Land of Israel. Expounding from Genesis's opening passages Rambam writes, "The entire universe belongs to Elohim. He created it and he granted it to whomever He deemed fit. It was His desire to give it to them (the nations) and then it was His desire to take it from them and give it to us (Israel)." This understanding is certainly echoed in ***Psalms 111:6; "He declared to His people the power of His works in order to give them the heritage of the nations."*** The seven Canaanite nations cannot accuse Israel of stealing land that was predestined to be taken by force for the purpose of showing YHWH's greatness.

Question: So how did Israel conduct itself when faced with these pagan nations occupying their land?

Answer: They bought blocks of land for generous sums of money. They allowed the Canaanites to co-exist with them, even allowing them to retain the heavenly portal (Temple Mount) to house a place of pagan worship. They even gave them and other foreign nations parts of Jerusalem to live in. After that they gave back sections of additional land because Canaanites violently protested the natural growth and success of Israel. In response Israel put up checkpoints and protective walls between them and the Canaanites, because the Canaanites started strapping bombs to their children and sending them into crowded marketplaces to detonate. Despite Israel receiving constant threats to its wellbeing in the form of kidnappings, terrorist bombings, missile launches and civil unrest they continued to seek avenues of peaceful co-existence that seemed to always make them worse off than they were before. Don't laugh. That's precisely what Israel is doing today. And as I've pointed out it's getting them nowhere. People are quick to say that Israel's secular government handles its enemies wrongly. The only problem is if you ask anyone who shares this view, particularly the average Christian, they will not be able to deliver any solution beyond what has been already proposed.

The Real Answer: YHWH commanded Israel to take possession of the land through repeated stringent militant action. ***Judges 1:17-18; "And Yahudah went with Shimeon his brother, and they killed the Kanaanites that inhabited Zephath, and utterly destroyed it. And the name of the city was called Hormah. Also Yahudah took Azah with its border, and Ashkelon with its border, and Ekron with its border."*** At times when Israel shrank away from the sword, even to the point of sparing some of their enemies YHWH was displeased. ***Numbers 33:55; "But if you will not drive out the inhabitants of the land from before you; then it shall come to pass, that those which you let remain shall be thorns in your eyes, and thorns in your sides, and shall distress you in the land in which you will dwell."***

Since Joshua's conquest of Canaan over 3200 years ago Israelites have lived in the land continuously, though for a considerable time in small numbers. When Mark Twain travelled through the Land in the 1900's he remarked on how it looked like the most forsaken place he had ever seen, as if cursed by G-d. ***Ezekiel 36:34:***

"And the desolate land shall be tilled, whereas it had been in ruin in the sight of all that passed by…" In less than sixty years from that time, as Judah began returning in greater numbers, the Land awoke from its slumber. Gradually a barren desert grew into a garden that yielded fruit and vegetable produce of such abundance and quality that Israel's economy increased to the eighth largest in the world. ***Ezekiel 36:35-36; "And they shall say, This land that was desolate has become like the Garden of Eden; and the waste, desolate and ruined cities have become fortified and inhabited. Then the gentiles that are left around you shall know that I YHWH rebuild the ruined places, and planted what had been desolate: I YHWH have spoken it, and I will do it."*** YHWH kept His promise.

With the labour pains of the Jewish holocaust over, the United Nations Security Counsel made history when they moved to vote Israel as a recognised nation in a single day fulfilling ***Isaiah 66:8; "Who has heard such a thing? Who has seen such things? Shall the earth be made to bring forth in one day? Or, shall a nation be born at once? For as soon as Tzion (Zion) travailed, she brought forth her children."*** After an exile by Rome in 135CE Israel, albeit almost exclusively represented by Jews, returned as masters of their own domain. ***Ezekiel: 36:24; "For I will take you out from among the gentiles, and gather you out of all countries, and will bring you into your own land."*** Scripture tells us that soon the lost sheep of the house of Israel will join them. ***Micah 4:2; "And many nations shall come, and say, Come, and let us go up to the mountain of YHWH, and to the Bayit (house) of the Elohim of Yaakov; and He will teach us His halachot (ways), and we will have our halacha in His paths: for the Torah shall go forth from Tzion (Zion), and the word of YHWH from Yahrushalayim (Jerusalem)."***

Who is the Real Owner of Any Land?

Man needs all inferior levels of creation to survive. He is nourished by the animal kingdom, which in turn is nourished by the inferior vegetative kingdom, which is nourished by the earth, which is nourished by the rain that falls from the heavens. Man has been created from the earth and remains dependant upon it until the day of his death. Each level of creation is a glimmer of a glimmer of a glimmer of the Divine.

A dispute arose between two tribes of Israel over the ownership of a piece of land. The heads of each tribe approached a rabbi to settle the dispute. The rabbi insisted he be taken out to the land in question. Upon arriving there he told all present that he must consult with the land itself. After placing his ear to the ground for a short time he arose and said, "Neither tribe owns this land. It owns you. For from the earth you were formed and to the earth you will return." At that, every member of the tribe departed in silence.

A substantial amount of Torah cannot be performed without actually dwelling in the Land of Israel. ***Numbers 33:53*** confirms that it is a commandment for Israel to take possession of the Land. A Torah observant believer in Yahshua as well as an Orthodox Jew are considered as not existing in their optimum natural state while they live outside the Land of Israel, much like Adam was not able to live in his primary state outside the Garden of Eden.

What amazes me is the world's current negative attitude toward modern-day Israel as they try in vain to explore avenues of peace whilst occupying just a small sliver of the Land. In contrast the Scriptures clearly show that Israel is commanded to take the entire Land to fulfill the promise made Abraham.

One has to wonder why the Church, the supposed new and improved spiritual Israel, cultivates its headquarters in Rome and why it continues to view itself as separate from YHWH's people that He foreknew despite the warning in ***Isaiah 56:2*** that says ***"Neither let the son of the ger (stranger), that has joined himself to YHWH, speak in this manner, saying, YHWH has utterly separated me from His people..."*** Or why the Church has fostered generations of the most vocal anti-semites in history and why it just stood idly by during the holocaust whilst preaching from a book that states, ***"For if you keep silent at this time, then shall their relief and deliverance arise for the Yahudim (Jews) from another place; but you and your abba's bayit (house) shall be destroyed..." (Esther 4:14)***

Have the words of the Christians' own Messiah fallen on deaf ears when he said to a woman who professed to worship the same Elohim as the Jews? ***"You worship you know not what: we know what we worship: for salvation is from the Yahudim (Jews)."(John 4:22)*** Or did the Sha'ul (Paul) speak in a vacuum when he said in ***Romans 3:1; "What advantage then has the Yahudi (Jew)? Or, what profit is there in brit-milah (circumcision)."***?

The nation of Israel's survival against all odds throughout the centuries is testimony that they were YHWH's people in ancient times just as much as they are His people today, though temporally blinded to Messiah. ***"I say then, did YHWH cast away His people? By no means. For I also am a Yisraelite, of the zera (seed) of Avraham, of the tribe of Benyamin. YHWH has not cast away His people whom He knew and chose beforehand."(Romans 11:1-2)*** One doesn't have to go as far back as the Scriptures to read about miraculous battles in which YHWH caused Israel to defeat enemies of far greater numbers and superior weapons. Between the time of June 5, 1967 to June 10, 1967 Israel fought and won a war against the combined forces of Egypt, Syria, Jordan and Iraq that is known as the Six Day War. The statistics of the war speak for themselves:

The Six Day War

The Reason Israel makes a preemptive strike against an assembled and ready to deploy army of Egyptian forces after their government expelled a United Nations Emergency Force (UNEF) from the Sinai Peninsula, which had been stationed there since 1957 to provide a peace-keeping buffer zone.

Force Capacity Egypt, Syria, Jordan, and Iraq unite with a collective strength of 280,000 troops and 812 combat aircraft and attack Israel who has 264,000 troops (incl. 214,000 reserve troops) and 197 combat aircraft.

The Result Israel receives 779 killed, 2,563 wounded, loses 15 troops as POWS and loses 19 aircraft.

The coalition of Arab nations receives 21,000 killed, 45,000 wounded, lose 6,000 as POWS and loses 400 aircraft.

The Yom Kippur War

The Reason This war was part of an ongoing dispute and began with a joint surprise attack by Egypt and Syria on the sacred Israeli holiday of Yom Kippur (Day of Atonement). Egypt and Syria sent legions of tanks across the cease-fire lines in the Sinai and Golan Heights, which had been captured by Israel in 1967 during the Six-Day War.

Force Capacity Egypt has collective strength of 800,000 troops, 2,400 tanks, 2,400 armoured carriers, 1,120 artillery units, 690 airplanes, 161 helicopters and 104 Navy vessels.

Syria has 150,000 troops, 1,400 tanks, 800–900 armoured carriers, 600 artillery units, 350 airplanes, 36 helicopters and 21 Navy vessels.

Iraq commits 60,000 troops, 700 tanks, 500 armoured carriers, 200 artillery units and 73 airplanes.

All together their collective force equals **1,010,000 troops**.

Israel has a force of **415,000 troops**, 1,500 tanks, 3,000 armoured carriers, 945 artillery units, 561 airplanes, 84 helicopters and 38 Navy vessels.

The Result Israel receives **2,656 killed**, 7,250 wounded, loses 400 tanks and loses 102 planes.

The coalition of Arab forces receives **15,000 killed**, 35,000 wounded, loses 2,250 tanks loses 432 planes.

"And it shall come to pass in that day that I will seek to destroy all the nations that come against Yahrushalayim (Jerusalem)." (Zechariah 12:9)

Conclusion

West Point Military Academy in the United States has surprisingly very little strategy analysis of the Six Day and Yom Kippur wars in their core curriculum, despite the miraculous nature of Israel's decisive victories against far superior numbers and weaponry. According to a three star general who taught military tactics and field strategies at West Point, the unofficial reason for side-stepping the Jewish wars was because of the obvious presence of divine intervention. His final comment to a querying Jewish cadet was, "G-d does not fit into military textbooks."

Ultimately the Promised Land is Israel's perpetual honeymoon destination. ***"You shall no more be termed: Forsaken*** ('azab {aw-zab'}); ***neither shall your land any more be termed Desolate*** (shimamah {shee-mam-aw'}**): *but you shall be called: My Delight Is In Her, Chephhtziybahh*** {khef-tzee'baw – literally "my darling"}**, *and your land Beulah-Married*** (or literally "Land of your husband"); ***for YHWH delights in you, and your land shall be married."*** Amein.

Chapter Twenty-Two

The Eradication of the Jew from Muslim Countries

IN THE ADVENTURE film, *Indiana Jones and the Kingdom of the Crystal Skull*, Dr. Jones, in one of his more academic moments, asks his university class to study the difference between "migration" and "exodus." This intrigued me, so, like a good student of the man whose name means "adventure," I decided to investigate. "Migration" refers to someone or something that moves from one specific location to another, while "exodus" refers to a population that leaves a long time inhabited location to a completely unknown or unfamiliar destination.

Perhaps there are no people who are as well acquainted with the concept of an exodus than the Jews. Their entire history is punctuated with forced removals from one location to another, with no guarantee of a trouble free existence at any destination.

So much has been made of the so-called Israeli mistreatment of the Palestinian people by the media, that it has overshadowed the mistreatment and eventual expulsion of a vast number of Jews who lived in Muslim countries for over 2500 years. Many of these Jews were born in regions well before Muslim conquests and before the Arabs came from Arabia. In fact 90% of world Jewry lived in regions now known as Arab countries right up until the 10th century. The ill treatment, and in some cases complete eradication of the Jew from Arab host countries makes Israel's current handling of Palestinian people look somewhat tame in comparison.

In 1947, when the UN announced that the Holy Land would be partitioned into separate Jewish and Muslims states, the climate became so difficult for Jews in Arab and North African countries that it caused approximately 856,000 of them to flee their homes from 1948 to 1976. Prior to this, Jewish communities flourished throughout the Arab and North African world. In 1900 a population of 410,000 Jews lived in Muslim countries. This figure grew steadily by 1947 to around 825,000. During this time few Jews returned to Judea1 (aka Palestine). By 1800 Jerusalem had a general population of around 8,750 people. Of this, there were approximately 2,000 Jews. As the general population grew to 22,000 by 1870, the number of Jews increased to roughly 11,000 and then 40,000 by 1905 from a total population of 60,000.

Before the declaration of a Jewish state, Jews lived quite comfortably under Arab rule. However, after the Holocaust, Jews predominantly from Europe and Russia gradually began returning to the Holy Land. The bitter sweet decision to partition Judea by the UN brought with it the death of 6000 defending Israelis and the persecution of thousands of Jews in the rest of the Arab world. Never let it be said that the UN resolution allowed the Holy Land to be handed over to Israel on a silver platter. On the contrary it was reacquired through blood, sweat and toil. Even the United States turned its back on Israel by imposing an arms embargo against them. In spite of this, IDF soldiers outnumbered 100 to 1, won their independence in 1948 by miraculously repelling and driving backward a combined force of seven Arab armies.

---

1 The region of Biblical Israel occupied by Jews today was called "Judea" before it was named "Palestine." More specifically, the area was previously called "Provincia Judaea" and was renamed "Provincia Syria Palaestina" by Emperor Hadrian. After the Emperor had put down the Jewish Bar Kochba revolt in 135AD he wanted to remove the name "Judaea" from the Land entirely. The word "Palaestina" comes from the Biblical word "Plesheth" (transliterated as "Philistine"). The word means "migratory invaders" and refers to the Philistines, who were actually Greeks that originated from Asia Minor. They had no ethnic, linguistic or historical connection to the Arabs.

Holocaust in the Middle East

The decision to partition the Land caused intense rioting against Jews in many Arab countries. Hundreds of Jews were killed and thousands imprisoned. Jewish owned businesses, residences and synagogues were looted and burned. Movement was restricted, curfews were implemented, citizenships were withdrawn and emigration to Israel was banned. Stock holdings were stolen, bank accounts frozen and property was confiscated. All manner of means to simply survive was taken away from the Jews. Interestingly, this happened less than a decade after the Holocaust.

From 1948 to the early 1970s, approximately 856,000 Jews were forced from their Arab residences. Of these, 600,000 permanently resettled in Israel. Today, their descendants make up 3.06 million of Israel's overall 5.8 million population. Jewish property and real estate that was left behind is estimated to be valued at $300 billion, not to mention the 100,000 square kilometers of land that was deserted, which incidentally equates to four times the size of the land of Israel. In 1948 the Jewish population in Arab countries was 881,000 and by 1976 there were only 25,620. Here are some figures of the Jewish populations in Arab/Muslim and Muslim countries prior to 1947 compared with today:

- In the Muslim country of Aden there were 8,000 Jews, today there are none.
- In the Muslim country of Algeria there were 140,000 Jews, today there are none.
- In the Muslim country of Bahrain there were 600 Jews, today there are around 30.
- In the Muslim country of Egypt there were 80,000 Jews, today there are less than 100.
- In the Muslim country of Iraq there were 140,000 Jews, today there are fewer than 100.
- In the Muslim country of Lebanon there were 20,000 Jews, today there are less than 100.

- In the Muslim country of Libya there were 38,000 Jews, today there are none.
- In the Muslim country of Morocco there were 265,000 Jews, today there are less than 7,000.
- In the Muslim country of Syria there were 30,000 Jews, today there are fewer than 30.
- In the Muslim country of Tunisia there were 105,000 Jews, today there are 1,500.
- In the Muslim country of Afghanistan there were 5,000 Jews, today there is 1.
- In the Muslim country of Iran there were 150,000 Jews, today there are 40,000.
- In the Muslim country of Pakistan there were 2,000 Jews, today there are none.
- In the Muslim country of Turkey there were 80,000 Jews, today there are 30,000.

Today, the number of Jews living in Arab countries has managed to climb back to approximately 85,860.

The bottom line is this: 45,000 Arabs have died over the past 80 years due to the Middle East Crisis. Almost all of these deaths were in direct response to attacks on Israel from neighbouring Arab countries and Muslim terrorist attacks. In contrast the number of Arab/Muslim and Muslim deaths during the same period due to internal strife numbers into the millions. The frequency of mass killings that occur in the Muslim world barely sees Western news headlines unless Westerners are involved. The terrorist attack in Mumbai is a prime example.

Why is it that Muslims are involved in 98% of all wars going on in the world today and the Jews are involved in only 1, yet their standing in the global media in relation to war is mud compared to Islam? Jews, in contrast to the Muslims, do not kill each other indiscriminately or habitually use civilians as human shields, yet they are accused of committing war crimes of holocaust proportions by a demographic that trains their young to see Jews as pigs and deal with them by killing innocent civilians with brainwashed suicide bombers.

Dr. Philip Hitti, a prolific Arab historian and author of the popular book, *The Arabs: A Short History*, made the following statement to the Anglo-American Committee of Inquiry in 1946: "There is no such thing as Palestine in history, absolutely not." Dr. Philip Hitti made this declaration as an official representative of the Muslim World. The concept of a historical nation called "Palestine" is as fabricated as a jolly red man delivering presents via flying reindeer to every household across the earth in a single night.

If someone persists with a belief that there was ever a legitimate nation called "Palestine," try responding with the following three simple questions:

- Who was the leader of "Palestine?" Who was its president, prime minister or king?
- Name one nation that had diplomatic relations with "Palestine."
- What was the currency of "Palestine?"

These questions should start anyone off in a pretty commanding position.

A Fictitious People with a Fictitious Name

The Palestine Liberation Organisation (PLO) was formed in 1964 in Cairo, Egypt, after an initial suggestion by a traitorous Jew to invent a fictitious nation under the name "Palestine." This idea was to create a mechanism whereby a thorn could be driven into the side of a proposed Jewish homeland. So successful was this plan, that much of the West is still sympathetic to a group of Arab terrorists who adopted a name from a people who originally hailed from a tribe of Greek sea-marauders known as the "Philistines" and who have no historical connection to the Arab world whatsoever. The whole situation is equivalent to an Arab family taking on the Western name "smith" and calling their existing area of habitation in the Middle East, "Smithfield."

Today, many Palestinians refuse to believe that Jews ever occupied Israel. This is despite millions of obvious archaeological evidences to the contrary. As it is, a tourist can find shards of Hebrew pottery (usually from clay oil lamps and urns) whilst walking with a tour group through a number of historical sites. Jerusalem is rich with over 3000 years of archaeological evidence of Jewish presence, yet their historical connection is still denied by the Arab media and even moderate Palestinian two state supporters.

Chapter Twenty-Three

The Baggage of Opinion

What is an opinion? Why do people have them? And why do places where many different opinions gather, tend to be places of unrest and dissention? Is an opinion a good thing? Do we need to have them at all? By now, having read this far, you might have a few opinions of your own. Do independent or mass agreed upon opinions in regard to YHWH's Word have any concrete place within the body of Moshiach?

According to one source an opinion is a person's ideas and thoughts towards something. It is an assessment, judgement or evaluation of something. An opinion is not a fact, because opinions are either not falsifiable, or the opinion has not been proven or verified. If it later *becomes* proven or verified, it is no longer an opinion, but a fact.

Conversations inhabited by opinions would not likely occur in the heavenly realm, especially when it comes to the way it operates. Think about it, two people having ascended to the throne room and on receiving glorification are not going to have a debate over the correct running on an aspect of the Temple service. It will be there, proceeding right in front of them and if there is a dispute the Almighty will settle it.

Opinion was first given birth to in the heart of the HayLale' ben Shakh'ar Yalal (HaSatan - the Accuser). ***"Ben-adam (Son of man), take up a lament concerning the (שַׂר Sar [Ruler]) of Tsor and say to him: 'This says the master*** (or sovereign) ***YHWH: "You were the model of perfection, full of chochmah (wisdom) and perfect in beauty. You were in Eden ha Gan (the Garden of Eden) Elohim; every precious stone adorned you: ruby, topaz and emerald, chrysolite, onyx and jasper, sapphire, turquoise and beryl. Your settings and mountings were made of gold;*** (He wore the choshen – breastplate – as High Priest of the Angels.)***: on the day you were created they were prepared. You were the Moshiach-like (anointed) Karuv (guardian) that covers*** (the Mercy seat of Heaven)***; for so I ordained you. You were on the Kadosh (Set-Apart) mountain of Elohim; you walked among the fiery (faceted) stones. You were blameless in your halachot (ways) from the day that you were created until iniquity was found in you. By the multitude of your merchandise*** (or trade) ***you were filled with violence, and you have sinned. So I will cast you out as the profane-one out of the mountain of Elohim, and I expelled you, O Karuv that covers, from the midst of the stones of fire. Your lev (heart) was lifted up because of your beauty, you have corrupted your chochmah (wisdom) by reason of your splendour: I will cast you to the ground, I will lay you before melechim (kings), that they may see you. You have defiled your sanctuaries*** (Angelic Houses of Worship) ***by the multitude of your iniquities, by the iniquity of your trade; therefore will I bring out a fire in your midst, it shall devour you, and I will bring you to ashes upon the earth in the sight of all them that see you. All they that knew you among the nations shall be astonished at you: you shall be a waste before them, and never shall you be again."'(Ezekiel 28:12-19)*** It was the most beloved of all the angels who developed an opinion that the Master YHWH should not receive all glory and praise alone. There is no need to say that HaSatan developed a differing opinion, just an opinion. An opinion by definition is a different view that is either willingly or unwillingly held without knowledge of a fact. To say that HaSatan had a different opinion to YHWH suggests that the Creator's view of things was also based on opinion. HaSatan's development of an opinion enabled him to falsely legitimise his rebellion. Unlike someone who is genuinely ignorant of the truth, he had to willingly withdraw his knowledge from truth. In doing this he retarded his ability to discern, by choosing to ignore the fact that even if he overthrew YHWH and killed Him, heaven forbid, his heart would stop beating in the next instant and all creation would cease to exist. This is how disruptive rebellion is to a person's mental perception.

Prior to his corruption, all HaSatan's views fell in complete harmony with YHWH's will. Over time he slowly developed a unique and disunited view. HayLale served as the High Priest of the angelic host. He wore the *choshen* (breastplate) and ***"...walked among the fiery stones..."*** and he was responsible for the Kadosh Places. But ***"[He] defiled [the] sanctuaries by the multitude of [his] iniquities."*** His opinion led to his destruction and disqualification as High Priest in the heavenly court. To solidify his opinion he rallied for supporters, eventually coaxing one-third of the heavenly host to follow him. This was echoed in Korach's Levite rebellion against Moshe in the desert ***(Numbers 16)***. He was against the validity of all Moshe's appointments, including A'aron's appointment as the kohen. He began a series of verbal exchanges with Moshe that grew into his gathering two hundred and fifty supporters. The result of this rebellion was not favourable to say the least. Before the sight of the whole congregation, Korach and all his supporters and their belongings became swallowed up as Sheol opened its mouth to them ***(verse 32-33)***.

Mankind has had a very long love affair with rebellion. The world thrives on it. Many of our countries were formed off the back of it. Rebellion is the fuel that pumps through our films, TV shows, music, histories and culture. Rebellion is defined as any form of open resistance to authority. It's usually fed by crisis junkies who create controversy because peace makes them miserable. Rebellion's close cousin is "sedition," which is an illegal action that incites resistance to lawful authority, whether done secretly or openly. Rebels that create sedition lurk with people who have abandoned a community. YHWH singles these out as His most hated. ***"These six things does YHWH hate: yes, seven are an abomination to Him: A proud look, a lying tongue, and hands that shed innocent dahm (blood), A lev (heart) that plans wicked imaginations, feet that are swift in running to mischief, A false witness that speaks lies, and he that sows***

discord among brothers." (Proverbs 6:16-19) Sedition is also listed as a "work of the flesh" in ***Galatians 5***.

Korach's challenge teaches us that rebellious tendencies can even follow us into the faith and drive us to intrude into areas YHWH may not wish to reveal to us. At times when He does not wish to reveal something to us by a specific date, we try to reason it out anyway. ***"The secret things belong to YHWH our Elohim: but those things that are revealed belong to us and to our children le-olam-va-ed (forever and ever), that we may do all the words of this Torah." (Deuteronomy 29:29)***

My Rebbe, Rabbi Robert Miller writes: "We do just the opposite of the counsel of YHWH and we wonder why our theology (and our very) lives (are) in a mess. We trust in ourselves; we lean to our own understanding; we pay 'lip service' to the authority of Yahweh while we 'bulldoze' our own way through life. So is it any wonder that when we come into the Community of Faith we bring the old, cracked, weather-beaten, leathery baggage of rebellion." ***"Trust in YHWH with all your lev (heart); and lean not to your own binah (understanding). In all your derachot acknowledge Him, and He shall direct your paths." (Proverbs 3:5-6)***

Opinions can be used as a means of raising prestige as it heralds a person as an independent thinker who has departed from a common viewpoint. An opinionated person is usually someone who perceives many agreeing views as commonly agreed upon opinions rather than commonly agreed upon facts.

However, this is different from an individual or people who depart from a normally accepted view that was always based on opinion. HaSatan has managed to dilute the truth enough to be able to float enough opinion to keep people busy arguing about correct doctrine for a lifetime.

A soldier who exerts independent thinking on the battle field (and who doesn't train with the rest of his team) will try to fill the gap of his ignorance with opinion and put the team's safety in jeopardy. How much more in the spiritual realm with believers who can't settle down in a congregation and don't know what the rest of the body is doing. Imagine a soldier who just drifts from one platoon to another on his own whim.

***Proverbs 18:2*; "A fool has no delight in binah (understanding), but only in revealing his lev (heart)."**

The Sadducees were an interesting sect of religious men. Today they no longer formally exist and neither do any of their writings. Some of their beliefs and even some references to their writings can be found in the Karaite movement. The word "Karaite" means "written," as if to denote going only by what is strictly written. The Karaites evolved from a sect of breakaway fundamentalist Sadducees. They exist today and in some cases have made deep inroads into the Messianic movement. Judas Iscariot was from a Karaite sect. Yahudah HaKaraite is translated as Judas Iscariot.

The Sadducees and the Karaites that evolved from them were very opinionated groups; even members within these sects harboured differing private opinions on certain Biblical texts, born out of their doctrinal view. This is all in spite of the warning in ***2 Peter 1:20; "Knowing this first that no prophesy of the Keetvay HaKadosh (Set-apart Scriptures) is of any private interpretation."***

Before Rabbi Sha'ul's encounter with the Almighty he was a clever, capable, wise and rational man who exuded confidence and performed his duties with all his enthusiasm.

But whilst heading a fully armed and equipped Nazarene Israelite hunting party he was struck by a great light which cast him off his horse and threw him to the ground. In this day and age we'd call this a "Close Encounter of the Second Kind." This means a visual and verbal contact by an extraterrestrial being.

Blinded, he immediately abandoned his task in Damascus and all his reasons for it. He returned neither to Tarsus nor to Jerusalem. He was like a computer in complete "reboot mode." The capability of the software was to stay the same but all the corrupting files he amassed were deleted.

When an opinionated view takes root in one individual it can quickly spread to an entire congregation. This can lead to a general laid back arrogance and false perceptions of superiority.

The congregation of Laodicea was in poor shape. The word "Laodicea" is a Greek word and means, "people of personal opinions." They exuded an over-confidence in regard to their status with the Almighty and became unable to recognise their own spiritual bankruptcy. ***Revelations 3:15-18; "I know your mitzvoth (love***

deeds) that you are neither cold nor hot: I desire that you were cold, or hot. So then because you are lukewarm, and are neither cold, or hot, I will vomit you out of My mouth. Because you say, I am rich, and increased with goods, and have need of nothing; and know not that you are wretched, and miserable, and poor, and blind, and naked: I counsel you to buy from Me gold tried in the fire, that you may be rich; and white raiment, that you may be clothed, so that the shame of your nakedness does not appear; and anoint your eyes with ointment, that you may see."

To avoid opinion rearing its ugly head in Scriptural matters, tag the topic that you're compelled to give your theory on with an immediate "to do." Then find time to study it in context with the text and find related Scriptures. Do this with the following principle in mind: ***Isaiah 28:10; "For precept must be laid upon precept, precept upon precept; line upon line, line upon line; here a little, and there a little."***

This piece-by-piece method of study avoids finding meanings that depart from context and maintains a message's unity to the Scripture's foundational text – the Torah. Then read Jewish, Messianic or Christian commentaries on the text. This can be the most enlightening process as you read other thoughts that reveal things you may never have noticed.

There's only one opinion that's ever going to matter to you, and that's YHWH's. Actually, it's not even His opinion; it is His completely accurate view of you tempered with the perfect measure of judgement and mercy.

Wherever there is opinion there is lack of knowledge. Opinion is the desire to make a decision or offer advice at the exclusion of knowledge. What's wrong with saying, "I just don't know. I'll have to go and study it"? Or more to the point, "You go and study it. It's your question."

Watchman Nee writes in the book, *Spiritual Authority*, "The primary evidence that one has met YHWH is in the disappearing of one's opinions and cleverness."

Avoda(h) – Hebrew word that means "work" can also mean "service," "ritual" or "Divine Service" (worship).

Baal Shem Tov – ("Master of a Good Name") Title given to Rabbi *Yisrael ben Eliezer* (1698-1760), the founder of Chassidic movement.

Ba'al Teshuvah – ("Master of Return") One who returns to Torah observance after a period of estrangement.

Beit HaMikdash – Hebrew word that means, "Set-apart" or "Holy House." Refers specifically to the Temple in Jerusalem (whether first, second [or soon to come] third Temple).

ChaBaD – This is an acronym for the Hebrew words *Chochmah*, *Binah* and *Da'at*, meaning Wisdom, Understanding, and Knowledge. It is also the name of an ultra- Orthodox Jewish community that formed in the 18th century in the town of Lyubavichi, Russia.

Ebionites – The Hebrew word Ebionite (Ebonim [plural]) literally means, "Poor One." Ebionites, like Nazarenes, followed Torah as it was "rightly divided" by Messiah Yahshua. However, unlike Nazarenes, they regarded Yahshua as not being immaculately conceived. They also largely rejected Sha'ul's teachings.

Golem (*goilem* – Yiddish) – A golem is a fully articulated human-like creature created entirely from clay. The word "golem" means "cocoon" and is derived from the word *gelem*, which means "raw material." One is known to have been made in Prague by Rabbi Judah Loew the Maharal in the 16th century. The first human, Adam is described in the Talmud as being a golem before Elohim breathed into his nostrils. (Tractate Sanhedrin 38b)

Great Pyramid of Giza (The) – The Great Pyramid was built on a flat topped mountain of fairly level granite bedrock called the Giza Plateau. If it had been built elsewhere in the area the ground would not have been able to support its massive weight. It is the largest and most elaborately built of nine great pyramids located about ten miles to the west of the modern city of Cairo.

Though the second largest pyramid that sits in a nearby southwesterly direction from the Great Pyramid appears higher, it is due to its locality on a slightly higher foundation. Further to the southwest again is the third pyramid accompanied by two very small crudely built copies that are largely in ruin.

These three major pyramids at Giza are completely devoid of Egyptian hieroglyphs inside and out and there has been no evidence of any Pharaoh ever being laid to rest in any of them. This is very significant because the three Pyramids along the Giza Plateau initially had nothing to do with the Egyptians. The Great Pyramid was originally called "The Pillar of Enoch." In Hebrew the word "pillar" is *Matsebhah* and refers to an object that is erected to commemorate something memorable. It and the other two pillars near it were designed by Noah's grandfather, Enoch, a man who walked with YHWH. ***"'Observe, Enoch, these heavenly tablets, and read what is written hereon, And mark every individual fact.' And I observed the heavenly tablets, and read everything which was written (thereon) and understood everything, and read the book of all the deeds of mankind, and of all the children of flesh." (1 Enoch 81:1-2) "Yea, I Enoch will declare [them] unto you, my sons: According to that which appeared to me in the heavenly vision, and which I have known through the word of the holy angels, and have learnt from the heavenly tablets." (1 Enoch 93:1-2)*** Enoch was the first to decipher the story of the Gospel in the stars and prophetically transfer that knowledge into the form of an enormous stone monument, known today as the Great Pyramid of Giza. ***"I know a mystery and have read the heavenly tablets, and have seen the holy books..." (1 Enoch 103:1)*** The gradual decline in the precision of the architecture of the first pyramid to the third represents man's gradual departure from holiness. That being said, the quality of the third pyramid is still leaps and bounds ahead of any other pyramid in the rest of Egypt.

The three pyramids on the Giza Plateau were built by the sons of Seth, the first under the direct instruction of Enoch and the next two by proceeding generations who worked from his plans. Their construction was achieved by manipulating the land in a similar authoritative fashion as YHWH (through Messiah) when he formed the very foundations of the earth. The cutting, transportation and positioning of the stones was most likely achieved through some form of harmonic vocal recitation. Studying the meticulous construction of another manmade wonder, King Solomon's Temple, and noting the way that life was restored in Genesis, gives some measure of indication as to how the three Pyramids on the Giza Plateau could have been physically built. To venture detailed theories as to how this was specifically done is not the aim of this work; rather it is to establish the purpose of the structures themselves; in particular the Great Pyramid as being a three-dimensional Torah scroll if you will. For now I will simply add that the role of utterance in the construction of the Pillar of Enoch and its two sister monuments is put forward due to the Creator's single reliance on verbal utterance in bringing every phase of creation into being.

More popular theories as to the method of construction and function of the Great Pyramid are problematic for a host of reasons. Conventionally dragging and floating 2.3 million 2.5 ton limestone blocks 934 km (700km air-line distance) and hauling them up a gradually diminishing ascending area of 146.59 metres within twenty years of conception to completion is not possible to achieve even with the use of modern technology today. In addition there has been no discovery of any remains of equipment, heavy or otherwise, that could have enabled the structures to be built as they originally appeared. In addition to this, the existence of pristinely hewn and fitted together internal granite stones that make up 5% of the Pyramid's total structure remains as an inescapable anomaly to all generally accepted academic theories as to the manner of their construction. This is because granite can only be cut awkwardly by steel, yet thousands of finely cut tons of it was produced in an age that only used small soft copper cutting implements. Today granite is only cut effectively with diamond.

Curious watermarks are still visible today on the Giza Pyramid to those with a keen eye. Thanks to the fabulous lithographs of the late Scottish landscape artist David Roberts, watermarks are clearly visible on his reproductions drawn in 1838 depicting the Sphinx and a largely intact limestone casing covering of the Great Pyramid, which prove their existence even before Noah's Flood. Part of Enoch's design plan was to have these structures withstand an impending flood. To do this he used a special organic material in the mortar that would resist dissolving under extreme environmental stresses. To this day the material has been unsuccessfully replicated in any known laboratory.

The Great Pyramid was built as a symbol of Mount Moriah (the primordial mound of creation) which resides at the centre of the Garden of Eden, the place where YHWH stares continually. All three pyramids at Giza were deliberately built to represent Orion's belt, chiefly represented by the three major mountains in Jerusalem - Mount Moriah, the Mount of Olives and Mount Zion.

The Pillar of Enoch was built with supernatural knowledge that was handed down to Enoch with the chief principle of:

- Teaching Torah
- Making man aware of the link between the physical and spiritual realm
- To foretell specific points and prophetic points in time
- To provide a portal from the spiritual and physical realm (like Mount Moriah).

"For You have set signs and wonders in the land of Mitzrayim (Egypt), <u>even to this day</u>, and in Yisrael, and among other men; and have made Your Name great, <u>even to this day</u>." (Jeremiah 32:20)

Josephus Flavius, in his *Antiquities of the Jews*, Book I, Chapter 2:9-10, wrote concerning the Great Pyramid and the Sphinx, "All these proved to be of good dispositions. They also inhabited the same country without dissensions, and in a happy condition, without any misfortunes falling upon them, till they died. They also were the inventors of that peculiar sort of wisdom which is concerned with the heavenly bodies, and their order. And that their inventions might not be lost before they were sufficiently known, upon Adam's prediction that the world was to be destroyed at one time by the force of fire, and at another time by the violence and quantity of water, they made two pillars, the one of brick, the other of stone: they inscribed their discoveries on them both, that in case the pillar of brick should be destroyed by the flood, the pillar of stone might remain, and exhibit those discoveries to mankind; and also inform them that there was another pillar of brick erected by them. Now this remains in the land of Siriad (Egypt) to this day."

"In that day shall there be an altar to YHWH in the midst of the land of Mitzrayim (Egypt), and a standing column at its border to YHWH. And it shall be for an ot (sign) and for a witness to YHWH tzevaoth (of hosts) in the midst of land of Mitzrayim (Egypt)." (Isaiah 19:19-20). Reference to "***...its border...***" means the border of Israel because according to Scripture Israel stretches from Egypt to the Euphrates River. And "***...the midst of...***" (more accurately translated as in the "***middle of***") refers to the middle of Egypt because the great Pyramid sits in its centre.

The outer mantle of the Great Pyramid was composed of 144,000 casing stones, which were symbolic of the end time 144,000 evangelists ***(Revelation 7:2-4)***.

The absence of the "capstone" on the Great Pyramid is also very significant. ***"The Stone that the builders rejected has become the Rosh Pina (Corner Stone) of the corner. This is YHWH's doing; it is marvellous in our eyes." (Psalms 118:22-23) "Therefore I say to you, The malchut (kingdom) of YHWH shall be taken from you, and given to a people bringing forth the fruits of it. And whoever shall fall on this Stone shall be broken: but on whomever it shall fall, it will grind him to powder and they will be broken apart." (Matthew 21:43-44)***

The prophetic timeline encoded within the measurements of the Great Pyramid of Giza (also cited in the teachings of the false prophet and founder of the Jehovah's Witness Movement, Charles Taze Russell) is derived from its geometrical features. It is worth noting that some of Russell's conclusions as to the Pyramid's prophetic meaning were wrong. ***Isaiah 19:19's*** statement that there, "***...shall there be an altar to*** YHWH ***in the midst*** (or middle) ***of the land of Mitzrayim (Egypt), and a standing column at the border to YHWH"*** is supported in ***Jeremiah 32:20*** which speaks of YHWH setting "***signs*** **and** ***wonders in the land of Mitzrayim (Egypt), even unto this day."*** The inclusion of "***...even unto this day***" stumps those who believe it is referring to the plagues in the time of the prophet Moshe.

The Great Pyramid is the only serious contender as YHWH's "***Witness.***" It is literally a storehouse of scientific, historic and prophetic truth with a testimony that is in perfect accord with Scripture sitting in the geographical centre of the surface of the world. "That monument stands in a more important physical situation than any other building erected by man," cited Henry Mitchell, the Chief Hydrographer of the United States Coast Survey in 1868. To say that the Great Pyramid was built as a tomb is like seeing Buckingham Palace and saying that it was built as a toilet block.

Every feature of the Great Pyramid's architecture (as with the Holy Temple) is supremely important because it outlines YHWH's plan of the Ages. The Great Pyramid represents the plan of YHWH completed by Messiah Yahshua who is the ***"precious corner-stone." (Isaiah 28:16) Zechariah 4:7*** refers to its placement at the top of the completed monument saying, ***"he shall bring forth the headstone of it with shouts of, favour, favour to it.'"***

Interestingly, an Arabian by the name of Caliph Al Mamoun, who was ignorant of an official "Entrance Passage" to the great Pyramid, forced an entry in hopes of finding treasure and in so doing paralleled a famous passage in Scripture. ***"I tell you the truth, the man who does not enter the sheep pen by the gate, but climbs in by some other way, is a thief and a robber." (John 10:1)*** The Great Pyramid has only one "Entrance Passage." Once inside the Great Pyramid one will immediately notice that the interior is predominantly made up of granite. This represents the gold as it is used in the Holy Temple. Thus the granite represents Set-apartness and the limestone represents that which is not Set-apart (common).

The sparse passages of the Great Pyramid have unique functions in relating YHWH's plan of salvation. From the entrance, the "Descending Passage" represents the spiritually declining life of man after "The Fall." The "Well" that sprouts out from it near "The Pit" represents Messiah's death, burial, and resurrection. Images show that the well literally looks like an explosion had burst it open from beneath signifying Messiah bursting the bonds of death ***(Acts 2:24)***, thereby opening up a way to eternal life ***(Hebrews 10:20)***. In November 2009, my wife and five other members of our tour group, including our Rabbi, went inside the Great Pyramid. We were not able to make our way into the descending passage, the pit, or the well, which was probably for the best if one realises their significance (with the exception of the well of course).

The huge granite plug stopping access to the "First Ascending Passage" represents the Old Covenant because without Set-apartness no one will see YHWH ***(Hebrews 12:14)***. This also symbolises the absence of the law of return of the adulterous bride (Israel) until the proclamation of the New Covenant in Jeremiah 31. Upon going inside the Great Pyramid through the Caliph Al Mamoun passage, my companions and I walked straight past this massive plug as we made our ascent toward "The Grand Gallery." This ascent was very confined, causing us to walk in a perpetual bow until we reached the Grand Gallery. **Prof. C. Piazzi Smyth,** an Astronomer-Royal for Scotland, wrote in his work *Our Inheritance in the Great Pyramid,* "From the north beginning of the Grand Gallery, in upward progression, begin the years of our Savior's life, expressed at the rate of an inch to a year. Three and thirty inch-years, therefore, bring us right over against the mouth of the Well." At precisely the moment we got to walk upright in the ascending passage we saw the point were the well opens out signifying Moshiach's enabling unmerited power (Grace). So from here we proceeded by grace symbolised by being enabled to walk in an upright fashion with an exceeding height overhead. It was truly amazing and an experience I won't easily forget.

John and Morton Edgar wrote in volume one of their book, *The Great Pyramid Passages and Chambers*[1] that "... (based) upon the work of Professor Smyth, many able minds have been awakened to search into the various problems presented by the Great Pyramid. Some of these investigators have claimed not only that it embodies great scientific truths, but also that it sets forth symbolically and by measurement the Divine plan of salvation-that, in fact, it is Messianic."

The Grand Gallery leads up into an entirely granite room called "The King's Chamber." At one end is an object known as "the coffer," which is an object that has the exact volume of the Ark of the Covenant with dimensions described in Scripture as 2.5 cubits by 1.5 cubits by 1.5 cubits (45 inches by 27 inches by 27 inches). This will be the resting place of the Ark of the Covenant that will be no

1 This volume was first published in 1910 and circulated among Jehovah's Witnesses who were called at that time "Bible Students." The book's distribution within this movement ceased in 1928.

longer remembered according to ***Jeremiah 3:16; "And it shall come to pass, when you are multiplied and increased in the land, in those days, says YHWH, they shall say no more, 'The ark of the brit (Covenant) of YHWH': neither shall it come to mind: neither shall they remember it; neither shall they visit it; neither shall that ritual be done anymore."*** The Ark of the Covenant will no longer be significant in people's minds because of the physical presence of the real capstone, Yahshua our King who will rule and reign during the great millennium. This time will not be the be-all-end-all age, but the final trial period (if you will) before the final restoration of a New Heaven and a New Earth. **With an understanding of the Great Pyramid's true significance, verses throughout Scripture come to life like never before.** ***Psalms 111:4; "He has made a memorial for His wonders." Job 38:5-6; "Do you know who determined its dimensions or who stretched the measuring line across it? On who laid its cornerstone…?" (Complete Jewish Bible – Translation by David Stern)***

Obviously there is much more information than what I have shared here about the Great Pyramid. But hopefully I have presented enough here to whet the appetite. YHWH has allowed The Great Pyramid and the Sphinx to be witnesses to His Greatness; and as a consequence, out of the Seven Wonders of the World only they remain to this day.

Halacha – Means "Way" or "Path."

Kabbalah – The word "Kabbalah" means "receive" and is the name given to esoteric, mystical or what I like to call 'high end Judaism.' Technically the term Kabbalah was first applied to a form of medieval Judaism that emerged in 12th century medieval Spain. But elements of its principles and practices can be traced back to the patriarch Abraham. The deeper revelations that Kabbalah has the potential to unlock from the Torah in no way compromise any surface meanings but conform to a strict cohesive pattern that adds further insight to the text. True Kabbalah should not be confused with the pop-culture counterfeit that is exhibited in the media today.

Minyan - "A count of 10 men" that signifies Elohim's minimal requirement of righteous people dwelling in the twin cities of Sodom and Gomorrah to avoid destruction. Orthodox Jews have many prayers that require a minyan for them to be chanted in a Synagogue.

Moshiach (Messiah) – The word "Moshiach" (sometimes spelt Mashiach) is the Hebrew word for "Messiah." However, there is some initial confusion about this subject because the word Messiah carries the meaning of "saviour" or "deliverer," whilst the word Moshiach means "anointed one." It is actually the common Christian term "Christ" that carries the equivalent meaning of "anointed one." The title Moshiach was given as a position of great nobility, which is evident in the title of the High Priest who was formally called the *Kohen Hamoshiach* (The anointed High Priest). In rabbinical literature *Melech Hamoshiach* (the King Messiah) refers to a Jewish leader that will redeem Israel. Throughout this work I have used the terms Moshiach and Messiah interchangeably to familiarise the reader with Hebrew words. It is most beneficial to become acquainted with as much Hebrew as possible, because there are root word meanings within existing words that hold additional information[2]. Even Martin Luther (1483-1546) knew the advantages of the Hebrew language when he made this often overlooked statement:

> "If I were younger I would want to learn this language [Hebrew], for without it one can never properly understand the Holy Scripture.... For that reason they have said correctly: 'The Jews drink out of the original spring, The Greeks drink out of the stream flowing out of the stream, the Latins, however, out of the puddle.'"

All the letters of the Hebrew language have a numerical equivalent. This process is called *Gematria*. The reason for this is to show

2 Many Hebrew words can be broken down into three-consonant root words. These roots contain a deeper insight to the word's meaning. The correct way to interpret Scripture is based on understanding this principle. Anyone familiar with a *Strong's Concordance* will note there are often cases where the same English word is used for different Hebrew roots. This means that words have a slightly different emphasis in meaning that can get lost in translation. For example, a big man can simply be described as "big" because Hebrew has a specific masculine world for "grown-up" *(gadol)*.

that Semitic words have a deeper level of meaning beyond normal linguistic capabilities. In other words, two different words that possess the same numerical value indicate that they hold a similar truth or carry a special relation. The numerical value of Moshiach exceeds the numerical value of the name Moshe (Moses) by thirteen. The difference between these words equals the same value of the Hebrew word *echad* (one) and the twelve tribes of Israel plus the tribe of Levi. The unity (or oneness) of Moshiach with Moshe and the 13 tribes of Israel is a chief principle of the faith.

Nazarenes (Ha-Natsarim) / Natsari (singular) – The name of a people who are joined to a sect of Judaism that recognises Messiah Yahshua ben Yoseph HaNazaret (Jesus the son of Joseph the Nazarene). Nazarenes were first referred to as a sect in ***Acts 24:5***. They were similar to the Ebionites who recognised Yahshua and maintained an adherence to Torah, but differed in that they also accepted his virgin birth and divinity. The word "Natsari" is used for any Torah observant person who also accepts Yahshua as Messiah, whether Jew or former Gentile.

Nazarite vow – A voluntary act of setting oneself apart to YHWH that is considered extremely sacred. This vow can be made by a man or a woman and involves abstaining from wine or any strong drink. A Nazarite is forbidden to cut the hair of his own head and must avoid contact with the dead during the entire duration and of the vow. This vow can be made for a lifetime or any shorter period of time. At the close of a Nazarite vow a burnt, sin and peace offering was to be presented at the door of the sanctuary. After these sacrifices were offered, the Nazarite would cut off his own hair and throw it into a fire under the peace offering according to ***Numbers 6:2-21***. Samson was a Nazarite from birth and was commanded to remain as one for the duration of his life in order to help insulate him from sin since he was required to interact with pagan women. The success of his mission was postponed due to sin enabling the Philistines to remain as a thorn in Israel's side until just before his death, which came about through repentance.

Petra – "Petra" is a Greek word meaning "rock" and is the name for an ancient city hewn into the rock of a large valley in Jordan that runs from the Dead Sea to the Gulf of Aqaba. It appears in Scripture as the Hebrew word *Se'lah* (also meaning "rock") or *Bozrah*, which means "sheep pen," referring to its eastern entrance that is only accessible via a long and narrow gorge. ***Ezekiel 20:33-38*** mentions a great purging of mankind and a gathering of all of Israel from the four corners of the globe to a desert location. Those who are led there will be taken note of as they ***"...pass under my*** (YHWH's) ***rod." "I will surely assemble, O Yaakov (Jacob), all of you; I will surely gather the remnant of Yisrael (Israel); I will put them together as the sheep of Bozrah, as the flock in the midst of their fold: they shall make great noise by reason of the multitude of men." (Micah 2:12-13)*** Israel will be gathered first to Judah and then later to a place of protection. ***"When you therefore shall see the abomination of desolation*** (aka The Golem), ***spoken of by Daniel the navi*** (prophet), ***standing in the Beit HaMikdash*** (Temple), ***(whoever reads, let him understand); Then let them who are in Yahudah*** (Judah) ***flee into the mountains." (Matthew 24:15-16)***.

The Prophet Moshe was protected within ***"...the cleft of the rock..."*** when YHWH passed by ***(Exodus 33:22)***. Similarly all Israel will be gathered again into the cleft of the rock for their own protection as YHWH makes war on her enemies.

Israel's passage, arrival and time in Petra will not be without incident as the armies of the Moshiach Neged (Anti-Messiah) attempt to slaughter them as they attempt to cross the Jordan River and enter Bozrah. YHWH parts the Jordan in seven parts ***(Isaiah 11:15)*** and Messiah is sent to Bozrah to counter attack the Moshiach Neged. ***Revelation 12:13-17; "And when the dragon (HaSatan) saw that he was cast to the olam (earth), he persecuted the woman*** (Israel) ***who brought forth the Male-Child. And to the woman was given two wings of a great eagle, that she might fly into the wilderness*** (Petra), ***into her place, where she is nourished for a time, and times, and half a time*** (3½ years), ***from the face of the serpent (HaSatan). And the serpent cast out of his mouth mayim (water) as a flood after the woman, that he might cause her to be carried away by the flood. And the ground helped the woman*** (Petra protects Israel), ***and the land opened her mouth, and swallowed up the flood, which the dragon (HaSatan) cast out of his mouth. And the dragon (HaSatan) was angry with the woman, and went make war with the remnant of***

her zera (seed) that shomer (hear) the mitzvoth (commandments) of YHWH, and have the testimony of Yahshua HaMoshiach."

Isaiah 43:19; "See, I (YHWH) ***will do a new thing*** (in our generation)***; now it shall spring forth; shall you not know it? I will even make a derech (way) in the wilderness, and rivers in the desert*** (of Moab and Edom)."

Isaiah 11:12-16; "And He (YHWH) ***shall set up a miraculous Banner for the nations and He shall gather the outcasts of Yisrael, and gather together the dispersed of Yahudah*** (The Jews) ***from the four corners of the earth. The envy also of Efrayim (Ephraim) shall depart, and the adversaries of Yahudah shall be cut off Efrayim shall not envy Yahudah (Jews), and Yahudah shall not trouble Efrayim. But they shall fly upon the shoulders of the Plishtim (Philistines) toward the west; they shall plunder them of the east together; they shall lay their hands upon Edom and Moab; and the children of Ammon*** (Jordan) ***shall be subjected and obey them*** (Jordan will become Israel's allies). ***And YHWH shall utterly destroy the tongue of the Mitzrayim (Egyptian) Sea; and with His mighty Ruach (spirit) shall He shake His hand over the river, and shall break it into seven streams, and shall cause Yisrael to trample it in their sandals. And there shall be a highway for the remnant of His people, who shall be left, from Ashshur; like as it was for kol (all) Yisrael in the day that they came up out of the land of Mitzrayim (Egypt)."***

Details of the battles that will be fought on the way and at the entrance to Petra are detailed in the Dead Sea Scrolls in the manuscript called "War of the Sons of Light and the Sons of Darkness."

Petra's enormity and its use as a previous refuge are also mentioned in ***1 Maccabees 5:24-26; "Judas Maccabeus and Jonathan his brother crossed the Jordan and went three days' journey into the wilderness. They encountered the Nabateans, who met them peaceably and told them all that had happened to their brethren in Gilead: 'Many of them had been shut up in Bozrah, Bosor, in Alema and Chaspho, Maked Carnaim' – all these cities were strong and large."***

Rabbi Judah Loew ben Bezalel ("Judah Loewe son of Bezalel") – Rabbi who lived in the 16th century who is widely believed to have created a golem to protect his community from riots incited by blood libel accusations. He is known in Judaism as the Maharal of Prague. Maharal is a Hebrew acronym for, "Our Teacher the Rabbi Loew." Rabbi Loew is also known for drawing upon Kabbalistic concepts in his sermons that were chiefly derived from the Zohar.

Rambam (Maimonides) – Acronym for "Rabbi Moses ben Maimon" (1135-1204). 12th century Jewish scholar, philosopher and physician, best known for his 14 part compendium of Jewish law called the Mishnah Torah.

Ramban (Nachmanides) – Acronym for "Rabbi Moses ben Nachman," famous Jewish scholar and philosopher (1194-1270).

Shimmushei Tehillim – (Practical Psalms) Shimmushei Psalms focus on the use of the Psalms to invoke healing and protection. While I do not espouse all the various forms of use of the Psalms or any other part of Scripture to achieve a supernatural result, I do firmly believe that the recital of specific Psalms for specific situations is not only permissible, but an ideal way of using them to combat and overcome certain physical and spiritual barriers in life.

Some examples of certain Psalm citations for specific purposes include:

Psalm 2 – To subdue a storm or wild sea

Psalm 5 – Combat Evil Spirits

Psalms 8 – Subdue a crying child

Psalm 12 – Vanquish temptation and nullify evil counsel

Psalms 21 – Maintain composure when standing before a spiritual or temporal authority

Psalms 23 – To receive correct interpretation of a dream

Psalms 26 – To receive peace whilst in distress or in prison

Psalms 6, 30, 41, 88 & 103 – Recovery from illness

Psalms 51 & 90 – Repentance

Psalms 119 – For the success of a son in his learning of Torah

Shimmushei Torah – (Practical Torah) According to a Midrash on the book of Psalms "(if)...the chapters of the Torah (were) given in their correct order, anyone who read them would have been enabled to raise the dead and work miracles; therefore, the Torah's true order has been hidden and is known only to Elohim." A medieval Jewish text was compiled out of this understanding and subsequently professes to list all the Torah that upon utterance enables one to achieve supernatural feats. Its recitation is to be performed with deep concentration and focus upon the Divine power of YHWH's names, which are contained throughout the entirety of the text. In actuality, all the Torah is formed from the many names of Elohim, out of which the merciful four-letter Tetragrammaton name, YHWH, can be enumerated. It is believed that this knowledge was transmitted directly from the Almighty to the Prophet Moshe and that it's widely accepted episodic order in the Five Books of Moses was arranged to give situational authoritative instruction and enable only the most devoted students to decipher its true order to perform such miraculous works.

Note: This author does not view serious works or students of Kabbalah as being necessarily contrary to the Scriptures or the Gospel of the Brit Chadashah (New Testament). Such genuine texts and scholars are merely the product of years of intense study of the Scriptures, which have unlocked levels of revelation that were privy to a great many of the Hebrew Patriarchs and to Messiah himself. The wayward depiction of so-called Kabbalists and Kabbalah groups in popular media is no different to the depiction of other so-called Bible based people and religious movements throughout the world today and cannot warrant grounds for a sweeping rejection of all kabbalistic literature without suitable investigation.

Star of David – Over the years I have weathered steady criticism by sincere, yet sincerely wrong returning and grafted-in Israelites who have criticised the Star of David as being a pagan symbol. To this end I feel it necessary to add a small entry that explains the origin and meaning of the Star of David to set minds at rest. This symbol is completely in harmony with Scripture and has its origin in the Davidic reign. It was a mark of Divine protection, given to David by YHWH. ***Psalms 18:36; "You have given me Your shield of***

***salvation.*"** The "six pointed star" is made up of two inverted superimposed paleo-Hebrew "daleths" (delets), the beginning and ending letter in King David's name.

> "The Magen David ("Shield of David") has six-points, which symbolise that (YHWH) rules over the universe and protects Israel from all six directions: North, South, East, West, Up and Down. A similar symbolism is found in reading the 'Shema.' ('Code of Jewish Law' O.C. 61:6)" - Rabbi Shraga Simmons

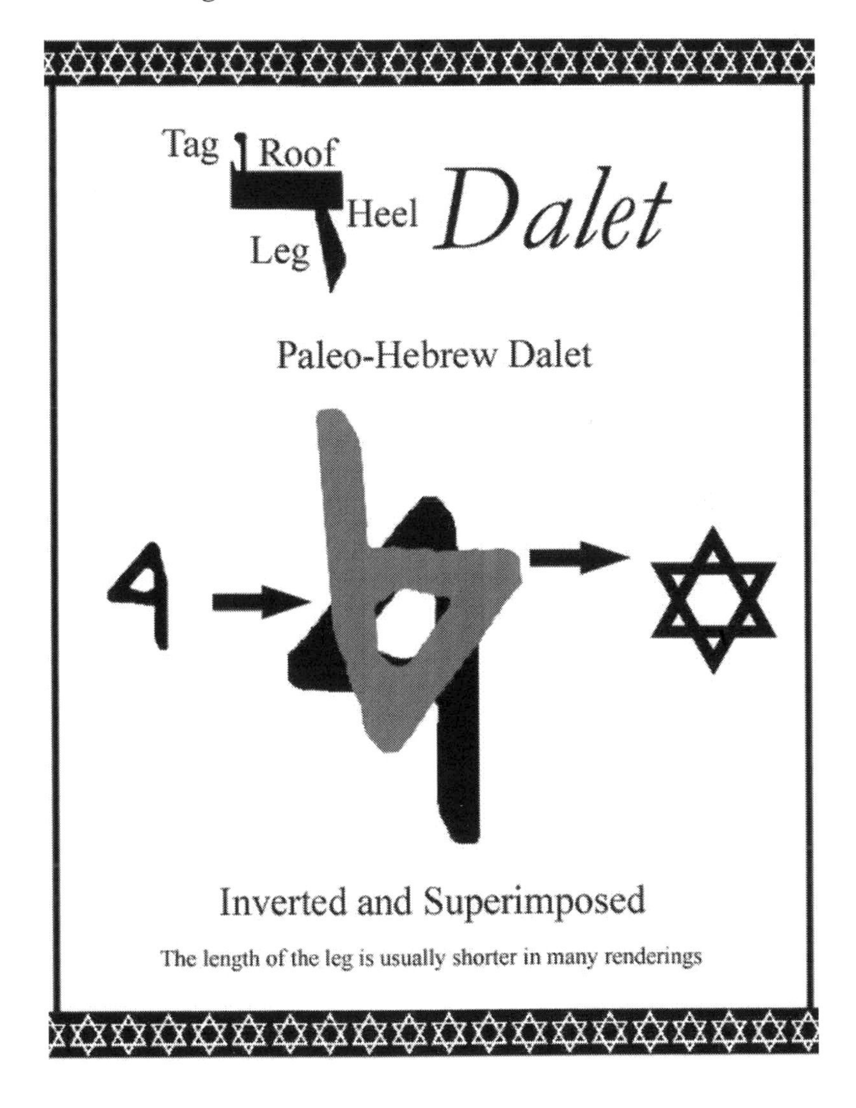

Though King David is believed not to have ever literally worn the symbol in battle, it was latter utilised by his descendants. During the 1st century Bar Kochba rebellion, Jewish troops equipped themselves with shields in the shape of two overlapping inverted triangles to signify that the Almighty shields them in war. Interestingly Bar Kochba means "son of the star." It is also believed that the Macabees adorned their battle gear with the Magen David and in the 1500s the threatened Jewish community in Prague flew a flag with a six pointed star.

Triangle based interlocking designs, as we know from the construction of the pillar of Enoch (aka The Great Pyramid), are the strongest forms of construction known to man. The triangles represent the reciprocal relationship between heaven and a future harmonic world summed up as, "as above, as below." The triangle facing down represents the flow of goodness down from heaven and the triangle facing up represents "good deeds" that will provoke Messiah Yahshua's return. The overall shape of the great Pyramid at Gaza, which was not built by Egyptians at all, was built based on this premise. So the foundation or premise for the Star of David has its origin in the Enochian period. When Yahshua returns it will be as if another pyramid descends from above to form a three dimensional Star of David.

The inner core of the Star of David represents the spiritual dimension whilst being surrounded by six equally sized directions. The centre hexagonal shape is the Shabbat, which is balanced by the six weekdays.

I have personally seen and photographed, not only the Star of David, but the Pentagram of Solomon carved on the arch of the ruined Natsarim Synagogue, which Yahshua taught at, on the shores of the Galilee. This partially erect structure still stands behind the remains of Kepha's (Peter's) parent's home. Surrounding the Synagogue is also the location of a large crumbling Yeshiva (house of study), which is evidence that the fishing community that Yahshua recruited students from was not a collection of poverty stricken fisherman, but that of a flourishing fishing business, whose profits went to constructing a once prestigious building that housed the school of Yahshua. This alone is ample evidence that the Star of

David and the Pentagram of Solomon was alive and well in Yahshua's day, and not a set of seventeen century afterthoughts that got attributed to Israel's beloved King David or his son.

Criticism of the Star of David calls into question the symbol of the early Natsarim (Offshoot Branch Watchmen) movement, which depicts a menorah interlocked with the Star of David and the fish symbol, the latter adopted exclusively by modern-day Christianity. This symbol has been discovered on pottery in the locality of Natsarim communities within Israel.

It grieves me that the memory of Jewish soldiers (both ancient and modern) have died in battle trying to uphold this standard and it gets branded as pagan by "Johnny come lately" Ephramites who usually also broadly criticise Rabbinic Judaism, but quite happily help themselves to small portions of it.

The Tanya – *Tanya* means "it was taught" (Aramaic). It is described as "...an incense to counter all the spiritual plagues besetting the generations just before the arrival of *Mashiach (Messiah).*" It is also known as *Likkutei Amarim*, which means "collection of statements." R. Zusya said, "With the *Tanya* the Jewish people will go out to greet the righteous *Mashiach.*"

The work itself teaches Torah based spirituality and psychology from a Chasidic perspective. Its style actually acquaints the reader with Kabbalistic principles but in a way that does not step outside the boundaries of Torah. As a result it is one of the few works that correctly and safely teaches practical Kabbalah by teaching what this author calls "high end" Torah.

Tzimtzumim – The function of the *Tzimtzum* was "to conceal from created beings the activating force within them, enabling them to exist as tangible entities, instead of being utterly nullified within their source."[3] According to Chassidic thought, when an educator, whose level of mind and understanding is almost completely removed and incomparable to his student, he has to "find" an idea that is simple enough to convey to the student. To do this he chooses a simplistic utterance, but at the same time retains all

3 From *The Tanya* ("It has been taught"). "The Tanya is the first schematic treatment of Hasidic moral philosophy and its metaphysical foundations." - *The Encyclopedia of Hasidism*, entry: Habad, Jonathan Sacks, pp. 161-164

the knowledge of who he really is ("thus the contraction is not a literal contraction").

Zohar – The word Zohar means "splendor" or "radiance." The work of the Zohar is considered to be the most important source for understanding the mystical levels of Torah. This concept is known as "Kabbalah." The book itself, compiled in written form around the 13th century in Spain, is essentially an intricate commentary on the First Five Books of the Bible (The Torah).

Bibliography

Benner, Jeff A.	***His Name is One***
Brenton, Sir Lancelot C.L.	***The Septuagint with Apocrypha*** (2005 Edition of 1851 printing)
Burns PhD, Dr. Cathy	***Hypnosis: Cure or Curse*** Sharing Publication (1993)
Chumney, Edward	***The Seven Festivals of the Messiah*** (2003 Edition) Treasure House
Collins, John J. & Robert A. Kugler	***Religion in the Dead Sea Scrolls*** (2000 Printing)
Dimony, Max I	***Jews, God and History*** ([2nd Edition] A Signet Classic 2004 printing)
Ederseim, Alfred	***The Temple - Its Ministry and Services*** (2004 Printing)
Eisnitz, Gail E.	***Slaughterhouse: The Shocking Story of Greed, Neglect, and Inhumane Treatment inside the U.S. Meat Industry***
Ginzberg, Lewis	***The Legends of the Jews, Volume II: From Joseph to Exodus. 1909***
Greenberg, Blu	***How to Run a Jewish Household*** (1983 Edition)
Hastings, James	***The Dictionary of the Bible***
Hayford, Pastor Jack W.	***The Spirit Filled Life Bible (NKJV)***
He-Chasid, Rabbi Judah ben Samuel. (translator: Finkel, Avraham Yaakov)	***Sefer Chasidim (The Book of the Pious)*** (Jason Aronson, 1997)
Friedman, Ph.D., David,	***They Loved the Torah*** (2001 Edition Paperback) Lederer Books
Jeffrey, Grant	***Heaven: The Mystery of Angels*** (Frontier Research Publications, Inc. [1990])
Koniuchowsky, Rabbi Moshe Y.	***The Restoration Scriptures Sacred Name Edition*** (2005, 2nd Edition)
Koster, C.J	***Come Out of Her My People*** (2004 Edition)
Kuehl, N. L.	***A Book of Evidence*** (1997) Electronic Publication

Josafat Ben-Ezra, Juan (Emmanuel Lacunza) — ***The Coming of the Messiah in Glory and Majesty*** (1827 English version)

LaHaye, Tim & Jenkins, Jerry B. — ***Left Behind*** (Tyndale House / 1995 Edition)

Lustiger, Dr. Arnold — ***Rosh Hashanah Machzor*** w/ Commentary adapted from the teachings of Rabbi Joseph B. Soloveitchik (First Edition / Aug 2007)

McDowell, Josh & Don Stewart — ***Handbook of Today's Religions*** (1983 Edition) Thomas Nelson Publishers

McIntosh, Dr. & Twyman, Dr. — ***The Archko Volume: or The Archeological Writings of the Sanhedrim & Talmuds of the Jews***

Metzger, Coogan — ***The Oxford Companion to the Bible*** (1993 Edition)

Nee, Watchman — ***Spiritual Authority*** (1972 Paperback Edition) Christian Fellowship Publishers, Inc New York

Overstreet, A. T. — ***Are Men Born Sinners? The Myth of Original Sin Chapter 3 - The Origin and History of the Doctrine of Original Sin*** (1995)

Razwy, Sayed A. A. & Ali, Abdullah Yusuf — ***The Qur'an Translation*** (Tahrike Tarsile Qur'an; 14 Edition)

Rodkinson, Michael L. — ***The New Babylonian Talmud*** (Translated and Revised Second Edition [Revised by Rev. Dr. Isaac M. Wise] 1903)

Simpson, Jacqueline — ***The Oxford Dictionary of English Folklore***

Steinsaltz's, Rabbi Adin — ***The Essential Talmud Vol 1-10*** (1918 Edition)

Strong, LL.D., S.T.D. James — ***Strong's Exhaustive Concordance of the Bible*** (1990 Edition)

Trimm, James Scott — ***Nazarene Jewish Manifesto*** (Second Edition)

Unger, Merril F. — ***Unger's Bible Dictionary***, Moody Press, Chicago, IL (1966)

Whiston, A.M. William — ***The Works of Josephus*** [Complete and Unabridged] (2007)

Wooten, Batya Ruth — ***Israel's Feasts and their Fullness*** (2002 Printing) Key of David Publishing

Webster, Merriam — ***Webster's Dictionary for Students*** (Federal Street Press; Student 2003 Edition)

News Articles

"Bikies' Code Makes Them Hard to Crack" By Gary Hughes / *The Australian* (June 23, 2007)

Internet Sites Sourced:

http://www.bibletopics.com/BIBLESTUDY/94.htm

http://www.gospeltruth.net/menbornsinners/mbsindex.htm

Ghosts of *SS Watertown* info sourced from:

http://paranormal.about.com/library/weekly/aa102102b.htm

A Perspective on Psalm 51:5 by William P. Murray, Jr.

http://www.biblical-theology.com/originalsin/ps51_5.htm

Practical Kabbalah – F. Levine

http://www.atomick.net/fayelevine/pk/index.php

Article: The Golem All Around Me by Rodger Kamenetz

http://www.beliefnet.com/story/33/story_3342_1.html

Mythological and Mysterious Creatures in the KJV

http://www.kjv-only.com/satyr.html

Specific Rabbinic Literature Sourced:

Source of Morning Blessings from ***ArtScroll Tranliterated Linear Siddur*** (weekday) Translation and commentary by Rabbi Nosson Scherman. Published by Mesorah Publications, LTD.

***Joshua • Judges* – The Rubin Edition** (The Early Prophets with a Commentary Anthologized from the Rabbinic Writings by Rabbi Nosson Scherrman

Moses Maimonides – The Guide for the Perplexed Translation from the original Arabic Text by M. Friedländer 9Second edition, Revised Throughout) PH.D Dover Publications, Inc New York

Other Bible Translations used within this work:

The Authorized Catholic Lain Vulgate (1592)

Complete Jewish Bible – Translation by David H. Stern

The Stone Edition TANACH – The Torah/Prophets/Writings (Artscroll Series) General Editors Rabbi Nosson Scherman / Rabbi Meir Zlotowitz (Second Edition 2007)

About the Author

Jason Jordan lives in NSW Australia with his wife Shabnam and their daughter Hannah. They joined themselves to the Commonwealth of Israel back in 2003 and attend a Nazarene Israelite congregation at Camden. Jason has a deep respect for the ultra Orthodox *ChaBaD* movement and studies under a Messianic Rabbi who was trained by them. In addition to the Scriptures, he regularly reads a wide range of rabbinic literature, including the *Chumash*, *Talmud*, *Zohar* and *The Tanya.* Whilst researching material for his second book, the author came to the conclusion that the *ChaBaD* teach a lifestyle that most closely resembles Messiah Yahshua, though they are temporarily blinded to his identity. Jason is sympathetic to this blindness and attributes it to a long running campaign by the Church to obscure Yahshua's Jewishness and his love for Torah. Jason is in no way associated with any denominational group that promotes Christianity, whether openly or under the banner of a Hebraic veneer.

7839188R0

Made in the USA
Lexington, KY
17 December 2010